D0170025

Democracy's Edges

Democracy is a flawed hegemon. The collapse of communism has left it without a serious institutional competitor in much of the world. In many respects this is, no doubt, a good thing. Democracy's flexibility, its in-built commitment to equality of representation, and its recognition of the legitimacy of opposition politics are all features of political institutions that should not lightly be discounted. But democracy has many deficiencies. It is all too easily held hostage by powerful interests; it often fails to protect the vulnerable or otherwise to advance social justice; and it does not cope well with a number of features of the political landscape. Intensely felt political identities, the drawing and redrawing of boundaries, and global environmental problems are among the most urgent. In short, although democracy is valuable it fits uneasily with many other political values and is in many respects less than equal to the demands it confronts.

In this volume (and its companion, *Democracy's Value*) some of the world's most prominent political theorists and social scientists present original discussions of these urgently vexing subjects. *Democracy's Edges* contains meditations on one of the most enduring problems of democratic politics: how to establish the boundaries of democratic polities democratically. *Democracy's Value* deals principally with the nature and value of democracy, with particular attention to the tensions between it and such goods as justice, equality, efficiency, and freedom. These books provide an accessible extension of the state-of-the-art in democratic theory.

IAN SHAPIRO is Professor of Political Science at Yale University. He has written widely on contemporary political and social theory, with particular recent emphasis on democratic theory. His books include *The Evolution of Rights in Liberal Theory* (1986), *Political Criticism* (1990), *Pathologies of Rational Choice Theory* (with Donald Green, 1994), *Democracy's Place* (1996), and *Democratic Justice* (1999). He has also edited numerous books, including, since 1992, the NOMOS series.

CASIANO HACKER-CORDÓN is a doctoral student at Yale University. His work centers on contemporary political philosophy and social theory.

Contemporary Political Theory

Series editor
Ian Shapiro

Editorial Board
Russell Hardin   Stephen Holmes   Jeffrey Isaac
John Keane   Elizabeth Kiss   Susan Moller Okin
Philippe Van Parijs   Philip Pettit

As the twenty-first century approaches, major new political challenges have arisen at the same time as some of the most enduring dilemmas of political association remain unresolved. The collapse of communism and the end of the Cold War in the east reflect a victory for democratic and liberal values, yet in many of the western countries that nurtured those values there are severe problems of urban decay, class and racial conflict, and failing political legitimacy. Enduring global injustice and inequality seem compounded by environmental problems, disease, the oppression of women, racial, ethnic and religious minorities, and the relentless growth of the world's population. In such circumstances, the need for creative thinking about the fundamentals of human political association is manifest. This new series in contemporary political theory is intended to foster such systematic normative reflection.

The series proceeds in the belief that the time is ripe for a reassertion of the importance of problem-driven political theory. It is concerned, that is, with works that are motivated by the impulse to understand, think critically about and address problems in the world, rather than issues that are thrown up primarily in academic debate. Books in the series will be interdisciplinary in character, ranging over issues conventionally dealt with in philosophy, law, history, and the human sciences. The range of materials and the methods of proceeding should be dictated by the problem at hand, not the conventional debates or disciplinary divisions of academia.

Democracy's Edges

Edited by

Ian Shapiro and Casiano Hacker-Cordón

CAMBRIDGE
UNIVERSITY PRESS

PUBLISHED BY THE PRESS SYNDICATE OF THE UNIVERSITY OF CAMBRIDGE
The Pitt Building, Trumpington Street, Cambridge, United Kingdom

CAMBRIDGE UNIVERSITY PRESS
The Edinburgh Building, Cambridge, CB2 2RU, UK
  http://www.cup.cam.ac.uk
40 West 20th Street, New York, NY 10011–4211, USA   http://www.cup.org
10 Stamford Road, Oakleigh, Melbourne 3166, Australia

© Cambridge University Press 1999

This book is in copyright. Subject to statutory exception and to the provisions
of relevant collective licensing agreements, no reproduction of any part may
take place without the written permission of Cambridge University Press.

First published 1999

Printed in the United Kingdom at the University Press, Cambridge

Typeset in 10/12pt Plantin   [CE]

A catalogue record for this book is available from the British Library

ISBN 0 521 64356 2 hardback
ISBN 0 521 64389 9 paperback

To the memory of Richard Ashcraft

Contents

List of contributors   *page* xi
Preface   xiii

1. IAN SHAPIRO and CASIANO HACKER-CORDÓN   1
    Outer edges and inner edges

Part I. Outer edges   17

2. ROBERT A. DAHL   19
    Can international organizations be democratic?
    A skeptic's view

3. JAMES TOBIN   37
    A comment on Dahl's skepticism

4. ELMAR ALTVATER   41
    The democratic order, economic globalization, and
    ecological restrictions – on the relation of material and
    formal democracy

5. RUSSELL HARDIN   63
    Democracy and collective bads

6. DAVID HELD   84
    The transformation of political community: rethinking
    democracy in the context of globalization

7. WILL KYMLICKA   112
    Citizenship in an era of globalization: commentary on Held

8. ALEXANDER WENDT   127
    A comment on Held's cosmopolitanism

9. BROOKE A. ACKERLY and SUSAN MOLLER OKIN   134
    Feminist social criticism and the international movement
    for women's rights as human rights

Part II.   Inner edges   163

10. DOUGLAS RAE   165
     Democratic liberty and the tyrannies of place

11. ELIZABETH KISS   193
     Democracy and the politics of recognition

12. IAN SHAPIRO   210
     Group aspirations and democratic politics

13. JEFFREY C. ISAAC, MATTHEW F. FILNER, and
     JASON C. BIVINS   222
     American democracy and the New Christian Right:
     a critique of apolitical liberalism

14. COURTNEY JUNG   265
     Between liberalism and a hard place

15. SUSAN L. HURLEY   273
     Rationality, democracy, and leaky boundaries: vertical vs
     horizontal modularity

Index   295

Contributors

Brooke A. Ackerly *Department of Political Science, University of California, Los Angeles*
Elmar Altvater *Department of Political Science, Free University of Berlin*
Jason C. Bivins *Department of Political Science, Indiana University*
Robert Dahl *Department of Political Science, Yale University*
Matthew F. Filner *Department of Political Science, Indiana University*
Casiano Hacker-Cordón *Department of Political Science, Yale University*
Russell Hardin *Department of Politics, New York University*
David Held *Department of Politics and Sociology, The Open University*
Susan Hurley *Department of Philosophy, University of Warwick*
Jeffrey Isaac *Department of Political Science, Indiana University*
Courtney Jung *Department of Political Science, The New School for Social Research*
Elizabeth Kiss *Kenan Ethics Program and Department of Political Science, Duke University*
Will Kymlicka *Department of Philosophy, University of Ottawa*
Susan Moller Okin *Department of Political Science, Stanford University*
Douglas Rae *School of Management, Yale University*
Ian Shapiro *Department of Political Science, Yale University*
James Tobin *Department of Economics, Yale University*
Alexander Wendt *Department of Politics, Dartmouth College*

Preface

This volume and its companion, *Democracy's Value*, grew out of a conference on "Rethinking Democracy for a New Century" held at Yale in February 1997. The conference was sponsored by Yale's Program in Ethics, Politics, and Economics, with financial support coming from Yale's Olmsted Fund, Castle Fund, and Kempf Fund. Thanks are due to Kellianne Farnham for going well beyond the call of duty in organizing the conference and helping us assemble the manuscript. We are also pleased to record our gratitude to John Haslam of Cambridge University Press for his interest in the project from the beginning, and for facilitating the timely appearance of the volumes.

IAN SHAPIRO

CASIANO HACKER-CORDÓN

1   Outer edges and inner edges

Ian Shapiro and Casiano Hacker-Cordón

An enduring embarrassment of democratic theory is that it seems impotent when faced with questions about its own scope. By its terms democracy seems to take the existence of units within which it operates for granted. It depends on a decision rule, usually some variant of majority rule, but the rule's operation assumes that the question "majority of whom?" has already been settled. If this is not done democratically, however, in what sense are the results that flow from democratic decision rules genuinely democratic? A chicken-and-egg problem thus lurks at democracy's core. Questions relating to boundaries and membership seem in an important sense prior to democratic decision-making, yet paradoxically they cry out for democratic resolution.

One need not consider such extreme cases as Northern Ireland, the former Yugoslavia, or the West Bank for evidence supporting this contention, though they surely do. Arguments about the legal status of Turkish "guestworkers" in Germany, removing full British citizenship from members of the Commonwealth, or denying public education to the children of illegal immigrants in California are all challenging to think about as matters of *democratic* politics partly because they render problematical assumptions about who constitutes the appropriate demos for majoritarian decision. Indeed, virtually every aspect of a country's policies dealing with immigrants or minorities can be shown to involve this paradox in some way. Democratic theorists often acknowledge the existence of the difficulty, but surprisingly little headway has been made in dealing with it to date.[1]

If the controversial character of political boundaries were to diminish over time, perhaps the chicken-and-egg problem would abate as well.

---

[1] As Dahl (1989: 3) puts it: "Advocates of democracy – including political philosophers – characteristically presuppose that 'a people' already exists. Its existence is assumed as fact, a creation of history. Yet the facticity of the fact is questionable. It is often questioned – as it was in the United States in 1861, when the issue was settled not by consent or consensus but by violence."

But events show few signs of being so generous to democratic theory's troubles. The past decade has seen a resurgence of identity politics in many parts of the world, ranging from the remnants of the Soviet empire through much of Africa – not to mention in long-established democracies such as Australia and Canada. In dozens of countries around the world, insurgent groups question the legitimacy of existing boundaries, demanding that they be redrawn so as better to reflect their aspirations. Sometimes these demands are limited to requests for bounded domains of sovereignty over certain matters within national boundaries, as with the Welsh Assembly and Scottish Parliament approved by referendum in 1997. Indeed many run-of-the-mill disputes about the distribution of authority within federal and confederal systems fall into this category. Often, however, the demand has involved insistence on full secession and the creation of new national states, as with the creation of the United States of America, Pakistan, or the Slovak republic. One only has to think of the demands for an independent Quebec, a Palestinian state, an Afrikaner Volkstaat, reunion of Russia with Belarus, an independent Chechnya, or a Kurdish republic – to name a few obvious cases – to be reminded that today's world is replete with would-be secessionists and unifiers who reject the democratic legitimacy of existing boundaries and seek to redraw them.

Even when boundaries are not in dispute, the international realities of power can render democracy's edges elusive. Transnational forces in today's world can have a greater bearing on national policies than the decisions of elected governments. National political choices are often trumped by the actions of such institutions as the World Bank, the International Monetary Fund, the United Nations, or the European Union. Such institutions often have political agendas of their own, ranging from privatizing and deregulating the global economy to imposing labor law and regulatory regimes on countries to which their governments may stand opposed. Some of these international institutions are subject to attenuated forms of popular control, but it is unclear that this rises to a level that accords them much democratic legitimacy.

Moreover, democracy's edges are often blunted by transnational forces that defy even indirect popular control. The decisions of currency speculators, multinational investors, and global mutual fund managers can render domestic governments at best reactive and at worst helpless before dynamics set in motion by private players on the international stage. Britain's 1991 sterling crisis, which forced withdrawal from the European exchange rate mechanism, was a dramatic illustration. But in a host of more mundane and less visible ways, democratic governments the world over find increasingly that their taxation, welfare,

employment, borrowing, and public expenditure policies are constrained by what they are bound to anticipate from fickle international
investors. A poignant instantiation of this trend is the 1990s fashion for
creating independent banks that "signal" stability to capital markets – a
euphemism for ceding democratic control of monetary policy to technocrats whose behavior can better be predicted by investors just because
they are insulated from mechanisms of democratic accountability.

The contributors to the present volume all speak to dimensions of this
reality. Some deal with the conventional boundary problem, advancing
possible solutions to the chicken-and-egg paradox it engenders. Some
are concerned with recasting the relations between democracy's decision
rules and its edges, to diminish the paradox's significance or make it
disappear. Some focus on transnational institutions, asking whether and
how they might be subjected to more meaningful popular control or
otherwise rendered legitimate within the ambit of democratic principles.
Some take up secessionist aspirations, and the role of transnational
institutions in undermining, or fostering, national democracy. Some
consider the capacity of democratic institutions, whether domestic or
international, to manage the environmental dangers that exhibit little –
and decreasing – interest in national boundaries. And some suggest that
the search for democracy's edges should lead us to reconsider the
meaning of democracy itself, drawing on developments in fields as
distant from the contemporary practice of political theory as the foundations of cognitive science. All are concerned to further our understanding of a perennial but neglected dimension of democratic theory
that has been thrown into sharp relief by the evolving power fluidities of
the late twentieth century.

I.   Outer edges

In chapter 2, Robert Dahl makes the case that democracy's outer edges
are likely to remain coterminous with those of the national state. Understanding democracy to require, at a minimum, a measure of popular
control over decision-making, he argues that there is an inverse relationship between efficacious popular control and consequential decision-
making. Whereas small groups can offer extensive popular control of
their decisions to their members, such groups will often be ineffectual in
determining outcomes in the world. By contrast, large entities may be
consequential in the world, but are difficult to control democratically.
Nation states are sufficiently large that meaningful democratic control of
them is exceedingly difficult, but Dahl argues that it is at least possible
in some areas. He thinks it instructive, when thinking about democracy

in international organizations, to note that foreign policy is one of the most difficult areas in which to achieve democratic control at the national level. What is at stake in foreign policy decisions is often by its nature inaccessible, and far removed from voters' everyday experience. The result is that popular control is limited to a kind of reactive activism. When foreign policies such as the United States' pursuit of war in Vietnam begin to have a widespread impact on people's daily lives they may rise up and oppose them; the rest of the time the policies will be left in the hands of elites.

International organizations such as the United Nations are substantially immune from even the limited popular control that is characteristic of foreign policy in national democracies. As a result, Dahl contends that we should not regard them as democratic at all. Better we should see international organizations for what they are: bureaucratic bargaining systems. This does not mean, for Dahl, that international organizations are undesirable. They may serve valuable purposes, perhaps indispensable ones. Indeed, some international organizations such as the UN may promote national democracy in parts of the world where it is presently lacking. Even in these cases, however, the international institutions themselves are unlikely to be democratic by Dahl's criterion. An important resulting challenge, that Dahl thinks has not yet been satisfactorily tackled by anyone, is to come up with plausible criteria for evaluating the legitimacy of undemocratic international institutions.

James Tobin brings an economist's perspective to bear on Dahl's challenge in chapter 3. He notes that most international institutions are not democratic in Dahl's sense because they result from treaty agreements among participating nations which generally have equal voting power regardless of their domestic populations. Tobin suggests a perspective for thinking about their legitimacy, drawing on the work of Hirschman (1970). Whether our sense of an institution's legitimacy should be linked to how democratic it is depends on the institution for Tobin. In particular, if the costs of exit from it are low, requiring it to operate democratically may be unnecessary and even unwise. Allowing members of transient groups a say in democratic governance may reasonably be judged unfair because of their different stakes in the collective decision. Like Dahl, Tobin sees the demands of international competition between national states as undermining democracy, particularly when this involves handing over monetary, exchange rate, and even fiscal policies to independent authorities so as to insulate them from the demands of electoral competition. Because there is no escape from the effects of international monetary and exchange rate regimes in the modern world, on Tobin's logic they ought to be subject to democratic control. The fact that they are not contributes to what is sometimes termed the "democratic deficit" of legitimacy in contemporary politics, and exacerbates domestic sources of democracy's erosion such as the role of money in shaping the public agenda.

Elmar Altvater furthers the skeptical critique of transnational democracy in chapter 4, by arguing that whether or not international political institutions are democratically designed, they are unlikely to be democracy-enhancing. Most supranational institutions have emerged partly as a result of, and partly in response to, the globalization of economic relations. More often than not, global economic institutions assist transnational economic forces in undermining national democratic sovereignty, contributing to the retrenchment of welfare states and of institutional protections for the vulnerable that have been hard won over generations of domestic democratic conflict in the world's older democracies. Moreover, the recent proliferation of electoral politics to many of the world's countries is itself affected by globalization, since people gain formal democratic rights without much substantive scope for policy-making. In these circumstances, democratization legitimates the processes of deregulation and privatization called for by those who control international economic institutions. While agreeing with Dahl and Tobin that globalization contributes to the democratic deficit in the older democracies, Altvater believes the prospects to be even bleaker in the younger ones, which are less well placed in the world economy.

Altvater also broaches what may be one of the most serious challenges to democratic politics – not to mention the human species – in the coming decades: heading-off planetary-wide ecological catastrophe. Even if one takes a comparatively benign view of the possibilities for transnational modes of democratic governance, Altvater notes that there is no obvious reason to suppose that such institutions will have the capacity to limit global economic growth to ecologically sustainable levels. On the contrary, in light of the political imperatives unleashed by the structured dynamics of economic globalization, the potential of "ecological democracy" is limited. Social movements and NGOs working for ecologically sensitive economic policies confront an incongruence between the boundaries which divide the world's peoples into separate national states – which set the internal space for formal democratic institutions – and the boundary of humanity's natural environment. The obstacles to effective political action are compounded in this area, because ecological questions are intertwined with distributive ones. The national state system preserves global inequalities of income and wealth that would have to be challenged as part of any serious attempt at international environmental regulation.

Russell Hardin takes up this question as part of a general discussion of democracy and collective bads in chapter 5. Although democracy's messy procedures have not generally been thought adequate to the handling of collective bads such as environmental pollution, Hardin alleges that in fact democracies have managed these problems better than autocratic states in the past several decades. At the same time as pollution was limited consistent with maintaining economic growth in the West, ecological disaster accompanied economic catastrophe in the East. The reason, Hardin argues, is that democracy is much better suited to solving coordination problems than to problems that exhibit significant distributive dimensions. Pollution problems were widely seen as universal bads in the Western countries, making collective response to them feasible. Unfortunately, the international environmental problems that are emerging as a by-product of globalization involve manifest distributive conflicts. Newly industrializing countries, with populations in the hundreds of millions or even billions, threaten to overwhelm the planet's capacity to support life if they develop on the same basis of cheap fossil fuels that the advanced countries utilized over the past 150 years. But if industrializing countries are to be diverted from cheap development paths, the costs of this diversion have to be distributed. This is what democracy does poorly.

Nor does Hardin think we can take heart from the European Union, NAFTA, and GATT as models for the sort of institutions that are required. Such institutions emerged to solve coordination problems: to eliminate barriers to better results that had emerged as by-products of the nation-state system, barriers that prevent economic and other activities that would have occurred spontaneously but for their presence. Solving international collective bads problems such as global environmental damage would require stronger transnational institutions, not the mere weakening of national institutions. Moreover, given the substantial distributive dimensions to such collective bads problems, it is unlikely that such institutions can be democratic if they are to be effective. Thus, despite national democracy's track record of relative success in managing domestic environmental problems, Hardin agrees with Altvater's pessimism when these problems take on an increasingly transnational character.

In contrast to these skeptical views, David Held argues in chapter 6 that democratic theory and politics can respond constructively to the challenges of globalization. Like Altvater, Held notes that the internationalization of many dimensions of social interaction – economic, cultural, and political – has circumscribed the nation state's policy autonomy in multiple ways with the result that many national governments increasingly play the role of "decision-takers" – they react to the actions of transnational players and more powerful foreign governments. Global financial markets, multinationals, and banking institutions can act, increasingly, in unilateral ways with decisive effects for national policies and strategies. Contrary to many discussions of these processes, however, Held is careful to distinguish the matter of nation states' *policy autonomy* from their sovereignty. Nor is it only multinational forces and institutions that circumscribe national policy autonomy. While emphasizing the crucial distinction between legal–political sovereignty and policy autonomy, Held illuminates how some of the world's governments are increasingly powerful beyond their spheres of legitimate sovereignty. They take decisions about trade, crime, environmental, and regulatory policy that have reverberations around the world. Such decisions affect populations whose governments may be impotent with respect to these policies, no matter how much recognition of national sovereignty may in fact be a well-observed (though qualified) norm in international relations.

Held's distinctive insight derives from his observation that the dynamics surrounding globalization are not as novel as they are often alleged to be. In important respects, he notes, they parallel developments that accompanied the emergence of the modern nation-state system over the past several centuries. It, too, involved the emergence of power relations that cut across traditional units of political authority: absolutist states that centralized power internally and operated on the Westphalian model externally; they acknowledged no superior authorities, limiting international law to rules of coexistence among formally equal entities in a Hobbesian order.

Held usefully points out that modern democracy emerged after absolutism, and to some degree as a response to it. The challenge of refashioning a democratic ideal that had originally been conceived for governing small homogeneous polities for a world of large heterogeneous nation states was met with the idea of representative government. It transformed democratic theory from a piece of quaint antiquarianism into an ideology equal to its age, shaping the form that democratization of the nation state was to take. What is needed now, he argues, is a comparably innovative idea, to respond to the globalization that is eroding national democratic polities. Held's candidate is the idea of a transnational democratic legal order or *Rechtstaat*: an international order that is circumscribed and legitimated by democratic public law. Democratizing international law will require "the establishment of a community of all democratic communities"; a kind of cosmopolitan community that can command the allegiance of all democrats. Held's suggestion is thus that a transnational democratic *Rechtstaat* might domesticate transnational authoritarian forces and institutions, just as representative government domesticated the absolutist state. Such domestication should not come at the expense of allegiance to democratic nation states on Held's account; rather, democrats should begin to discern that they are citizens of multiple polities to which allegiances are multiply owed. But the basic elements of a transnational rule of law system are essential to this endeavor, and democrats should see it as a central – if not primary – obligation in the coming decades to work toward its creation.

In chapter 7 Will Kymlicka takes issue with the view that globalization is eroding the capacity for meaningful democratic citizenship at the domestic level. Kymlicka argues that there is greater room for optimism regarding the prospects for domestic citizenship than he takes Held to suggest. Not only do nation states still possess considerable decision-making autonomy, he argues, but their citizens still prize this autonomy, which allows them to act in distinctive ways, reflective of their national political cultures and inherited solidarities. So much is recognized, if not emphasized, by Held. But, in so far as citizens no longer find political participation meaningful, Kymlicka contends, the explanation has little to do with globalization. Rather, it is traceable to flaws in the electoral and legislative systems which existed prior to, and independent of, globalization, and which can be remedied whenever we find the political will to do so. A flourishing democratic citizenship at the national level remains a viable possibility within Western democracies, despite globalization. Concurring with the position advanced by Dahl and Altvater, Kymlicka also questions the view that whatever democratic deficit exists at the national level can be redeemed by democratizing the transnational institutions which increasingly shape important economic, environmental, and security decisions. The preconditions for mass participation in transnational organizations do not yet exist, and it is difficult, he argues, to see how they could arise in the foreseeable future

Alexander Wendt explores these ideas further in chapter 8. He distinguishes *cosmopolitan democracy*, in which individuals cast votes in the governance of transnational institutions, from *international democracy*, in which sovereign states are the voting members. The former is less likely to be attainable than the latter in the medium term, in Wendt's view, for several reasons. Although powerful constituencies – particularly in the financial world – are open to political globalization, other relevant forces are hostile to it. States are jealous guardians of the sovereignty created by the Westphalian system which remains the order of the day in international politics. Populations have been socialized into national political orders, so that they tend to be hostile to the trans-nationalization of political power. Accordingly, Wendt argues that international state formation should be expected to differ from the domestic state formation of the early modern period to which Held alludes. Unlike the process by which political power was concentrated in the hands of centralized states, often through conquest, the path-dependencies of sovereignty may lead to *de facto* internationalization of the state without much *de jure* internationalization. More likely than institutions of world government, we should expect that state power will increasingly be dispersed or "de-centered" among nominally independent states. On Wendt's account, it is likely to be a long time – if ever – before there is any centralized apparatus of international governance, any commanding heights of institutional power for transnational democrats to capture. For this reason Wendt is skeptical about how far Held's comparison between domestic and international state formation holds.

Reflecting on this limitation leads Wendt to pose the question whether international democracy should be deemed as objectionable by democrats as Dahl and others have suggested. International democracy, on Wendt's account, depends on a notion of group rights. Although democrats often count themselves hostile to the idea of group rights, Wendt notes that there is an important sense in which the group is inevitably prior to the individual in democracies. Just because of the chicken-and-egg problem, individual democratic rights are bound to be parasitic on some form of group membership. Moreover, Wendt speculates that if one surveyed people asking them to imagine a cosmopolitan democracy, many of those who are unalterably opposed to group rights within their country would want strong protections for their nation at the international level, whether this took the form of federalism, subsidiarity, governance based on an international "Senate" rather than "House," or other institutions to shield national identities. Protecting groups among nations may be more compelling than it is within them from the standpoint of democratic theory, on Wendt's view, and should not be dismissed as a viable basis for transnational democratic legitimacy.

In chapter 9 Brooke Ackerly and Susan Moller Okin argue that although globalization threatens democracy in some respects, in others it may actually enhance democratic possibilities. Their case study is the international women's movement, particularly those parts of it that have sought to redefine the notion of human rights, embraced by many international institutions and national governments, so as to include explicit acknowledgment of women's rights. Although globalization has had a mixed impact on democratization, activists around the world have combined global awareness and communication with knowledge of the real, diverse, and dispersed local experiences of women, to make international policy on human rights more inclusive of them. In their organizing around women's issues or for women's interests, activists have developed a method of social criticism that makes use of deliberation without relying on the ideal conditions required by deliberative democratic theorists. Using the example of the women's rights as human rights movement, Ackerly and Okin describe the methods that activists in the real world have used to try to make international fora more inclusive. While in general skeptical about the democratic credentials of transnational politics in the contemporary world, Ackerly and Okin's paper aims to call attention to a democratic bright spot on the landscape of non-democratic global organizations.

II.   Inner edges

Douglas Rae refocuses our attention from democracy's outer edges to its undernoticed inner ones in chapter 10. A central development in what he describes as the United States' evolving spatial economy since World War II has been the growth of "enclave-seeking" behavior by large numbers of those who have the wherewithal to engage in it. Until the 1940s, urban residential locations were sought after because they offered privileged access to nodes of heavy transportation and employment around which prosperity revolved. Growing inner-city density meant declining quality of life, however, and suburban commuting presented itself as a logical alternative, buttressed by subsidized road systems and motor-vehicles affordable to the middle class. In most northeastern and mid-western cities the white middle-class flight to the suburbs coincided with the exodus of poor blacks from the south, away from segregation and in search of economic opportunity. This migrating population filled the inner-city vacuums left by the white middle class, accelerating the pace of their departure. The result was that migrating blacks exchanged the south's *de jure* segregation for a new and no less potent form of *de facto* apartheid. This trend has accelerated since the 1970s, as the incomes and life chances of poor blacks have diverged ever more sharply from those of the middle class and the wealthy.

Rae goes on to argue that the information revolution and the "home office" phenomenon that has accompanied it reinforce spatial segregation patterns, as those who are not members of the substantially black urban poor have fewer and fewer reasons to set foot in inner cities at all. Whether made inaccessible by fact of distance or by "gated communities" – privately guarded enclaves of which there are now upwards of

50,000 in the United States – they live lives in which their democratic liberties are protected by the space from which they are able to exclude others. The flipside of this is that the only truly public realm left is the inner city, public in the sense that no one needs resources to enter it. There democratic liberties exist in principle only, since people who must live in it lack the minimal protected space that even negative freedom requires. They lack the freedom to move about without fear of violence, the chance for meaningful educational aspiration for their children, the realistic possibility of competing for employment or accumulating assets, and the right to participate on more or less equal terms in collective decisions that impose laws on themselves and their families. Thus deprived of the basic incidents of democratic liberty, for practical purposes they are excluded from democratic citizenship. On Rae's account we do not need to travel far to discover democracy's edges. They are all around us – or, rather, we are all around them. In this world of "segmented democracies," those who are excluded are tyrannized both by being kept out and because in their daily lives the basic problem of political order is unresolved. For them no less than for the states confronting one another in the international realm of which Held writes, the Hobbesian threat is unconstrained by democratic principles.

What of those who seek to transform democracy's inner edges into its outer edges by reconstituting accepted boundaries? In contrast to Tobin's suggestion that this problem may be beyond resolution within the confines of democratic theory, Elizabeth Kiss and Ian Shapiro advance different, though complementary, democratic ways of tackling subgroup aspirations in the next two chapters. In chapter 11 Kiss argues for case-by-case scrutiny of subgroup claims. She focuses on specific alleged harms rather than desires for self-expression. Such harms can include cultural and symbolic harms, but the onus should be on the claimant, in her account, to establish that this is so. Context is all; each case must be understood in all its idiosyncratic complexity in order to determine which subgroup claims should be recognized, and how this can be done democratically. Kiss illustrates this approach by considering the demands for recognition by the Hungarian minority in Romania, where the peculiarities of the particular harms they confront suggest remedies that are not easily generalized to other circumstances.

Shapiro also thinks context is critical to evaluation of subgroup aspirations, but in chapter 12 he makes the case that democratic theory none the less suggests the appropriateness of some general criteria for evaluating them. He begins by noting that much of the philosophical literature on this subject is artificial in defining the problem as an abstract consideration of what different groups and subgroups might be alleged to "want." In reality, he argues, because group rights are typically asserted by political parties and leaders with particular goals, their claims can be fairly evaluated only when those goals are taken into account. Appropriate criteria for evaluating demands for group rights – up to and including rights of secession – have to do with their likely impact on democratic politics, where this is understood to require inclusive participation of those affected by collective decisions and the toleration of loyal opposition within a democratic order. Shapiro explores these criteria by reference to a variety of recent competing group aspirations in South Africa and the Middle East. He notes that although some conflicting group claims cannot be satisfied simultaneously, some can. In zero-sum situations, preference should be given to the groups that fare better by the democratic criteria, but the more valuable institutional challenge is to find ways of transforming group aspirations that are incompatible with democracy so that they can be realized consistently with it. Developing this claim leads Shapiro to a more general discussion of the foundations of politicized group identities, and of institutional arrangements that are more and less likely to induce these identities to evolve in democratic directions.

An alternative to re-engineering threatening identities so as to render them compatible with democracy is to keep them out of politics altogether. Pursuing this goal, by creating and fortifying inner limits to the domain of legitimate politics, distinguishes the enterprise of liberal democracy from other variants of the species. To this end, an alleged moral of the English and European wars of religion, taken to heart by the authors of the Establishment Clause of the First Amendment to the United States Constitution, is that mutual insulation of religious and public identities from one another can afford valuable protection to both. Such institutional "gag rules" are held by liberal democrats to be essential to both political legitimacy and stability (Holmes 1988). The most sustained recent defense of this view is perhaps John Rawls's insistence that the edges of legitimate politics are those of "public reason"; that in a world of multiple competing conceptions of the good the only arguments that should hold sway in shaping public institutions are those that appeal to an "overlapping consensus" of the different competing views. This "political, not metaphysical" approach eschews the thought that the state should aspire to adjudicate among different comprehensive world views; rather it should recognize as valid public arguments only those that rest on premises that adherents of the competing views can all affirm (Rawls 1993).

This is the view taken up and found wanting by Jeffrey Isaac, Matthew Filner, and Jason Bivins in chapter 13. They make the case that the liberal democratic view, which came of age during the postwar era of relative growth and prosperity in most Western countries, is less appropriate for the world that we know now which is marked by harder times and a resurgence of identity politics. In today's world, they argue, liberalism's overlapping consensus is in danger of collapsing, as groups such as the New Christian Right discover that the consensus in question seems to include secular and moderate religious world-views while excluding their more fundamentalist ones. The liberal democratic impulse is to push such groups out of public life, often fortifying this stance with heavy reliance on judicial review rather than accountable democratic institutions. Isaac, Filner, and Bivins agree with those who say that this undermines liberal democracy's legitimacy. They argue instead for constructive democratic engagement with such groups. By enticing them into public debate on their own terms, they argue, democrats are more likely to get fundamentalists to consider alternative views than their own than by adopting strategies of exclusion. Moreover, they argue, such engagement could open the way to exploring common interests in other matters that are currently over-determined by a polarizing identity politics.

Courtney Jung takes issue with Isaac, Filner, and Bivins's argument in chapter 14. On the one hand, she argues that they reify religious identity politics as a fixed feature of the political landscape that must be accommodated into the political order lest they undermine it. In fact, she argues, identities become politicized or depoliticized in response to the incentives built into institutions and the activities of political entre-preneurs. There are always choices to be made as to which forms of politicization to permit and encourage, and some are more sustaining of democracy than others. On the other hand, she argues, religious funda-mentalism is peculiarly recalcitrant from a democratic point of view because it is often by its terms hostile to principles of inclusive toleration that democracy requires. Fundamentalists make use of these principles in opposition (perhaps while complaining that the principles are loaded against them), but on coming to power they seldom extend such inclusive toleration to their opponents. This should not surprise us, on Jung's account, because it is part of the nature of fundamentalist commitments that they involve insisting on the truth of single compre-hensive doctrines, rendering them particularly resistant to the sorts of institutional engineering discussed by Kiss and Shapiro in earlier chap-ters. From Jung's point of view Isaac, Filner, and Bivins are thus naive to suppose that fundamentalists can be domesticated by the constructive engagement they propose, or that fundamentalists are likely to be diverted from their central focus on identity politics by coalition-building on other questions. The better course, for democrats, may indeed be to seek out ways of depoliticizing their aspirations.

In different ways the discussions by all our contributors question the conventional view that plotting democracy's edges is exogenous to the operation of democratic principles. On the one hand, even when questions about borders are settled, they may be perceived to lack legitimacy if they have been imposed without reference to democratic considerations or cannot be revised in democratic ways. Moreover, many dilemmas of inclusion and exclusion will remain, suggesting that no democratic theory worth the name can regard boundary questions as wholly exogenous. By their nature boundaries reproduce inequalities in decision-making power that can always be questioned by reference to democratic values. On the other hand, the chicken-and-egg problem, while real, can be approached in more or less democratic ways, and with consequences that are better or worse from the standpoint of democratic values. These reflections naturally raise the question taken up by Susan Hurley in chapter 15: is it perhaps not better to conceive of the boundary problem as wholly endogenous to democracy's operation? Jurisdictional decisions have implications for democratic values of self-determination, autonomy, respect for rights, equality, and contestability, and they are best made, arguably, so as to preserve or maximize these values.

Hurley's point of departure is by analogy to the role of rationality in competing views of cognitive science. On traditional accounts, the mind is seen as depending on vertically modular underlying processes, in which different modules perform stages of processing, passing the resulting representations on to the next module for further processing. Perceptual modules extract information from inputs about such things as color, motion, and location, and once they have been processed through the vertical scheme they are combined in cognition, the central module that interfaces between perception and action. This is where the processes occur on which rational thought and deliberation depend. Rationality is conceived of as an internal process, the manipulation of internal symbols passed on by prior modules. Against this vertical view, Hurley and others have advanced a horizontally modular view, in which the mind is conceived of as layer upon layer of content-specific networks. The layers, which are dedicated to specific tasks, are dynamic: they extend from input through output and back through input in various feedback loops. On the horizontally modular view, vertical boundaries, such as those around sensory or cognitive or motor processes, or indeed around the organism as a whole, do not disappear; but they are relatively permeable or leaky. Rationality, on this account, can no longer be conceived as wholly internal. Since there is no linear sequence of separate stages, rationality is instead reconceived as emerging from a complex system of decentralized, higher-order relations of inhibition, facilitation, and coordination among different horizontal layers. It is a higher-order property of complex patterns of adaptation between organisms and their structured environments.

Hurley suggests that whereas the exogenous view of the boundary question is similar to the vertically modular view of the mind, the endogenous view parallels the horizontally modular view. She explores the implications of this fertile comparison, recasting many traditional questions about democracy's edges along the way. Among the advantages of Hurley's approach are that it encourages us to consider the ways in which democracy in some domains of collective life affects it in other domains, and in particular how varying amounts of democracy in transnational activities and organizations affects the chances for democracy at the national level. Democracy, on this view, is conceived of as an emergent property of a complex, globally distributed, dynamic system or network. Democracy need not be perceived in internal and procedural terms, wedded to vertical modularity. It can coexist with, and even depend on, horizontal relationships among different components of the system. Institutional design – or redesign – challenges can thus be considered in their parts but also in relation to the system as a whole, so that it – as well as they – might gradually evolve in more democratic directions. Hurley's philosophical outlook thus supports and renders coherent several of the enterprises argued for in different ways by the other contributors to this volume. Her suggestive elaboration of it offers a host of novel avenues for theorizing about democratic innovation in the future.

REFERENCES

Dahl, Robert A. 1989. *Democracy and its Critics*. New Haven and London: Yale University Press.
Hirschman, Albert O. 1970. *Exit, Voice and Loyalty*. Cambridge, MA: Harvard University Press.
Holmes, Stephen. 1988. "Gag rules or the politics of omission." In Jon Elster and Rune Slagstad (eds.), *Constitutionalism and Democracy*, pp. 19–58. Cambridge: Cambridge University Press.
Rawls, John. 1993. *Political Liberalism*. New York: Columbia University Press.

Part I

Outer edges

2 Can international organizations be democratic? A skeptic's view[1]

Robert A. Dahl

Can international organizations, institutions, or processes be democratic? I argue that they cannot be. Any argument along these lines raises the question, "What is democracy?" or, better, "What do I mean by democracy?" If I can say what democracy is, presumably I can also say what democracy is not, or to put it another way, what is not a democracy.[2] In brief: an international organization is not and probably cannot be a democracy.

Democracy

Yet to say what democracy is and is not is far more difficult than we would like. This is so for many reasons, of which I will offer three.

First, as we all know, the term democracy has been and continues to be used indiscriminately.[3] Although the word may be applied most frequently to a form of government, it is not restricted to forms of government. What is more, government itself is a protean term. Not only do states have governments; so also do economic enterprises, trade unions, universities, churches, voluntary associations, and other human organizations of infinite variety, from families and tribes to international organizations, economic, military, legal, criminal, and the rest. Even when the word democracy is applied to governments, and further restricted to the government of a state, the concept unfolds into several complex dimensions.[4] In usage, then, the meaning of the term is

---

[1] I am indebted to Martin Gilens for polling data on American opinion and to Bernt Hagtvet and Rune Premfors for providing me with articles, published and unpublished, on the referenda on membership in the European Union in the Nordic countries and Austria.

[2] For another reflection on this question, see Schmitter and Karl 1991.

[3] In his neglected but excellent analysis of the meaning of democracy, Jens Christophersen (1966) provides us with several dozen different usages, many by illustrious writers, and many of them mutually inconsistent.

[4] In my own work, for example, a minimally coherent and adequate assessment seems to me to require descriptions of ideal criteria, their moral justifications, different forms of actual political institutions that we call democratic (which is to say, more or less

virtually unbounded – indeed so unrestricted that it has even been used to signify dictatorship.[5]

To explain why international institutions and processes will be non-democratic, I intend to consider just two of the innumerable aspects of democracy. These are democracy as a system of popular control over governmental policies and decisions, and democracy as a system of fundamental rights.

When we consider democracy from the first and probably the most familiar point of view, we interpret it as consisting of rule by the people, or rather the demos, with a government of the state that is responsive and accountable to the demos, a sovereign authority that decides important political matters either directly in popular assemblies or indirectly through its representatives, chosen by lot or, in modern democracies, by means of elections. Viewing democracy from the second point of view, we interpret it as providing an extensive body of rights. These are of at least two kinds. One consists of rights, freedoms, and opportunities that are essential to popular control and the functioning of the democratic institutions themselves, such as freedom of speech and assembly. The other consists of a broad array of rights, freedoms, and opportunities that, though arguably not strictly essential to the func-tioning of democratic institutions, tend to develop among a people who govern themselves democratically, such as rights to privacy, property, a minimum wage, non-discrimination in employment, and the like.

One may value democracy from either point of view, or, more likely, from both, and of course for other reasons as well. However that may be, I am going to focus mainly on the first perspective, democracy as a system of popular control over governmental policies and decisions,[6] and I will offer several reasons for believing that whatever kind of government may prevail in international organizations it will not be recognizably democratic in that sense. The famous democratic deficit that has been so much discussed with respect to the European Union is not likely to be greatly reduced in the EU; elsewhere the deficit is likely to be far greater.

---

democratic by ideal standards), chiefly democratic polyarchy, and some conditions favorable or unfavorable for the emergence and stability of actual democratic political systems.

[5] "The most explicit occurrence," according to Christophersen, "is Babeuf's statement that the terms 'democracy' and 'Robespierrism' were identical, and the latter term signified a revolutionary dictatorship, or a strict and merciless emergency rule, which was to crush anything that barred the victory of revolution" (Christopherson 1996: 304). Lenin and his followers also equated dictatorship of the proletariat with democracy, or proletarian democracy.

[6] Though a more detailed analysis might benefit from sharper distinctions, I will use the terms policies, decisions, and policy decisions indiscriminately.

The second problem in saying what democracy is and is not is to determine how and where to locate the threshold or cut-off. It is not very useful to treat democracy as if we could specify a sharp, clear line between democracy and non-democracy. Imagine that we had two scales for democracy rather like scales for measuring temperatures. One would run from a theoretical system that is perfectly or ideally democratic to a theoretical system that is completely non-democratic; the other would run from actual or real-world systems that sufficiently meet ideal democratic criteria to be called democracies to the most extreme non-democratic systems that we actually observe in human experience. An analogy might be a thermometer used for weather and one going from absolute zero to the boiling point of water. If we were to place the two democracy scales alongside one another, systems at the top of the scale for measuring actual democracy would surely fall considerably short of the top of the scale on which we would locate an ideal democracy – and so too, no doubt, at the bottom. At what point on the scale of actual political systems are we justified in designating a political system as democratic or non-democratic? Unfortunately the transition from democracy to non-democracy is not like the freezing point of water. None the less, even if the threshold is pretty hazy, I want to argue that international systems will lie below any reasonable threshold of democracy.

A third difficulty in defining democracy arises because, in practice, all democratic systems, with the exception perhaps of a few tiny committees, allow for, indeed depend on, delegation of power and authority; the citizen body delegates some decisions to others. Size and complexity make delegation essential. Despite all their concern for maintaining the authority of the assembly, even Athenians could not avoid delegation. In modern representative democracies, or what I sometimes call polyarchies, the extent of delegation is enormous, in theory running from the demos to its elected representatives to higher executives to top administrators and on down the lengthy bureaucratic hierarchy. To what extent the demos effectively controls important final decisions has been, of course, a much disputed empirical question, not to say a crucial ideological issue. But we would agree, I think, that, in practice, delegation might be so extensive as to move a political system beyond the democratic threshold.[7]

I believe this is very likely to be true with international organizations and institutions, including the European Union (hereafter, the EU).

[7] Guillermo O'Donnell (1994) distinguishes "democratic" systems, in which office-holders are held accountable to voters through competitive elections, and "delegative democracy" in which they are held accountable by one another.

The problem

If that judgment were shown to be justified, a democrat might say, we cannot in good conscience support such delegation of power and authority by democratic countries to international organizations and institutions. Yet this answer will not do. In both democratic theory and practice a fundamental dilemma lurks half hidden, ordinarily just out of view. Other things being more or less equal, a smaller democratic unit provides an ordinary citizen with greater opportunities to participate in governing than a larger unit. But the smaller the unit the more likely that some matters of importance to the citizen are beyond the capacity of the government to deal with effectively. To handle these broader matters, the democratic unit might be enlarged; but in doing so the capacity of the citizen to participate effectively in governing would be diminished. To put it loosely, one might say that although your government gains more control over the problem, your capacity to influence that government is diminished.

At the extreme limit, a democratic unit of, say, twenty people, could provide every member with unlimited opportunities to participate in its decisions and little or no delegation would be necessary. Yet the government would have no capacity to deal effectively with most matters that were important to the members. At the other extreme, a world government might be created in order to deal with problems of universal scope, such as poverty, hunger, health, education, and the environment. But the opportunities available to the ordinary citizen to participate effectively in the decisions of a world government would diminish to the vanishing point. To speak in this case of "delegating authority" would simply be a misleading fiction useful only to the rulers.[8]

Optimists and skeptics

In the latter half of the twentieth century this dilemma has reappeared because of the increasing use of international organizations, institutions, and processes to deal with matters that are beyond the effective capacities of the government of a single country. So the question arises: to what extent can the ideas and practices of democratic government be applied to international organizations, institutions, and processes? Those who believe that democracy can be extended to the international realm offer an optimistic answer. International institutions not only should be democratized but actually can be (Archibugi and Held 1995;

---

[8] For my earlier explorations of this dilemma, see Dahl 1967: 953–70, 1989: 317ff and 1994, and Dahl and Tufte 1973: 13ff.

Held 1995). An opposing view is offered by skeptics such as Philippe Schmitter (1996), who argues that even within "the emerging Europolity" (which is surely the most promising international site for democratization) a recognizably democratic political system is unlikely to develop. For reasons I am going to present here, I share Schmitter's skepticism, although I take a somewhat different path to reach a similar conclusion.

My skepticism applies not just to the European Union but even more to international organizations in general. I do not mean to say that we should reject the benefits of international organizations and institutions. The benefits may sometimes even include assistance in fostering democratization in non-democratic countries. But I believe we should openly recognize that international decision-making will not be democratic. Whether the costs as measured in democratic values are outweighed by gains as measured in other values, and perhaps even by gains in the democratization of non-democratic countries, obviously depends, among other things, on how much one values democracy. Overarching judgments are likely to be either vacuous or highly controversial. The only point I wish to press here, however, is that international policy decisions will not ordinarily be made democratically.

My argument is simple and straightforward. In democratic countries[9] where democratic institutions and practices have been long and well established and where, as best we can tell, a fairly strong democratic political culture exists, it is notoriously difficult for citizens to exercise effective control over many key decisions on foreign affairs. What grounds have we for thinking, then, that citizens in different countries engaged in international systems can ever attain the degree of influence and control over decisions that they now exercise within their own countries?

Foreign affairs and popular control: the standard version

Scholars and other commentators have observed for many years that exercising popular control over foreign policy decisions is a formidable problem. Consider the United States. In the standard version[10] foreign

---

[9] To prevent definitional overload I omit a discursus on what I mean by a "democratic country." Different scholars using similar but not identical criteria tend to converge on about the same list of countries. I simply use the term to refer to the twenty or so countries in which the political institutions of polyarchy, as I have described them elsewhere, have existed since 1950 or earlier, and other countries in which they now exist at about the same level as in these "old" democracies.

[10] The classic and still highly relevant study is Almond 1950.

affairs are remote from the lives, experiences, and familiar knowledge of ordinary citizens. Although a small "attentive public" may exist "before whom elite discussion and controversy takes place" (Almond 1950: 139), a great many citizens lack knowledge of foreign affairs, certainly in depth.[11] Concrete experience, personal familiarity, social and professional ties, knowledge of relevant histories, data, and trends are weak or entirely lacking and are replaced, if at all, by flickering images drawn from radio, television, or newspaper accounts. In addition, the sheer complexity of many international matters often puts them beyond the immediate capacities of many, probably most, citizens to appraise. The upshot is that crucial foreign policy decisions are generally made by policy elites without much input from or accountability to the majority of citizens.[12]

The US decision in late 1993 to adopt NAFTA closely fits the pattern. A week before the vote on NAFTA in the House of Representatives, 79 percent of those surveyed in a CBS/New York Times poll were unsure or did not know whether their Congressional representative favored or opposed NAFTA. "Some Americans felt strongly about NAFTA. But the vast majority neither understood it nor cared enough about it to become well informed. As a result, public opinion was effectively neutralized on the issue and had little effect on the final outcome" (Newhouse and Mathews 1994: 31–2; see also Molyneux 1994: 28–30).

Americans are not unique.[13] Is it realistic, for example, to expect

---

[11] In surveys in the US from the 1930s to 1994, 553 questions concerned foreign affairs. Of these, "14 percent were answered correctly by at least three-quarters of survey respondents ... An additional 28 percent of the items were correctly answered by between half and three-quarters of those asked ... [M]ore than half could be answered by less than half the general public. 36 percent of the questions were known by only one-quarter to one-half of those asked. In the 1940s, this included knowledge about the forms of government of Sweden and Yugoslavia ... and that the United States was sending military aid to Greece. Finally, nearly a quarter of the items could be answered by fewer than one-fourth of those asked. These little known facts included knowing that the United States was sharing information about the atomic bomb with England and Canada in the 1940s ... knowing about how many soldiers had been killed in Vietnam in the 1960s, knowing how much of the federal budget goes to defense of foreign aid in the 1970s ..." (Delli Carpini and Keeter 1996: 82–6).

[12] I am going to use terms like political elites, policy elites, and political leaders and activists despite their lack of precision. Almond (1950: 139ff) distinguished four types of foreign policy elites: political, administrative and bureaucratic, interest, and communication elites. The more inclusive term "political class" widely used in Italy (*la classe politica*), which might also be useful, is too rarely used in English to be helpful here.

[13] Whether Americans are less well informed on foreign affairs than citizens in some European countries is hard to say, since differences in the knowledge of citizens in different countries seems to vary so much with the particular item. See table 2.8 and table 2.9 in Delli Carpini and Keeter 1996: 90–1.

citizens in European countries to develop informed judgments about European Monetary Union and its desirability? The editors of *The Economist* recently observed that "public debate on the subject has been dismally poor right across Europe ... Far from engaging in argument, the pro and anti tribes ignore each other resolutely" (*The Economist* 1996: 17).

One response to the standard account might be: So what? If the average citizen is uninterested in foreign affairs and not fully competent to make informed judgments, is it not better to leave the matter to the political leaders and activists?

We can take it as axiomatic that virtually all decisions by any government, including a democratic government, are disadvantageous to some people. If they produce gains, they also result in costs. If the trade-offs in advantages and disadvantages were identical for everyone, judgments involved in making collective decisions would be roughly equivalent to those involved in making individual decisions; but the trade-offs are not the same for everyone. Typically costs and benefits are distributed unevenly among those subject to a decision. So the perennial questions arise: What is the best decision? Who can best decide? How?

A part of the perennial answer is that the proper criterion for government decisions is the public good, the general interest, the collective good, and other similar, though perhaps not strictly equivalent, formulations. But as we all know, how to define the public good and how to achieve it are formidable problems.

Proposed solutions to the problem of the public good seem to fall into two rough categories: substantive and procedural. Substantive solutions offer a criterion, such as happiness, welfare, well-being, utility, or whatever; a metric or measure that can be summed or aggregated over the persons concerned; and a distributive principle for determining what constitutes a just or justifiable allocation of the good among persons. Procedural solutions offer a process for determining and validating decisions, such as majority rule, or a full-blown democratic process, or guardianship, or judicial determination, and so on. On closer examination, however, neither substantive nor procedural solutions are sufficient; each requires the other. Because substantive solutions are not self-enacting, they require procedures for determining the substantively best outcomes; and because procedures, including democratic procedures, are means to ends, not ends in themselves, their justification depends on more than purely procedural values.

In practice all substantive solutions are contested, indeed highly contested; none commands general acceptability, except perhaps in a purely formulaic way, such as Pareto optimality or the greatest good of the greatest number. In the absence of full agreement on substantive criteria, many people in democratic countries tend to accept procedural solutions as sufficient, at least most of the time. When we disagree, they might say, then let the majority decide, if not directly then through our representatives; though to be acceptable, the majority decision must not only follow proper procedures but must also lie within some generally agreed on boundaries as to rights, liberties, minimal standards of justice, and so on.[14]

As a practical matter, the problem of determining the general good would be easier to solve in a political unit containing a highly homogeneous population. At the limit of complete homogeneity, differences in the impact of collective decisions would vanish, but of course that limit is rarely if ever reached, even in a unit as small as a family. In any case, an increase in the size of a political unit is usually accompanied by an increase in the diversity of interests, goals, and values among the people in the unit. Thus when a democratic unit is enlarged to include new territory and people, the demos is likely to become more heterogeneous. Diversity in turn tends to increase the number of possible political interests and cleavages based on differences in economic position, language, religion, region, ethnic or racial identity, culture, national affiliation, historical memories, organizational attachments, and others.

As the number of persons and the diversity of interests increase, the idea of a common good or general interest becomes ever more problematic. Earlier I mentioned some of the cognitive and emotional obstacles to popular control over foreign policy decisions. These make it harder for citizens to perceive and understand the situations, conditions, needs, wants, aims, and ends of other citizens who are distant and different from themselves in crucial respects. Even if they acquire some grasp on these matters, their incentives to act for the benefit of the distant others when it may be to their own cost or disadvantage are weak or nonexistent. Beyond the boundaries of one's own intimate attachments, altruism is uncommon, and as a steady state among many people it is too feeble to be counted on. In sum, among a large group of persons with varied and conflicting ends, goals, interests, and purposes, unanimity is unattainable, disagreement on the best policy is to be expected, and civic virtue is too weak a force to override individual and group interests.[15]

---

[14] The process of deliberation in democratic decision-making, to which democratic theorists have been giving increased attention, can be seen as a crucial procedural stage necessary if democratic decisions are to be substantively justifiable. See Guttman and Thompson 1996 and Fishkin 1991.

[15] I have elaborated on this question in Dahl 1987 and 1995.

If the public good on foreign affairs were rationally demonstrable, if in fine Platonic fashion the elites possessed the necessary rationality and sufficient virtue to act on their knowledge of the public good, and if ordinary citizens had no opinions or held views that demonstrably contradicted their own best interests, then a defensible argument might be made that the political leaders and activists should be entrusted with decisions on foreign affairs. But on international issues the public good is as rationally contestable as it is on domestic questions and we have no reason to believe that the views of elites are in some demonstrable sense objectively correct. Yet the weight of elite consensus and the weakness of other citizens' views means that the interests and perspectives of some, possibly a majority, are inadequately represented in decisions. Views that might be strengthened among ordinary citizens if these views were more effectively brought to their attention in political discussion and debate remain dormant. The alternatives are poorly explored among ordinary citizens, if not among the policy elites. Yet if citizens had gained a better understanding of their interests and if their views had then been more fully developed, expressed, and mobilized, the decisions might have gone another way.

These conditions probably exist more often on foreign affairs than on domestic issues. Sometimes elites predominantly favor one of the major alternatives; many citizens are confused, hold weak opinions, or have no opinions at all; and those who do have opinions may favor an alternative that the political leaders and activists oppose. So public debate is one-sided and incomplete, and in the end the views and interests of the political leaders and activists prevail.

To provide a satisfactory account of the empirical evidence bearing on this conjecture would be a large undertaking, all the more so if one attempted to compare the experiences of several democratic countries. The best I can offer are several scattered pieces of evidence:

- As I have already indicated, the US decision about NAFTA appears to fit the pattern pretty well.
- Support for European unification was markedly higher among "opinion leaders" than among non-leaders in twelve European countries from 1973–91 (Wessels 1995: 143–4, tables 7.2 and 7.3). From evidence for changes in support over time, one author concludes that:

a system of internationalized governance such as the EC could not expect support if there were no political leaders and activists, political parties, and attentive publics who care about it. That does not turn the European integration process into a process independent of mass opinion. Quite the contrary: because support and legitimacy are necessary, élites and political actors have to work to secure them. (Wessels 1995: 162)

The revised standard version: occasional activation

In the standard version, the views of elites tend to prevail, particularly when they pretty much agree. But suppose that the policy on which they agree is seen to cause or threatens to cause great harm to the interests, goals, and well-being of a large number of citizens. We need only recall the Vietnam War, in which US policy was initially made almost exclusively by "the best and the brightest," the elite of the elites, until the human waste and futility of the war became so evident as to create intense public opposition *and* a broadening split among the political leaders and activists. On such occasions, political leaders and activists are sharply divided, ordinary citizens are activated, mass publics develop strong views about foreign affairs, and public opinion becomes highly influential in key foreign policy decisions (Aldrich, Sullivan, and Bordiga 1989).

It is misleading to say, for example, that Americans never become involved in foreign affairs. Answering the standard Gallup question, "What do you think is the most important problem facing this country today?" in about one-third of the 150 surveys from 1935 to 1985 Americans ranked foreign affairs highest. At least once in each of eighteen years during that fifty-year interval Americans put foreign affairs highest. Not surprisingly, the importance of foreign affairs soared during wars: World War II, Korea, Vietnam. In short, their responses were appropriate to the circumstances.[16] While support for the war effort during World War II was widespread among elites and the general public, during the wars in Korea and Vietnam elite opinion, at least in some highly influential quarters, lagged behind general public opinion.

In Europe, questions about a country's relations with the EU and its predecessor, the European Community, have led to the political

---

[16] Thus, in 1939, the public concerns of Americans began to shift from domestic to foreign affairs, moved to first place after Hitler invaded Poland, were replaced at the end of World War II by domestic matters, which in turn were replaced by Cold War worries in the late 1940s. "From that point until the early 1960s, foreign affairs dominated public concern, ranking first in 48 of 56 surveys and often commanding over 50 percent of the public ... In 1963 the hegemony of foreign affairs was interrupted by the emergence of the civil rights movement ... until foreign affairs, boosted by the Vietnam War, regained the top position in 1965. From 1960 to 1970 Vietnam and other international issues dominated public concern. The only exception occurred in August 1967, when race riots pushed social control to the forefront...With minor exceptions, economics has completely dominated public concerns for the last 10 years [1974–84], often capturing 60 percent of the public" (Smith 1985).

activitation of a large part of the electorate,[17] aroused intense passions, and produced sharp divisions within the general population, sometimes in opposition to the predominant views of the political leaders and activists. Political activation and sharp divisions were particularly visible in the referendum in Norway in 1972 on membership in the EC, in France in 1992 on ratifying the Maastricht Treaty, and in Norway and Sweden in 1994 on membership in the EU. In all four referenda, citizens disagreed as sharply in their views of what would be best for themselves and their country as they would on divisive domestic issues. Voters in the French referendum on Maastricht split almost evenly (51 percent yes to 49 percent no) along class and occupational lines.[18] By small majorities Norwegians rejected membership in the EC in a referendum in 1972 and again in the EU in 1994. In public argument, advocates of the economic, security, and cultural advantages of the EU were in conflict with opponents who tended to stress such values as democracy, absence of red-tape Brussels bureaucracy, environmental protection, welfare state values and policies, counter-culture as well as gender equality. Analysis of the vote reveals significant differences among Norwegians. "No" votes were concentrated more heavily in the northern and western periphery; in fishing and farming communities; among church members, women, and those working in primary industries or in the public sector, particularly in social and public health services. "Yes" votes were concentrated more in urbanized areas, particularly in the area around Oslo, and among voters with university education or higher incomes. Voters who identified themselves as supporters of the Christian, Agrarian, or Left Socialist parties preponderantly opposed EU membership, while both Labor and Conservative voters strongly supported it.[19] The referendum in Sweden appears to have divided voters in a somewhat similar fashion. It is worth noting, by the way, that Swedish surveys revealed that within a year the majority in favor had declined to a minority, though by then the die was cast.

---

[17] The turnout on the EU referendum in Austria was 82 percent, which exceeded the general election of 1994; in Finland, 74 percent, about the same as in the election of 1991; in Sweden, 83.3 percent, about 3.5 percent lower than in the immediately preceding general election; in Norway, 89 percent, which exceeded turnout in all previous elections (Jahn and Storsved 1995).

[18] The "no" vote was 70 percent among farm laborers, 62 percent among farmers, and 60 percent among urban manual workers. Lower white collar workers and persons in crafts and small business split almost evenly. People in big business, management, professions, academics, scientists, teachers, and health and social workers voted in favor by substantial majorities (Brulé 1992).

[19] Cf. Petterson, Jenssen, and Listhaug 1996; Hansen 1996; Bjorklund (n.d.). Although the various factors tend to overlap, multiple regression analysis indicates that those listed had significant independent effects.

The revised standard version of the influence of public opinion on foreign policy, then, would read something like this: although citizens in democratic countries are usually less interested in foreign affairs than in domestic issues, in some circumstances they can become activated and play an influential or even decisive role in key foreign policy decisions. A policy is likely to activate citizens if it causes or threatens to cause such severe harm to the interests, goals, and well-being of a large minority, or even a majority, of citizens that they become aroused in opposition, political activists arise to champion their cause, and political leaders are themselves split. The question then begins to look very much like a hard-fought domestic issue. If the threatened costs of the policy are fairly obvious, concrete, and immediate, while the promised gains are abstract, theoretical, and distant, leaders in favor of the policy may ultimately lose.

Yet even in the revised standard version, such issues are rare: in Vietnam, casualties brought the costs home while the promised gains, like preventing the dominoes of South and Southeast Asia from falling, were to most Americans remote, uncertain, and highly theoretical. So, too, joining the EU pits assurances of long-run and somewhat abstract gains for some Europeans against more specific and understandable losses perceived by others.

But foreign policy decisions like these are uncommon. Even NAFTA did not activate many voters, despite the efforts of its opponents to generate fears of its consequences. As a result, most Americans gave it scant attention. In effect, the decision was made by political leaders and activists without much influence by ordinary citizens.

International organizations and processes

If popular control is formidably difficult within democratic countries, surely the problem will be even harder to solve in international institutions. If Norway had joined the EU, would its citizens be able to exercise anything like the degree of influence and control over the decisions in Brussels and Strasbourg that they have over the decisions of their own parliament and cabinet? Swedish citizens may now have more influence on the policy decisions of the EU than Norwegians, but would anyone contend that they exercise as much influence in the European Parliament as they do in their own? Or Danes? That these are small and relatively homogeneous countries only reinforces the point. Scale and heterogeneity matter. But the same question might be asked about a larger country such as Britain.

To achieve a level of popular control that is anywhere near the level already existing within democratic countries, international organizations would have to solve several problems about as well as they are now dealt with in democratic countries. Political leaders would have to create political institutions that would provide citizens with opportunities for political participation, influence, and control roughly equivalent in effectiveness to those already existing in democratic countries. To take advantage of these opportunities, citizens would need to be about as concerned and informed about the policy decisions of international organizations as they now are about government decisions in their own countries. In order for citizens to be informed, political and communication elites would need to engage in public debate and discussion of the alternatives in ways that would engage the attention and emotions of the public. To insure public debate, it would be necessary to create an international equivalent to national political competition by parties and individuals seeking office.[20] Elected representatives, or functional equivalents to them (whatever they might be), would need to exercise control over important international bureaucracies about as well as legislatures and executives now do in democratic countries.

How the representatives of a hypothetical international demos would be distributed among the people of different countries poses an additional problem. Given huge differences in the magnitude of the populations of different countries, no system of representation could give equal weight to the vote of each citizen and yet prevent small countries from being steadily outvoted by large countries; thus all solutions acceptable to the smaller democracies will deny political equality among the members of the larger demos. As with the United States and other federal systems, acceptable solutions may be cobbled together as one has been for the EU. But whatever compromise is reached, it could easily be a source of internal strain, particularly in the absence of a strong common identity.

Strain is all the more likely because, as I have already said, just as in national democracies most decisions are bound to be seen as harming the interests of some people, so too in international organizations. The heaviest burden of some decisions might be borne by particular groups, regions, or countries. To survive these strains, a political culture supportive of the specific institutions would help – might indeed be necessary. But developing a political culture takes time, perhaps many generations. In addition, if policy decisions are to be widely acceptable and enforceable among the losers, then it is probable that some common identity, equivalent to that in existing democratic countries, would have to

---

[20] Although his conclusions are somewhat more hopeful than mine, Ramón Vargas-Machuca 1994 addresses some of the problems.

develop. On present evidence, even Europeans do not now possess a common identity.[21] How then can we reasonably expect one to grow elsewhere?

In sum: if it is difficult enough for ordinary citizens to exercise much influence over decisions about foreign affairs in their own countries, should we not conclude that the obstacles will be far greater in international organizations? Just as many important policy decisions in democratic countries are in effect delegated by citizens to the political elites, will not the citizens of countries engaged in an international association delegate effective control to the international policy elites? And will not the extent of delegation in international organizations go well beyond any acceptable threshold of democracy?

Conclusions

To say that international organizations are not and are not likely to be democratic is not to say that they are undesirable. It seems evident that they are necessary to many of the same human needs and goals that advocates of democracy contend are best served by democratic governments, and, as I said at the beginning, they can sometimes assist a non-democratic country to make the difficult transition from a highly undemocratic to a more democratic government. In addition, international organizations can help to expand human rights and the rule of law, the other important aspect of democracy that I emphasized earlier. Even measured against some loss in democratic control, these are important potential gains.

Despite these possible advantages I see no reason to clothe international organizations in the mantle of democracy simply in order to provide them with greater legitimacy.

But if their governments cannot be justified as democratic, how can they be justified? In the current world there are not many alternatives to democracy as a source of legitimacy. Autonomous hierarchies are hard to justify, though justifications do exist. The hierarchies of business enterprises acquire legitimacy because they are believed to be useful to the operation of predominantly privately owned market economies, which nowadays are almost universally regarded as preferable to any

---

[21] "As an economic, political, and administrative construction, Europe evidently elicits evaluative attitudes, but not a real community of belonging of the kind experienced in nation states. If the European Union is able, in the future, to generate a new system of belonging, it is difficult to imagine, from what we know, what it will be like. ... For the present, a European identity is a vanguard phenomenon" (Duchesne and Frognier 1995: 223).

feasible alternative.[22] Other hierarchies in the private or non-profit sectors in democratic countries – including universities, research centers, hospitals, some religious organizations, and many others – justify the non-democratic aspects of their governments as necessary on the ground that their governors are greatly superior in knowledge and expertise to those they govern, and adequately concerned for the well-being of those subject to their decisions.

As long as, and in fact longer than, the idea of democracy and the practise of popular government have existed, so too has an alternative view, according to which rule by an elite of guardians possessed of greatly superior knowledge and virtue is definitely superior to democracy. Although we who advocate democracy reject this view as invalid when it is applied to the government of a state, including the government of a nation state or a country, is the argument for guardianship valid in governing international organizations? If not, and if as I have argued here democracy is unattainable in international organizations, what alternative would be left? Or, should I say, what alternative would be right?

Although the answer to that question is unclear to me, I would like to suggest some parts of an answer.

1. We should be wary of ceding the legitimacy of democracy to non-democratic systems. In the course of this century we have already witnessed many attempts to cloak non-democratic systems in the mantle of democracy. We have had "authentic" democracy, "true" democracy, "proletarian" democracy, "people's" democracy, "stock-holder" democracy, and many others. All of these were in fact non-democratic forms of bureaucratic, hierarchic, or authoritarian rule. If international organizations are not democratic, then are we not obliged to speak the truth about them?

2. Yet if the governments of international organizations are not democracies, what are they? I suggest that we treat them as *bureaucratic bargaining systems*. Just as rulers in most authoritarian governments are to some extent and in some ways responsive to the opinions and desires of those over whom they govern – even corporate managers cannot indefinitely ignore the desires of their subordinates – so leaders in bureaucratic bargaining systems cannot indefinitely ignore

---

[22] I agree that in a democracy there are no feasible alternatives to a predominantly (not completely!) market-oriented economy. I also believe that the existing hierarchies in business enterprises are not necessary or legitimate, and the arguments in their defense seem to me unsatisfactory. See, e.g., Dahl 1985. At present, views along these and similar lines are clearly those of a fairly small minority. Should they become widely shared in the future, then of course the governments of most existing business would be in deep trouble.

the limits set by the opinions and desires of the governed. But if such a highly attenuated kind of responsiveness were sufficient to render a political system "democratic" then I do not see how any political system could ever be non-democratic.

3. In weighing the desirability of bureaucratic bargaining systems in international organizations, the *costs to democracy* should be clearly indicated and taken into account. Even if we conclude that the gains, or expected gains, outweigh these costs, that is no reason to ignore them entirely. The "democratic deficit" described by critics of the bureacratic bargaining system for governing the European Union should be seen as a likely cost of all international governments.

4. Supporters of democracy should resist the argument that a great decline in the capacity of national and subnational units to govern themselves is inevitable because globalization is inevitable. To be sure, the forces leading to greater internationalization of the economic, political, military, social, and cultural spheres of human life appear to be extremely powerful. However, I do not see how we can know with confidence the extent to which globalization is inevitable or contingent. The last three centuries are a graveyard packed with the corpses of "inevitable" developments. Instead of yielding to triumphal claims of inevitablity, we should evaluate each situation on its own merits.

5. If we judge that important human needs require an international organization, despite its costs to democracy, we should not only subject its undemocratic aspects to scrutiny and criticism but also try to create proposals for greater democratization and insist that they be adopted.[23]

6. Finally, in so far as the government of an international organization continues indefinitely as an undemocratic bureaucratic bargaining system, are we not obliged to develop criteria against which to judge it? We do have some useful criteria for judging how well a government measures up to democratic standards, even if we may disagree on details. But what standards should we use to appraise an international organization after we have concluded that it is desirable despite the costs to democracy imposed by its bureaucratic bargaining system of government? And on what grounds are we to justify any alternative standards that we may propose? These may be difficult, and even embarrassing, questions, but I do not believe we should evade them by describing undemocratic systems as democratic.

[23] Such proposals have in fact been advanced by scholars who are more optimistic than I about democratizing international organization. See, for example, Held 1995: chap. 12.

REFERENCES

Aldrich, John H., John L. Sullivan, and Eugene Bordiga. 1989. "Foreign affairs and issue voting: do presidential candidates 'waltz before a blind audience'?" *American Political Science Review* 83(1): 124–41.

Almond, Gabriel. 1950. *The American People and Foreign Policy.* New York: Harcourt Brace.

Archibugi, Daniele and David Held (eds.). 1995. *Cosmopolitan Democracy, An Agenda for a New World Order.* Cambridge: Polity Press.

Bjorklund, Tor. n.d. "Change and continuity: the 'no' majority in the 1972 and 1994 referendum concerning Norwegian membership in the EU" (ms).

Brulé, Michel. 1992. "France after Maastricht." *The Public Perspective* 4(1): 28–30.

Christophersen, Jens A. 1966. *The Meaning of Democracy.* Oslo: Universitetsvorlaget.

Dahl, Robert A. 1967. "The city in the future of democracy." *American Political Science Review* 61: 953–70.

1985. *A Preface to Economic Democracy.* Berkeley: University of California.

1987. "Dilemmas of pluralist democracy: the public good of which public?" In Peter Koslowski (ed.), *Individual Liberty and Democratic Decision-making*, pp. 201–14. Tubingen: J. C. B. Mohr.

1989. *Democracy and its Critics.* New Haven: Yale University Press.

1994. "Democratic dilemma: system effectiveness versus citizen participation." *Political Science Quarterly* 109: 23–34.

1995. "Is civic virtue a relevant ideal in a pluralist democracy?" In Susan Dunn and Gary Jacobsohn (eds.), *Diversity and Citizenship*, pp. 1–16. Lanham, MD: Rowman and Littlefield.

Dahl, Robert A. and Edward R. Tufte. 1973. *Size and Democracy.* Stanford: Stanford University Press.

Delli Carpini, Michael X. and Scott Keeter. 1996. *What Americans Know About Politics and Why It Matters.* New Haven: Yale University Press.

Duchesne, Sophie and André-Paul Frognier. 1995. "Is there a European identity?" In Oskar Niedermayer and Richard Sinnott (eds.), *Public Opinion and International Governance*, pp. 193–226. New York: Oxford University Press

The Economist. 1996. "The wrong design." 14 December, p. 17.

Fishkin, James. 1991. *Democracy and Deliberation.* New Haven: Yale University Press.

Guttman, Amy and Dennis Thompson. 1996. *Democracy and Disagreement.* Cambridge, MA: Harvard University Press.

Hansen, Tore. 1996. "The regional basis of Norwegian EU-resistance" (ms).

Held, David. 1995. *Democracy and the Global Order, From the Modern State to Cosmopolitan Governance.* Stanford: Stanford University Press.

Jahn, Detlef and Ann-Sofie Storsved. 1995. "Legitimacy through referendum? The nearly successful domino-strategy of the EU referendums in Austria, Finland, Sweden and Norway." *West European Politics* 18: 18–37.

Molyneux, Guy. 1994. "NAFTA revisited: unified 'opinion leaders' best a reluctant public." *The Public Perspective, A Roper Center Review of Public Opinion and Polling* (January/February): 28–30.

Newhouse, Neil S. and Christine L. Mathews. 1994. "NAFTA revisited: most Americans just weren't deeply engaged." *The Public Perspective, A Roper Center Review of Public Opinion and Polling* (January/February): 31–2.

O'Donnell, Guillermo. 1994. "Delegative Democracy." *Journal of Democracy* 5(1): 56–69.

Pettersen, Per Arnt, Anders Todal Jenssen, and Ola Listhaug. 1996. "The 1994 EU referendum in Norway: continuity and change." *Scandinavian Political Studies* 19(3): 257–81.

Schmitter, Philippe C. 1996. "Is it really possible to democratize the Euro-polity." Unpublished.

Schmitter, Philippe and Terry Lynn Karl. 1991. "What democracy is . . . and is not." *Journal of Democracy* 2(3): 75–88.

Smith, Tom W. (1985). "The polls: America's most important problems, Part I: National and international." *Public Opinion Quarterly* 49: 264–74.

Vargas-Machuca, Ramón. 1994. "How to be larger and more accountable: the paradoxical challenge of European political parties." A paper presented at the Center for Advanced Study in the Social Sciences of the Juan March Institute, Madrid, on 15–17 December.

Wessels, Bernhard. 1995. "Support for integration: elite or mass driven?" In Oskar Niedermayer and Richard Sinnott (eds.), *Public Opinion and International Governance*, pp. 137–62. Oxford: Oxford University Press.

3   A comment on Dahl's skepticism

James Tobin

Dahl discusses several aspects of the feasibility of democracy in an international setting. He is pessimistic, convincingly so. Let me mention some thoughts about his topic that may reflect the disciplinary perspective of an economist.

Governance of international institutions

Typically the members are nation states, and the organization operates under a constitution agreed by treaty among them. The members are often vastly different in population, and they are usually not all democracies. What would democratic governance mean? Even if all members were democracies, they would not be likely to agree that each member have votes proportionate to its population. For example, the countries whose pecuniary contributions are essential to the functioning of the World Bank and International Monetary Fund are not about to let China run these institutions. Germany and France are not about to let the new euro central bank be run by a board of EU member representatives with votes weighted by population.

Exit as a substitute for voice

Albert Hirschman (1970) pointed out that internal democracy is not the only possible source of moral legitimacy for an institution. If membership is voluntary, if "exit" is permissible and not terribly costly, then governance by "voice" of members is not essential. Indeed it may be unfair to let members with transient attachments participate in governance on equal terms with those having long records of "loyalty" – a third Hirschman concept. Exit is fair when competing institutions exist or can be established. Equity requires democracy when exit is infeasible or very costly. Of course the costs of exit and transfer to an alternative institution are matters of degree, and accordingly various pragmatic mixtures of voice and exit are appropriate.

Regretfully I have never shared Dahl's enthusiasm for democracy of employees, or of employees, customers, and share-owners, as a principle of governance of business enterprises. Nor would I – or I think he – favor analogous democratic governance of universities by majorities of all members of the community.

If "exit" does not work, the answer within a single jurisdiction has to be anti-trust policy or other regulations and protections imposed by a democratic polity. In many cases, especially in the international context Dahl is discussing here, neither competition among parallel institutions nor democratic governance is feasible, and we are left with what Dahl calls bureaucratic bargaining systems to exert the supervision of the broader polity.

Unions and federations, and constitutions

Unrestricted majority rule could be disastrous for minorities, for equality of citizens before the law, and for the continuation of democracy itself. That is why constitutions are essential. And that is why devolutions of decisions on local issues to democratic governments of diverse smaller entities could ideally protect minorities against majoritarian tyranny without giving any of them extra weight in national decisions. The ideal is elusive. Nation states are typically federations; their constitutions are the contracts of union or federation and constituent governments, as well as the rights of citizens. The United States Senate is an undemocratic aberration in our constitution, but without such a compromise the union might not have been formed and might not survive demographic and economic shifts.

As Dahl suggests, we must expect similar compromises in the governance of the European Union. The European Parliament represents head-counts irrespective of boundaries between members, but that is probably a reason why it will never have sovereign power.

Which populations are entitled to be sovereign democratic states?

This seems to me a thorny problem in democratic theory. Majority rule and self-determination, yes, but for whom? Does geography identify a sovereign nation? Ethnicity? Religion? History? Are the British Isles inclusive of Ireland, Scotland, and Wales a legitimate unit, the pre-1914 United Kingdom a feasible federation? Irish nationalists, with the support of a majority of residents of the island, claimed the whole of

Ireland. The aggregate Protestant majority of six northern counties wanted to stay in the UK and succeeded. But Catholic majorities in two of those counties preferred the Free State. Democratic theory does not tell us how the area should be divided among separate sovereign democracies, whether or not they can be federally joined.

The modern world is full of similar conflicts – Yugoslavia, Chechnya, Somalia, Sudan, Rwanda and Burundi, the Congo, Liberia, Armenia and Azerbaijan, Kurdistan, etc. – and unfortunately they generally become bloody. Actually it is hard to think of nations whose boundaries were not determined by force and invasion, as natural and sacred as they seem to current residents.

Commitment and credibility

Dahl wonders whether a sovereign democratic government can credibly commit the state beyond its own term in agreements with other countries. Of course dictators can change their minds too, as Hitler and Stalin did. Actually, nations do generally respect treaty obligations, even though the agreements were made by governments of opposing parties. (However, the United States Congress has made our government an exception by its unwillingness to pay UN dues).

The problem of inconstancy in policy as a result of political swings extends beyond foreign policy. In electoral competition, parties and candidates are judged term by term, election by election, on their promises and achievements. Yet governments do many things and pass many laws of longer lives and still longer effects. Zig-zags and stop-goes between ideologically and programmatically extreme parties are a potential threat. Socialize after one election, privatize after the next? Business and finance – the Bond Market! – communities insist on the need for credibility, which is strongly emphasized in economic theory these days. Powerful interests say, in effect, "We must have credible monetary, fiscal, financial, tax policies, or else we won't play."

The result is a strong movement to remove important economic policies from democratic politics. In the US the Federal Reserve becomes more and more independent. Congress is chronically on the brink of proposing to the states a constitutional amendment requiring balance of the federal budget. In the UK, the 1997 Labor government has for the first time given the Bank of England operating independence in monetary policy. In Europe, the Treaty of Maastricht will deprive members of the EU of independent monetary, exchange rate, and fiscal policies. These trends endanger democracy by narrowing the scope of democratic choice.

REFERENCE

Hirschman, Albert O. 1970. *Exit, Voice, and Loyalty: Responses to Decline in Firms, Organizations, and States*. Cambridge, MA: Harvard University Press.

4   The democratic order, economic globalization, and ecological restrictions – on the relation of material and formal democracy

Elmar Altvater

Introduction: three dilemmas of democratic order

In the democratic order, in principle, citizens make political decisions under conditions of freedom and equality. Procedures and rhythms of this decision-making follow from a historically specific spatio-temporal regime constituted in a long-lasting process since the beginnings of the "age of liberalism." The spatial boundaries of sovereign nation states define a limited territory within the "pluriverse" (Schmitt 1963: 54) of nation states. The territory endows citizens with rights (and duties) of participation in decision-making procedures. But because citizens also are involved in economic activities, they are construing an economic space which transcends the limited political territory. The contradiction between economic boundlessness and political limitedness with regard to time and space of action has already been conceptualized by Adam Smith (Rosanvallon 1988). Today the contradiction between political territoriality and economic (global) space has become a common argument in the discourse on "globalization."

In addition to formal and procedural dimensions of participation, the equality of citizens is material and substantial. After World War II the substance of material citizens' rights emanated from the collective welfare state in the form of individual claims which within the United Nations system are considered social, economic, and cultural rights ("human rights of second generation"). In the postwar period, they have become prerequisites of the modern democratic discourse and in some cases they claim the dignity of constitutional principles. But recently globalization processes, including the dissolution of political sovereignty on the one hand and the ecological crisis on the other, have undermined claims to substantial rights. The democratic order therefore faces a number of new dilemmas, which will be discussed in the following.

(1) Beetham (1993) suggests four theorems that explain the relationship between markets and democracy: (1) the "necessity" theorem, which explains the necessity of a democratic order for the market to function well; (2) the "analogy" theorem, which outlines how the liberal democracy and free market are following analogous principles; (3) the "superiority" theorem, which says that, in terms of providing freedom to citizens, the market is superior; and (4) the "disability" theorem which, in contrast to the necessity theorem, would show how liberal democracy is a hindrance to the free market's efficiency. This model suggests that in the market citizens count only if they have money. The more dollars, German marks or Japanese yen they have in their purse in the "dollar-ballot-democracy," the more important they and their vote may be. In the democratic "political market," however, the rules of "one man, one vote" are valid, that is, the conditions of strict equality of citizens pertain: all voices are equally loud, independent of the citizens' bank accounts.

The equality of *citoyens* in politics discussed by Marx thwarts the inequality between *bourgeois* and *prolétaire* as do the welfare state's minimal standards of social equality, and to a certain extent the claims of economic and social human rights in international politics. In part, this may be because the formal democratic order's substantial standards are minimal and therefore acceptable everywhere, i.e., "for all its problems, failures, and ambiguities, democracy has won the day in the sense that it has no serious political competitor in the modern world" (Shapiro 1996: 3), or as Winston Churchill said: the democratic order still remains the best of the worst. Democracy, at least in principle, has no enemies in the "new world order." "Global democratization" in the analysis of the "Group of Lisbon" (Gruppe von Lissabon 1997) is one of the most striking and unchallenged characteristics of globalization. A democratic political system belongs to the conditionalities of "good governance" requested by international institutions (such as the World Bank or the IMF or the EU). Humanity moved closer to Kant's ideal of "everlasting peace" in democratic societies because there is a congruence between those who decide on war and peace and those who have to bear the consequences of warfare. Thus the democratic question seems to be depoliticized, if politics consists of applying the binary logic of friend or foe (and of the "clash" between them (Schmitt 1963)). But it was never that easy, let alone during the "Cold War" when national identity, for many, was built on the definition of a hostile and threatening alternative.

(2) More important for the question of the procedural rationality of democracy is the contradictory nature between national borders of

politics and the globalized economy's boundlessness. It can be traced back to the emergence of modernity after the Renaissance, the great expeditions and the triumph of the "European rationality of world domination" (Max Weber). In the historical process of the "Great Transformation" (Polanyi 1957 [1944]) since the seventeenth century, the economy breaks away from social control and subjugates society to the capitalist accumulation's laws and acquisition's inherent rationality. As Beetham (1993) convincingly showed, this rationality is not fully compatible with political rationality, even in the formal sense of the democratic process. Economic decision-makers either deny political territoriality or take it as an opportunity for arbitrage speculation, and, that is, integrate it into the global economic space as a part of it and thus reduce it to an economic calculus. Thus their instrumental, formal economic rationality surpasses political deliberations and the "bed" of social relations, disembedding them, as Polanyi (1957 [1944]) suggests. This contradiction between formality and materiality of social (and political) decisions, well known since Max Weber, is apparently intensifying at the end of the twentieth century and involving an increasing tension between globalization and nation states, "systemic constraints," and political deregulation. These indicate the political-administrative system's loss of control of essential economic variables.

(3) This leads us to the third problem of democratic rationality. For the determination of application ranges and duration of the procedures, democracy requires coordinates in space and time to secure "governability," since, of course, governability can never refer to the global system as a whole.[1] Borders are already necessary to secure the formal democratic working of the procedures. In addition, they are the framework within which *substantial* rights of both individuals (human rights) and peoples (peoples' rights) can be asserted and maintained.[2] The

---

[1] Governability has to be distinguished from governance. The latter is a project of a global reach as the establishment of the "world commission on global governance" clearly shows (Commission on Global Governance 1995). The change of discourses is interesting: in the 1970s the "trilateral commission" tried to spell out the prerequisites of overcoming non-governability and the re-establishment of conditions of governability of Western nation states. The "commission on global governance" twenty years later in the 1990s, however, is aiming to the establishment of "soft" global rules for new forms of institutionalized global cooperation between states, private economic actors, international organizations, and NGOs. (For the trilateral commission see Sklar 1980; for global governance see Commission on Global Governance 1995; Falk 1995.)

[2] This is the basic idea of social and socialist democracy. Lelio Basso, for instance, considers that it is a "fundamental element of socialism" that "conscious and responsible participation" (Basso 1980: 18) have to be possible according to the needs and interests of human beings. It is obvious that this kind of participation prerequisites a limited territorial basis.

rationality of participation is established not only formally, but substantially. The participants in the "democratic game," with all its paradoxes and dilemmas, therefore are equipped with, first, an integrity as persons and thus, second, specific, not just formal, but substantial rights. These rights are historical "achievements," in most cases the outcomes of social and political conflicts, which have become social and political standards. "Western" rationality, which forms the background of formal democracy and the rational choice discourse, has a substantial historical basis: the trinity of (1) capitalist social forms, (2) the use of fossil energy with all the technology which is necessary to transform this energy into work, and last but not least (3) the tradition of rationality, of enlightenment (Altvater 1994).

However, standards become "positional goods" (Harrod 1958; Hirsch 1980) the higher their level and the more they are intentionally generalized. As far as they generate substantial claims, certain rights (in a material sense) cannot be democratized, they are "oligarchic" or "positional": while everybody can equally participate in voting, this is not possible with regard to the participation in the consumption of natural resources. This is the tragedy, so to speak, of the democratic process: the formal "rules of the game" are not matched by the "stake in the game." This discrepancy is decisive: here, the "rules of the game," i.e., the rules of *formal* democracy, bend for *substantial* reasons. In the social sciences, the dilemma has been described by Garrett Hardin as the "tragedy of the commons" (Hardin 1968) and can also be applied to the rationality of democratic procedures.[3] Consequently, the rules of the "democratic game" cannot be sufficiently discussed without considering *historical (and therefore political) space and time and the (ecological) carrying capacity of the (global) commons.* Far away from their boundaries, substance does not matter for formal rules of decision-making; near to the limits of growth (or to the boundaries of the "environmental space" (Wuppertal Institut 1996)) they are of decisive importance and must be taken into account.

Having outlined the problem, we are going to discuss in the following first section the problems arising from economic globalization for the sovereignty of the nation state. Obviously the perforation of national

[3] The conclusion which Garrett Hardin has drawn from his statement must not be accepted (the transformation of the commons into private property). When the carrying capacity of resources and sinks tend to be overloaded, two different reactions are possible: either not all human beings can use natural resources on the level obtained by "Westerners" (the oligarchic solution) or all human beings, inclusive of "Westerners," have to adapt their levels of consumption (the democratic–egalitarian solution) to the carrying capacity of nature.

borders is shaping democracy's space and time, and thus the *meaning of sovereignty* is changing. Whereas these tendencies might be labeled as the "traditional democratic question," in the second section we deal with the "new democratic question," i.e., with the emergence of *new ecological boundaries* which again are reshaping the space and time of democracy, but in a quite different way than that indicated in the preceding section.

Territoriality and globality

The contrast between politics and economics, though aggravated dramatically by globalization, is woven into the capitalist world system's long history, since the fifteenth century in Europe, as nation states and world markets were formed together. Nation states are defined by borders, which they set and defend, both domestically, by the exclusion of those who are considered as not belonging to the citizenry, and externally, against other nation states and their citizens. Thus, the question of citizenship on the one hand and the organization of the "pluriverse" of sovereign nation states, i.e., the constitution of an international order, on the other hand come in. The solution was the establishment of the "Westphalian order" (established 1648 in the peace treaty of Münster and Osnabrück) of mutual respect of nation states, which allows the distinction between friend or foe. From the viewpoint of the nation state, the world of states is divided according to those within and those without, who are to be fought, anticipated as enemies, and potentially the objects of "total war" (Schmitt 1963: 102). It is obvious that the friend–foe construct under the threat of "total war" does not permit deliberative democratic procedures.

More complex, however, is the economic principle of competition, in so far as the economic sphere is characterized by competitors, not (political) enemies. Thus, with the exception of a bilateral monopoly, political binary logic is not applicable in the economic space. The deregulated market follows its unbound rationality and offers, according to Karl Polanyi, not a friendly utopia, because of its social and ecological destructiveness, while Adam Smith, Auguste Comte, or Herbert Spencer since the eighteenth century only perceive progress as a triumphant march of the industrial–commercial principle. So Smith and the liberal thinkers argue for free markets regulated by the "invisible hand" whereas Polanyi argues for the "visible hand," for political and social regulation of the economic sphere. Consequently, where economic rationality in its pure form is *deregulation*, the pure form of political rationality is *regulation*. Economic deregulation undermines political sovereignty and thus the capacity of political regulation and vice versa: political regulation is a means of "re-embedding" and "binding" economic rationality.

The nation state is becoming an inalienable institution of the modern capitalist market economy. Liberal thinkers in the tradition of Adam Smith are fully aware that the state is executing important functions of a society. In Book V of Volume II of the *Wealth of Nations* Smith discusses necessary "expences" of defense, justice, public works, and public institutions "for facilitating the Commerce of the Society" (Smith 1976 [1776]: II/244), of institutions for the education and instruction and, last but not least, of supporting the "Dignity of the Sovereign" (Smith 1976 [1776]: II/338). Following this argument a totally depoliticized market economy is impossible. Therefore a society never can predominantly rely on the functioning of the "invisible hand"; hence, the necessary institutions of the political sphere need rules. First, these rules include procedures for recruiting persons, appointing positions in the political-administrative system, as well as training, education, and control of bureaucrats and bureaucracy. Second, they include the legitimation of political decisions through adequate procedures. Third, they involve questions of the relation between economic freedom and political equality under the conditions of globalization. And, fourth, they involve always topical questions, of the limits of citizen's action (framework and rule of law), of the state towards society (the formation of the "constitutional state"), and the definition of human and peoples' rights. In other words: even if for reasons of economic efficiency the state is necessary to regulate the market economy, society itself has to be able to control the state, the institutions, as well as their personnel. Thus, in our first analysis, procedures regulating the citizen's freedom and equality could be characterized in a *formal* and procedural sense as democratic: "What is a democracy if not a set of rules (the so-called rules of the game) for the solution of conflict without bloodshed?" (Bobbio 1987: 193). But is it so unequivocal and simple?

Because societies are territorially constituted, including formal decisions on the distribution and control of "state power," deregulation involves the partial loss of sovereignty. The democratic process suffers a diminishing role in socially and economically relevant political decision-making. This is because state borders, defining the spatial and temporal reach for the set of formal rules and procedures, are a prerequisite of the territorial *congruence* of decision-making. This is the only way a nation can be conceived as a "community of fate" (Held 1991). The procedural set of rules obliged to this principle – in the minimal sense of Bobbio – nearly defines a democratic system of checks and balances: thus, not only is the representation of the different and antagonistic social interests within the nation state's institutional system maintained in principle, but the exchange between government and subjects is also part of the rules. Therefore, the sphere of the nation state is a prerequisite for the congruence of decision-makers and the persons concerned, of voters and those elected, and, thus, for the efficacy of democratic procedures.

Under the pressure of economic globalization this situation is being changed. Due to the dissolution of the unity between state territory and citizenry, the congruence more and more disappears. The previously clear territorial properties of the state, national power, and people are fading away. The unequivocal allocations of rights and duties as well as the rules of participation in decisions and the mechanisms of legitimation are no longer clear. In times of transnational migration, questions of how civic rights emerge or disappear finds no easy or definite answers. Migration makes the modern invention of (national) citizens seem even more artificial, since fewer and fewer people living in a territory are united in language, origin, religion, ethnic origin, etc.

Politically, globalization and concomitant deregulation also means that, first, privatized decision-making is "de-politicized": it no longer needs citizens' legitimation. The "unconstitutional powers" in the economy or the world of media needs merely present an attractive market supply to the *customers*, yield a profit to the *shareholders*, and achieve a high audience rating; they have only to obey the rules of the economic (and media) sphere. The unconstitutional powers are not tied to political decisions; the citizens – who form a political community – are primarily interesting as economic subjects, particularly as consumers. Hence, globalization raises completely new questions which were not on the agenda as long as the "systemic constraint of the world market" was not a serious question and the sovereignty of the state over a certain territory was a natural and self-explanatory assumption.

Not just political decisions, but also economic decisions made within one nation state turn out to exert effects in other nation states. This problem has been known for some time and has been discussed thoroughly, for example in respect to the influence of transnational corporations on governmental decisions in developing countries. German Bundesbank decisions on the prime rate affect employment and exchange rates from Portugal to Poland, which has been interpreted as a sign of increasing global interdependence as well as of the extraordinary power of certain central banks, i.e., of monetary institutions on democratic procedures. The power of central banks and governments,

however, is not autonomous and politically constituted. They hardly
have any other political option thar to follow the external course
determined by "the capital markets." These economic constraints
restrict the political space. Mexico suffered an especially drastic experience in this respect in December 1994: the reduction of short-term
capital due to decisions (raising of interest rates) made by the US
Federal Reserve System halved the value of the Mexican currency
within a mere two weeks. The idea of sovereignty having a territorial
character is rendered ridiculous in times of globalization. In shaping the
governing institutions of Mexico, the World Bank, the IMF, and the US
Treasury assumed primary importance (NACLA 1997: 13). A comparable story can be told about Asian countries losing control over the
"national" economy and therefore losing political sovereignty *vis-à-vis*
financial markets and institutions as a consequence of the financial crash
in 1997/8.

Certainly, this general statement must not be made without men-
tioning that the nation states' loss of sovereignty is asymmetrical. The
already mentioned example of the German Bundesbank shows that only
a few play first fiddle in the "concert of the nation states" and that many
other less mighty states have to follow their tune. While within the
United Nations system the 200 or so nation states are formally considered equal, in the "new world order" the G7 countries set the tone; even
the "Group of Lisbon," which is harshly critical of the process of
globalization, seriously holds to the rule of the G7 as a "desirable
option" for global governance (Gruppe von Lissabon 1997: 124).
However, the "logic" of state action under the conditions of economic
globalization has changed compared to the so-called "Westphalian
order" of the "pluriverse" of states. This logic is no longer imperialist in
the traditional sense (of Lenin and Luxemburg). It is no longer primarily
all about increasing the political power of the nation state (and/or
territorial, colonial expansion) and direct economic exploitation of
colonial peoples, but about advantages of the respective nation in the
market competition within the geo-economy (Luttwak 1994). These
advantages are relevant with regard to the appropriation of a larger or
smaller share of the global surplus being produced (Holloway 1993;
Altvater and Mahnkopf 1996). Politics in the geo-economy is losing its
territorial foundations and thus its "infrastructural power" (Mann
1984). It cannot condition the citizen's social action when the national
political-administrative systems themselves are conditioned by the
process of globalization.

The ecological crisis also has consequences on the form and substance
of democracy. The radioactive fall-out in Chernobyl not only affected

national citizens in the Ukraine, but *global citizens* from the Scandinavian countries to Poland, Germany, and even to the United States. Their health is more or less strongly threatened, but they cannot react to this as national citizens in any substantially and procedurally decisive way. The idea of the sovereign nation state as a "national community of fate" (Held 1991) has become an anachronism in view not only of economic globalization and the global media world, but also as a consequence of the global ecological crisis. Democratic procedures in the age of global social and ecological problems are rendered questionable merely because the time-frame (nuclear material half-life periods of several tens of thousand years) and the expansion in space (across the whole planet Earth) have become far too big for the "human dimension" of rational decision-making. The congruence of decision, concern, and control has gone. It is impossible to decide on the effects of the radioactive fall-out from Chernobyl or the construction and use of the atomic bomb democratically.

At first sight, the connection between *globalization, deregulation*, and *depoliticization* presents a paradox for the "democratic question." Authoritarian political systems lose their "sense" in view of the authority of the world market. They simply become dysfunctional and make room for formal democratic systems. For political power counts less and less compared to economic power. The transition from the "bureaucratic authoritarian state" (O'Donnell, Schmitter, and Whitehead 1986) to democratic political systems in Latin America during the 1980s (the "abertura") and in Eastern Europe about one decade later ("transformation" or "transition") are a politically adequate reaction to globalization and can therefore be compared, despite many differences. In all cases, the transition – quite different from previous history – took place in a surprisingly orderly fashion, nearly without violence, and without the representatives of the authoritarian regimes clinging to their power and defending it violently. They readily became acquainted with democratic regimes – and vice versa. This is evident in the amnesty laws in Argentina, Chile, and Brazil as well as in the consistency of political elites in many former "socialist" countries.

The direct repression of authoritarian political systems (Latin American dictatorships of the developing state; "socialist" planning economies in Central and Eastern Europe) has been replaced by the "systemic constraint" imposed by the world market, no less effective and harsh than the previous authoritarian political regimes. The politics of democratic governments nowadays often consist of more or less intelligent "structural adjustment" to the challenges of the world market – and often enough are demanded by the world market's institutions, the IMF,

the World Bank, G7, etc., and associated by interested political con-
sultancies.[4] With limited sovereignty over (global) economic procedures,
the nation state cannot enforce political aims – not even with authoritarian measures – or carry out macroeconomic (national) plans (as in
Brazil during the 1970s) against microeconomic powers. The rationality
of economic deregulation supersedes the rationality of political regulation. Therefore, capitalism and democracy are actually compatible.
Economic opening and political opening are conditioning each other.
For highly developed countries to manage competitiveness on the world
market, democratic participation on the national level, and (welfare
state) systems for social security all at once is comparable to squaring
the circle (Dahrendorf 1995), and this is even more so for less developed
countries.

Meanwhile, in all international institutions in which the mighty
Western societies are involved, there is consent on the fact that countries
seeking membership in international institutions, or aid from the international community or association to the EU, NATO, OECD, etc.,
need to pass the "democracy test," in order to secure human rights as
well as ecological minimum standards. Democratic accountability and
the respect of human rights are understood as unrenounceable ingredi-
ents of "good governance." The international system is about not only
economic and social structural adjustment, but also political democratization, unequivocal law administration, and compliance with individual
(and economic, social, and cultural) rights in the very formal sense
outlined above. This again sheds light on the above-mentioned correspondence between the functioning mode of the economic and the
political order, respectively. Even Shell had to declare that compliance
with human rights was one of the corporation's aims, following the
débâcle with Brent Spar and the international outrage over its responsibility for the ecological devastations in the Nigerian Ogoni country, and
especially, its involvement with the military junta who murdered Ken
Saro Wiwa. Is this a recognition of the "good market" principle (Kay
1996), where the securing of profits is moderated by a discourse on
democratic participation and human rights, and where the working of

---

[4] Stephen Volk, in respect to the state and democracy in Latin America, describes how the
nation state's "central role changed from one of encouraging development and providing
public services to overseeing the foreign debt and implementing IMF-inspired structural
adjustments." Quoting Jorge Nef he adds: "The 'highly transnationalized and weak'
state acts as a 'liquidator of its own bankruptcy,' and the process depoliticizes,
demobilizes, privatizes, and insures that any democratic opening will be limited . . . Latin
America today faces the reality that the basic terms not just of its broadly construed
political economy but of the details of its state budget and social trade-offs are often
determined outside its borders" (Volk 1997: 10).

the market is tamed by democratic forms of people's participation (Beetham's (1993) "necessity-theorem")? Or is this an expression of the market's superiority, i.e., of a new form of congruence of market and democracy which relies no more on territorial space, but on political and economic action functioning according to a similar logic? Politics of the state in the geo-economy differ from those of the sovereign national state. The state makes sure that the *competitiveness* of the *national* economy is maintained in the *global competition* and, if possible, improved ("national competition state"). Politics and economics become homologous, such that politics follow the economic logic. In the global currency competition, at least, the nation states are competing to attract highly mobile and volatile financial capital. The borders of a currency-space seem to be more important than the territorial borders of the political unit. In societies exposed to the world market's systemic constraints, formal democracy costs nothing. On the contrary, it reduces social frictions and thus economic transaction costs. The substantial political participation claims of the people (or a collective) fall into the emptiness left by deregulation, within which the individual market participants hang around. In view of the authority of the market, the *substance* of political democracy turns out to be rather thin, even if the *form* is strong.[5]

---

[5] Some think an expansion of the democratic principle to the world society could help and thus turn the inferiority of the democratic principle in its superiority with regard to the market. This entails a delusive hope for a world state (Knieper 1991; critically, with a reference to Kant, Narr, and Schubert 1994), which could only be authoritarian, should it be established. For the distance between citizen and state (the political and administrative system) is geographically, but mainly culturally and concerning the political mechanisms of participation, far too big; it allows no congruence between decision, concern, and control. As for the improvement of "global governance," things are different. This refers to the necessary forms and institutions for the regulation of global processes, an ensemble of market control, hierarchic guidance, and the operation of social networks (cf. Altvater and Mahnkopf 1996: chap 15; Messner 1995; Commission on Global Governance 1995). All should be involved in the process of governance, but a large part of humanity are economically excluded. How can the "interdependence between organizations ... continuing interaction between network members, caused by the need to exchange resources and negotiate shared purposes, game-like interactions, rooted in trust ... a significant degree of autonomy from the state" (Rhodes 1996: 660) be accomplished, if interdependence becomes dependence, if interaction does not help because some of the actors have no resources, if the distances are too big for trust to develop, and if, finally, the autonomy of the state is only the reverse of the dependence on the mechanisms of world economy? Thus a "world state" is a "no starter": a system of global governance, however, is only a weak and contradictory response to the challenges of economic globalization.

Dissolution of old and the establishment of new borders: democracy and the environmental space

Under the conditions of economic globalization, the political space within which democratic deliberations and procedures can be carried out and governability can be secured becomes diffused. But crossing frontiers in the course of capitalist accumulation has led not only to the creation of a world economy out of "national economies," new limits have also been erected in the process. Sensitive observers have been spotting these new limits on the far horizon for some time, but until recently it has not played a role for the attitude and behavior of the people and has attained a name only a short time (nearly three decades) ago: the limit of the "carrying capacity" of ecosystems or of the "environmental space" of planet Earth. This limit is being recognized as a global environmental crisis. Resources are limited in an objective way due to the limitations of planet Earth, even if the limits are politically constituted by the people's discursive practices, i.e., by social subjects (Harvey 1996). Evidence of the interplay between objective challenges and subjective discursive practices is given by the ozone hole and the CFC regime, the greenhouse effect and climate conferences, the destruction of rain forests and the G7 pilot program, the decrease in arable land and the FAO, and especially, the extinction of species – which cumulatively could effect an evolutionary catastrophe – and of course the global environmental debate since UNCED in Rio de Janeiro. The nature of planet Earth is not a free good, but a "positional good," i.e., as more and more people participate in it, its quality is more and more deteriorated for all.

This substantial change leads to a number of consequences: First, it is hardly sensible to determine the central political concept of "power," as Franz Neumann and others did half a century ago:

The concept of power comprises two constituent facts: domination of nature and domination of human beings. Domination of nature is intellectual domination which results from the recognition of the lawfulness of the external nature. This knowledge is the foundation of the productivity of society. This domination has no power. As such, it does not include domination of other human beings. (Neumann 1978 [1950]: 385)

This quotation shows that a discourse can lose its validity in a very short time (in less than half a century). The assumption that domination of nature is powerless and thus practically unpolitical cannot be maintained if the ecological and feminist discourse (e.g., Plumwood 1992) and the discourse of critical Marxism (e.g., O'Connor 1988; Grundmann 1991) are considered in view of the recognized limits of the environmental space. The domination of knowledge over nature only helps increase productivity so long as the consequences of energy and material throughput within the environmental space can be benignly neglected. Limits to increasing productivity are inevitable as resources are exhausted and the spheres of planet Earth are polluted and contaminated. It could even be that the productivity of labor, its increase being the fundamental principle of capitalist market economy and modern society since the writings of Adam Smith, has to be reduced for ecological reasons (radical reduction in the use of fossil energy – apart from an "efficiency revolution" in energy which so many hope for).

Therefore, in contrast to the economic tendencies of dissolving (political) borders, new ecological borders are emerging. They have an objective character, but their relevance is constituted only in the course of a globalized discourse on ecological sustainability (for this aspect see Harvey 1996). The "societal relation to nature" does actually allow different forms of dealing with the borders of the environmental space; the premises under which they are constituted are contested, but nevertheless the natural carrying capacity or the environmental space exhibit new borders. They are discursively constructed after the limits of the state territory have been deconstructed by economic processes of globalization. Consequently, the democratic question is radicalized from two antagonistic sides. First, on the one side is the globalization of the economy and the information media which perforate traditional political borders. On the other, the ecological crisis creates new borders which cannot, in the long term, be ignored. This leads to the traditional question of how to make compatible a boundless (globally) expanding and deregulated market and the limited place (territory) of politics. The *new* question is directed to the effects of the limits of the environmental space on the possibilities of participation, the legitimation of institutions, the representation of interests, and, finally, on the governability of the limited environmental space under the auspices of the politically borderless, "disembedded," and deregulated economic processes.

Second, ecological limits are not congruent with national borders, and therefore, political subjects do not gain their political identity in disputes concerning the establishment of territorial borders and social limits. Traditional citizens wear a "national uniform" which equips them with rights and duties on the state territory. As actors in the environmental space (e.g., in environmentalist movements), however, they face other borders: the restrictions on the use of natural resources in production and consumption. This is not a question of different political party affiliations, but of lifestyle and mode of production. Politics in the nation state and politics in the environmental space thus differ in principle, especially under the aspect of economic globalization. On the one hand, there is a strong and even overpowering tendency towards deregulation, and, on the other hand, there is the unconditional necessity of regulating the society's relation to nature.

When considering democracy and rationality, the theoretical field is formed by the triangle of the globalized economic space, the political space whose borders are more and more perforated, and the new borders of the environmental space. First, the space of politics in the course of globalization, and subsequently the place of democracy, is compressed. This could be the reason for the far-reaching weariness about politics observed in most countries. Why participate in democratic procedures of legitimation and representation if economic processes have already been predecided, can only be confirmed politically *post factum*, and can hardly be changed? If decisions have been made according to the criteria of the market, there is no more space for an application of criteria of political justice, even if they are constructed individualistically.[6] The coordinates in space and time of politics are thus by no means congruent with those of the market or those of material and energy transformations. Democracy, even as a formal set of rules, prerequisites a substantial, secure base. "Western" democratic systems are based on individual and collective wealth, industrialization, urbanization, qualification, and the like.

In the 1950s Lipset (1959: 75) had already referred to the substantial preconditions of formal democracy: "The more well-to-do a nation, the greater the chances that it will sustain democracy." Przeworski holds that, taking empirical findings into account, a democratic order never failed after World War II in a country with a per capita income of more than US$4,335 (Przeworski 1994).[7] Three conclusions now are possible. The first disconnects the argumentative links between substantial and formal democracy. It is possible then to apply the rules of rational decision-making in a democratic order without any reference to substantial constraints. The quoted statements about substantial minimum standards of a formal democratic order are perhaps of a practical

---

[6] This is, by the way, one of the great dangers related to the European integration process according to the criteria of Maastricht. The monetary conditions for the entrance into the monetary union have vastly restricted the scope of political decisions and increased the pressure on social standards in all EU countries. Thus democracy's place is shrinking.

[7] Under the assumption of equal distribution a per capita income of c. US$4,400 for a world population of ca. 6 billion requires a global GNP of ca. US$26,500 billion. This is less than the present gross global product and only half of the stock of financial derivatives on global financial markets. This comparison demonstrates that the substantial democratic question today is more that of distribution than that of production and productivity.

relevance, but theoretically they are not decisive. The second conclusion follows the optimistic position that in the long run mankind will find solutions to any shortage or scarcity of resources and therefore always be able to provide a better standard of life to more people in the world. The limits of the environmental space do not count, productivity and welfare increases are not only desirable but also possible. Third, having enough evidence on the limits of the environmental space, it is clear that the substantial preconditions of formal democracy cannot be established for all societies on the globe at the level of the "Western lifestyle." Then the formal, parliamentarian democracy in most parts of the world is a most fragile order because of its naturally conditioned substantial deficiencies.

An inclination to that constellation of the concomitance of democratic and non-democratic places on the globe is constituted by the fact that the reserves of fossil energy (oil, gas, coal) are unequally distributed, so the use of fossil energies needs a worldwide logistic system which requires so much technological and organizational competence, finances, economic know-how, transport facilities, and political relationships, which can only be procured by highly developed industrial countries for an unforeseeable time. The tendency to – unequal – globalization by no means results just from the functioning of the financial system, but also from the logic of the energy system of the capitalist mode of production: if no equality is possible on Earth under these conditions, then the possibilities of democratic participation are also unequally distributed. The way the social relation to nature is organized in space therefore has consequences for the possibilities of industrial democracy; these depend on whether they refer to *production* or *extraction* economies. In any case, the possibilities for applying democratic procedures are better in complex production economies than in simple extraction societies.

Western democracy could only be globalized if the "Western way of life" could be globalized. Or, thermodynamically: far from the entropic equilibrium, all possibilities of development and democratic participation are open. At the limits of environmental space, however, the environmental goods needed for production and consumption become "oligarchic goods" (Harrod 1958), i.e., reserved for a money oligarchy which secures its access to resources with monetary measures (and therefore following the economic rationality of achievement and not the political rationality of freedom combined with equality) and excludes everybody else – unless the principle of global justice is reigning and the then-demanded reduction of the level of nature use can also be enforced in the industrialized countries. Therefore, economic globalization is a mighty tendency, but it is impossible that the *situation of globality*, i.e., a world society based on reciprocity if not on solidarity, could be achieved in the *process of globalization* (detailed in Altvater and Mahnkopf 1996).

But are there possibilities for attempts towards an ecological democracy, i.e., democratic deliberations and participation within the limits of the environmental space (limits of resources and sinks) mentioned in the beginning? There are, and they can be identified with regard to procedures, subjects and forms. The procedures of democracy are partially transnationalized, when the territory of the nation state is no longer the place for which the democratic procedure was designed. In the world of nation states, the place of democracy was identical with the nation state's territory. In the course of globalization and the withering away of territorial places of democratic deliberations, democracy is becoming – as mentioned before – a placeless procedure. The territorial placelessness of democracy, however, is substituted for new *communication nets*, which are not only of virtual nature in the Internet; democratic deliberations find new places, taking account of the consequences of new limits of new functional spaces.

In traditional democracies, political parties are the main mediators between society and state institutions. The "democracy of parties," however, supplies insufficient chances of participation when dealing with questions to which the political institutional system of the nation state cannot find any sufficient answers. This is the case with the articulation of locally restricted and temporary issues, for which civic interest groups are established. There have always been groups fighting against the destruction of "their" environment, very often in a NIMBY ("not in my backyard") manner. With the far-reaching capitalization of modern societies and the consequent dramatic environmental devastation, also in connection with the colonialization of the living worlds, the once locally limited, temporary, and singular protest has expanded to an ubiquitous and permanent feature of modern (and post-modern) societies. The once local and temporarily "single-issue" interest groups are then transformed into permanent social movements and then also into parties on the one hand and into non-governmental organizations (NGOs) on the other hand.[8] Parties are still (even in unifying Europe) tied to a (national) territory; new social movements and even more pronouncedly, "non-governmental organizations," are not. They represent

---

[8] Non-governmental organizations, as far as they are lobby organizations, operate in the forefield of (nation) state bureaucracies, have often been coestablished by the latter to improve "governance" in environmental or developing policy. Therefore, besides NGOs labels such as GONGOs (government-owned NGOs) or GRUNGOs (government-run NGOs) and the like are used in order to differentiate in the complex world of NGOs.

certain social interests (especially the conservation of nature) much more directly and flexibly than parties. They become important actors of environmental policy.

The forms of democratic processes change when organizations of "civil society" speak directly without relying on parties which usually filter strongly the intervention as they carry it into the state institutions. Between market and state, the civil society speaks. This concept has a long tradition. It characterizes the space of social life which is not constituted by the state (unlike the "società politica" or the "ideological and repressive state apparatus"). Even this concept of civil society, whether in Hegelian or Gramscian tradition, has a territorial dimension which coincides with the nation state. With sovereignty being undermined and "società politica" subsequently changing its meaning, the horizon of the civil society is expanded beyond the respective national borders. The procedures are mostly discursive, i.e., the result is principally open. Only one thing is indisputable: the "insight into the necessity" of politics subjected to harsh ecological restrictions facing the limits of the (global) environmental space. The knowledge of the necessity of ecological sustainability thus determines the discourse on the rationality of the market, as well as the discourse on the procedures of democracy: what would the necessary reduction of the use of natural resources by up to 90 percent (in highly industrialized, rich countries such as Germany, according to calculations by the Wuppertal Institute 1996), actually imply for the organization of substantial (and industrial) democracy, for a regime based on the "pact for production and productivity" between capital and labour (Sinzheimer 1976)? When ecological limits challenge the substance of participation, which rationality is able to guide formal democratic procedures?

Industrial democracy under the conditions of ecological sustainability

For decades in the Western societies, industrial democracy has made increasing income the norm. Even where income increases have been lacking for several years, as in the US for a majority of workers during the Reagan era, and as in most Western European countries in the 1990s, they still are considered a rule and real wage cuts considered an exception. Income increases are easier to achieve if the monetary (and physical) surplus (i.e., if productivity) increases. The higher labor productivity has a positive effect on capital productivity, the rate of profit and economic growth, and on the competitive position in the world market because unit labor costs can be reduced. The increase in productivity is more than just a "historical mission" of the capitalist mode of production, as Marx thought. It forms the common reformist "production interest" of all actors in the capitalist society: the trade unions, the entrepreneurs, and the governments (Sinzheimer 1976). The productivity increase is the starting and finishing point of the social democratic reform policy which has made history in this century (1) against the conservative perseverance, on the one hand, and (2) against the attempts to transcend the system in "socialist" societies, on the other. The unwritten "pact for productivity" between labor and capital, between trade unions and entrepreneurs – and of governments, parties, and parliaments – forms the common ground of a joint "production interest." Dependent workers have been able to participate in the enterprise to some extent, and have an influence on the economic development through their trade unions. These possibilities vary from country to country; they are a theme for comparative policy analysis. But, irrespective of the exact settlement, they show that workers and their organizations are able to exercise rights and are thus political legal subjects and not just objects of the capitalist production and accumulation process and the entrepreneurial management and disposition power. The welfare state is practically the substantial materialization of formal democracy. This is pointed out by Hobsbawm (1995) rightly and emphatically.

This is a result of the social and economic transformations in the "Fordist mode of production and regulation." Fordism is not only a technical and social innovation but also includes a new relation to external nature compared with pre-Fordist modes of production and regulation (Altvater 1992 and 1993). This aspect is mostly ignored in studies on Fordism which concentrate either on the organization of wage- and labor-relations or elaborate on macroeconomic conditions of market supply and demand, of money and economic policy. A crucial variable in these deliberations are unit labor costs and therefore the relationship between wage and productivity increases. More than ever before in history, nature in the Fordist age is trimmed by artifacts of human beings in order to increase productivity. The high input of energy, mineral, and agrarian resources, as well as the technical and social system of transforming energy and material, are the vehicles for a considerable increase in labor productivity – and thus wealth – which again, as Lipset (1959) said, forms the material foundation of the formal democratic procedures. Like labor in industry, nature is now also *really subsumed* to capital, i.e., subjugated to the logic of accumulation to a greater extent and more efficiently than ever before in human history. This leads to the paradoxical result that the meaning of (industrial) labor for the social, economic, and political institutions – for culture as a whole – increases considerably, and at the same time, due to the fossilist characteristic of Fordism, the biological energy of labor is increasingly substituted by machines which operate with fossil energy resources and correspondingly complex systems of energy transformation. Accumulation of capital thus means release of living labor, even if discharges have been compensated by new jobs in "golden times" of high economic dynamics. For ecological reasons at least, it is impossible to stimulate growth rates in such a way that releases of labor due to productivity increases can be compensated on a permanent basis without a reduction of working hours and thus changing the social form of labor, the relation between labor time and disposable time, etc. And in the long run, a stable "post-Fordist" order can only rely on non-fossil (and non-nuclear) renewable (i.e., solar) energy. Different modes of production provoke new forms of life and thus new forms of participation. Since even formal democracy is part of a comprehensive system it is not unaffected by the indicated ecological challenges.

At the limits of the environmental space the link between productivity growth (i.e., increasing material and energy output per labor input) and rising wages (i.e., increasing consumption of energy and material per capita) is ecologically disconnected. The increase in productivity cannot be achieved without an increase in the consumption of natural resources. Even the "efficiency revolution" advanced by ecological technocrats cannot change this. The combustion of fossil energy is known to be mainly responsible for the greenhouse effect, the modern transport systems (roads, airports, etc.) for the destruction of livelihoods, the waste produced for the contamination of solid soils and water reserves, the destruction of ecosystems for the extinction of species, etc. All these effects of fossil Fordism are well known. Universally threatened by non-class-specific dangers, the even "dispersion of misery," the risk would also be democratic. Democratization in the sense of being affected evenly and unspecifically ("smog is democratic," says Ulrich Beck (1995)) leads to universalization and, simultaneously, trivialization of dangers.

If increase in productivity has to be limited because the combustion of fossil energy and the use of material have to be reduced, then the conditionality of industrial democracy radically changes and overwhelms the actors. In this situation, one could be inclined to understand the crisis of the welfare state as a "trick of history": the *ecologically* inevitable reductions of nature use are *economically* enforced by global competition, and obviously nobody can escape the "systemic constraint of the world market." The constraint, no doubt, exists, but it has its perfidy: its effects are unequal. Those who have money (i.e., hard currency) are not or only minimally exposed to it, while those who have to earn money by working feel it full blast. The oligarchic (or pluto-cratic) possibilities to buy nature with money are still maintained.

This principal inequality (in each national society as well as in the whole world) is not a good precondition for the development of demo-cratic institutions. In a substantially unequal world, where 20 percent of humanity have access to 80 percent of the resources and 80 percent of humanity can only use 20 percent for themselves (UNDP 1994), no formal democratic procedure is able to have a compensatory effect. The freedom of deciding the future is here open only to those who control alternatives and are not obliged to comply with predicament. Therefore, even the establishment of global structures of governance is difficult. One effect is that ecological sustainability is either not or only possible under conditions of extreme global inequality, and thus the basic requirement of applicability of democratic procedures is not fulfilled. A democratic order at the limit of ecological carrying capacity can no longer be based on a common Fordist *production interest*.

Conclusion

At the limits of the environmental space the contradiction of the principles of economic inequality and democratic equality, introduced at the beginning of this essay, is aggravated. For ecological reasons it is impossible that the modern expectation of ever-increasing well-being following the development path of Western democracies becomes a reality. On the contrary, it is more necessary to reduce the level of the use of natural resources, i.e., also the level of productivity and thus monetary income. The procedures of free choice in the market, as well as in the political space, are not able to deal with the problem of positional goods adequately. The dilemma of the democratic discourse which was shown at the beginning of this essay can only be solved under the usual premises of a congruence of political and economic ranges and of unlimited carrying capacity of nature. When economic dynamics constitute a globalized market and dissolute political spaces of a territorially defined nation state and when ecological limits to welfare production are set up, then the procedural rules of democracy do not remain unaffected. Freedom of choice can be assumed to be rational only in so far as basic prerequisites of equality are fulfilled. The assumption that after the pre-1989 experiences of "actually existing socialism" the old contradiction between freedom and equality has been resolved in favor of freedom proves to be too simple to serve as a guide to democratic discourse.

REFERENCES

Altvater, Elmar. 1992. *Der Preis des Wohlstands*. Münster: Westfälisches Dampfboot.
1993. *The Future of the Market*. London: Verso.
1994. "Die Ordnung rationaler Weltbeherrschung oder: Ein Wettbewerb von Zauberlehrlingen." *PROKLA 95 – Zeitschrift für kritische Sozialwissenschaft*, 24: 1.
Altvater, Elmar and Birgit Mahnkopf. 1996. *Grenzen der Globalisierung. Ökonomie, Politik, Ökologie in der Weltgesellschaft*. Münster: Westfälisches Dampfboot.
Basso, Lelio. 1980. *Socialismo e rivoluzione*. Milan: Fetnell.
Beck, Ulrich. 1995. *Ecological Politics in an Age of Risk*. Cambridge: Polity Press.
Beetham, David. 1993. "Four theorems about the market and democracy." *European Journal of Political Research* 23: 187–201.
Bobbio, Norberto. 1987. *The Future of Democracy*. Cambridge: Polity Press.
Commission on Global Governance. 1995. *Our Global Neighbourhood*. Oxford: Oxford University Press.
Dahrendorf, Ralf. 1995. *Quadrare il cerchio. Benessere economico, coesione sociale e libertà politiche*. Roma and Bari: Laterza.
Falk, Richard. 1995. "Liberalism at the global level: the last of the independent commissions?" *Millennium: Journal of International Studies* 24(3): 563–76.
Grundmann, Reiner. 1991. "The ecological challenge to Marxism." *New Left Review* 187.
Gruppe von Lissabon. 1997. *Grenzen des Wettbewerbs. Die Globalisierung der Wirtschaft und die Zukunft der Menschhei*. Neuwied: Luchterhand-Verlag.
Hardin, Garrett. 1968. "The tragedy of the commons." *Science* 162: 1243–8.
Harrod, Roy. 1958. "The possibility of economic satiety – use of economic growth for improving the quality of education and leisure." *Problems of United States Economic Development (Committee for Economic Development)* 1: 207–13.
Harvey, David. 1996. *Justice, Nature, and the Geography of Difference*. Oxford: Blackwell.
Held, David. 1991. "Democracy, the nation-state and the global system." *Economy and Society* 20(2): 138–72.
Hirsch, Fred. 1980. *Die sozialen Grenzen des Wachstums*. Reinbek: Rowohlt.
Hobsbawm, Eric. 1995. *Das Zeitalter der Extreme. Weltgeschichte des 20. Jahrhunderts*. Wien and München: Hanser.
Holloway, John. 1993. "Reform des Staats: Globales Kapital und nationaler Staat." In *PROKLA 90 – Zeitschrift für kritische Sozialwissenschaft* 23, H.1: 12–33.
Kay, John. 1996. "The good market." *Prospect* (May): 39–43.
Knieper, Rolf. 1991. *Nationale Souveränität. Versuch über Ende und Anfang einer Weltordnung*. Frankfurt: Fischer.
Lipset, Seymour M. 1959. "Some social requisites of democracy: economic development and political legitimacy." *The American Political Science Review* 53(1).
Luttwak, Edward. 1994. *Weltwirtschaftskrieg. Export als Waffe – aus Partnern werden Gegner*, Reinbek bei. Hamburg: Rowohlt.

62   *Elmar Altvater*

Mann, Michael. 1984. "The autonomous power of the state." *Archives Européennes de Sociologie* 25: 2.
Messner, Dirk. 1995. *Die Netzwerkgesellschaft. Wirtschaftliche Entwicklung und internationale Wettbewerbsfähigkeit als Probleme gesellschaftlicher Steuerung.* Köln: Weltforum Verlag.
NACLA. 1997. *Report on the Americas* 30(4).
Narr, Wolf-Dieter and Alexander Schubert. 1994. *Weltökonomie. Die Misere der Politik*, Frankfurt am Main: Suhrkamp.
Neumann, Franz. 1978 (1950). "Die Wissenschaft der Politik in der Demokrate." In Alfons Söllner (ed.), *Wirtschaft, Staat, Demokratie. Aufsätze 1930–1954.* Frankfurt: Suhrkamp.
O'Connor, James. 1988. "Capitalism, nature, socialism. A theoretical introduction." *Capitalism, Nature, Socialism. Journal of Socialist Ecology* 1: 11–45.
O'Donnell, Guillermo, Philippe C. Schmitter, and Laurence Whitehead. 1986. *Transitions from Authoritarian Rule.* 3 vols. Baltimore and London: The Johns Hopkins University Press.
Plumwood, Val. 1992. "Feminism and ecofeminism: beyond the dualistic assumptions of women, men and nature." *The Ecologist* 22(1): 8–13.
Polyani, Karl. 1957 (1944). *The Great Transformation.* Boston: Beacon Press.
Przeworski, Adam. 1994. Paper presented at the International Congress of Political Science, Berlin, August 1994 (German version: "Ökonomische und politische Transformationen in Osteuropa: Der aktuelle Stand." *PROKLA – Zeitschrift für kritische Sozialwissenschaft* 25: 130–51).
Rosanvallon, Pierre. 1988. *Le libéralisme économique. Histoire de l'idée de marché.* Paris: Editions du Seuil.
Rhodes, R. A. W. 1996. "The new governance: governing without government." *Political Studies* 44(4): 652–67.
Schmitt, Carl. 1963. *Der Begriff des Politischen. Text von 1932 mit einem Vorwort und drei Corollarien.* Berlin: Duncker & Humblodt.
Shapiro, Ian. 1996. *Democracy's Place.* Ithaca and London: Cornell University Press.
Sinzheimer, Hugo. 1976. *Arbeitsrecht und Rechtssoziologie.* Gesammelte Aufsätze und Reden, hrsg. von Otto Kahn-Freund und Thilo Ramm mit einer Einl. von Otto Kahn-Freund, 2 Bde. Frankfurt and Köln: Suhrkamp.
Sklar, Holly. 1980. *Trilaterialism: The Trilateral Commission and Elite Planning for World Management.* Boston: South End Press.
Smith, Adam. 1976 (1776). *An Inquiry into the Nature and Causes of the Wealth of Nations.* Edited by Edwin Cannan. Chicago: The University of Chicago Press.
UNDP. 1994. *United Nations Development Programme: Human Development Report 1994: New Dimensions of Human Security.* New York: Oxford University Press.
Volk, Stephen. 1997. "Democracy" versus "democracy." *NACLA. Report on the Americas* 30(4): 6–12.
Wuppertal Institut für Klima, Umwelt, Energie. 1996. *Zukunftsfähiges Deutschland. Ein Beitrag zu einer global nachhaltigen Entwicklung.* Edited by von Bund and Misereor. Basel, Boston, and Berlin: Birkhäuser.

5   Democracy and collective bads[1]

Russell Hardin

Supporters of democracy might take special pleasure in noting how well democratic decision-making, even as messy as it typically is, has handled several problems of the generation of collective bads, such as air and water pollution.[2] Many autocratic states, which are often thought to have advantages in pushing through difficult policies, have been environmental disasters while Western democracies were actually improving their environments even while continuing economic growth. At the same time, democratic states – especially, but not only, the United States – have been relatively poor at handling distributive issues such as poverty and equal opportunity. These contrary results are inherent in the nature of democracy and the kinds of problems at stake. This fact bodes ill, oddly, for international handling of collective bads.

Democracy is particularly good at handling problems of coordination, sometimes including relatively difficult problems of coordination within the context of standard collective actions. It is generally poor at handling more conflicted issues, such as, especially, straight distributional issues. The regulation of many collective bads in our time falls on both sides of the democratic divide. In so far as these problems are purely domestic, as in the pollution of, say, Lake Tahoe, they are relatively easily seen as coordination problems by at least the bulk of the relevant population. In so far as they are very substantially international, as in the destruction of the ozone layer or acid rain, however, they often have massive distributive implications that would make their resolution difficult even in domestic politics but that make resolution extremely difficult in

[1] Prepared for presentation at the conference, "Rethinking Democracy for a New Century," Yale University, 28 February–2 March 1997. Work on this paper has been supported by New York University, the Guggenheim Foundation, the Center for Advanced Study in the Behavioral Sciences, and the National Science Foundation (grant # SBR-9022192). I am grateful to all of these splendid agencies for their support. I am also grateful to the participants in the Yale conference and in the Rational Choice Seminar at the Center for Advanced Study for comments on an earlier draft and especially to Susan Hurley, Susan Moller Okin, and Steven Weber, who wrote lengthy comments.
[2] On air pollution in the United States, see, e.g., *Scientific American* (1977).

63

international politics. In domestic politics, they could, in principle, be handled by simple voting or by majoritarian representative legislation. In international politics, they must be handled through voluntary cooperation on the part of many states and, thus, they face the standard problem of the logic of collective action. Even worse, they face that problem in a normative context in which fairness as well as mere cooperation is often thought to be at issue.

Although there might be good abstract arguments for the use of democratic procedures to serve the general interest of each citizen, in actual democratic decisions it is almost invariably the case that some are losers while others are winners. A rare exception to this aspect of democracy as it actually works is the choice of whether to defend a nation under attack from outside. At least in the logic of the interests at stake, another very broad class of exceptions is, or may soon be, the general losses that all might suffer from such collective bads as environmental degradation. If collective action to overcome the generation of collective bads must be spontaneously, voluntarily motivated, we generally can expect such action to fail. In general, we expect it to succeed only for very small groups and for groups, such as labor unions, that have sanctioning power, to some extent, just as states have. When, however, it is determined by democratic vote with the backing of government to enforce the collective choice, we should often expect most individuals who vote to vote for enforcement, just as they might be expected to vote to defend their nation from attack.

Again, in the larger international system in which individual nations are unable to secure themselves against collective bads, however, the problem of collective action might be replayed at the higher level of states, because it may not be in the interest of a single nation independently to adopt self-regulative policies. I wish to investigate the nature and logic of democratic incentives in the face of such nested collective action problems of overcoming collective bads. In general, one might suppose that geographically very large nations, such as the United States, Russia, Brazil, Canada, Australia, and China, might have greater interest in regulation directly for their own benefit, so that domestic politics might suffice for some regulation in these nations, as it also might for the new European Union. Of course, even in these cases the levels of regulation that would be popularly chosen would likely vary with levels of prosperity. Contemporary Chinese would presumably be willing to suffer a larger trade-off of higher rates of pollution for higher rates of economic growth than would contemporary Americans.

Most nations in the world, however, could not plausibly justify the expense of certain environmental regulations merely for their own benefit, because almost all of the benefit would accrue to the people of other nations. This is most conspicuously true, perhaps, for the use of ozone-depleting chemicals. Ozone depletion is almost wholly internationalized, although nations such as the United States and Australia can reasonably see the problem of ozone depletion as particularly costly to their citizens, many of whom, with their fair skins and nearly tropical locations, may be especially susceptible to harms from the increased ultraviolet radiation that comes through the depleted ozone layer.[3] But other problems of, for example, ocean and air pollution are also predominantly internationalized for many nations that contribute to these problems.

Democracy and collective goods and bads

The contemporary understanding of collective goods and collective action comes from two main sources: Paul Samuelson's theory of public goods, especially as spelled out by Mancur Olson, and the game theoretic prisoner's dilemma (Samuelson 1954; Olson 1965; Hardin 1982: chap. 2). It is partly a response to the traditional interest group theory in politics. In the traditional group theory, it was taken for granted that, if a group of individuals share an interest in having some good provided, then they will individually act to see to its provision (Bentley 1908; Truman 1971 [1951]). This is a fallacy of composition. Just because a group is composed of individuals, it does not follow that the group will behave as individuals would. It is now generally accepted that, as in the prisoner's dilemma and Olson's logic of collective action, individuals may commonly not act in ways that further their group interest. Instead, they commonly free-ride on the efforts of others or their group fails altogether.

The theory of collective goods

In Samuelson's theory, public goods differ from ordinary marketable goods in two ways. They are joint in supply and relevant individuals cannot be excluded from consuming them. If a good is joint in supply, then it can be made available to all comers just as cheaply as to one person. If individuals cannot be excluded from consuming a good, it

---

[3] The seriousness of this problem may be less than has been supposed until recently. The worst implication of increased UV radiation exposure has been thought to be an increase in melanoma, a deadly cancer, an association that has been questioned by some findings. The lesser harm of superficial skin cancers, which are generally treatable, is far less ominous than a dramatic increase in melanoma.

cannot be sold only to those who pay for it. Jointness implies that a good can be most efficiently sold at a zero price, because that is the marginal cost of adding an additional consumer of it. Non-excludability implies that it cannot be sold at all once it has been made available to anyone.

In actual fact, there are few if any goods from whose enjoyment individuals cannot be selectively excluded, if necessary at gun-point. Hence, there are few if any goods that are strictly public in Samuelson's sense (Snidal 1979). Yet there are many goods exclusion from which would be very costly so that it might make little sense actually to exclude anyone. The chief reason for providing many goods collectively rather than privately is that it is more efficient to do so, that is, the total costs of providing them collectively to those who would be willing to pay for them privately are less than the costs of providing them privately to those same people. If we can vote to get government to provide us such a good through our tax payments, we save over the inefficiency of private provision. It would still be wrong to call the goods "public goods" in Samuelson's strict sense, because exclusion is possible. But exclusion can be costly enough that one might think of the efficiency gains from collective provision as a meta-public good.

In general, there may also be few if any goods that are genuinely joint in supply, because there are typically crowding effects that reduce the value that additional users can get from a good. Once, it seemed reasonable to suppose that water was in unlimited supply because the supply could not be exhausted by ordinary users. Today, the limits on water supplies and, perhaps especially, on water quality are urgent problems.

Hence, it makes little sense to speak of Samuelson's pure cases in ordinary politics. Rather, the issue is merely that of collective provision, which can be a problem for ordinary goods that could also be marketed but which we choose, for whatever reason, to allocate collectively.

If our problem is simply that of collective provision, then it often has the strategic structure of the prisoner's dilemma for n-persons. The narrow interest of each individual is not to contribute to the provision of the collective good of the group but the overall interest of all individuals is to secure the good even despite the costs to individuals of providing it. If the group must act strictly from voluntary, spontaneous choice, it may be expected therefore to fail to provide itself with its good. But a group with near unanimity on the assessment of its collective interest and the sharing scheme for providing its good can generally be expected to succeed if it has sanctioning power to get its members to do what they agree to do. The first success of unions is to gain such sanctioning power. The point of the early organization of the medical and legal professions in the United States was to gain such sanctioning power by gaining legal authority to regulate medical and legal certification. On a Hobbesian account, government similarly has as its central point the power to sanction those who do not cooperate in the maintenance of social order that supposedly all desire. If we democratically choose to provide ourselves collectively with some good, we can commonly expect our government to force us to carry through on our own desire.

In the traditional group theory of politics, it is commonly supposed, as an empirical fact, that groups organize in contest with each other over relevant resources. My group wants some benefit and it attempts to get that benefit from your group or, perhaps more commonly, from the general revenues. A casual canvass of the literature on such groups suggests that this is a roughly accurate view of many of the most effective and most important groups in American politics. Unions organize against owners, often directly and often through the intermediary power of government. Business interests organize to gain benefits from the tax code, the tariff, or direct subsidies from government. Citizen groups organize to gain concessions from business and government. There are other groups that organize merely to provide a good that is general, rather than specific to themselves. For example, Schattschneider (1960) cites such groups as those that oppose the death penalty. There are many groups that organize around divisive religious issues, such as abortion. But it seems evident that the noise of groups in American politics is primarily from those organized adversarily to gain benefits at cost to others.

Collective bads

A public good in Samuelson's sense is a good from whose enjoyment relevant individuals may not be excluded, although they can typically exclude themselves. For example, I cannot readily be excluded from listening to a radio program broadcast openly, although I can simply leave my radio turned off and thereby exclude myself. A public bad is, contrariwise, a bad from which individuals cannot exclude themselves. For example, if the air of my city has been polluted with harmful chemicals, I cannot readily exclude myself from that pollution while living in the city.

Instead of speaking of public bads, I will speak of collective bads. As with collective goods, the issue is not whether a bad is public in Samuelson's technical sense. Rather, what matters is how we deal with a particular bad. Unlike goods, however, bads may be collective in two quite different ways. The analog of the way in which goods can be collective is that bads can be collectively regulated or eliminated. But many of them can also be collectively generated. We face certain bads at all only because we produce them in the first instance. Hence, we might collectively both produce and regulate or eliminate a bad.

Through sophistic definition, one can easily reduce the regulation of collective bads to the provision of collective goods in some sense. We can relabel a collective bad problem as a collective good problem by saying that the collective good is simply the regulation that eliminates the collective bad. Vice versa, one might suppose that the absence of a collective good is a bad, so that the provision of the good is tantamount to elimination of the bad. All of this might especially seem to make sense because both problems are strategically equivalent to the n-person prisoner's dilemma when it is genuinely beneficial for all relevant persons to provide the good or eliminate the bad.

There are, however, at least two compelling general reasons for not reducing our two categories to one. The first of the general reasons is that most of the things that we nominally call bads are genuine harms and we have little difficulty distinguishing them from goods in ordinary language, even though a sophist might confuse ordinary speakers into thinking they have been getting it wrong all along. The second is that the definitional difference, stated above, between goods and bads is clear and compelling: I cannot be excluded from the enjoyment of the former and I cannot exclude myself from the burden of the latter.[4]

Still, a sophist might insist, the actual provision of a collective good or the elimination of a collective bad is all one in kind strategically. Here one must concede the case. There is, however, an empirical difference in the range of goods and bads of greatest interest that makes their provision or elimination distinctively different. Hard-fought collective goods problems in our time have mostly been about goods that could be provided by agencies outside the beneficiary group without action by the members of the group. The most important collective bad issues of our time are endogenously generated, and they can best be regulated by endogenous changes of behavior by the groups that generate them and suffer from them, as discussed below.

Endogenous vs exogenous generation and provision

A collective good or bad can be generated either endogenously by the members of the group that is affected by it or exogenously by other

---

[4] For further discussion of the complexity of incentives in dealing with collective bads, see Hardin 1982: 61–6. Also see Sonnemans *et al.*, 1998.

agencies or even by nature. This is an important distinction here because the collective bads of greatest interest in international politics appear typically to be endogenously generated bads, as are air and water pollution, global warming, and damage to the ozone layer. It is important to keep clear that the point of this distinction is *not that the bads are endogenous in the sense of being produced by the United States or China, but rather in the much more micro sense that they are produced by the persons who would benefit from their regulation.* The people who create such a bad are roughly also the people who suffer from it – there is, metaphorically, no division of labor. For example, automotive pollution, which is about half of the air pollution problem in the United States, is primarily generated by individuals' actions. Hence, one way to eliminate the bad is to get the people who generate it to stop doing so on their own behalf. This device entails a fairly strong causal connection between the regulation and the generation of a typical collective bad.

As noted above, the collective goods of greatest interest in American domestic politics have been goods that could be provided by someone other than the beneficiaries of them – that is, exogenously. Under present technological constraints, such bads as automotive air pollution virtually require endogenous regulation – they cannot be eliminated exogenously. Neither the public good nor the game theoretic representation of the problem as a prisoner's dilemma captures this differential aspect of collective action for commonplace goods and bads. In the game theoretic representation, for example, the payoffs are in value, in utiles, or in ordinal preference rankings rather than in actions or objective benefits. What is at stake in the difference between endogenous and non-endogenous elimination of a bad is individual actions whose consequence is to affect the values of the payoffs.

Again, collective bads that are endogenously aggregated from individual actions can be regulated through constraints on individual actions. To regulate or eliminate such a bad it is insufficient for one person to take action. All or most, or at least many, must change their behavior if we are to succeed in regulating or eliminating the bad. Many of the political collective goods most commonly discussed in the literature can, at least in principle, be provided by a single actor or external agency to benefit all. Hence, in actual practice these collective goods are commonly produced only indirectly by the relevant collective while endogenously generated collective bads are produced directly and can only be eliminated directly. For common collective goods, the individuals pay taxes or fees and government or another agency provides the good or service. For endogenously generated collective bads, many individuals change some specific behavior and the bad is reduced or eliminated.[5] Commonly, of course, the behavior that produces some bad is regulated coercively by government to give individuals strong incentive to change their behavior.

Both goods and bads can be either endogenously or exogenously regulated or provided. For a collective good that can be produced endogenously on behalf of those who produce it, consider the good of the election of someone to public office. Such election requires votes from many, who cannot benefit from the election unless enough of them take part to produce a margin of victory. Similarly, the solidarity that a union needs in order to bargain successfully on behalf of workers can typically only be endogenously created among the workers themselves. But such collective goods as a national highway system or a general health care system can be provided exogenously to the group of those who benefit from them. Indeed, for such goods it seems implausible to think of providing them endogenously (although it is not implausible to think of them as provided on a market rather than collectively). A mixed case is a common roadway through an area with separate houses along its way. The roadway could be maintained either endogenously by the action of every homeowner caring for a relevant stretch of the road or exogenously by the state, which would pay its costs from tax revenues or fees, which could be levied on the homeowners but could also be raised from others. Similarly, many local irrigation systems in Vietnam were traditionally maintained endogenously through the individual efforts of the beneficiaries (Scott 1976; Popkin 1979; cf. Hardin 1982: 75).

Consider examples of the range of collective bads from endogenously to exogenously generated. At one extreme, automotive air pollution is essentially endogenously generated and it can be reduced by changing the behavior that generates it. (In a science fiction world, we might imagine handling such pollution exogenously with giant air filters.) At the other extreme, a large asteroid striking the earth would be a collective bad that is exogenously generated. To eliminate such a bad would require action not unlike that which would be necessary to provide an ordinary collective good, such as a highway program: governmental bodies must take action. Hence, regulation would be exogenous.

---

[5] It is at least conceivable that, say, water pollution could be handled more effectively by some central agency that actually cleaned the water rather than by changing the behavior of those who pollute it. In that case, the bad could be exogenously eliminated even though it is endogenously generated. It does not seem likely that such exogenous management of the major collective bad problems of our time will soon, if ever, become feasible.

Between these polar cases is a particular disease. One can call a disease a collective bad, because it is harmful and because it afflicts a collective. In so far as the problem of disease is a problem of nature and is not endogenously created by those who suffer from it, it poses a problem of providing relevant controls – vaccination, treatment – to make life better for people than it would be in the natural state. Polio or smallpox was arguably such a natural, or exogenous, disease. But, of course, it can be true that a disease is in part problematic because it is endogenously created or spread because individuals behave in such ways as to spread it, as seems to be true of AIDS. In so far as the way to handle a disease is through changes in spontaneous human behavior to stop its spread, then that behavior produces an endogenously generated collective bad. In such a case the bad might be regulated through endogenous actions of changed behavior.

We can also canvass the spectrum from endogenously to exogenously regulated collective bads. In addition to the cases of the previous paragraph, consider the mixed cases of exogenously produced but endogenously regulated *and* of endogenously produced but exogenously regulated bads. At least in principle, generation and regulation can be unrelated, although there might be natural affinities for certain bads. Endogenously produced but exogenously regulated bads are relatively common. For example, garbage is endogenously generated by the general population but for the most part it is exogenously treated by large public facilities (see further, Hardin 1998). Exogenously produced but endogenously regulated bads of significance are not so common. A particularly celebrated instance was the elimination of schitosomiasis by Chinese peasants who methodically eliminated the schistosome-carrying snails from waterways and rice paddies.

Table 5.1 represents the array of extreme or ideal types of endogenously and exogenously determined collective bads. It is an empirical, and not an analytical, claim that the collective goods at issue in American policy-making in recent decades have largely been goods that could most sensibly be provided exogenously. The collective bads at issue have largely been endogenously produced bads whose regulation has often involved endogenous changes in behavior to reduce their incidence and severity. Hence, one can say that bads are typically endogenously generated and regulated while goods are typically exogenously produced. In international politics, collective bads seem to loom much, much larger than collective goods. The international collective bads are almost entirely bads that are endogenously produced and that, with present technology, must be, if at all, endogenously regulated through changes in behavior. Collective action problems in international politics

Table 5.1. *Types of collective bad problems*

	Endogenously resolved	Exogenously resolved
Endogenously generated	Auto pollution	Garbage
Exogenously generated	Schistosomiasis	Asteroid

are therefore, as an empirical matter, distinctively different from those of domestic politics.[6]

Many important classes of collective goods can be provided internationally despite massive free-riding by many, most, or even almost all nations. The creation of a satellite communication system can be done by a single nation with benefit to virtually all nations. The invention of new technologies might be seen as a good that can be done by some to the benefit of all. (Regulation of flight patterns or of the airwaves is sometimes seen as a collective good, but such problems are more sensibly seen as matters of coordination rather than instances of the prisoner's dilemma. For such coordination problems, a big first-mover can often establish a pattern that then gives later arrivers incentive simply to go along with the established coordination, so that there is no need for most beneficiaries of the coordination to participate in establishing it.)

Similarly many non-endogenously generated collective bads can be regulated or eliminated internationally despite massive free-riding. For example, control of certain diseases is of sufficient interest to the United States that it alone might underwrite the costs of research and vaccination to eliminate those diseases not only in the United States but in virtually the entire world, because the diseases might threaten citizens of the United States so long as they are endemic anywhere in the world.[7] In such a case, one might rightly suppose that the costs of providing the good of vaccination are radically smaller than the costs of bearing the burden of the diseases, as was surely true in the eradication of smallpox and as seems likely to be true in the case of polio and perhaps other, especially new, diseases, such as AIDS. Similarly, the collective bad of an asteroid striking the earth might be prevented by the action of

---

[6] Note that it would make little sense to construct a parallel two-by-two table of collective goods. Goods can be endogenously or exogenously provided, as discussed in the text, just as bads can be endogenously or exogenously resolved, but there is no parallel sense in which goods *problems* are endogenously or exogenously generated.

[7] This is the brunt of a recent report, "America's vital interest in global health," issued by the Institute of Medicine of the National Academy of Sciences. The report concludes that "the Government and businesses need to do … more to protect the American people as well as populations elsewhere" from the threat of emerging diseases (*New York Times* 1997).

the United States or Europe, with all other nations as coincidental beneficiaries.

The elimination or regulation of many of the most urgent collective bads of our time, however, cannot be accomplished well without the joint participation of many nations in the effort through changing behavior of their own citizens. For endogenous bads, other nations cannot do, say, China's share of the pollution reduction. Others can subsidize China to make doing its share more palatable, but in the end China and the Chinese must do it. For such bads there is a direct causal connection between generation and regulation. We regulate the bad by stopping its generation. This is true only of collective bads that are endogenously generated and endogenously resolved.

The causal connection between generation and regulation of a particular collective bad often means that the regulation of the bad is Pareto efficient or very nearly so because of the way the costs of regulation are parceled out to beneficiaries of it. For example, each automobile driver pays extra for pollution control equipment and for higher-priced, less-polluting fuel, and each driver benefits from the overall pollution reduction. If the result of regulation is very nearly universally preferred to non-regulation by a substantial margin, individual benefits may typically outweigh individual costs of the regulation. As noted below, there might be some drivers for whom the benefit of pollution control does not outweigh their own costs of bringing it about, but for most drivers in, say, greater Los Angeles the individual benefits arguably outweigh the individual costs. Such regulation also has a strong element of fairness. The cost of the regulation is borne by the producers of the bad in proportion to how much of it they produce. Those who drive more, and hence pollute more, pay more for the reduction in pollution.

Domestic collective bads and the quasi-consensual politics of coordination

The problem of endogenously generated collective bads, as opposed to traditional collective goods, creates an odd asymmetry that has not substantially been addressed in democratic theory, perhaps because the problem is essentially new in the scale of its significance. Even when collective goods seem to be of interest to very broad groups (such as virtually all children in the case of universal education or fluoridation of water), there is often objection to their provision. The use of government for paternalistic purposes provokes opposition from many, such as libertarians, those hostile to big government, and fiscal conservatives. Libertarians, for example, contend that these goods can be provided through the market to those who want them without imposing on those who do not want them.

A strategic difference between traditional problems of collective goods and the problem of collective bads is that some of the latter are of nearly universal interest to all citizens (as is the collective good of the system of justice even in the views of libertarians, conservatives, and those hostile to big government). This consideration makes these problems potentially easy to resolve democratically. Many traditional paternalistic policies can be seen as responses to collective, rather than individual, problems and these may therefore be similar in kind to the burgeoning problem of dealing with collective bads. For paternalism in many traditional contexts, the issue that bothers libertarians is that what the state thinks is good for me may not be what I think is good for me. A remarkable feature of public bads is that there might well be little or no disagreement about the interests individuals have in overcoming them. (There might, of course, be differences over how to deal with them, because one resolution might benefit me more and another might favor you, as discussed further below.) Hence, depending on the form that the policies take, environmental policies might not be seen as objectionably paternalistic. Moreover, for endogenously generated bads, it makes clear, non-paternalistic sense that the state regulate behavior of *others* on my behalf, as it regulates potentially criminal activity of others.

The collective bads that beleaguer contemporary life are objective features of our environment that are objectively, not merely aesthetically, bad and that virtually everyone agrees are bad. Whether they are bad enough to justify the costs of preventing them is not similarly a matter of simple agreement. But the very idea of the state's forcing me to work a limited number of hours in the day, to invest for my retirement, or to educate my children to a certain age provokes opposition because some people genuinely do not think those policies are beneficial for them net of their costs in taxation. If government could overcome environmental problems of smog and fouled water supplies without significant cost to citizens and without the creation of powerful government agencies, there might be no, or at most slight, opposition to the actions. (It would probably be foolish to suppose there would be no opposition. Even fluoridation of drinking water for the benefit of children was opposed with extraordinary energy and venom by the parents of many of those children in American cities in the 1950s and 1960s. The politics of stupidity can intrude at any time.)

There are two complications that make the issues politically difficult. First, the costs can be borne in various ways, so that groups have strong interests in pushing the costs onto others. Second, people weigh the costs and benefits differently. This second complication is most easily framed for problems in which there is an almost inherently natural way to allocate costs to the producers of a particular externality. For example, auto pollution can be greatly reduced, and has been, by requiring that manufacturers design autos with reduced emissions per mile by burning fuel more cleanly, by adding equipment to reduce certain emissions, and by redesigning vehicles to weigh less so that they require less fuel to operate. All of these devices for reducing pollution add to the costs of vehicles and to the per-gallon costs of fuel (which might be offset by the reduced consumption of fuel per mile of driving). Suppose a wealthy and a poor person drive 10,000 miles per year. The costs of the poor person's contribution to reducing pollution might now be nearly as great as those of the wealthy person, yet the poor person might genuinely not value the reduction in pollution as highly as the wealthy person does – it is merely a cost of living, and the poor person faces a disproportionately large contribution to her costs of living from cleaning up her auto emissions.

The distributive problem of auto pollution is even worse than this, however. Although the well-off may not intend to push the costs more heavily onto the poor than onto themselves, a policy that pushes costs onto producers of the pollution does just this. The poor must pay proportionately more than the well-off to reduce their automotive emissions for two reasons. First, they typically drive older cars for which the costs of reduction per mile of driving are larger than for the new cars that the well-off more commonly drive, for reasons independent of their concern (if any) for environmental harms. Second, even if their per-mile costs of pollution abatement were the same as those for the well-off, this would still require a larger percentage of their overall income.

International collective bads

There is a peculiar difference between the traditional problems of securing collective goods and at least some of the contemporary problems of blocking collective bads. The latter are often inherently not national problems – they cross borders, they even straddle hemispheres. Democratic theory has virtually always been conceived at the level of relatively small populations in well-defined areas. Its expansion to cover large nations has been an evolutionary result in the older democracies and a move by analogy rather than by reinvention in such newer democracies as that of India with its population of, now, about a billion people. In our time there are two contrary forces underway that either expand or shrink the scope of democracy. The growth of ethnic politics has led to the splitting of nations into smaller units, as most dramatically in the case of the former Soviet Union, while the growth of concern with the benefits of larger markets and their efficiencies has led to the union of nations into larger blocks, as most dramatically in the case of the European Union (EU).

Pooling decisions at higher levels, as in the European Union, is what the international regulation of contemporary collective bads requires. The pooling of the EU, NAFTA, GATT, and similar supranational unions is designed to overcome institutional barriers to better results, barriers that get in the way of economic and other activities that would spontaneously happen if those barriers were not in the way. This is fundamentally a coordination problem rather than a problem of the provision of a collective good. Indeed, to date, successful resolution of international problems has typically been resolution of coordination problems. Contemporary collective bads will require institutional devices to motivate changes in action by individuals and institutions. It will require creation of stronger, international institutions rather than the weakening of extant, national institutions.

Arguably, the European Union entails an overall reduction in governmental power to the benefit of individual and corporate actors. The standard debate over the Union refers to the growing strength of government in Brussels, as though the issue were an old libertarian issue of the growth of government. The actual implication of that Union, at least for the short term, however, is the weakening of national government controls over individuals and non-governmental corporate bodies.

There would be grievous conceptual and measurement problems in determining whether the EU gains more or less power than the individual national governments, taken together, lose. But a simple and compelling indicator of who loses and who gains is that individuals and corporate actors gain substantially, both economically and in other ways such as freedom to travel and live and work at will throughout the nations of the Union. It seems implausible that overall governmental control over individuals – which is the core concern of libertarianism – has grown. Surely it has been reduced. This is not to say that the power that individual nations had over individuals was beneficial to anyone or was deliberately exercised for some nationally beneficial reason. Much of it was almost certainly not. It was often like the power of the bureaucrat, which, according to a joke that is too true to be entirely funny, is no power but the power to deny any reasonable request. Nations essentially just got in the way of individuals and corporations to make certain actions harder than they need have been.

Again, the change entailed in regulating contemporary international collective bads has virtually the opposite character: it seems likely to involve intrusions to block individual actions of many kinds. At the very least, it involves the creation of artificial incentive structures to alter behavior relatively unobtrusively.

At the international level all environmental problems are similar to the US national problem of auto pollution, whose principal harms are borne by Americans, who must bear the costs of reducing those harms. Of course, some of the harms are externalized to the larger world, especially the larger world of the northern hemisphere, and some of the regulatory costs are also externalized through the standardization of automotive design in the international market so that, say, Singaporeans drive cleaner cars and have to use more expensive fuel in them irrespective of whether they would want to do so. If each nation is responsible for reducing its industrial emissions, some nations cannot sensibly be thought to see it as their interest to bear the costs of the reduction even if that means no other nation reduces emissions either.

Hence, it is not conceivable to defend any international policy on reduced emissions without making interpersonal comparisons of the evaluation of the costs and benefits of such reductions. Straightforward policies are not likely to be Pareto improving. In some abstract sense, we might be convinced that there are policies that would be Pareto improving in that they would reduce pollution for virtually everyone without imposing costs on anyone that outweighed that person's own benefits from the reduction. But standard results in choice theory suggest that we cannot expect to reach agreement on the conclusion that any actually proposed policy is Pareto improving. It would be in the interest of, say, Brazil or China or the United States to assert that its own interest would be harmed by any given policy that allocated costs in a particular way.

Moreover, only in a world of relative equality could we suppose that such claims must be specious. Even without strategic misrepresentation of evaluations, we cannot expect to resolve the international problems with easy agreement because of deep inequalities. For example, suppose the Chinese economy is soon generally a market economy, with a small government role in the actual production of ordinary goods and services. Also suppose the government insists that its people do not value clean air enough to stop using coal in antiquated generators that are especially polluting. Finally, suppose that cleaning up the environment means, at least in large part for the short term, buying new equipment from abroad and using other fuels that would be internationally marketable, so that, whether they are imported or merely not exported, their use involves substantial losses of Chinese capital. Among the chief financial losers from any policy to clean up the environment would be various industrialists, but Chinese workers could also lose if the displacement of capital reduced rates of economic growth.

One might suppose that the transition of poorer nations to higher productivity could be subsidized by wealthier nations in ways that would benefit both. It would benefit the wealthier nations by reducing the externalities they would suffer from dirtier economic production in the poorer nations – but this is likely to be a chimera at present costs of technologies for environmental protection. The population of Africa alone is almost twice, and those of India and China are each almost four times, that of the United States. The wealthy nations of North America, Europe, Japan, and Australia have a small fraction of the population of the poor nations now hoping for rapid economic growth. Substantial per capita subsidies to the poorer nations would require massive per capita contributions from the wealthier nations.

Welfarist politics over collective bads

The central claims of libertarianism turn on something roughly like a market vision of the prospering of individuals. We all would do better making our own choices for our lives than we would having our lives collectively determined. The provision of collective goods has long posed the standard objection to libertarian claims, and it is a compelling objection for many such goods, such as the provision of a justice system, without which the market would work less well and individuals would be less prosperous. Historically, the problem of blocking collective bads has not been as important as that of providing collective goods. We are now in, or are perhaps entering an era in which arguably the problem of collective bads will loom very large and will trump libertarian claims that we should leave many areas of activity entirely up to free choice by individuals. Hence, even from an individualist perspective of concern for individual welfare independently of comparison to others' welfares, we may suppose the state should act to block collective bads. To the extent this is true, collective bads pose a problem for democracy *simpliciter* independently of any theory of justice. Theories of justice might be implicated in specific policies for the regulation of collective bads, but the demand for addressing them is already compelling as a purely welfarist concern.

Domestically, many of the collective bad problems of our time might be conflictual as between certain industrial interests and typical citizens but not between large opposing groups of citizens. They are unlike distributional issues that generally divide the population into large groups with opposing interests. While politics over these issues may be hard fought and often indeterminate, straight democratic counting of interests might nevertheless often be expected to yield a generally agreeable result. Submitting these issues to more nearly democratic decision might therefore be expected to lead to predictable outcomes in favor of environmental regulation of some kinds. The chief conflict that cannot be encapsulated in ordinary democratic accounting is intergenerational. Our generation might readily see it as in our interest to benefit from the greater apparent productivity that comes from externalizing some of our production and consumption costs onto future generations.

This is not to say that there are no intragenerational distributional issues in the resolution of various collective bad problems. There are, of course. For example, even if air pollution from automotive exhaust were entirely a domestic rather than partly an international problem, the current solutions to the problem have substantial distributional effects, as discussed above from merely the domestic level. Unfortunately, the general distributional implications of pollution abatement at the international level are even more skewed. Americans at the time of the heyday of smoke-stack industrial development, without which contemporary economic structures would not likely have come into being, polluted massively. Poor nations, such as India, Bangladesh, Kenya, and many others, can expect to become prosperous on their own only by swallowing, as Americans did, environmental harms along with the benefits of production. As they do so, they will share those harms with others.

"Property rights" in international pollution

In a tradition that is not merely Lockean, it is commonly supposed that those who stake out an area first have a strong normative claim on it thereafter. The notion of national sovereignty, which is primarily a concern of the third world, is a variant of this principle of the rightness of prior ownership. In part, such a principle could be seen as essentially a convention that settles issues that would otherwise be destructively in conflict, so that, on the whole, all are better off from the stability of expectations and reduction of conflict that follows from virtually any form of property rights.

There is a sense in which the advanced industrial nations staked out a claim on the world's atmosphere and water during the past two centuries and that they have left little of these resources for those who come after them who wish to use the atmosphere and water of the world in similar ways. In John Locke's (1963 [1690]: paras. 27 and 33) argument for the normative derivation of claims of ownership from prior use, there is a condition, the Lockean proviso, that, if taken very seriously, cannot be met in our world. The proviso states that I have the right to some property if, after my appropriation of it, there is enough and as good left for others. Those who staked out claims to farmland in Iowa cannot be said to meet this proviso because there is very little farmland as good as Iowa. Similarly, those who put substantial pollutants into the air and into major water resources, including international rivers and the seas, left little further carrying capacity in those resources for others to use after them.

If the Chinese and Indians pollute at per capita levels today that rival the per capita levels of the United States in the era 1880–1960, they must bear huge burdens domestically and must externalize huge burdens to the rest of the world. Except for the massive problems of polluting energy sources, they might be expected to accomplish industrial growth at earlier American levels without polluting at American levels because technology has improved and become much cleaner. But since the scale of their current combined populations is roughly twenty times that of the United States at the beginning of its industrial growth, they probably cannot be expected to match American levels of growth without polluting far more in absolute terms than the United States did, especially if they rely on using abundant supplies of cheap coal for energy.

Naturally, Americans and Europeans concerned with overburdening the environment tend to focus relatively heavily on the responsibility of nations for their rates of population growth. Poor nations focus rather on national responsibilities for per capita rates of energy consumption and pollution. Population is treated more nearly as a domestic problem by poor nations and as an international problem by wealthy nations. It is both, but the difference in emphasis is essentially a distributional issue. Again, democracy is not good at handling distributional issues, and international democracy, which is exceedingly weak, cannot be expected to handle international distributions except in so far as wealthy nations choose to act more or less altruistically toward impoverished nations.

Concluding remarks

As the problem of collective bads has not been a major concern of democratic theory, so too the problem of nested collective actions has not been addressed in democratic theory, perhaps because democratic theory has not yet gone international. When applied to a domestic population, democracy seems to yield relatively easy results of uniform policies on such issues as collective bads and occasional collective goods. We stipulate that cars will meet various anti-pollution standards and then let individuals freely decide, within this constraint, what cars they buy. We do not necessarily have to enforce the policies against individuals to change their behavior. The central problem of nesting collective actions at different levels is that this relatively easy resolution is not possible at the higher level of international politics. When the issues have differential effects, especially distributional effects, at the international level, we cannot simply vote by some kind of majority decision procedure and then expect every nation to follow through as virtually every US citizen might be expected to follow through on Environmental Protection Agency directives.

The creation of larger, supranational governmental bodies such as the European Union may, however, make environmental regulation easier because such unification "domesticates" some of the relevant problems of collective bads. Instead of seeing its own polluting activities as largely internationalized, each nation of the Union can increasingly see its problem as merely the general problem of the larger Union, and at that level democratic choice might relatively easily reach consensus on regulation. A side advantage of supranational organizations intended for the resolution of simple coordination problems in economic activities may be to domesticate some problems of collective bads enough to make them consensually, democratically resolvable. This prospect should give many western European leaders greater incentive to broaden the Union by including the polluting states of eastern Europe – because much of the cost of the eastern pollution is visited on the western nations. In the short term, however, economic differences might make such resolutions harder by making them seem redistributive, because levels of economic development differ substantially from east to west.

Note that this resolution of the European problems of collective bads is far from creating a generally powerful supranational government. The nations could merge little more than economic policy, although there are likely to be, as there have been, more or less inseparable social issues that the Union might be forced to address. But it would not require a supranational police force to control compliance with environmental policies, because these could be coupled with other economic policies that have beneficial consequences. The bad to be regulated would be collective and its regulation would require more or less universal endogenous changes in behavior. But the policing of those changes in behavior would be done by each domestic government, and each domestic government would have its policies dyadically enforced by negotiation with each member state of the larger Union rather than by centralized directive, for which there might be no authority.

Not to couple environmental and other economic policies would inherently undercut the point of the Union, which is to make internal trade and production efficient across all the nations of the Union. Very dirty production in one nation would allow that nation to externalize its costs of production to the other nations, through pollution that crosses borders, thus lowering its production costs and increasing its benefits from marketing its production more competitively. National leaders who suppose that their nation must yield economic advantages in submitting to a Union whose members are not all equally advanced and productive have reason to temper their nationalist inclinations with concern for gaining ways to control the generation of collective bads in the less developed nations of the Union.

As argued above, the focus of collective action problems in international politics is distinctively different from that of domestic politics. Collective bads that are endogenously generated and that must be endogenously regulated are now, and for the near future of a generation or more, the main concern in the international politics of collective action. In a democratic political order with sanctioning power, consensus that some pattern of behavior produces a severe bad implies good prospects for regulation of the bad. In a quasi-anarchy of states with only dyadic rather than centralized sanctioning power, a similar consensus may be less effective in motivating regulation. The best hope for regulation may lie in regional and other supranational organizations of states to address issues of economic relations.

These organizations form relatively successfully because their central problem is merely coordination. Although there are conflictual issues at the edges and in the details of the coordination, coordination is the modal incentive structure. Once such organizations are established, they can effectively use the value of coordinating with them as a dyadic sanction against those who do not join in resolutions of other issues that are not merely coordination. By increasing the geographical reach of policies on various issues, they can come much closer to domesticating collective bads that cross borders and that, therefore, would allow member states to externalize the burdens of the bads they produce to other states. At the regional level, there might therefore be consensus on regulating some bad that none of the member states would have an interest in regulating on its own. A moderately anarchic world of geographically very large nations and large regional organizations of nations might therefore be expected to handle international collective bads relatively well, even if perhaps not as well as could a functioning democracy with central power.

REFERENCES

Bentley, Arthur. 1908. *The Process of Government.* Chicago: University of Chicago Press.
Hardin, Russell. 1982. *Collective Action.* Baltimore, MD: The Johns Hopkins University Press.
1998. "Garbage out, garbage in." *Social Research* 65: 9–30.
New York Times. 1997. 22 June, I, p. 12.
Locke, John. 1963 (1690). "The second treatise of government," in *Two Treatises of Government.* Edited by Peter Haslett. Cambridge: Cambridge University Press.
Olson, Mancur, Jr. 1965. *The Logic of Collective Action.* Cambridge, MA: Harvard University Press.
Popkin, Samuel L. 1979. *The Rational Peasant: The Political Economy of Rural Society in Vietnam.* Berkeley: University of California Press.
Samuelson, Paul A. 1954. "The pure theory of public expenditure." *Review of Economics and Statistics* 37: 387–9.
Schattschneider, E. E. 1960. *The Semi-sovereign People.* New York: Holt, Rinehart and Winston.
Scientific American. 1977. April: 27.
Scott, James C. 1976. *The Moral Economy of the Peasant.* New Haven: Yale University Press.
Snidal, Duncan. 1979. "Public goods, property rights, and political organizations." *International Studies Quarterly* 23: 532–66.
Sonnemans, Joep, Arthur Schramm, and Theo Offerman. 1998. "Public good production and public bad prevention: the effect of framing." *Journal of Economic Behavior and Organization* 34: 143–61.
Truman, David B. 1971 (1951). *The Governmental Process: Political Interests and Public Opinion.* New York: Knopf.

6   The transformation of political community: rethinking democracy in the context of globalization

David Held

This chapter focuses on the changing nature of political community in the context of globalization – in brief, the growing interconnectedness, and intensification of relations, among states and societies. The chapter has a number of parts. In the first part, I explore the changing forms of political association and, in particular, the rise of the modern nation state as a background against which modern conceptions of democracy developed. With this in mind, I examine some of the key assumptions and presuppositions of liberal democracy; above all, its conception of political community. In the second part, I explore changing forms of globalization. In my view, globalization has been with us for some time, but its extent, intensity, and impact have changed fundamentally. In the third and final part of the essay, the implications of changing forms of globalization are explored in relation to the prospects of democratic political community. A particular conception of democracy is elaborated, a form of transnational democracy, which, it is argued, is more appropriate to the developing structure of political associations today. The future of democracy is set out in cosmopolitan terms – a new democratic complex with global scope, given shape and form by reference to a basic democratic law, which takes on the character of government to the extent, and only to the extent, that it promulgates, implements, and enforces this law. This is by no means a prescription for the end of the nation state or the end of democratic politics as we know it – far from it. Rather, it is a recipe for the enrichment of democratic life (see Held 1995 and 1996). It is argued that only by buttressing democracy, within and across nation states, can the accountability of power in the contemporary era be strengthened.

Changing forms of political life

At the turn of the first millennium human associations developed in relative isolation. The most deeply rooted ancient civilizations, particularly the Chinese, Japanese, and Islamic, were "discrete worlds" (Fernández-Armesto 1995: chap. 1). While they were, of course, highly sophisticated and in many respects culturally complex worlds, they had relatively little contact with one another, although they were not without some forms of direct interchange (Mann 1986; Watson 1992; Fernández-Armesto 1995). For example, various types of trade flowed across cultures, civilizations, and early state forms, linking the economic fortunes of different societies together as well as acting as a conduit for ideas and technological practices. Extensive trading networks often connected the ancient civilizations in great loops of cause and effect (see Abu-Lughod 1989). One of the most remarkable examples of this was the Chinese development of massive fleets which, from the thirteenth century, were able to trade and explore vast sections of the seas, making possible an extensive pattern of trade with Europe in luxury goods such as silk, silver, and slippers (Kennedy 1988: 7; Fernández-Armesto 1995: 134). But in spite of these interchanges, the ancient civilizations developed largely as a result of "internal" forces and pressures; they were separate and to a large extent autonomous civilizations.

These civilizations were shaped by imperial systems which stretched over scattered populations and territories. Some, notably the Chinese, retained identifiable institutional forms over long periods, and benefited from an accumulation and concentration of coercive means – above all, of military and war-making capacity. When this capacity waned, empires disintegrated. The deployment of military strength was uppermost in the creation and maintenance of frontiers or territorial boundaries, though the latter were often in flux and shifted according to patterns of alliances, rebellion, and invasion. Empires were culturally diverse and heterogeneous, ruling over a plethora of communities and societies.

I shall argue later that the early development of trade routes, or select military and naval operations, or cultural contacts across societies, is quite different from the contemporary pattern of sustained and deepening interchange among states and societies. But first, it is necessary to underline how these early discrete worlds were slowly altered and enveloped by Europe's changing political and economic structures – structures which engendered a very particular conception of political community which was to grip the political imagination.

The roughly 30 million people who lived across the European land mass a thousand years ago did not conceive of themselves as a connected people (Tilly 1990: 38). The larger power divisions that crystallized masked the area's fragmented and decentered nature. Those who prevailed over territories did so above all as military victors and conquerors, exacting tribute and rent; they were far from being heads of state governing clearly demarcated territories and peoples. To the extent that we can talk of a European political system at all at this time, it was one marked by overlapping and divided authority, distinguished by interlocking ties and obligations, with networks of rule fragmented into many small, autonomous parts (Poggi 1978: 27). Political power tended to be local and personal in focus, generating "a social world of overlapping claims and powers" (Anderson 1974: 149). Some of these claims and powers conflicted; and no ruler or state was sovereign in the sense of being supreme over a given territory and population (Bull 1977: 254). While the Church helped give "Europe" what overarching unity it had, tensions were rife and war was frequent.

The proximate sources of modern political community, that is of the modern nation state, were absolutism and the interstate system it initiated. In condensing and concentrating political and military power in its own hands, and in seeking to create a central system of rule, absolutism paved the way, from the sixteenth century onward, for a secular and national system of power. The concentration of power set in motion a series of developments which were of great significance to the history of political communities: (1) the growing coincidence of territorial boundaries with a uniform system of rule; (2) the creation of new mechanisms of law-making and enforcement; (3) the centralization of administrative power; (4) the alteration and extension of fiscal management; (5) the formalization of relations among states through the development of diplomacy and diplomatic institutions; and (6) the introduction of standing armies (see Anderson 1974: 15–41; Giddens 1985: chap. 4; Mann 1986: chaps. 12–15). Absolutism helped set in motion a process of state-making which began to reduce the social, economic, and cultural variation *within* states and expand the *variation* among them, i.e., it helped to forge politica. communities with a clearer and growing sense of identity – national identity (Tilly 1975: 19).

By the end of the seventeenth century Europe was no longer simply a mosaic of polities. For the "consolidated independent sovereignty of each individual state ... was at the same time part of the process of overall inter-state integration" (Giddens 1985: 91). A concomitant of each and every state's claim to uncontestable authority was the recognition that such a claim gave other states an equal entitlement to autonomy and respect within their own borders. The development of state sovereignty was part of a process of mutual recognition whereby states granted each other rights of jurisdiction in their respective territories and communities. Sovereignty established an *entitlement* to rule over a bounded territory, although whether such rule was effective – that is, whether a state possessed sufficient *autonomy* to articulate and achieve its objectives in relation to other key agencies and forces – was always another matter. But in the world of relations among states, the principle that all states have equal rights to self-determination became paramount in the formal conduct of states towards one another. Of course, at issue was largely the formal relations among the most powerful states – the rights and privileges of sovereignty were by no means granted to all those peoples and communities with whom these states came into contact, within and beyond Europe (see below).

The emergent international "society of states" was articulated by a new conception of international law which has been referred to as the "Westphalian model" (after the Peace of Westphalia of 1648). While it can be disputed that all the elements of the model, as described below, were intrinsic to the treaties signed at the Peace of Westphalia, this dispute need not be examined here (see Krasner 1995; Keohane,1995). For the model can be taken to depict a developing trajectory in international law which did not receive its fullest articulation until the late eighteenth and early nineteenth centuries when territorial sovereignty, the formal equality of states, non-intervention in the domestic affairs of other recognized states, and state consent as the basis of international legal obligation became the core principles of international society (see Crawford and Marks 1998).

The model represents an emerging community of territorial, sovereign states which settle their differences privately and by force if necessary; which engage in diplomatic relations but otherwise minimal cooperation; which seek to place their own national interest above all others; and which accept the logic of the principle of effectiveness, that is, the principle that might eventually makes right in the international world – appropriation becomes legitimation. The model of Westphalia can be summarized by the following points (see Cassese 1986: 396–9; Falk 1969):

1. The world consists of, and is divided by, sovereign states which recognize no superior authority.
2. The processes of law-making, the settlement of disputes and law enforcement are largely in the hands of individual states.
3. International law is oriented to the establishment of minimal rules of coexistence; the creation of enduring relationships among states and peoples is an aim, but only to the extent that it allows national objectives to be met.
4. Responsibility for cross-border wrongful acts is a "private matter" concerning only those affected.
5. All states are regarded as equal before the law: legal rules do not take account of asymmetries of power.

6. Differences among states are often settled by force; the principle of effective power holds sway. Virtually no legal fetters exist to curb the resort to force; international legal standards afford minimal protection.

7. The minimization of impediments to state freedom is the "collective priority."

This new order of states, while providing a framework for the integration of the state system, simultaneously endorsed the right of each state to autonomous and independent action. As one commentator aptly noted, states were "not subject to international moral requirements" because they were held to represent "separate and discrete political orders with no common authority among them" (Beitz 1979: 25). In this conception, the world consists of separate political powers pursuing their own interests, backed ultimately by their organization of coercive power. Although strictly illegal in Westphalian terms, the resort to coercion or armed force by non-state actors also became an almost inevitable by-product of this order; for communities contesting established territorial boundaries had little alternative but to resort to arms in order to establish "effective control" over the area they sought as their territory, and in that way made their case for international recognition (see Baldwin 1992: 224–5).

Of course, the principles and rules of the Westphalian system did not translate simply into one conception of international order (see Held 1995: chap. 4; Hall 1996), and the consolidation of the modern system of nation states has not been a uniform process, affecting each region and country in a similar way. From the outset this process has involved great costs for the autonomy and independence of many peoples, especially in extra-European civilizations. In fact, the spread of the modern state system has been consistently characterized by both "hierarchy" and "unevenness" (see Falk 1990: 2–12). Europe's global empires, starting with the European voyages of discovery led by the Iberian monarchies in the fifteenth century and culminating, perhaps most dramatically, in the scramble for Africa in the late nineteenth century, are adequate testimony to this. None the less, it is against the background of the forging of the modern state system that the nature and form of modern political community, and of democratic politics in particular, has to be understood.

Those who contested absolutism in Europe and struggled to establish an impersonal system of power, the rule of law, and greater accountability of political authority could take the emergent political communities for granted, or at least that there were communities to fight over. As Hawthorn has argued, "absolutist states were, in their absolutism, states. They controlled their territories and the population within them. And even if they did not emerge from an already existing political community, they almost always served to create one. Those who came later to contest them, whether in France in the later 1780s, or in Chile, South Korea or South Africa in the later 1980s, could take that community for granted, or at least could take it that there was a community to be fought for" (Hawthorn 1993: 344). Elsewhere, the context of community has not always been so fortuitous either for the development of centralized administrative power or for the establishment of greater accountability (see Held 1993: part IV; Potter, Goldblatt, Kiloh, and Lewis 1997). Where states successfully carved out political communities, by building upon old "ethnic cores," and/or by linking communities together, and/or by forging new political relations, they provided an impetus to the development of a discourse about the nature of modern political community, about the meaning of membership in it, and about proper form and limits of political power – in short, about democracy.

Until the eighteenth century, democracy was, of course, generally associated with the gathering of citizens in assemblies and public meeting places. From the late eighteenth century, it was beginning to be thought of as the right of citizens to participate in the determination of the collective will through the medium of elected representatives (Bobbio 1989). The theory of representative democracy fundamentally shifted the terms of reference of democratic thought: the practical limits that a sizeable citizenry imposes on democracy, which had been the focus of so much critical (anti-democratic) attention, were thought to be removable. Representative democracy could now be celebrated as both accountable and feasible government, potentially stable over great territories and time spans (see Dahl 1989: 28–30). As one of the best-known advocates of the representative system put it, "by ingrafting representation upon democracy" a system of government is created that is capable of embracing "all the various interests and every extent of territory and population" (Paine 1987: 281). Representative democracy could even be heralded, as James Mill wrote, "as the grand discovery of modern times" in which "the solution of all difficulties, both speculative and practical, would be found" (quoted in Sabine 1963: 695). Accordingly, the theory and practice of democratic government broke away from its traditional association with small states and cities, opening itself to become the legitimating creed of the emerging world of modern nation states. Of course, who exactly was to count as a legitimate participant, or a "citizen" or an "individual," and what his or her exact role was to be in this new order, remained either unclear or unsettled in many of the leading theories of representative democracy (Held 1996). It was only with the actual achievement of citizenship for all adults, men and women, that liberal democracy took on its distinctively contemporary form: a cluster of rules and institutions permitting the broadest participation of citizens in the selection of representatives who alone can make political decisions, that is, decisions affecting the whole community (see Bobbio 1987: 66; Dahl 1989: 221, 233).

Built, as it was, upon an emerging conception of the modern nation state, the development of liberal democracy took place within a fairly delimited conceptual space (cf. Walker 1988; Connolly 1991; McGrew 1997). Modern democratic theory and practice was constructed upon Westphalian foundations. National communities, and theories of national communities, were based on the presupposition that political communities could, in principle, control their destinies and citizens could come to identify sufficiently with each other such that they might think and act together with a view of what was best for all of them, that is, with a view of the common good (Sandel 1996: 202). It was taken for granted that, bar internal difficulties, the demos, the extent of the franchise, the form and scope of representation, and the nature and meaning of consent – in fact all the key elements of self-determination – could be specified with respect to geography: systems of representation and democratic accountability could be neatly meshed with the spatial reach of sites of power in a circumscribed territory. Moreover, as a consequence of this, clear-cut distinctions could be elaborated – and national institutions built upon – the difference between "internal" and "external" policy, between domestic and foreign affairs. The vast majority of the theories of democracy, liberal and radical, assumed that the nature and possibilities of political community could be elaborated by reference to national structures and national possibilities, and that freedom, political equality and solidarity could be entrenched in and through the nation state. This became the cornerstone of modern democratic thought.

Of course, the construction of a national democratic community was often deeply contested as different social, economic, and cultural groups fought with each other about the nature of this community and about their own status within it. If it had not been for the extensive and often violently suppressed struggles of working-class, feminist, and civil rights activists in the nineteenth and twentieth centuries, a genuinely universal suffrage would not have been created in many countries (see Potter, Goldblatt, Kiloh, and Lewis 1997). In addition, the construction of a national democratic identity has often been part of an attempt to bind people together in order to gain or enhance particular interests. The requirements of political action have led to attempts to deploy national identity as a means of ensuring the coordination of policy, mobilization, and legitimacy (see Breuilly 1982: 365ff). That nationalist elites actively sought to generate a sense of nationality and a commitment to the nation – a "national community of fate" – is well chronicled (see Smith 1995). Yet, the conditions of state making and of nationalism or of nation building never fully overlapped. And, of course, there was considerable theoretical dispute about how national self-government should be understood; liberal, republican, and radical views diverged.

None the less, the theory of democracy, particularly as it emerged in the nineteenth and twentieth centuries, could take for granted the link between the demos, citizenship, electoral mechanisms, the nature of consent, and the boundaries of the nation state. The fates of different political communities may be intertwined, but the appropriate place for determining the foundation of "national fate" was the national community itself. In the contemporary era the key principles and practices of liberal democracy are associated almost exclusively with the principles and institutions of the sovereign nation state. Further, modern democratic theory and democratic politics assumes a symmetry and congruence between citizen-voters and national decision-makers. Through the ballot box, citizen-voters are, in principle, able to hold decision-makers to account; and, as a result of electoral consent, decision-makers are able to make and pursue law and policy legitimately for their constituents, ultimately, the people in a fixed, territorially based community. Accordingly, the heart or "deep structure" of the system of democratic nation states can be characterized by a number of striking features, which are, broadly: democracy in nation states and non-democratic relations among states; the entrenchment of accountability and democratic legitimacy inside state boundaries and pursuit of reasons of state (and maximum political advantage) outside such boundaries; democracy and citizenship rights for those regarded as "insiders," and the frequent negation of these rights for those beyond their borders.

Changing forms of regional and global enmeshment

At the centre of the dominant theoretical approaches to democratic politics is an uncritically appropriated concept of the territorial political community. The difficulty with this is that political communities have rarely – if ever – existed in isolation as bounded geographical totalities; they are better thought of as multiple overlapping networks of interaction. These networks crystallize around different sites and forms of power – economic, political, military, cultural, among others – producing diverse patterns of activity which do not correspond in any simple and straightforward way to territorial boundaries (see Mann 1986: chap. 1). The spatial reach of the modern nation state did not fix impermeable borders for other networks, the scope and reach of which have been as much local as international or even global. Modern political communities are, and have always been, locked into a diversity of processes and structures which range in and through them. The theory and practice of the democratic sovereign state has always been in some tension with the actuality of state sovereignty and autonomy. National political communities do not always make and determine decisions and policies simply for themselves, and governments do not always make policies and decisions exclusively for their citizens (see Offe 1985). The freedom of action of particular political communities has always been, to varying degrees, constrained. How should one understand these patterns of interconnections, and their changing form over time? And how should one understand their political implications, in particular, for sovereignty, autonomy, and the democratic political community?

The term "globalization" captures some of the changes which shape the nature of the political and the prospects of political community; unpacking this term helps create a framework for addressing some of the issues raised above. Globalization can be understood, I believe, in relation to a set of processes which shift the spatial form of human organization and activity to transcontinental or interregional patterns of activity, interaction and the exercise of power (see Held, McGrew, Goldblatt, and Perraton 1999). It involves a stretching and deepening of social relations and institutions across space and time such that, on the one hand, day-to-day activities are increasingly influenced by events happening on the other side of the globe and, on the other, the practices and decisions of local groups or communities can have significant global reverberations (see Giddens 1990). It is possible to distinguish different historical forms of globalization in terms of: (1) the extensiveness of networks of relations and connections; (2) the intensity of flows and levels of activity within these networks; and (3) the impact of these phenomena on particular bounded communities. It is not a case of saying, as many do, that there was once no globalization, but there is now; rather, it is a case of recognizing that forms of globalization have changed over time and that these can be systematically understood by reference to points 1–3 above. Such an historical approach to globalization contrasts with the current fashion to suggest either that globalization is fundamentally new – the "hyper-globalization school," with its insistence that global markets are now fully established (see Ohmae 1990) – or that there is nothing unprecedented about contemporary

levels of international economic and social interaction since they re-
semble those of the gold standard era – the "skeptical school" (see Hirst
and Thompson 1996).

Globalization is neither a singular condition nor a linear process.
Rather, it is best thought of as a multidimensional phenomenon involving domains of activity and interaction that include the economic,
political, technological, military, legal, cultural, and environmental.
Each of these spheres involves different patterns of relations and activities. A general account of globalization cannot simply predict from one
domain what will occur in another. It is extremely important, then, to
keep these distinctive domains separate and to build a theory of
globalization and its impact on particular political communities from an
understanding of what is happening in each and every one of them. It is
neither feasible nor desirable to set out such a theory here, but a number
of historical contrasts can usefully be drawn, and placed alongside some
illustrative material, in order to explore the changing impact of globalization on the nature and prospects of political community. This provides
the backdrop for rethinking the nature of democracy in the context of
globalization.

While early modern colonialism criss-crossed many parts of the
world, and the expansion of the European–Atlantic maritime empires
forged deep connections between regions, the historical watershed in
the growing enmeshment of political communities probably lies in the
period of the last half of the nineteenth century. The impetus to global
processes, both in terms of stretch and intensity, was provided by the
rapid expansion of Europe, and by the contest over the terms of this
expansion and the struggle by various regional centres to contain it
(Geyer and Bright 1995). Undoubtedly, the rapidly developing empires
of Britain and of other European powers were the most powerful agents
of globalization in the late nineteenth century. By the end of that
century the spread of the British Empire had been so great that it
comprised nearly a quarter of the land surface of the world and included
more than a quarter of the population. The British Empire, to borrow a
phrase, "stretched long fingertips over the world" (Fernández-Armesto
1995: 264). At issue was not simply an acceleration of European
expansion along a continuum that ran back through earlier centuries,
but a new ordering of relations of domination and subordination among
various parts of the world.

European colonialism had often been propelled by a spirit of "pio-
neering expansionism," aided and abetted by an interest in the exploitation of local conditions and infrastructures. In Africa, the imperialists
succeeded best when they followed the recommendations of an English

parliamentary committee: "adopt the native government already existing; being content with controlling their excesses and maintaining
peace between them" (quoted in Fernández-Armesto 1995: 419; see
Pakenham 1992). The management and control of massive overseas
territories would have been exorbitantly expensive and deeply imprac-
tical without the use of existing political structures and resources. Until
innovatory developments in the infrastructure of communication and
travel were widely available – new breeds of fast steamers, morse code,
the telegraph, cable links, and, later, radio – highly dispersed territories
remained hard to communicate with and were vulnerable to independently minded colonial administrators and/or shifting local circumstances about which the imperial centres might know too little, too late.
Although changes in the technology of communication and travel were
far from a panacea for the political elites and classes in London, Paris,
and elsewhere, without investing in them and deploying them wherever
practicable they thought they could not fully manage their overseas
interests and personnel (see, for example, Pakenham 1992: chap. 3).

But perhaps more than anything else, this period of expansion should
be understood as the start of a shift from imperial and territorial forms
of control, which were deeply contested and fought over, to new,
distinctive, non-territorial forms of power and domination. Slowly,
during the late-nineteenth and early-twentieth centuries, European
empires altered their modes of control from mechanisms of direct
administration within empires to new forms of infrastructural interaction and control. Geyer and Bright put the point thus: "through
spatial expansion and occupation ... a new effort, with new capabilities,
to synchronise global time and co-ordinate interactions within the world
... [was] made possible by the formation of communications-based
systems of control (the gold standard, the global deployment of maritime force ...) that began to ... [enmesh] the world in global circuits of
power by the end of the century" (1995: 1047). European states moved
beyond the mere extension of their power over others to the formation
of direct and sustained organization which might give them infrastructural control of others. Over time, regimes of personal order and direct
control, with their haphazardness and uncertainies, gave way to new
transnational forms of organization and activity. These were often
marked by more anonymous systems of power – managed and controlled by new international organizations and/or multinational corporations – which began to develop a life of their own, independently of the
nation states from which they were initiated. Instead of territorial
empires stretching over many regions and seeking to subject them to a
single political system, a new political order began to develop based on a

proliferation of international organizations, transnational practices, and networks of exchange (in industry and banking, in information and communication, in travel and cultural interchange) (see Murphy 1994). The influence of Western commerce, trade, and political organization outlived direct rule, giving rise to new patterns of non-territorial globalization – globalization without territory (see Pieterse 1997).

From the foundation of the International Telegraph Union in 1865, a plethora of international organizations developed with responsibility for regulating and ordering diverse domains of activity including trade, industrial infrastructure, agriculture, labor, public order and administration, elements of individual rights, health, and research. At issue was not the creation of a single institution or authority to manage world affairs, but rather the establishment of regulatory regimes for, in principle, the predictable and orderly conduct of pressing transnational processes. By 1914 many aspects of global affairs had been brought within the terms of these offices and rule systems. Accordingly, a new infrastructure for the regulation and control of economic, social, and cultural affairs was slowly founded, stimulating telegrams, letters, and packages to flood the international networks by the beginning of the twentieth century (see Murphy 1994: chaps. 2 and 3).

Virtually all countries in the world became enmeshed in and functionally part of a larger pattern of global flows and global transformations (Nierop 1994: 171). Goods, capital, people, knowledge, communications, and weapons, as well as crime, culture, pollutants, fashions, and beliefs, readily moved across territorial boundaries (see McGrew 1992). Transnational networks, social movements, and relationships extended through virtually all areas of human activity. The existence of interregional systems of trade, finance, and production bound together the prosperity and fate of households, communities, and nations across the world. Far from this being a world of "discrete civilizations," it became a fundamentally interconnected global order, marked by dense patterns of exchange as well as by power, hierarchy, and unevenness.

Against this background, the meaning and place of political community, and particularly of the democratic political community, needs to be re-examined. At least two tasks are necessary in order to pursue this objective. First, it is important to illustrate some of the fundamental alterations in the patterns of interconnectedness among political communities and the subsequent shifts in the structure and form of political community itself. Secondly, it is important to set out some of the political implications of these changes. In what follows, I start by illustrating some of the transformations which have brought a change in the organization and meaning of political community. Clearly, these are indicative transformations only; they obviously fall short of a systematic account (see Held, McGrew, Goldblatt, and Perraton 1999).

(1) Among the significant developments which are changing the nature of political community are global economic processes, especially growth in trade, production, and financial transactions, organized in part by rapidly expanding multinational companies. Trade has grown substantially, reaching unprecedented levels, particularly in the post-World War II period. Not only has there been an increase in intra-regional trade around the world, but there has also been sustained growth among regions as well (see Perraton, Goldblatt, Held, and McGrew 1997). More countries are involved in global trading arrangements, for instance, India and China, and more people and nations are affected by such arrangements. If there is a further lowering of tariff barriers across the world, these trends are likely to continue and to further the extension, intensity, and impact of trade relations on other domains of life. The expansion of global financial flows has, moreover, been particularly rapid in the last ten to fifteen years. Foreign exchange turnover has mushroomed and is now over 1.2 trillion dollars a day. Much of this financial activity is speculative and generates fluctuations in prices (of stocks, shares, futures, etc.) in excess of those which can be accounted for by changes in the fundamentals of asset values. The enormous growth of global financial flows across borders, linked to the liberalization of capital markets from the late 1970s, has created a more integrated financial system than has ever been known.

Underpinning this economic shift has been the growth of multinational corporations, both productive and financial. Approximately 20,000 multinational corporations now account for a quarter to a third of world output, 70 percent of world trade, and 80 percent of foreign direct investment. They are essential to the diffusion of skills and technology, and they are key players in the international money markets. In addition, multinational corporations can have profound affects on macroeconomic policy. They can respond to variations in interest rates by raising finance in whichever capital market is most favorable. They can shift their demand for employment to countries with much lower employment costs. And in the area of industrial policy, especially technology policy, they can move activities to where the maximum benefits accrue. None of this is to say that multinational corporations are simply "footloose" or stateless operators. Multinational direct investment is often undertaken to ensure a presence in local markets; it is frequently marked by significant start-up costs, and corporations are often committed to particular markets for the medium or long term. In addition, many domestic markets are too substantial for these companies simply to ignore them. Accordingly, multinational corporations play a much more central role in national and international economic transactions than they have done in previous periods. "In particular, they have established international networks of coordinated production that is historically unique, and have done so across a wider range of sectors than in the past ... their actions and interests shape the flow, form and location of investment, the conduct of trade and the development of technologies" – all significant matters for individual national communities (Goldblatt, Held, McGrew, and Perraton 1997: 73). Against this background, the traditional claims of democratic theory – above all, the claims to the possibility of a circumscribed, delimited self-determining community of citizens – begin to appear strained.

It is easy to misrepresent the political significance of the globalization of economic activity. There are those, earlier referred to as the "hyper-globalizers," who argue that we now live in a world in which social and economic processes operate predominantly at a global level (see Ohmae 1990; Reich 1991). According to these thinkers, national political communities are now immersed in a sea of global economic flows and are inevitably "decision takers" in this context. For many neo-liberal thinkers, this is a welcome development; a world market order based on the principles of free trade and minimum regulation is the guarantee of liberty, efficiency, and effective government (see Hayek 1960: 405–6). By contrast, however, there are those who are more reserved about the extent and benefits of the globalization of economic activity. They point out, for instance, that for all the expansion in global flows of trade and investment, the majority of economic activity still occurs on a more restricted spatial scale – in national economies and in the OECD countries. They also point out that the historical evidence suggests that contemporary forms of international economic interaction are not without precedent – and they refer to the gold standard era for some substantial and interesting comparisons (see Hirst and Thompson 1996; cf. Perraton, Goldblatt, Held, and McGrew 1997).

But the claims of the hyper-globalizers and their critics misstate much of what is significant about contemporary economic globalization for politics. Nation states continue to be immensely powerful, and enjoy access to a formidable range of resources, bureaucratic infrastructural capacity, and technologies of coordination and control. The continuing lobbying of states by multinational corporations confirm the enduring importance of states to the mediation and regulation of economic activity. Yet it is wrong to argue that globalization is a mere illusion, an ideological veil, that allows politicians simply to disguise the causes of poor performance and policy failure. Although the rhetoric of hyper-globalization has provided many an elected politician with a conceptual resource for refusing political responsibility, globalization has significant and discernible characteristics which alter the balance of resources – economic and political – within and across borders. Among the most important of these is the tangible growth in the enmeshment of national economies in global economic transactions (i.e., a growing proportion of nearly all national economies are involved in international economic exchanges with an increasing number of countries). This increase in the extent and intensity of economic interconnectedness has altered the relation between economic and political power. One shift has been particularly significant: "the historic expansion of exit options for capital in financial markets relative to national capital controls, national banking regulations and national investment strategies, and the sheer volume of privately held capital relative to national reserves. Exit options for corporations making direct investments have also expanded ... the balance of power has shifted in favour of capital *vis-à-vis* both national governments and national labour movements" (Goldblatt, Held, McGrew, and Perraton 1997: 74). As a result, the autonomy of democratically elected governments has been, and is increasingly, constrained by sources of unelected and unrepresentative economic power. These have the effect of making adjustment to the international economy (and, above all, to global financial markets) a fixed point of orientation in economic policy and of encouraging an acceptance of the "decision signals" of its leading agents and forces as a, if not the, standard of rational decision-making. The options for political communities, and the costs and benefits of them, ineluctably alter.

(2) Within the realms of the media and culture there are also grounds for thinking that there is a growing disjuncture between the idea of the democratic state as an independent, accountable centre of power bounded by fixed borders – in this case, a centre of national culture, able to foster and sustain a national identity – and interlinked changes in the spheres of media and cultural exchange. A number of developments in recent times can be highlighted. English has spread as the dominant language of elite cultures throughout the world: it is now the dominant language in business, computing, law, science, and politics. The internationalization and globalization of telecommunications have been extraordinarily rapid: international telephone traffic has increased over fourfold between 1983 and 1995; there has been a massive increase in transnational cable links; there has been an explosion in satellite links; and the Internet has provided a remarkable increase in the infrastructure of horizontal and lateral communication capacity within and across borders. Moreover, substantial multimedia conglomerates have

developed, such as the Murdoch empire and Time Warner. In addition, there has been a huge increase in tourism – for example, in 1960 there were 70 million international tourists, while in 1994 there were nearly 500 million. And in television and film there are similar trends.

None of the above examples, or the accumulative impact of parallel cases, should be taken to imply the development of a single global, media-led culture (consider the impact of Star television in India), but certainly, taken together, these developments do imply that many new forms of communication media range in and across borders, linking nations and peoples in new ways. The creation and recreation of new forms of identity – often linked to consumption and the entertainment industries – are not to be underestimated. In this context, the capacity of national political leaders to sustain a national culture has become more complex and difficult. Even China, for example, where the authorities sought to restrict access to and use of Western media, films, and the Internet, has found this extremely difficult to do, especially with regard to young people. All independent states may retain a legal claim to "effective supremacy over what occurs within their territories," but this is significantly compromised by the growing enmeshment of "the national" with transnational influences (see Keohane 1995). The determination of political community and the nature of political identity within it become less a territorial matter and more a matter of transaction, exchange, and bargaining across a complex set of transnational networks. At the very least, national political communities by no means simply determine the structure, education, and cultural flows in and through which their citizens are cultivated. Citizens' values and judgments are now formed in a complex web of national, international, and global cultural exchange. (This situation is not entirely without precedent if considered in the context of the spread of world religions: see Held, McGrew, Goldblatt, and Perraton 1999: chap. 7, for some notable comparisons.)

(3) Environmental problems and challenges are perhaps the clearest and starkest examples of the global shift in human organization and activity, creating some of the most fundamental pressures on the efficacy of the nation state and state-centric democratic politics. There are three types of problems at issue:

a) the first is shared problems involving the global commons, i.e., fundamental elements of the ecosystem – among the most significant challenges here are global warming and ozone depletion;

b) a second category of global environmental problems involves the interlinked challenges of demographic expansion and resource consumption – pressing examples under this heading include desertification, questions of biodiversity, and threats to the existence of certain species;

c) a third category of problems is transboundary pollution such as acid rain, or river pollutants, or the contaminated rain which fell in connection with Chernobyl.

In response to the progressive development of, and publicity sur-rounding, environmental problems in the last three decades, there has been an interlinked process of cultural and political globalization as illustrated by the emergence of new cultural, scientific, and intellectual networks; new environmental movements with transnational organiza-tions and transnational concerns; and new institutions and conventions such as those agreed in 1992 at the Earth Summit in Brazil. Not all environmental problems are, of course, global; such an implication would be entirely false. But there has been a striking shift in the physical and environmental conditions – that is, in the extent and intensity of environmental problems – affecting human affairs in general. These processes have moved politics dramatically away from an activity which crystallizes first and foremost around state and interstate concerns. It is clearer than ever that the fortunes of political communities and peoples can no longer be simply understood in exclusively national or territorial terms. As one commentator aptly noted, "in the context of intense global and regional interconnectedness, the very idea of political com-munity as an exclusive territorially delimited unit is at best unconvincing and at worst anachronistic. In a world in which global warming connects the long-term fate of many Pacific islands to the actions of tens of millions of private motorists across the globe, the conventional territorial conception of political community appears profoundly inadequate. Globalization weaves together, in highly complex and abstract systems, the fate of households, communities and peoples in distant regions of the globe" (McGrew 1997: 237). Political communities are locked into a diversity of processes and structures which range across them. It can be no surprise then that national communities do not make decisions and policies exclusively for themselves, and that governments today do not simply determine what is right or appropriate for their own citizens alone. While it would be a mistake to conclude that political commu-nities are without distinctive degrees of division or cleavage at their borders, they are clearly shaped by multiple cross-border interaction networks and power systems. Thus, questions are raised both about the fate of the idea of political community and about the appropriate locus for the articulation of the democratic political good. The proper "home" of politics and democracy becomes a puzzling matter.

(4) Changes in the development of international law have placed

individuals, governments and non-governmental organizations under
new systems of legal regulation. International law recognizes powers and
constraints, and rights and duties, which have qualified the principle of
state sovereignty in a number of important respects; sovereignty *per se* is
no longer a straightforward guarantee of international legitimacy. Entrenched in certain legal instruments is the view that a legitimate state
must be a democratic state that upholds certain common values (see
Crawford 1994). One significant area in this regard is human rights law
and human rights regimes.

Of all the international declarations of rights, the European Convention for the Protection of Human Rights and Fundamental Freedoms
(1950) is particularly noteworthy. In marked contrast to the Universal
Declaration of Human Rights and the subsequent UN Covenants of
Rights, the European Convention was concerned, as its preamble
indicates, "to take the first steps for the collective enforcement of certain
of the rights stated in the Universal Declaration." The European
initiative was and remains a most radical legal innovation: an innovation
which, against the stream of state history, allows individual citizens to
initiate proceedings against their own governments. Within this framework, states are no longer free to treat their own citizens as they think fit
(see Capotorti 1983: 977). Human rights regimes have also been
promoted in other regions of the world, partly in response to United
Nations encouragement that such rights should be entrenched at
regional levels (see Evans 1997).

Each of the main UN human rights covenants has now been ratified
by over 140 out of 190 states, and more are expected to ratify them.
Increasing numbers of states appear willing to accept, in principle,
general duties of protection and provision, as well as of restraint, in their
own procedures and practices (see Beetham 1998). Clearly these commitments are rarely backed by coercive powers of enforcement.
However, the demands of the new international human rights regimes –
formal and informal – have created a plethora of transnational groups,
movements, agencies, and lawyers all engaged in reworking the nature
of national politics, national sovereignty, and state accountability.

In international law, accordingly, there has been a gradual shift away
from the principle that state sovereignty must be safeguarded irrespective of its consequences for individuals, groups, and organizations.
Respect for the autonomy of the subject, and for an extensive range of
human rights, creates a new set of ordering principles in political affairs
which can delimit and curtail the principle of effective state power.
Along with other international legal changes (see Held 1995: chap. 5),
these developments are indicative of an alteration in the weight granted,

on the one hand, to claims made on behalf of the state system and, on the other hand, to those made on behalf of an alternative organizing principle of world order, in which an unqualified state sovereignty no longer reigns supreme.

(5) While all the developments described so far have helped engender a shift away from a purely state-centered international system of "high politics" to new and novel forms of geogovernance, a further interesting example of this process can be drawn from the very heart of the idea of a sovereign state – national security and defense policy. There has been a notable increase in emphasis upon collective defense and cooperative security. The enormous costs, technological requirements, and domestic burdens of defense are contributing to the strengthening of multilateral and collective defense arrangements as well as international military cooperation and coordination (see Held, McGrew, Goldblatt, and Perraton 1999: chap. 2 for an elaborate discussion). The rising density of technological connections between states now challenges the very idea of national security and national arms procurement. Some of the most advanced weapons-systems in the world today, e.g., fighter aircraft, depend on components which come from many countries.[1] There has been a globalization of military technology linked to a transnationalization of defense production. And the proliferation of weapons of mass destruction makes all states insecure and makes problematical the very notions of "friends" and "enemies."

Even in the sphere of defense and arms production and manufacture, the notion of a singular, discrete, and delimited political community appears problematic. Indeed, even in this realm, any conception of sovereignty and autonomy which assumes that they denote an indivisible, illimitable, exclusive, and perpetual form of public power – embodied within an individual state – is increasingly challenged and eroded.

Democracy and globalization: in sum

At the end of the second millennium, as indicated previously, political communities and civilizations can no longer be characterized simply as "discrete worlds"; they are enmeshed and entrenched in complex structures of overlapping forces, relations, and movements. Clearly, these are often structured by inequality and hierarchy, but even the most powerful among them – including the most powerful nation states – do not remain unaffected by the changing conditions and processes of

---

[1] I am indebted to Anthony McGrew for this point.

regional and global entrenchment. Five central points can be noted to help characterize the changing relationship between globalization and democratic nation states. All indicate an increase in the extensiveness, intensity, and impact of globalization, and all suggest important points about the evolving character of the democratic political community.

First, the locus of effective political power can no longer be assumed to be national governments – effective power is shared, bartered, and struggled over by diverse forces and agencies at national, regional and international levels. Second, the idea of a political community of fate – of a self-determining collectivity – can no longer meaningfully be located within the boundaries of a single nation state alone. Some of the most fundamental forces and processes which determine the nature of life-chances within and across political communities are now beyond the reach of nation states. The system of national political communities persists of course; but it is articulated and re-articulated today with complex economic, organizational, administrative, legal, and cultural processes and structures which limit and check its efficacy. If these processes and structures are not acknowledged and brought into the political process themselves, they will tend to bypass or circumvent the democratic state system. Third, there is a growing set of disjunctures between the formal authority of the state – that is, the formal domain of political authority that states claim for themselves – and the actual practices and structures of the state and economic system at the regional and global levels. These disjunctures indicate that national communities do not exclusively program the action and decisions of governmental and parliamentary bodies, and the latter by no means simply determine what is right or appropriate for their own citizens (see Held 1995: chaps. 5 and 6; cf. Offe 1985: 286ff).

Fourth, it is not part of my argument that national sovereignty today, even in regions with intensive overlapping and divided political and authority structures, has been wholly subverted – not at all. But it is part of my argument that there are significant areas and regions marked by criss-crossing loyalties, conflicting interpretations of rights and duties, interconnected legal and authority structures, etc., which displace notions of sovereignty as an illimitable, indivisible, and exclusive form of public power. The operations of states in increasingly complex regional and global systems both affects their autonomy (by changing the balance between the costs and benefits of policies) and their sovereignty (by altering the balance between national, regional, and international legal frameworks and administrative practices). While massive concentrations of power remain features of many states, these are frequently embedded in, and articulated with, fractured domains of political authority. Against this background, it is not fanciful to imagine, as Bull once observed, the development of an international system which is a modern and secular counterpart to the kind of political organization found in Christian Europe in the middle ages, the essential characteristic of which was a system of overlapping authority and multiple loyalties (Bull 1977: 254–5).

Fifth, the late twentieth century is marked by a significant series of new types of "boundary problem." If it is accepted that we live in a world of overlapping communities of fate, where the trajectories of each and every country are more tightly entwined than ever before, then new types of boundary problem follow. In the past, of course, nation states principally resolved their differences over boundary matters by pursuing reasons of state backed by coercive means, but this power logic is singularly inadequate and inappropriate to resolve the many complex issues, from economic regulation to resource depletion and environmental degradation, which engender an intermeshing of "national fortunes." In Zimbabwe, it is said, many villagers used to believe that weather patterns were due to "acts of God" and, accordingly, climate shifts had to be accepted; today, the same people believe that their weather is affected by Western energy policy, patterns of pollution as well as some local practices, and, of course, some bad luck. In a world where powerful states make decisions not just for their peoples but for others as well, and where transnational actors and forces cut across the boundaries of national communities in diverse ways, the questions of who should be accountable to whom, and on what grounds, do not easily resolve themselves. Overlapping spheres of influence, interference, and interest create fundamental problems at the centre of democratic thought, problems which ultimately concern the very basis of democratic authority.

Rethinking democracy in the context of globalization

In the liberal democracies, consent to government and legitimacy for governmental action are dependent upon electoral politics and the ballot box. Yet the notions that consent legitimates government, and that the ballot box is the appropriate mechanism whereby the citizen body as a whole periodically confers authority on government to enact the law and regulate economic and social life, become problematic as soon as the nature of a "relevant community" is contested. What is the proper constituency, and proper realm of jurisdiction, for developing and implementing policy with respect to health issues such as AIDS or BSE (Bovine Spongiform Encephalopathy), the use of nuclear energy, the management of nuclear waste, the harvesting of rain forests, the use of non-renewable resources, the instability of global financial markets, the reduction of the risks of chemical and nuclear warfare? National boundaries have traditionally demarcated the basis on which individuals are included and excluded from participation in decisions affecting their lives; but if many socio-economic processes, and the outcomes of decisions about them, stretch beyond national frontiers, then the implications of this are serious, not only for the categories of consent and legitimacy but for all the key ideas of democracy. At issue is the nature of a constituency (how should the proper boundaries of a constituency be drawn?), the meaning of representation (who should represent whom and on what basis?), and the proper form and scope of political participation (who should participate and in what way?). As fundamental processes of governance escape the categories of the nation state, the traditional national resolutions of the key questions of democratic theory and practice are open to doubt.

Against this background, the nature and prospects of the democratic polity need re-examination. I have argued elsewhere that an acceptance of liberal democratic politics, in theory and practice, entails an acceptance of each citizen's equal interest in democracy; that is, a recognition of people's equal interest in self-determination (Held 1995: part III). Each adult has an interest in political autonomy as a result of his or her status as a citizen with an equal entitlement to self-determination. An equal interest in political autonomy requires, I have also argued, that citizens enjoy a common structure of political action. A common structure of political action entails a shared enjoyment of a cluster of rights and obligations. This cluster of rights and obligations has traditionally been thought of as entailing, above all, civil and political rights and obligations. Again, elsewhere, I have argued that this cluster has to bite more deeply than civil and political rights alone; for the latter leave large swathes of power untouched by mechanisms of access, accountability, and control. At stake, in short, is a recognition that a common structure of political action requires a cluster of rights and obligations which cut across all key domains of power, where power shapes and affects people's life-chances with determinate effects on and implications for their political agency.

I think of the cluster of rights and obligations that will create the basis of a common structure of political action as constituting the elements of a democratic public law. If power is to be held accountable wherever it is located – in the state, the economy, or cultural sphere – then a common structure of political action needs to be entrenched and enforced through a democratic public law. Such a notion, I believe, can coherently link the ideas of democracy and of the modern state. The key to this is the notion of a democratic legal order – an order which is bound by democratic public law in all its affairs. A democratic legal order – a democratic *Rechtstaat* – is an order circumscribed by, and accounted for in relation to, democratic public law.

The idea of such an order, however, can no longer be simply defended as an idea suitable to a particular closed political community or nation state. We are compelled to recognize that we live in a complex inter-connected world where the extent, intensity, and impact of issues (economic, political, or environmental) raise questions about where those issues are most appropriately addressed. Deliberative and deci-sion-making centres beyond national territories are appropriately situ-ated when those significantly affected by a public matter constitute a cross-border or transnational grouping, when "lower" levels of decision-making cannot manage and discharge satisfactorily transnational or international policy questions, and when the principle of democratic legitimacy can only be properly redeemed in a transnational context (see Held 1995: chap. 10). If the most powerful geopolitical interests are not to settle many pressing matters simply in terms of their objectives and by virtue of their power, then new institutions and mechanisms of account-ability need to be established.

In the context of contemporary forms of globalization, for democratic law to be effective it must be internationalized. Thus, the implementa-tion of what I call a cosmopolitan democratic law and the establishment of a community of all democratic communities – a cosmopolitan community – must become an obligation for democrats; an obligation to build a transnational, common structure of political action which alone, ultimately, can support the politics of self-determination.

In this conception, the nation state "withers away." But this is *not* to say that states and national democratic polities become redundant. There are many good reasons for doubting the theoretical and empirical basis of claims that nation states will disappear. Rather, withering away means that states can no longer be, and can no longer be regarded as, the sole centres of legitimate power within their own borders, as is already the case in diverse settings. States need to be articulated with, and relocated within, an overarching democratic law. Within this frame-work, the laws and rules of the nation state would be but one focus for legal development, political reflection, and mobilization. For this frame-work would respecify and reconstitute the meaning and limits of sover-eign authority. Particular power centers and authority systems would enjoy legitimacy only to the extent that they upheld and enacted democratic law.

Thus, sovereignty can be stripped away from the idea of fixed borders and territories. Sovereignty would become an attribute of the basic democratic law, but it could be entrenched and drawn upon in diverse self-regulating realms, from regions and states to cities and local associations. Cosmopolitan law would demand the subordination of regional, national, and local sovereignties to an overarching legal framework, but in this framework associations would be self-governing at different levels. A new possibility is anticipated: the recovery of an intensive and more participatory democracy at local levels as a complement to the public assemblies of the wider global order; that is, a political order of democratic associations, cities, and nations as well as of regions and global networks. I call this elsewhere the cosmopolitan model of democracy – it is a legal basis of a global and divided authority system, a system of diverse and overlapping power centres, shaped and delimited by democratic law (Held 1995 and 1996). However the model is specified precisely, it is based upon the recognition that the nature and quality of democracy within a particular community and the nature and quality of democratic relations among communities are interlocked, and that new legal and organizational mechanisms must be created if democracy is to prosper.

In this system of cosmopolitan governance, people would come to enjoy multiple citizenships – political membership in the diverse political communities which significantly affect them. They would be citizens of their immediate political communities, and of the wider regional and global networks which impacted upon their lives. This cosmopolitan polity would be one that in form and substance reflected and embraced the diverse forms of power and authority that operate within and across borders and which, if unchecked, threaten the emergence of a highly fragmented, neo-medieval order.

It would be easy to be pessimistic about the future of democracy. There are plenty of reasons for pessimism; they include the fact that the essential political units of the world are still based on nation states while some of the most powerful socio-political forces of the world escape the boundaries of these units. In reaction to this, in part, new forms of fundamentalism have arisen along with new forms of tribalism – all asserting the a priori superiority of a particular religious, or cultural, or political identity over all others, and all asserting their sectional aims and interests. In addition, the reform of the UN that is currently contemplated by the most powerful countries is focused on efforts to include other powerful countries, above all, Germany and Japan. This would consolidate the power of certain geopolitical interests, but at the expense of many other countries which have some of the fastest rates of economic growth and some of the largest populations. I believe this position to be unsustainable in the long run.

But there are other forces at work which create the basis for a more optimistic reading of democratic prospects. An historical comparison might help to provide a context for this. In the sixteenth and seventeenth centuries, Europe was marked by civil conflict, religious strife, and fragmented authority; the idea of a secular state, separate from ruler and ruled, and separate from the Church, seemed an unlikely prospect. Parts of Europe were tearing themselves to pieces and, yet, within 150–200 years, a new concept of politics became entrenched based around a new concept of the state. Today, we live at another fundamental point of transition, but now to a more transnational, global world. There are forces and pressures which are engendering a reshaping of political cultures, institutions, and structures. First, one must obviously note the emergence, however hesitatingly, of regional and global institutions in the twentieth century. The UN is, of course, weak in many respects, but it is a relatively recent creation and it is an innovative structure which can be built upon. It is a normative resource which provides – for all its difficulties – an enduring example of how nations might (and sometimes do) cooperate better to resolve, and resolve fairly, common problems. In addition, the development of a powerful regional body such as the European Union is a remarkable state of affairs. Just over fifty years ago Europe was at the point of self-destruction. Since that moment Europe has created new mechanisms of collaboration, human rights enforcement, and new political institutions in order not only to hold member states to account across a broad range of issues, but to pool aspects of their sovereignty. Furthermore, there are, of course, new regional and global transnational actors contesting the terms of globalization – not just corporations but new social movements such as the environmental movement, the women's movement, and so on. These are the "new" voices of an emergent "transnational civil society," heard, for instance, at the Rio Conference on the Environment, the Cairo Conference on Population Control, and the Beijing Conference on Women. In short, there are tendencies at work seeking to create new forms of public life and new ways of debating regional and global issues. These are, of course, all in early stages of development, and there are no guarantees that the balance of political contest will allow them to develop; but they point in the direction of establishing new modes of holding transnational power systems to account – that is, they help open up the possibility of a cosmopolitan democracy.

REFERENCES

Abu-Lughod, Janet. 1989. *Before European Hegemony*. Oxford: Oxford University Press.
Anderson, Perry. 1974. *Passages from Antiquity to Feudalism*. London: Verso.
Baldwin, Tom. 1992. "The territorial state." In H. Gross and T. R. Harrison (eds.), *Jurisprudence: Cambridge Essays*. Oxford: Clarendon Press.
Beetham, David. 1998. "Human rights as a model for cosmopolitan democracy." In Daniele Archibugi, David Held, and Martin Köhler (eds.), *Re-imagining Political Community*, pp. 58–71. Cambridge: Polity Press.
Beitz, Charles. 1979. *Political Theory and International Relations*. Princeton: Princeton University Press.
Bobbio, Norberto. 1987. *Which Socialism?* Cambridge: Polity Press.
  1989. *Democracy and Dictatorship*. Cambridge: Polity Press.
Breuilly, John. 1992. *Nationalism and the State*. Manchester: Manchester University Press.
Bull, Hedley. 1977. *The Anarchical Society*. London: Macmillan.
Capotorti, F. 1983. "Human rights: the hard road towards universality." In R. St J. Macdonald and D. M. Johnson (eds.), *The Structure and Process of International Law*, pp. 970–81. The Hague: Martinus Nijhoff.
Cassese, Antonio. 1986. *International Law in a Divided World*. Oxford: Clarendon Press.
Connolly, William. 1991. "Democracy and territoriality." *Millennium* 20(3).
Crawford, James. 1994. *Democracy in International Law*. Cambridge: Cambridge University Press.
Crawford, James and Susan Marks. 1998. "The global democracy deficit: an essay in international law and its limits." In Daniele Archibugi, David Held, and Martin Köhler (eds.), *Re-imagining Political Community*, pp. 72–90. Cambridge: Polity Press.
Dahl, Robert A. 1989. *Democracy and Its Critics*. New Haven: Yale University Press.
Evans, Tony. 1997. "Democratization and human rights." In Anthony McGrew (ed.), *The Transformation of Democracy?* pp. 122–48. Cambridge: Polity Press.
Falk, Richard. 1969. "The interplay of Westphalian and Charter conceptions of the international legal order." In Cyril Black and Richard Falk (eds.), *The Future of the International Legal Order*, Vol. 1, pp. 32–70. Princeton: Princeton University Press.
  1990. "Economic dimensions of global civilization." Working paper, pp. 1–22. Princeton: Princeton University, Center for International Studies.
Fernández-Armesto, Felipe. 1995. *Millennium*. London: Bantam.
Geyer, Michael and Charles Bright. 1995. "World history in a global age." *American Historical Review*, 100(4): 1034–60.
Giddens, Anthony. 1985. *The Nation-State and Violence* (Vol. II of *A Contemporary Critique of Historical Materialism*). Cambridge: Polity Press.
  1990. *The Consequences of Modernity*. Cambridge: Polity Press.
Goldblatt, David, David Held, Anthony G. McGrew, and Jonathan Perraton. 1997. "Economic globalization and the nation-state: shifting balances of power." *Soundings* 7: 61–77.

Hall, John. 1996. *International Orders: An Historical Sociology of State, Regime, Class and Nation*. Cambridge: Polity Press.

Hawthorn, Geoffrey. 1993. "Sub-Saharan Africa." In David Held (ed.), *Prospects for Democracy: North, South, East, West*, pp. 330–54. Cambridge: Polity Press.

Hayek, Friedrich A. 1960. *The Constitution of Liberty*. London: Routledge and Kegan Paul.

Held, David. (ed.) 1993. *Prospects for Democracy: North, South, East, West*. Cambridge: Polity Press.

   1995. *Democracy and the Global Order: From the Modern State to Cosmopolitan Governance*. Cambridge: Polity Press.

   1996. *Models of Democracy* (2nd edn). Cambridge: Polity Press.

Held, David, Anthony McGrew, David Goldblatt, and Jonathan Perraton. 1999. *Global Transformations: Politics, Economics and Culture*. Cambridge: Polity Press.

Hirst, Paul and Thompson, Grahame. 1996. *Globalization in Question*. Cambridge: Polity Press.

Kennedy, Paul. 1988. *The Rise and Fall of the Great Powers*. London: Unwin.

Keohane, Robert. 1995. "Hobbes's dilemma and institutional change in world politics: sovereignty in international society." In Hans-Henrik Holm and Georg Sorensen (eds.), *Whose World Order?* pp. 165–86. Boulder, CO: Westview Press.

Krasner, Stephen. 1995. "Compromising Westphalia." *International Security* 20(3): 115–51.

McGrew, Anthony G. 1992. "Conceptualizing global politics." In Anthony G. McGrew, Paul G. Lewis *et al.*, *Global Politics*, pp. 1–30. Cambridge: Polity Press.

   (ed.) 1997. *The Transformation of Democracy?* Cambridge: Polity Press.

Mann, Michael. 1986. *The Sources of Social Power*, Vol. I. Cambridge: Cambridge University Press.

Murphy, Craig N. 1994. *International Organization and International Change: Global Governance since 1850*. Cambridge: Polity Press.

Nierop, Tom. 1994. *Systems and Regions in Global Politics*. London: John Wiley.

Offe, Claus. 1985. *Disorganized Capitalism*. Cambridge: Polity Press.

Ohmae, Kenichi. 1990. *The Borderless World*. London: Collins.

Paine, Thomas. 1987. *The Thomas Paine Reader*. Harmondsworth: Penguin.

Pakenham, Thomas. 1992. *The Scramble for Africa*. London: Abacus.

Perraton, Jonathan, David Goldblatt, David Held, and Anthony McGrew. 1997. "The globalization of economic activity." *New Political Economy* 2(2): 257–77.

Pieterse, Jan N. 1997. "Going global: futures of capitalism." *Development and Change*, 28(2): 367–82.

Poggi, Gianfranco. 1978. *The Development of the Modern State*. London: Hutchinson.

Potter, David, David Goldblatt, Margaret Kiloh, and Paul Lewis (eds.). 1997. *Democratization*. Cambridge: Polity Press.

Reich, Robert. 1991. *The Work of Nations*. New York: Simon and Schuster.

Sabine, George H. 1963. *A History of Political Theory*. London: Harrap.

Sandel, Michael. 1996. *L?mocracy's Discontent*. Cambridge, MA: Harvard University Press.

Smith, Anthony. 1995. *Nati?ns and Nationalism in a Global Era*. Cambridge: Polity Press.

Tilly, Charles (ed.) 1975. *The Formation of National States in Western Europe*. Princeton: Princeton University Press.

  1990. *Coercion, Capital and European States, AD 990–1990*. Oxford: Blackwell.

Walker, Robert B. J. 1988. *One World, Many Worlds*. Boulder, CO: Lynne Reinner.

Watson, Adam. 1992. *The Evolution of International Society*. London: Routledge.

Will Kymlicka

The literature is replete with discussions of the impact of globalization on us as workers, consumers, investors, or as members of cultural communities. Less attention has been paid to its impact on us as citizens – as participants in the process of democratic self-government. This is a vitally important issue, for if people become dissatisfied with their role as citizens, the legitimacy and stability of democratic political systems may erode.

This question in fact arises at two levels – domestically, and transnationally or globally. David Held's chapter provides a clear and balanced assessment of the possible consequences of globalization for citizenship at both levels. In effect, Held argues that globalization is eroding the capacity for meaningful democratic citizenship at the domestic level, as nation states lose some of their historic sovereignty and become "decision-takers" as much as "decision-makers." If meaningful citizenship is to exist in an era of globalization, therefore, it will require democratizing those transnational institutions which are increasingly responsible for important economic, environmental, and security decisions.

In this short commentary, I would like to pursue a couple of Held's points in more depth. While I do not disagree with any of his substantive claims, I would like to suggest that there is more room for optimism regarding the prospects for domestic citizenship than he suggests, but perhaps less ground for optimism about global citizenship.

Domestic citizenship

First, then, let me consider the impact of globalization on citizenship at the domestic level. Like many commentators, Held argues that globalization is reducing the historic sovereignty of nation states, and so undermining the meaningfulness of participation in domestic politics. There is obviously some truth in this, but how extensive is the problem? Held gives a nuanced account of this process of globalization, and explicitly distances himself from the more exaggerated claims about the "obsolescence" of the nation state which are made by the "hyper-globalizers" (p. 97, above). Yet I think that Held too, in his own way, may overstate the situation.

It is certainly true that industrialized nation states have less elbow-room regarding macroeconomic policy today than they did before. (It is doubtful whether Third World states ever had much elbow-room in this area.) This became painfully clear to Canadians when a left-wing government was elected in Canada's largest province (Ontario), and announced a policy of reflationary public spending to reduce unemployment. The response from international financial markets (and bond-rating services) was rapid and severe, and the government quickly dropped the proposal. This made all Canadians aware of how truly dependent we had become on the "men in red suspenders," as our finance minister called Wall Street brokers.

But there are two possible explanations for this phenomenon. Some people see the loss of control by nation states over macroeconomic policy as an inherent and permanent feature of the new world order, which we simply have to learn to live with. This, implicitly at least, is Held's view. But other people argue that the dependence on international financial markets is not an inherent feature of globalization, but rather a contingent result of international indebtedness. On this view, states which run up large foreign debts lose control over their macroeconomic policy. We are now so accustomed to governments running up billions of dollars in deficits every year that we take it as normal, even inevitable, that governments owe hundreds of billions of dollars in debt to people outside the country. But it is insane to think that a country can run up such debts for twenty years, and not have it affect their fiscal autonomy. If you put yourself in massive debt to other people, you lose some control over your life.

We will shortly be in a position to test these two hypotheses, since we are witnessing a steep decline in international indebtedness in many countries. What we see in Canada today, for example, as in many other countries, is a shift towards balanced budgets, and a reduction in the debt-to-GDP ratio. As a result, Canada is less dependent on foreign capital today than it has been for any time in the last fifteen years. As of 1998, the Canadian government will not have to borrow money from the men in red suspenders, and in 1999 will actually have a budget surplus. I believe that Canada is now regaining much (though not all) of its earlier macroeconomic autonomy, including the option of adopting a jobs-creation program, which is being seriously debated in Canada.

I think that Held also exaggerates the issue of capital mobility – i.e., the fear that companies will move their operations to whatever country offers the lowest taxes or wages. This is supposed to put dramatic limits on the extent to which countries can adopt more generous unemployment insurance programs, health and safety legislation, parental leave, or minimum wages. Here again, there is obviously some truth to this concern, but we need to keep it in perspective. A reporter in a large US city recently selected at random a number of companies in the Yellow Pages and asked each of them whether they had thought about relocating to another country. The number who said "yes" was negligible. The option of moving overseas is irrelevant for large sectors of the economy – health care, education and training, construction, most retail, most services, agriculture, and so on. The issue of capital mobility is most relevant for mid-to-large manufacturing companies employing low-skilled workers. This is not an insignificant portion of the economy, but it has been a declining percentage for a long time, and it is difficult to see how Third World countries can ever develop except by competing in this sector. The loss of some of these low-skilled manufacturing jobs is inevitable, and perhaps even desirable from the point of view of international justice so long as there are fair transition programs for those people thrown out of work; but there is no reason to think that large numbers of companies in other sectors will pack up and move if the government tells them to provide better parental leave to their workers.

So there remains considerable scope for national policy-making. Moreover, and equally importantly, countries continue to exercise their autonomy in very different ways, reflecting their different political cultures. Even if globalization puts similar pressures on all countries, they need not – and do not – respond in the same way. In his survey of social policy in OECD countries, Keith Banting notes that globalization puts great pressure on nation states both to respond to the social stresses created by economic restructuring and to the demands of international competitiveness. None the less, despite fears of a race to the bottom or an inexorable harmonization of social programs, the share of national resources devoted to social spending continues to inch upwards in OECD nations. While all welfare states are under pressure, "the global economy does not dictate the ways in which governments respond, and different nations are responding in distinctive ways that reflect their domestic politics and cultures" (Banting 1997).

I believe that citizens often care deeply about maintaining these national differences in social policy, and they provide considerable motivation for political participation in domestic politics. For example, the differences between Canadian and American approaches to social policy are increasing, not decreasing, and for Canadian citizens, these differences are worth keeping, and fighting for.

This points to another overstatement in Held's analysis. He argues that globalization is undermining the sense that each nation state forms "a political community of fate" (p. 102, above). I think he is vastly overstating the situation here. It is certainly true that "some of the most fundamental forces and processes which determine the nature of life chances" cut across national boundaries (p. 103, above), but what determines the boundaries of a "community of fate" is not the forces people are subjected to, but rather how they respond to those forces, and, in particular, what sorts of collectivities they identify with when responding to those forces. People belong to the same community of fate if they *care* about each other's fate, and want to *share* each other's fate – that is, want to meet certain challenges together, so as to share each other's blessings and burdens. Put another way, people belong to the same community of fate if they feel some sense of responsibility for one another's fate, and so want to deliberate together about how to respond collectively to the challenges facing the community. So far as I can tell, globalization has not eroded the sense that nation states form separate communities of fate in this sense.

For example, as a result of NAFTA, North Americans are increasingly subjected to similar economic "forces and processes." But there is no evidence that they feel themselves part of a single "community of fate" whose members care about and wish to share each other's fate. There is no evidence that Canadians now feel any strong sense of responsibility for the well-being of Americans or Mexicans (or vice versa). Nor is there any evidence that Canadians feel any moral obligation to respond to these challenges in the same way as do Americans or Mexicans (or vice versa). On the contrary, Canadians want to respond to these forces *as Canadians* – that is, Canadians debate amongst themselves how to respond to globalization, and they do so by asking what sort of society Canadians wish to live in, and what sorts of obligations Canadians have to each other. Americans ask the same questions amongst themselves, as do the Mexicans.

The economic forces acting on the three countries may be similar, but the sense of communal identity and solidarity remains profoundly different, as have the actual policy responses to these forces. Despite being subject to similar forces, citizens of Western democracies are able to respond to these forces in their own distinctive ways, reflective of their "domestic politics and cultures," and most citizens continue to cherish this ability to deliberate and act as a national collectivity, on the basis of their own national solidarities and priorities.

So I do not accept the view that globalization has deprived domestic politics of its meaningfulness. Nation states still possess considerable autonomy; their citizens still exercise this autonomy in distinctive ways, reflective of their national political cultures; and citizens still want to confront the challenges of globalization as national collectivities, reflective of their historic solidarities, and desire to share each other's fate. These facts all provide meaning and significance to domestic political participation.

I would not deny that many citizens in Western democracies feel dissatisfied with their political participation, but I would argue that the main sources of dissatisfaction with citizenship in Western democracies have little to do with globalization, and in fact long predate the current wave of globalization.[1] In Canada, for example, we have an electoral system which systematically deprives smaller regions of effective political representation in Canadian political life. We have also been unable to regulate campaign financing, with the result that the political process is increasingly seen as heavily skewed towards wealthy individuals and pressure groups. Nor have we changed party nomination procedures to reduce the systematic under-representation of women, Aboriginals, visible minorities, or the working class.

Moreover, Canada has a ridiculously centralized legislative process, in which the real power rests in the hands of a few people in the inner cabinet. We have no meaningful separation between the executive and legislative functions of government, and we have rigid party discipline. As a result, individual members of parliament, whether they are in the governing party or the opposition, have no real input into legislation – at least, much less influence than their counterparts in the American Congress. Parliamentary committees are supposed to provide a forum for input into the legislative process, but they are widely seen as a joke. For most Canadians, therefore, their elected MP is important only for constituency service, not as a conduit to the legislative process. What is the point in making one's views known to one's MP, when individual MPs seem to have no role in the legislative process?

These are the real problems with the political process in Canada – these are at the root of people's increasing sense that they have no real voice in political life. So far as I can tell, they have little to do with globalization. Globalization is not the cause of these problems, nor is there anything in globalization which prevents us from dealing with them.

---

[1] The following discussion draws in part on Kymlicka 1997.

Consider the fate of the recent Canadian Royal Commission on Electoral Reform and Party Financing, which studied these issues in depth, and which issued a number of perfectly sensible recommendations about how to make our political system more equitable, and more responsive to the needs and opinions of Canadians (Royal Commission 1991).[2] There is nothing in the discipline of economic globalization or the rules of international regulatory agreements which prevent us from acting on these recommendations. There is nothing in NAFTA, or in our commitments to the UN or the WTO, which prevents us from adopting these recommendations tomorrow.

Yet little has been done to implement them. This is partly because it is rarely in the interest of governing parties to reform a process which put them in power; but it is also partly because we citizens have not demanded that government make it a priority. Whether as individual citizens, members of advocacy groups, or commentators in the media, Canadians have let the government off the hook for improving the democratic process. There is much we can do to protect and enhance our role as citizens, and if we decide not to, the fault lies not in globalization, but in ourselves.

I have focused on the flaws in Canada's political process, but I think we would find very similar problems in other countries – i.e., electoral systems which systemically produce unrepresentative legislatures; over-centralized legislative decision-making; excessive role of wealth in determining power and influence; and so on. These are the real causes of citizens' dissatisfaction with the political process. Globalization is not the cause of these problems, nor does it prevent us from solving them.

Indeed, far from depriving domestic citizenship of its meaningfulness, globalization may actually be helping to renew it in important respects. For example, globalization is opening up the political process to new groups. Existing legislative and regulatory processes have been captured by entrenched interest groups for a long time now, but their traditional power bases are being eroded by globalization, and previously excluded groups are jumping in to fill the void (Simeon 1997: 307).

Also, globalization, far from encouraging political apathy, is itself one of the things which seems to mobilize otherwise apathetic people. Consider the vigorous debate over free trade in Canada, or the debate in Denmark over the Maastricht Treaty. This should not be surprising, since decisions about how to relate to other countries are themselves an important exercise of national sovereignty.

[2] I discuss some of these issues in more depth in Kymlicka 1993: 61–89.

This is perhaps clearer in the European context than in North America. It is quite clear, for example, that the desire of Spain or Greece to join the EU was not simply a matter of economic gain. It was also seen as a way of confirming their status as open, modern, democratic, and pluralistic states, after many years of being closed and authoritarian societies. Similarly, the decision about whether to admit new countries from Eastern Europe to the EU will be decided not just on the basis of economic gain, but also on the basis of moral obligations to assist newly democratizing countries, and on the basis of aspirations to create a Europe free of old divisions and hatreds.

In other words, decisions by national collectivities to integrate into transnational institutions are, in part, decisions about what kind of societies people want to live in. Being open to the world is, for many people, an important part of their self-conception as members of modern pluralistic societies, and they autonomously decide to pursue that self-conception through various international agreements and institutions. Such decisions are not a denial of people's national identity or sovereignty, but precisely an affirmation of their national identity, and a highly valued exercise of their national sovereignty.

The best example of this, perhaps, is the desire of former communist countries to join European organizations. It would be a profound misunderstanding to say that the decision by Baltic states to join the Council of Europe is an abridgment of their sovereignty. On the contrary, it is surely one of the most important symbolic affirmations of their new-found sovereignty. One of the most hated things about communism was that it prevented Baltic nations from entering into such international alliances, and acting upon their self-conception as a "European" country. Latvia's decision to join the Council of Europe was a way of declaring: "now we are a sovereign people, able to act on our own wishes. No longer can anyone tell us who we can and cannot associate with." Sovereignty is valued because it allows nations to act on their interests and identities, and the freedom to enter European organizations is an enormously important example of this sovereignty for Baltic nations.

These examples show, I think, that globalization often provides options which nations value, and decisions about whether and how to exercise these options have become lively topics for national debate. Globalization does constrain national legislatures, although the extent of this is often exaggerated. But globalization also enriches national political life, and provides new and valued options by which nations can collectively promote their interests and identities.

Cosmopolitan citizenship

So globalization need not undermine the scope for meaningful democratic citizenship at the national level. By contrast, I am rather more skeptical about the likelihood that we can produce any meaningful form of transnational citizenship. I think we should be quite modest in our expectations about transnational citizenship, at least for the foreseeable future.

I heartily agree with many aspects of Held's conception of "cosmopolitan democracy." In particular, I endorse efforts to strengthen the international enforcement of human rights, and I accept Held's idea that the rules for according international recognition to states should include some reference to democratic legitimation. Principles of democracy and human rights should indeed be seen as "cosmopolitan" in this sense – i.e., each state should be encouraged to respect these principles.

But I am more skeptical about the idea that transnational institutions and organizations can themselves be made democratic in any meaningful sense. Can we even make sense of the idea of "democratizing" such institutions? When thinking about this question, it is important to remember that democracy is not just a formula for aggregating votes, but is also a system of collective deliberation and legitimation. The actual moment of voting (in elections, or within legislatures) is just one component in a larger process of democratic self-government. This process begins with public deliberation about the issues which need to be addressed and the options for resolving them. The decisions which result from this deliberation are then legitimated on the grounds that they reflect the considered will and common good of the people as a whole, not just the self-interest or arbitrary whims of the majority.

Arguably, these forms of deliberation and legitimation require some degree of commonality amongst citizens. Collective political deliberation is only feasible if participants understand and trust one another, and there is good reason to think that such mutual understanding and trust require some underlying commonalities. Some sense of commonality or shared identity may be required to sustain a deliberative and participatory democracy.

But what sort of shared identity? If we examine existing democracies to see what sorts of commonalities have proven necessary, I think we would find that deliberative democracy does *not* require a common religion (or common lifestyles more generally); a common political ideology (e.g., right versus left); or a common racial or ethnic descent. We can find genuinely participatory democratic fora and procedures which cut across these religious/ideological/racial cleavages.

When we turn to language, however, things become more complicated. There are of course several multilingual democracies – e.g.,
Belgium, Spain, Switzerland, Canada. But if we look at how democratic
debates operate within these countries, we find that language is increasingly important in defining the boundaries of political communities, and
the identities of political actors.

There is a similar dynamic taking place in all of these countries, by
which: (a) the separate language groups are becoming more territorialized – that is, each language has become ever-more dominant within a
particular region, while gradually dying out outside that region (this
phenomenon – known as the "territorial imperative" – is very widespread);[3] and (b) these territorialized language groups are demanding
increased political recognition and self-government powers through
federalization of the political system. (These processes of territorializa-
tion and federalization are of course closely linked – the latter is both the
cause and the effect of the former.) Political boundaries have been
drawn, and political powers redistributed, so that territorialized
language groups are able to exercise greater self-government within the
larger federal system.

Held argues that globalization is undermining the territorial basis of
politics, and that territory is playing a less important role in the
determination of political identity (p. 99, above). I think this is simply
untrue, at least in the context of multilingual states. On the contrary,
language has become an increasingly important determinant of the
boundaries of political community within each of these multilingual
countries, and territory has become an increasingly important determinant of the boundaries of these language groups. These countries are
becoming, in effect, federations of territorially concentrated, self-governing language groups. These self-governing language groups often
describe themselves as "nations," and mobilize along nationalist lines,
and so we can call these countries "multination states."

There are good reasons to think that these "national" linguistic/
territorial political communities – whether they are unilingual nation
states or linguistically distinct subunits within multination states – are
the primary forum for democratic participation in the modern world.
They are primary in two distinct senses. First, democracy within
national/linguistic units is more genuinely participatory than at higher
levels which cut across language lines. Political debates at the federal

---

[3] On the territorial imperative in Belgium, see Lejeune 1994: 171–86 and Senelle 1989:
51–95; on Switzerland, see Mansour 1993: 109–11. For a more general theoretical
account of the "territorial imperative" in multilingual societies, see Laponce 1987 and
1993: 23–43.

level in multination states, for example, or at the level of the EU, are almost invariably elite-dominated.

Why? Put simply, democratic politics is politics in the vernacular. The average citizen only feels comfortable debating political issues in their own tongue. As a general rule, it is only elites who have fluency with more than one language, and who have the continual opportunity to maintain and develop these language skills, and who feel comfortable debating political issues in another tongue within multilingual settings. Moreover, political communication has a large ritualistic component, and these ritualized forms of communication are typically language-specific. Even if one understands a foreign language in the technical sense, without knowledge of these ritualistic elements one may be unable to understand political debates.[4] For these and other reasons, we can expect – as a general rule – that the more political debate is conducted in the vernacular, the more participatory it will be.

There are of course "public spaces" and forms of civil society which cut across language lines. However, these tend to be issue specific and/ or elite dominated. If we look for evidence of a genuinely popular process of "collective will formation" – or for the existence of a mass "public opinion" – we are likely to find these only within units which share a common language (and a common media using that language). John Stuart Mill (1972 [1861]: 392), writing in the mid-nineteenth century, argued that genuine democracy is "next to impossible" in multilingual states, because if people "read and speak different languages, the united public opinion necessary to the workings of representative institutions cannot exist." The evidence from Europe suggests that linguistic differences remain an obstacle to the development of a genuine "public opinion." As Dieter Grimm notes, it is the presence of a shared mass media, operating in a common language, "which creates the public needed for any general opinion forming and democratic participation at all," and

the absence of a European communication system, due chiefly due to language diversity, has the consequence that for the foreseeable future there will be neither a European public nor a European political discourse. Public discourse instead remains for the time being bound by national frontiers, while the European sphere will remain dominated by professional and interest discourses conducted remotely from the public.[5] (Grimm 1995: 296)

---

[4] In other words, the sort of fluency needed to debate political issues is far greater than the sort of knowledge needed to handle routine business transactions, or for tourist purposes.

[5] This same dynamic can be seen even within the various multilingual states in Europe, where it has become increasingly obvious that "public opinion" is divided on language lines.

There is a second sense in which these "national" units are primary – namely, they are the most important forum for assessing the legitimacy of other levels of government. Members of these national units may wish to devolve power upwards – to the federal level in multination states, or to the European Union – just as they may wish to devolve power downwards to local or municipal governments. As I noted earlier, such upward (or downward) devolutions of power are to be expected, since they will often be in the national interest of these collectivities. But the legitimacy of these devolutions of power is generally seen as dependent on the (ongoing) consent of the national unit (and this consent will only be given if these devolutions of power do not undermine the ability of the national unit to maintain itself as a viable, self-governing society). Decisions made by larger units – whether they are federal policies in multination states, or EU policies – are seen as legitimate only if they are made under rules and procedures which were consented to by the national unit, and similarly changes to the rules are only legitimate if they are debated and approved by the national unit. Members of these national collectivities debate amongst themselves, in the vernacular, how much power they wish to devolve upwards or downwards, and periodically reassess, at the national level, whether they wish to reclaim some of these powers. The legitimate authority of higher-level political bodies depends on this ongoing process of debate and consent at the national level. These decisions are made on the basis of what serves the national interest (and not on the basis of what serves the interests of, say, Europe as a whole).[6]

So the evidence suggests that language is profoundly important in the construction of democratic political communities. It has in fact become increasingly important in defining political communities, and these language-demarcated political communities remain the primary forum for participatory democratic debates, and for the democratic legitimation of other levels of government.

This is not to deny the obvious fact that we need international political institutions which transcend linguistic/national boundaries. We need such institutions to deal not only with economic globalization, but also with common environmental problems and issues of international security. At present, these organizations exhibit a major "democratic deficit." They are basically organized through intergovernmental

---

[6] In other words, the existence of political authority at higher levels is not seen as morally self-originating or self-justifying, but rather as conditional on the consent of the constituent national units. By contrast, the right of the national unit to self-government is seen as morally self-originating, and as not requiring the consent of any other level of government.

relations, with little, if any, direct input from individual citizens. Held suggests that this is a serious problem, which can only be resolved by promoting new forms of "cosmopolitan citizenship" which enable individuals and non-government groups to participate directly in transnational organizations (pp. 104–8, above). For example, in the EU, there is considerable talk about increasing the power of the Parliament, which is directly elected by individual citizens, at the expense of the Commission and Council of Ministers, which operate through intergovernmental relations.

I am not so sure that there is a serious problem here, or that Held's suggestion is realistic. It seems to me that there is no necessary reason why international institutions should be directly accountable to (or accessible to) individual citizens. To be sure, if international institutions are increasingly powerful, they must be held accountable. But why can we not hold them accountable *indirectly*, by debating at the national level how we want our national governments to act in intergovernmental contexts?

It seems clear that this is the way most Europeans themselves wish to reconcile democracy with the growth of the EU. There is very little demand for a strengthened EU Parliament. On the contrary, most people, in virtually all European states, show little interest in the affairs of the European Parliament, and little enthusiasm for increasing its powers.

What they want, instead, is to strengthen the accountability of their *national* governments for how these governments act at the intergovernmental Council of Ministers. That is, citizens in each country want to debate amongst themselves, in their vernacular, what the position of their government should be on EU issues. Danes wish to debate, in Danish, what the Danish position should be *vis-à-vis* Europe. They show little interest in starting a European-wide debate (in what language?) about what the EU should do. They are keenly interested in having a democratic debate about the EU, but the debate they wish to engage in is not a debate with other Europeans about "what should we Europeans do?" Rather, they wish to debate with each other, in Danish, about what we Danes should do. To put it another way, they want Denmark to be part of Europe, but they show little interest in becoming citizens of a European demos.

This is not to say that increasing the direct accountability and accessibility of transnational institutions is a bad thing. On the contrary, I support many of Held's suggestions in this regard. I agree that NGOs should have an increased role at the UN and other international bodies (pp. 107–8, above), and I support the idea of a global civil society, in which people seek to mobilize the citizens of other countries to protest violations of human rights or environmental degradation in their own country. But it is misleading, I think, to describe this as the "democratization" of transnational institutions, or as the creation of democratic citizenship on the transnational level. After all, these proposals would not create any form of collective deliberation and decision-making that connects and binds individuals across national boundaries.

For example, I am a member of Greenpeace, and support their efforts to gain a seat at the table of UN organizations, and their efforts to mobilize people around the world to stop acid rain, the burning of tropical rainforests, or illegal whaling, but this does not involve anything which we could recognize as democratic citizenship at the transnational level. The fact that Greenpeace has a seat at the table of the UN or the EU, or that Canadian members of Greenpeace write letters protesting Japan's whaling policy, does not change the fact that there is no meaningful forum for democratic deliberation and collective will-formation above the level of the nation state. I can try to influence Brazil's deforestation policy, but that does not mean that Brazilians and Canadians are now citizens of some new transnational democratic community. Transnational activism is a good thing, as is the exchange of information across borders, but the only forum in which genuine democracy occurs is within national boundaries.

Transnational activism by individuals or NGOs is not the same as democratic citizenship. Moreover, attempts to create a genuinely democratic form of transnational citizenship could have negative consequences for democratic citizenship at the domestic level. For example, I am not convinced that it would be a good thing to strengthen the (directly elected) EU Parliament at the expense of the (intergovernmental) EU Council. The result of "democratizing" the EU would be to take away the veto power which national governments now have over most EU decisions. Decisions made by the EU Parliament, unlike those made by the Council, are not subject to the national veto. This means that the EU would cease to be accountable to citizens through their national legislatures. At the moment, if a Danish citizen dislikes an EU decision, she can try to mobilize other Danes to change their government's position on the issue. But once the EU is "democratized" – i.e., once the Parliament replaces the Council as the major decision-making body – a Danish citizen would have to try to change the opinions of the citizens of every other European country (none of which speak her language). For obvious and understandable reasons, few Europeans seek this sort of "democratization." For Danish citizens to engage in a debate with other Danes, in Danish, about the Danish position *vis-à-vis* the EU is a familiar and manageable task, but for Danish citizens to engage in a debate with Italians to try to develop a common European position is a daunting prospect. In what language would such a debate occur, and in what fora? Not only do they not speak the same language, or share the same territory, they also do not read the same newspapers, or watch the same television shows, or belong to the same political parties. So what would be the forum for such a trans-European debate?

Given these obstacles to a trans-European public debate, it is not surprising that neither the Danes nor the Italians have shown any enthusiasm for "democratizing" the EU. They prefer exercising demo-cratic accountability through their national legislatures. Paradoxically, then, the net result of increasing direct democratic accountability of the EU through the elected Parliament would in fact be to undermine democratic citizenship. It would shift power away from the national level, where mass participation and vigorous democratic debate is possible, towards the transnational level, where democratic participation and deliberation is very difficult. As Grimm argues, given that there is no common European mass media at the moment, and given that the prospects for creating such a Europeanized media in the foreseeable future "are absolutely non-existent," dramatically shifting power from the Council to the Parliament would "aggravate rather than solve the problem" of the democratic deficit (Grimm 1995: 296).

In short, globalization is undoubtedly producing a new civil society, but it has not yet produced anything we can recognize as transnational democratic citizenship. Nor is it clear to me that we should aspire to such a new form of citizenship. Many of our most important moral principles should be cosmopolitan in scope – e.g., principles of human rights, democracy, and environmental protection – and we should seek to promote these ideals internationally. But our democratic citizenship is, and will remain for the foreseeable future, national in scope.[7]

REFERENCES

Banting, Keith. 1997. "The internationalization of the social contract." In Thomas Courchene (ed.), *The Nation State in a Global/Information Era*, pp. 255–86. Kingston, Canada: John Deutsch Institute for Policy Studies, Queen's University.
Grimm, Dieter. 1995. "Does Europe need a constitution?" *European Law Journal* 1(3): 282–302.
Kymlicka, Will. 1993. "Group Representation in Canadian Politics." In Leslie Seidle (ed.), *Equity and Community: The Charter, Interest Advocacy, and Representation*, pp. 61–89. Montreal: Institute for Research on Public Policy.

[7] For further elaboration of this theme, see Kymlicka forthcoming.

1997. "The prospects for citizenship: reply to Simeon." In Thomas Courchene (ed.), *The Nation State in a Global/Information Era*, pp. 315–25. Kingston, Canada: John Deutsch Institute for Policy Studies, Queen's University.

Forthcoming. "From Enlightenment cosmopolitanism to Liberal nationalism." In Steven Lukes and Martin Hollis (eds.), *The Enlightenment: Then and Now.* London: Verso.

Laponce, Jean. 1987. *Languages and their Territories.* Toronto: University of Toronto Press.

1993. "The case for ethnic federalism in multilingual societies: Canada's regional imperative." *Regional Politics and Policy* 1(3): 23–43.

Lejeune, Yves. 1994. "Le fédéralisme en Belgique." In Leslie Seidle (ed.) *Seeking a New Canadian Partnership: Asymmetrical and Confederal Options*, pp. 171–86. Montreal: Institute for Research on Public Policy.

Mansour, Gerda. 1993. *Multilingualism and Nation Building.* Clevedon: Multilingual Matters,.

Mill, John Stuart. 1972 (1861). *Considerations on Representative Government, in Utilitarianism, Liberty, Representative Government.* Edited by H. B. Acton. London: J. M. Dent.

Royal Commission on Electoral Reform and Party Financing. 1991. *Reforming Electoral Democracy: Final Report*, Vols. 1 and 2. Ottawa: Supply and Services.

Senelle, Robert 1989. "Constitutional reform in Belgium: from unitarism towards federalism." In Murray Forsyth (ed.), *Federalism and Nationalism*, pp. 51–95. Leicester: Leicester University Press.

Simeon, Richard. 1997. "Citizens and democracy in the emerging global order." In Thomas Courchene (ed.), *The Nation State in a Global/Information Era*, pp. 299–314. Kingston, Canada: John Deutsch Institute for Policy Studies, Queen's University.

8   A comment on Held's cosmopolitanism

Alexander Wendt

In his thought-provoking chapter David Held argues that we need to rethink our traditional, state-centric understanding of democracy in a more cosmopolitan direction because the forces of globalization are gradually eroding the territorial, Westphalian conceptualization of political community upon which it is based. I agree with Held on both counts. However, I think he does not emphasize sufficiently the role that the institution of sovereignty will play in channeling the impact of globalization, creating path-dependencies which raise both empirical and normative questions about the possibility of cosmopolitan democracy. If a non-territorial democracy does evolve, for the forseeable future it seems much more likely to be a democracy of states than of individuals, an "international" rather than "cosmopolitan" democracy, and this might even be normatively acceptable in a way that an analogous democracy at the domestic level based on groups is not.

I have divided my remarks into two parts, focusing first on how we get from the here of a world of sovereign states to the there of a non-territorial democracy, and then on some normative issues that arise when we get there.

From here to there

Held's chapter, and the book on which it builds (Held 1995), offers a strong and nuanced account of the many forces in the late twentieth century that are eroding purely territorial conceptions of political community and creating transnational "communities of fate." However, saying that national conceptions of community are being eroded by globalization is not the same thing as saying that transnational ones are being created. Here we need to distinguish more explicitly between the objective and subjective bases of community, between the reality of transnational common fate, which is increasing, and perceptions of common fate, which are lagging. It is perceptions of community that are crucial for democracy. Moreover, perceptions of transnational common fate vary a great deal within nation states, and these variations may have significant implications for the evolution of non-territorial forms of democratic governance. Very crudely, we might divide these perceptions into three groups.

(1) Furthest along in the awareness of common fate is probably capital. Not all elements of the capitalist class, to be sure, since fractions of capital that are entirely domestic in their orientation are not so keen on globalization, but the multinational fraction of capital is growing rapidly and seems increasingly conscious of its borderless quality.

(2) Somewhat further behind in their awareness of common fate are states, with those in the West being the most integrated. With the end of the Cold War, in their security relationships Western states may have finally transcended balance of power politics and begun to establish a collective security system, though much obviously depends on the future of Russia and its relationship to NATO. Due to their structural dependence on capital, however, it is in their economic relationships that Western states have gone furthest toward a recognition of common fate, having almost entirely abandoned a territorial, mercantilist orientation in favor of economic integration, manifested in ever-freer trade policies and openness to transnational capital flows. In both the military and economic spheres, therefore, at least Western states seem increasingly to be internationalizing their core functions, and building a sense of collective identity.

Yet there is another side to states' perceptions of common fate that may inhibit this kind of collective identity formation, which stems from the legacy of the institution of sovereignty. In 1648 European states agreed to recognize each other's sovereignty, and that mutual recognition has since been extended to states everywhere. This has had a pacifying effect on international politics by inducing states to exhibit a measure of self-restraint in their relations with each other, and as such is a key enabling condition for transnational community; it is hard to build community in a war of all against all. Realists might argue that the institution of sovereignty means that states will resist the formation of collective identities altogether. In my view it is more likely that sovereignty will affect the form that integration takes when it does happen. In particular, it may mean that states will be more protective of their formal, *de jure* sovereignty than their empirical, *de facto* sovereignty, more concerned with protecting form than content, since it is the former which is the basis of their identity as players in the international system. If so, states will be especially reluctant to cede powers formally to transnational agencies, even as they continue to engage in forms of *de facto* and informal cooperation that have functionally equivalent effects.

This suggests that the process of state formation at the international level will be quite different than that which occurred at the domestic level in the early modern period. Rather than concentrating political power in the hands of a centralized state, often through conquest, the path-dependencies created by the institution of sovereignty may lead to a *de facto* internationalization of the state without much *de jure* internationalization (Wendt 1994). Rather than creating a world government, state power will be increasingly dispersed or "de-centered" across nominally independent state actors. That could have an important implication for cosmopolitan democracy, which is that it may be a long time before there is any centralized apparatus of governance, any commanding heights of state power, for transnational democrats to capture; and the absence of such a center, the fact that there is "no there there," will in turn make it more difficult to hold transnational state power accountable than it was state power in domestic politics.

(3) This brings me to the impact of globalization on a third actor, which, for want of a better word, let us call "the people." A good case can be made that those who are ultimately most affected by globalization, and therefore would presumably benefit the most from cosmopolitan democracy, are also the ones who are least enthusiastic – relative to capital and states – about the idea of international community upon which any such democracy would have to be based. In Europe mass opinion is considerably more nationalistic and anti-integration than elite opinion. The same is true in the United States, where there is a deeply rooted populist culture of isolationism that is hostile to the UN, NAFTA, WTO, and international involvement generally. As globalization deepens and people become more aware of its costs, these tendencies might get stronger, such that rather than embracing a more cosmopolitan identity, "the people" may use their power at the ballot box as a weapon against globalization, bringing the whole process crashing down in a reassertion of nationalism. From this perspective, in short, territorial democracy looks like a potentially serious barrier to the emergence of cosmopolitan community.

In sum, then, to the extent that a perception of transnational community is being born, it is much more a community of capital and states than of peoples. Moreover, there is little reason to think that this community will be very democratic, at least in the individualistic or cosmopolitan sense, since a cosmopolitan democracy has no real constituency or advocates. None of the three actors has much interest in democratizing transnational power – not capital or states, since they *are* transnational power, and not peoples because they are hostile to the whole idea of transnational community in the first place. All of this suggests that the emergence of a truly cosmopolitan democracy, if it ever happens, will occur only very late in the process of globalization, in response to the emergence of clear and identifiable centers of transnational power. In this respect cosmopolitan democracy may be like democracy at the domestic level, which also emerged only after the consolidation of political power in absolutist states gave the people something to mobilize against. But given the de-centered character of transnational power it may be much longer before such a clear perception of threat takes hold. I am not sure I would go as far as Robert Dahl that international organizations cannot be democratic even in principle,[1] but I would argue that we are in for a long period in which there may be an increasing sense of community internationally, but one that is not very democratic. This suggests a "guardianship" model of international governance, or even a bureaucratic–authoritarian one, not a democracy.

One solution, which is arguably in states' interest if they are to avoid a legitimation crisis, would be to try to convince their peoples that globalization is good for them. One way to do this, noted by Dahl in his contribution to this volume, would be to try to ground the legitimacy of international organizations in things other than democracy – for example, in the fact that they promote peace or economic growth. Alternatively, states could try to change their peoples' identities in a more transnational direction. Territorial conceptions of community, after all, are a social construction due in no small part to state policy over the past several centuries. If states set out to "*re*imagine" political community through internationalized education policies or the creation of transnational collective memories then perhaps they might be able to build a constituency for cosmopolitan democracy (Shore 1996; cf. Anderson 1983). The notion of states as a "vanguard" for cosmopolitan democracy might not be a particularly democratic or appealing idea, but as Ian Shapiro points out, one can sometimes get democracy-enhancing outcomes by undemocratic means (Shapiro 1996: 213–19, 249–61).

Once we are there

I want to conclude by more briefly raising the normative issue of what a future non-territorial democracy should look like once we get there, and in particular the question of what unit should be privileged in the assignment of rights, or, alternatively, how the rights of different kinds of units should be balanced.

---

[1] See chapter 2 of this volume.

The answer to this question may be less obvious than it seems. On the surface democratic theorists are virtually unanimous that individuals should be the fundamental unit of democratic accountability. However, they almost always take as given that democracy should be a territorial phenomenon with clear boundaries delimiting who is inside and outside the demos, and in that sense the most fundamental unit of contemporary democratic theory in practice is actually the group or community rather than the individual, since it is only within communities that individuals are treated as basic.

David Held is one of the first to call our attention to the role of tacit territorial assumptions in traditional democratic theory, yet he too seems to suggest that cosmopolitan democracy will ultimately be a democracy of individuals, not of groups. In this respect his view is very much a liberal or individualistic one, though qualified by his recognition that individuals are subject to forms of power outside the public sphere which should be made democratically accountable as well. The latter is an attractive notion in theory, but it is not clear how it would work in practice. Who would decide who is affected by power relations, especially in the absence of a centralized world government, and by what criteria? It is a large question, but in the absence of clear, institutionally practical answers it is hard to know if cosmopolitan democracy is a good idea, let alone whether it is possible.

Apart from the practical problems of making the individual the basic unit of cosmopolitan democracy, however, there is another problem, which is that it is less obvious at the global than the domestic level that the individual *should* be the basic unit of accountability. If one did a survey of contemporary moral intuitions on this matter, for example, I suspect most people – at least in the West – would be strongly opposed to two principles that are normally associated with a liberal world-view. One is the free movement of people. At the domestic level this is seen as a basic human right, yet even among liberals probably few would accept that this right extends to the free movement of people *across borders*, i.e., open immigration,[2] on the grounds that this would reduce standards of living and undermine community values. The other problematic principle is "one person, one vote." This, too, is seen as a basic human right at the domestic level, but most people would probably be loath to extend it to the idea that voters in the much more populous Third World should have a say over what happens in the West, on the grounds that this could lead to a tyranny of the majority. Instead, one can imagine our respondents demanding, as a condition for their entry into a

---

[2] Joseph Carens (1995) is an important exception.

cosmopolitan democracy, strong constitutional protection for the survival of their distinct cultural communities, in the form of global governance based on a "Senate" rather than "House" model, significant local control over education, wages, and welfare, and so on. On both scores, then, the result would in effect be to affirm the priority of group rights over individual rights, where the group is understood in national or state-centric terms. Indeed, one might even argue that our respondents would in effect be tacitly affirming a principle of "separate development" in the world system which would have many of the same effects on the global level, even if unintended, as apartheid did in South Africa – keeping people tied to their land and institutionalizing vast inequalities of wealth and power (cf. Kohler 1995).

In this light a thorough-going cosmopolitan might argue that we should not indulge our survey respondents in designing a cosmopolitan democracy because their views are merely an artifact of having grown up in, and been socialized to, territorial or national communities, and as such have no particular normative standing. On the other hand, however, it might also be argued that there are stronger normative grounds for privileging group rights in the global than the national context, for at least three reasons. One is that the attachment of individuals today to territorial or national definitions of community is very real, even if it is a social construction, and this attachment has been used even by liberals to justify group rights (Tamir 1993; Kymlicka 1995). A second reason why different standards might apply is that the contracting entities in any future structure of global governance will almost certainly be states, and states are unlikely to enter such a structure without strong guarantees of local autonomy. If the alternative to guarantees is that states reject global governance altogether, then insisting on a first-best, purely cosmopolitan democracy will not only fail, but could prevent even a second-best, "international" democracy – the best being the enemy of the good.[3] Finally, recognition of group identity might also have the effect of reassuring individuals that the cultural attachments which give their lives much of their meaning will be respected at the global level, reducing their fear of being engulfed by a global community and thereby paradoxically enabling them to contemplate joining it (Wendt 1999: chap. 7; cf. Honneth 1996). I do not know how one should balance these communitarian considerations against the need to respect individual human rights, but they do suggest that the problem of achieving such a balance is likely to be an even more pressing problem for global democratic theory than it has been for domestic.

---

[3] In this light see Robert Goodin's (1995) suggestive remarks about the "theory of second-best."

REFERENCES

Anderson, Benedict. 1983. *Imagined Communities*. London: Verso.

Carens, Joseph. 1995. "Aliens and citizens: the case for open borders." In Will Kymlicka (ed.), *The Rights of Minority Cultures*, pp. 331–49. Oxford: Oxford University Press.

Goodin, Robert. 1995. "Political ideals and political practice." *British Journal of Political Science* 25: 37–56.

Held, David. 1995. *Democracy and the Global Order*. Stanford: Stanford University Press.

Honneth, Axel. 1996. *The Struggle for Recognition*. Cambridge, MA: MIT Press.

Kohler, Gernot. 1995. "The three meanings of global apartheid: empirical, normative, existential." *Alternatives* 20: 403–13.

Kymlicka, Will. 1995. *Multicultural Citizenship*. Oxford: Oxford University Press.

Shapiro, Ian. 1996. *Democracy's Place*. Ithaca: Cornell University Press.

Shore, Chris. 1996. "Transcending the nation state? The European Commission and the (re)-discovery of Europe." *Journal of Historical Sociology* 9(4): 473–96.

Tamir, Yael. 1993. *Liberal Nationalism*. Princeton: Princeton University Press.

Wendt, Alexander. 1994. "Collective identity formation and the international state." *American Political Science Review* 88(2): 384–96.

1999. *Social Theory of International Politics*. Cambridge: Cambridge University Press.

9 Feminist social criticism and the international movement for women's rights as human rights

Brooke A. Ackerly and Susan Moller Okin

As many of the chapters in this volume indicate, some aspects of globalization present challenges to our accustomed ideas about democracy. For many, globalization means the global movement of capital and the increased exploitation of labor. In those places around the world where labor is inexpensive, global capitalists have set up manufacturing. In those places where labor is relatively expensive, the threat of possible relocation of production enhances capital-owners' bargaining position *vis-à-vis* labor. Where economic power is easily translated into political power, such globalization poses problems for democracy. In places where the World Bank and IMF have imposed structural adjustment policies, the poor who benefit from entitlements have suffered and, in the name of maintaining political control, governments have imposed constraints on democratic freedoms. In these ways, globalization can be seen as promoting antidemocratic tendencies.

However, there are some aspects of globalization that, far from endangering democracy, present new opportunities for democratic participation and popular influence to emerge and to affect international law-making. Increased population mobility opens up opportunities for people from very different cultures to mingle with and learn from each other. Vastly faster and less expensive means of long-distance communication, global media, and greater levels of interest in global issues enable and encourage groups and individuals to communicate. Ideas generated at the grass roots spread to, and influence, international diplomats and policy-makers and, in turn, ideas adopted in international fora are able to affect people's thinking and their daily lives with unprecedented speed. Whether governments are less or more democratic, institutions of civil society such as non-governmental organizations (NGOs) play an important role in the transmission of information and ideas from the grass-roots level up through regional representatives to the level of international conferences and policy-making. Not all United Nations members are democratic nations; nor are UN representatives democratically elected. Therefore, although the General Assembly and World Conferences of the UN function under democratic norms, popular participation in international decision-making is both limited and uneven. In this paper, we look at the activism of grass-roots and international NGOs in the "women's rights as human rights" movement of the last decade as an example of increased democratic influence on international political decisions.[1]

We relate the story of the women's rights as human rights movement within the framework of feminist social criticism recently developed by Ackerly (1999). Building on the work of feminist activists and scholars around the world, Ackerly has developed a feminist method of social criticism that respects diversity yet has critical teeth. The activists and scholars of the women's rights as human rights movement have been effective feminist social critics who have influenced political decisions with regard to women's rights around the world. Their success has been imperfect, but we argue that it has been significant enough to demonstrate both the use of the feminist method of social criticism and to suggest strategies for future critics' efforts to influence national and international public policy. It can also help to shed light on how, in the afterglow of the three UN Conferences of the early 1990s, held in Vienna (1993), Cairo (1994), and Beijing (1995), activists for women's rights as human rights can hope to maximize the effect of the significant changes in international law regarding women's rights that emanated from these meetings.

While drawing from theories of deliberative democracy, culturally relativist communitarianism, and essentialism, the feminist method of social criticism also addresses the problems of each. Unlike most theories of deliberative democracy, its model of "deliberative inquiry" can be adopted and put to use by those who do not live in an ideal world of equality and near-perfect knowledge. Unlike culturally relativist theories, it subjects shared practices and common meanings to "skeptical scrutiny," alive to the dangers of domination and subordination, and interrogating them from multiple perspectives.[2] Unlike most

---

[1] Manfred Nowak and Ingeborg Schwarz roughly define NGOs as organizations that are "essentially understood to be more or less independent of state power structures, which does not necessarily exclude state funding" and "non-profit-orientated and devoted to the realization of relevant sociopolitical goals, such as peace, environmental protection, development cooperation, human rights, etc." (1994: 3).

[2] Early versions of feminist standpoint theory argued that the perspective of the less powerful group should be privileged in social decision-making. Recognizing the diversity among women and questioning their unity as a group, more recent feminist standpoint theorists respect diversity within and across groups rather than privilege a particular view. As Patricia Hill Collins (1997) notes, standpoint theory was born in response to

essentialist theories, which claim (almost a priori) that certain human goods are universally applicable, it utilizes a list of "guiding criteria" that are in a general sense universal, but that always require local interpretation (Ackerly 1999).

Activists in the women's rights as human rights movement have practiced the feminist methodology of social criticism at the local, regional, and international levels. In particular, NGOs have played a crucial role in promoting deliberative inquiry among previously silent or silenced women and devised tactics for bringing their information to broader deliberative fora including international UN conferences. The movement has also engaged in skeptical scrutiny along two dimensions: on the one hand, scrutiny of the prevailing conception of human rights itself; on the other, scrutiny of customary laws and practices of cultures which conflict with women's rights as human rights. This two-pronged scrutiny, too, has been largely the work of NGOs and, in some cases, individual activists and feminist scholars. This scrutiny and the change that followed it depended upon prior engagement in deliberative inquiry at various levels that ranged from the grass roots to the global. Finally, most strands of international feminism have, in the last, crucial decade, coalesced around a single guiding criterion: the basic feminist premise that all human beings, female and male, are of equal worth and are therefore equally worthy of dignity and respect. The way in which this has been most often stated is "that women should not be disadvantaged because they are women" (Charlesworth 1994; see also Soares, Costa, Buarque, Dora, and Sant'Anna 1995). Despite differences in the specific meaning of this criterion in a variety of cultural circumstances, it has been unifying for feminists and has enabled them to build alliances.[3]

In combination, deliberative inquiry, skeptical scrutiny, and guiding criteria are a formula for working towards social change, but they do not guarantee it. However, the women's rights as human rights activists have gone beyond social criticism. As well as being social critics, they have also been strategic in their efforts to bring about social change in local practices and global understanding, and to promote enforcement of women's rights as human rights. An important part of their strategy has

the knowledge/power framework of a particular time. Since then, feminist theory and practice have evolved.

[3] As Margaret Keck and Kathryn Sikkink show, whereas earlier arguments framed in terms of discrimination against women had limited effects on international discussions of human rights, arguments focused on violence against women, which appealed to their basic human worth and dignity, have broken the barriers to the full recognition of women's rights as human rights (Keck and Sikkink 1998).

been to influence debate by improving and broadening public information about women's rights. Specifically, they have used two tactics to influence international sympathies and to affect the formulation and adoption of international policies.

One of these tactics is the use of testimonials by specific women whose human rights had been violated, usually in ways that would have been neither detectable nor remediable under the old, androcentric conception of human rights. This testimony, or bearing witness, which occurred in its most dramatic and effective form at the Vienna Conference in 1993, and which was rendered even more effective because of the attention drawn to it by the media, played a crucial role in preparing the way for the recognition of women's rights as human rights that was arguably the most important outcome of that Conference. The other tactic of the movement has been its skillful use of politics in the conventional sense of the term. Starting as early as the Rio Earth Summit in 1990, representatives of women from many parts of the world, working through NGOs, learned to use tactics such as daily caucuses and lobbying, especially during the regional preparatory meetings, but also at the Conferences themselves. Since there were powerful conservative forces at work at most of the Conferences (but especially Cairo and Beijing), led by the Papacy and some delegations from Islamic nations, these political skills were essential to the gains that were made. None of these modes of action, however, would have been effective, or even possible, had they not been accompanied or preceded by use of the feminist critical method. The women's rights as human rights movement, which rapidly became a complex global network, made use of deliberative inquiry, skeptical scrutiny, and the guiding criterion of the equal worth of all human beings to author social criticism that was respectful of diversity and yet had critical teeth. The movement's activists then used the tactics of public testimonials as well as more conventional politics to effect change in attitudes and awareness around the world and in the formal documents of the UN Conferences.

Thus, we argue that the NGOs of the women's rights as human rights movement used the feminist critical methodology. Further, they took strategic advantage of global communications, media, and international interest to enhance international awareness of violations of women's human rights and to transform the human rights agenda to be more inclusive of women's rights more broadly understood. They were effective at doing so in part because they combined the use of testimonials and more conventional politics.

Feminist social criticism

There are three parts to the feminist method of social criticism: deliberative inquiry, skeptical scrutiny, and guiding criteria. These are not chronological stages of social criticism but, rather, three aspects of it that women have used in conjunction to lay the groundwork for collective, inclusive, and uncoerced social change. First, we define them, and then demonstrate how they are put to critical use by actors in the women's rights as human rights movement.

Deliberative inquiry is the practice of generating knowledge through collective questioning, exchange of views, and discussion among critics and members of the society. Unlike most theorists' versions of deliberative democracy, this version can help enable social change in the context of real world conditions of inequality and imperfect information. Deliberative inquiry serves two broad and complementary purposes. First, it promotes, in a relatively safe forum, collective expression, learning, and understanding among those who have previously been silenced. Second, having developed their self-knowledge and understanding of the obstacles they face, the previously silent then use their new knowledge to promote deliberative inquiry in the broader society where their views were formerly excluded. While the first form of deliberative inquiry may or may not have the impact of influencing the broader society, deliberation in the secured forum may enable women to formulate strategies and tactics for promoting deliberative inquiry in the broader society.[4]

Feminist social critics or activists may foster deliberative inquiry to promote analysis of issues and interpretation of cultural norms, to promote deliberative exchange in the broader society, and to promote institutional change. They may provide a safe haven for women to share their experiences and ideas and identify their collective resources; or they may assist in using the knowledge so gained to promote social change. Both are examples of the use of deliberation to enable collected knowledge to promote social change in conditions of social inequality.

Skeptical scrutiny is an attitude toward existing and proposed values, practices, and norms that requires one to examine their existing and potentially exploitable inequalities. Unlike the method typical of culturally relativist theories, which confine the role of the critic to the interpretation of "shared meanings,"[5] the subjection of shared practices and commonly accepted meanings to skeptical scrutiny illuminates previously concealed relations of domination and subordination, and

---

[4] See Verta Taylor's account of abeyance processes and organizations in inhospitable political environments (Taylor 1989).

[5] See Michael Walzer 1983 and 1993, from which the quoted phrase is drawn.

interrogates them from multiple perspectives. This aspect of the critic's methodology forces the critic to seek out all those who may be silenced by coercive values, practices, and norms. Skeptical scrutiny has critical meaning only contextually. It is a practice of critics, not a principle. It urges critics to question (not all at once for fear of undermining the foundations of society, but to question none the less) whether any and all aspects of community norms, values, and practices (no matter how "accepted" they are) presume, reinforce, cause, or exploit power inequalities to the detriment of the less powerful. Skeptical scrutiny has led feminist activists and scholars to question everything, including the basic institutions of government, the family, and religion.

The feminist method of social criticism employs skeptical scrutiny in conjunction with its other two parts: deliberative inquiry and guiding criteria. The social critic cannot practice skeptical scrutiny without making use of deliberation coming from multiple perspectives – especially that of those most silenced. Otherwise, it is impossible to determine which cultural values, practices, and norms are shared by all, and which are shared by some and forced on others, by means of violence, economic dependency, an enculturated sense of inferiority, or other means. The combined perspectives of inside, outside, and "multisited" critics better facilitate the analysis of potentially or actually oppressive practices, values, and norms than the singular perspective of a sole critic, no matter how unique her perspective may be.[6]

The guiding criteria are a list of minimum standards, or a single standard, that critics can use to challenge existing values, practices, and norms. There is great variety in how feminist activists and scholars have articulated and used their lists. Some (including some women's human rights activists) have articulated universal lists (Bunch 1990); others (such as a union for self-employed women in India) have articulated local lists (Rose 1992). One version of the guiding criteria – which Ackerly (1999) argues satisfies both, and the content of which she has derived from the lists of many social critics around the world – is a general list of what people ought to be able to choose to do. It is a universal list based on the guiding criteria used by social critics in many countries, from local and international activists to the authors of formal UN Declarations and delegation members at UN Conventions. Despite its broad base of sources and its attempt at gaining universal acceptance,

[6] The multisited critic has the unique perspective of an individual who has been an insider and an outsider; she has acquired local knowledge about more than one group, she is able to move between groups and take their various perspectives, and she is generally self-conscious about her unique perspective (Ackerly 1999). Okin uses the term "inside/outside critic" in much the same way (1997 and 1998).

the list requires local interpretation and prioritization by critics working in each particular context.[7] Though some individual activists in the women's rights as human rights movement have drafted and made use of such lists, the movement as a whole, as we noted earlier, has tended to rely on the general guiding criterion of men's and women's equal human worth. Like any list of criteria, the single criterion needs to be used in conjunction with deliberative inquiry and skeptical scrutiny in order to be a constructive guide to social criticism in a particular context. In the case of human rights, as we shall see, a set of existing guiding criteria have had to be subjected to skeptical scrutiny by feminist social critics, using the general feminist criterion, in order to become less androcentric and to become women's human rights as well as men's.

The work of the activists upon which the method of social criticism is based is called "feminist" *because* it presumes the equal worth of all human beings – male and female – and because these activists are "agents effecting change in their own condition" as well as that of many other women who have not been able to express their views (Soares, Costa, Buraque, Dora, and Sant'Anna 1995: 302). Our definition of feminism is consistent with the current wave led by Third World women's scholarship, focusing on women's power and empowerment (for example Basu 1995; Chowdhry 1995; Barriteau 1995; Pala 1977; Sen and Grown 1987; Smiley 1993). Not all those who use this method embrace the label "feminist." Nor do all those who embrace the label "feminist" use this method. However, activists around the world working toward the enhancement of women's lives or, more specifically, the recognition of women's human rights, use all three aspects of the feminist critical methodology – deliberative inquiry, skeptical scrutiny, and guiding criteria – even though many among them do not describe themselves as feminists.

Women's rights as human rights

In her account of the women's international human rights movement, Hilary Charlesworth distinguishes between those who wish to expand the interpretation and use of the existing human rights paradigm such that the ways in which women's human rights are violated are addressed by human rights law, and those who argue for women's particular rights such as reproductive freedom (Charlesworth 1994). The first might be

---

[7] Ackerly proposes and discusses the specific contents of a provisional list, in *Political Theory and Feminist Social Criticism* (1999).

called advocates of "women's human rights" and the latter advocates of "women's rights." In our account of the movement, we prefer to refer to "women's rights as human rights," which encapsulates both terms, but which also connotes a challenge to the paradigm of human rights law as being based on a typically male experience of life. Human rights law needed to be transformed, its anti-discrimination basis needed to be problematized, and its application needed to pay attention to the life experiences of women under patriarchy. The equal worth of all human beings is significant as a guiding criterion for women's rights as human rights advocates because it is a universal mandate that requires local interpretation to be culturally relevant and critically useful.

At first glance at the international human rights documents, one might wonder why the movement of the last decade to get women's rights fully recognized as human rights was necessary. The Universal Declaration of Human Rights (1948) protects women from discrimination:

Everyone is entitled to all the rights and freedoms set forth in this Declaration, without distinction of any kind, such as race, colour, sex, language, religion, political or other opinion, national or social origin, property, birth or other status. (Article 2)

The International Covenant on Civil and Political Rights (1966) also protects women from discrimination:

Each State Party to the present Covenant undertakes to respect and to ensure to all individuals within its territory and subject to its jurisdiction the rights recognized in the present Covenant, without distinction of any kind, such as race, colour, sex, language, religion, political or other opinion, national or social origin, property, birth or other status. (Part II, Article 1.1)

Likewise, the UN Convention on the Rights of the Child (1989) protects girl children and their mothers from discrimination:

States Parties shall respect and ensure the rights set forth in the present Convention to each child within their jurisdiction without discrimination of any kind, irrespective of the child's or his or her parent's or legal guardian's race, colour, sex, language, religion, political or other opinion, national, ethnic or social origin, property, disability, birth or other status. (Article 1.1)

Thus from the United Nations' Declaration of Human Rights in 1948 on, discrimination on the basis of sex was prohibited by international human rights law. However, the anti-discrimination paradigm was not sufficient to respond to many of women's specific important needs. In spite of the wording cited above, the "individual" whose human rights were protected was clearly, though not explicitly, the male head of a household. Two (now obvious) indicators of this are that the state was perceived as the most likely violator of human rights and that, while the privacy of one's family life was considered to need protection as a right, protection from the violations of one's rights by others within one's home was not treated as a right.

Even where the existing human rights could have been interpreted as protecting women, governments and human rights organizations focused on those violations that have been publicly and historically recognized. As Rebecca Cook notes, until recently, "there has been an unwillingness by traditional human rights groups to focus on violations of women's rights and a lack of understanding by women's groups of the potential of international law to vindicate women's rights" (Cook 1994: 3).

In 1979, the UN passed a special Convention on the Elimination of All Forms of Discrimination Against Women (CEDAW). The CEDAW goes much further than any of the other UN human rights documents in enumerating the ways in which women's human rights are violated. It identifies the ways in which women are discriminated against formally and informally in social, political, and economic practices. It departs from gender-neutral language where necessary or appropriate. It explicitly identifies the potential for women to be discriminated against and harmed in their own homes, in the workplace, and in public places, by family members, employers, and political actors. The content of the CEDAW was an advance for women. However, it was signed by far fewer countries, and with more reservations expressed, than any other human rights document. Moreover, limited resources have been devoted to enforcing it. Many of the states that have signed and ratified it continue to discriminate against women in their laws and even more extensively in their practices (Mayer 1995).

The anti-discrimination paradigm of the UN human rights documents including the CEDAW (which was closely modeled on the Convention against Racial Discrimination) is now recognized as, in many respects, inappropriate to the task of addressing inequalities of gender. As Charlesworth argues, "A more fundamental treatment of the skewed nature of the international human rights system would redefine the boundaries of the traditional human rights canon, rather than tinkering with the limited existing model of nondiscrimination" (1994: 60). Such redefinition of the concept would "more readily ... reach violations of human dignity that dominate women's lives, such as domestic violence" (Charlesworth, paraphrased by Cook 1994: 7). As we shall show, some rethinking of specific human rights was necessary in order to use them to address even basic rights violations commonly experienced by women. Feminists working on women's rights as human rights have, thus, advocated both tinkering with the existing model such that existing human rights law can be applied to protect women and transforming the paradigm of international human rights law, in order to expand its scope such that women are protected by it.

Women around the world acting locally, regionally, and internationally, typically in efforts coordinated through NGOs, have begun to transform accepted interpretations of human rights. These women have made constructive use of globalization to affect understandings of women's rights as human rights internationally and in their own countries. Their success was first formally recognized at the World Conference on Human Rights in Vienna in 1993 and further formalized, codified, and adopted as the "Platform for Action" at the World Conference on Women in Beijing in 1995. They continue to work toward these transformations in their home countries around the world.

Deliberative inquiry

In all of this critique and political action, the role of NGOs has been absolutely crucial. As two scholars of human rights in general have noted: "Non-Governmental Organizations (NGOs) have become indispensable in the work of human rights protection" (Nowak and Schwarz 1994: 3). But NGOs have played a particularly large part in the recognition of women's rights as human rights. NGOs have been important critics, in that their intercessions have been vital for, first, creating safe spaces for women to voice their previously silent (or silenced) accounts of their experiences and, second, in bringing public awareness to the fact that many of these women's experiences, though previously not understood as cases of violations of human rights, were in fact such violations.

NGOs of all sizes and with many different original purposes have played a crucial role in eliciting from women information about their experience and about the difficulties they have to contend with on a daily basis. For example, NGOs are often engaged in grass-roots level work aimed at the improvement of women's well-being – whether through the improvement of working conditions or the provision of such things as health care, credit, or legal aid. In Gujarat, India, a large, women-run NGO, the Self-employed Women's Association (SEWA) demonstrates the role NGOs can serve in promoting women's self-knowledge and their ability to effect public policy affecting their lives (Selliah 1989; Bumiller 1990; Rose 1992). In Gujarat, as in many parts of the Third World, most women are self-employed or work for a piece rate at home. When women are such contracted workers, any solitary worker is expendable; consequently, women are easily coerced by business owners and middlemen to accept low wages and wage cuts. SEWA fought against this by challenging the government interpretation of "trade union," which had required union members to be employed in the formal economy and, in 1972, SEWA was registered as a trade union of self-employed workers. By participating in SEWA trade groups, otherwise marginalized women are able to have a public voice. For example, women in Gujarat who subcontract to roll cigarettes acted collectively and successfully struck against their employers in order to receive minimum wages (Rose 1992). The trade groups were further strengthened by child care, legal aid, cooperative banking, and other services for SEWA members. Further, SEWA lobbied the government to finance the maternity benefit program which it had established and to provide life insurance through the SEWA Co-operative Bank to self-employed workers. Through SEWA's work at the grass-roots level, the surrounding society and government came to have a greater understanding of the lives and needs of self-employed women workers.

SEWA's success and information combined with that of other NGOs has enhanced international understanding of the gendered constraints on women's being able to live a life of equal worth to that of men. In the course of such work, NGOs have facilitated discourse amongst women, both subnationally and internationally and, by this and other means, they have uncovered numerous examples of rights violations experienced by women that did not fit the traditional human rights paradigm. NGOs such as SEWA mobilize social activism so that women can empower themselves in their families and communities, improve maternal and child health, and improve women's income and working conditions. Successful development organizations provide models for means of addressing the previously invisible violations of women's human rights. Regardless of their immediate goals, many NGOs tend to promote deliberative inquiry amongst their members, enabling them to share their experiences, to learn from each other about the problems that women, despite their different cultures and life circumstances, often have in common, and to propose solutions to their problems. Despite the variety of women's experiences and needs around the world, many development NGOs' work is guided by a belief in the fundamental equal worth of all human beings. Through their work, they have contributed important information to the women's rights as human rights movement.

NGOs working expressly in the women's rights as human rights movement also make use of deliberative inquiry. Leading up to the Vienna Conference, within countries, local NGOs held meetings at which women shared the ways in which their human rights had been violated. At one such meeting of 2,000 women in Secunderabad, India, women spoke out against child marriage, domestic violence, dowry murder,[8] and the economic exploitation of women in the home and society (Bunch and Reilly 1994: 125). Another meeting in Nepal combined the sharing of the experiences of women workers, bonded women, trafficked women, and women victims of domestic violence with group discussions (Bunch and Reilly 1994: 126).

Some international NGOs, too, were specifically set up to work on issues concerning women's rights as human rights. Some examples are Women Living Under Muslim Laws, the Center for Women's Global Leadership, and Women's Rights Watch. Such organizations played a key part in preparations for the Vienna Conference on Human Rights. They organized a huge petition drive of 900 organizations from 124 countries translated into 24 languages (Bunch and Reilly 1994: 130–1). Those signing "call upon the 1993 United Nations World Conference on Human Rights to comprehensively address women's rights at every level of its proceedings ... [and] demand that gender violence, a universal phenomenon which takes many forms across culture, race and class, be recognized as a violation of human rights requiring immediate action" (Bunch and Reilly 1994: 131). The petition was signed (in some cases with thumbprints) by nearly 500,000 women (Bunch 1994; Bunch and Reilly 1994: 135).

One of the main challenges faced by women's rights as human rights activists has been that there is so little agreement, from state to state and from culture to culture, about what constitutes discrimination against women. As Cook has written, however, "[t]he understanding of discrimination against women evolves with insights, perspective, and empirical information on how women are subordinated by different legal, social, and religious traditions" (1994: 11; see also Keck and Sikkink 1998). Working with women at the grass roots for decades enabled those in NGOs to gain such insights, perspective, and empirical information, through the deliberative inquiry that occurred in the course of their day-to-day work. They found that many women who worked extremely long hours trying to provide subsistence for their families were living in dire poverty. They found that such women often suffered doubly (as poor people and as women) from the effects of environmental degradation and from the constraints of structural adjustment programs. They found that many women were suffering from physical violence or the continual threat of such violence and that, during peacetime, their own homes

---

[8] Dowry murder refers to the murder of a woman by her husband (or occasionally her in-laws) that occurs in the context of arguments or threats about either the non-payment of dowry or what is considered insufficient payment of dowry. The murder often takes the form of a kitchen stove fire that is claimed to have been accidental.

were the most dangerous places for them to be. They found that many women were bearing more children than they wished to, and that many – half a million per year, globally – were dying from preventable pregnancy-related causes. They found that both inheritance systems and the provision of basic education were heavily prejudiced against girls, in many regions of the world. Much of this information about the problems that were realities in many women's daily lives was gathered through the NGOs' direct contacts and dialogue with the women they sought to help (Bruce 1989; Sen 1990a and 1990b; Tinker 1990).

Feminist social criticism can create the conditions for voices that are otherwise silent to emerge. NGOs and other international networks used information gained from such deliberative inquiry among previously unheard women as evidence of the ways in which women's rights have been formally and informally denied, and conveyed this knowledge from one part of the world to another. They provided the information, first garnered from women's experiences at the grass-roots level, to regional meetings, and eventually, to the three vast international Conferences of the early 1990s – Cairo, Vienna, and Beijing. Each of these Conferences was attended by unprecedented numbers of women, the vast majority of whom came as representatives of hundreds of local and international NGOs. Collected at the international fora, the shared knowledge from NGOs around the world gave a human face to the violations of women's human rights around the world. The local and international NGOs of the women's rights as human rights movement used deliberative inquiry to share information that led them to identify their common opposition to violence against women across cultures. Opposition to violence on the basis of women's equal human worth and dignity became a guiding criterion shared by activists opposed to practices as diverse as "rape and domestic battery in the United States and Europe, female genital mutilation in Africa, female sexual slavery in Europe and Asia, dowry death in India, and torture and rape of political prisoners in Latin America" (Keck and Sikkink 1998: 171). Thus, deliberative inquiry resulted in radical challenge to the existing human rights paradigm.

Skeptical scrutiny and the guiding criteria

The information gathered by NGOs through their direct contact with the women they served was important in the reconceptualization of prevailing conceptions of human rights. What was learned was that many of the violations of women's human rights and freedoms as enumerated in the 1948 Universal Declaration – the right not to be tortured (Article 5), to be recognized as a legal person (Article 6), to mobility (Article 13), to marry according to own's own choice (Article 16), to own property (Article 17), to choose one's religion and beliefs (Article 18), to public assembly (Article 20), to political participation (Article 21), to social security (Article 22), to choose one's work (Article 23), to paid holidays (Article 24), to a basic standard of living (Article 25), and to education (Article 26) – happen in homes or in local communities. Moreover, Article 12, which prohibits "arbitrary interference with ... privacy, family, home ...," has been interpreted as a constraint on states' ability to *protect* women and children in their homes from such violations of their rights. Further, as Charlesworth notes, what are sometimes called "third generation" rights – collective or group rights of "peoples" such as the right to "self-determination" or to "cultural development" – have been "invoked, and supported, recently in a number of contexts to allow the oppression of women" (1994: 75).

Knowledge about the lives of women, gathered and disseminated through deliberative inquiry, catalyzed national and international skeptical scrutiny of many of these rights. What good was the right to physical security from violence from the state and its agents, for example, to women subjected to continual or random violence from their own husbands or fathers? What good was the right to "equal pay for equal work" (Article 23) to a woman who toiled all day at various tasks, such as childcare, housework, the fetching of water and fuel, and subsistence farming, that were neither paid at all nor even (*because* they were performed by women) valued as "work"? What use were even fundamental liberties such as freedom of movement or association (Articles 13 and 20) to women whose freedom was radically constrained by childbearing and childcare responsibilities or cultural practices confining women to family compounds? What use is freedom of marriage (Article 16) to women in contexts where fathers have the accepted – even legally enforceable – right to choose their husbands? Of what use were formal political rights, such as the right to vote (Article 21), in a cultural context in which women were assumed to be subordinated to men and, in practice, did not exercise the right to vote? Becoming increasingly convinced that there was no way for women to enjoy their human rights in the public spheres of politics and the market unless they are valued as equal human beings in the private spheres of family life and community practice, the NGOs realized that societies and the world needed a fundamental reconceptualization of human rights.

Thus, in the context of the women's rights as human rights movement, one of the most valuable assets has also constituted one of the most daunting challenges: to use existing human rights law to *transform* human rights law. That is to say, a great deal of skeptical scrutiny of the human rights paradigm itself was needed in order to transform what were called "human" rights into guiding criteria that could promote and conserve the advancement of women's rights as human rights.

Scrutinizing existing human rights law in practice to re-evaluate its appropriateness for protecting women's rights as human rights led activists to challenge not only accepted notions of public and private, but also collective or group rights. Some communities and nations used the arguments of indigenous or group rights activists to argue for their rights to protect and perpetuate "traditional" practices that might otherwise be considered oppressive to women. Ann Elizabeth Mayer gives a particularly thorough account of the ways in which Muslim nations, US conservatives, and the Vatican used arguments of divinely ordained traditional law to deny women's freedoms (Mayer 1995). By contrast, and in challenge to such appeals to tradition, culture, and religion, women's rights as human rights activists scrutinized traditional customs, cultures, and religions for sex bias and sources of women's oppression.

The challenge for national or local activists living and working within such contexts is to speak for themselves in locally specific ways so that their arguments cannot be undermined by the accusation of being under foreign or Western influence. The challenge for international activists is to support local activists but not to undermine their voices by speaking for them. In 1993, Alice Walker's book and Pratibha Parmar's film by the same title, *The Warrior Marks*, drew Western media attention to the problem of female genital mutilation, but the international attention, from Westerners in particular, functioned in part to undermine those who had been active locally in the Sudan and elsewhere. Western critics of female genital mutilation have sometimes been accused of essentializing based on a Western definition of feminity. In comparison, critics native to, even if exiled from, the country in which such abuses of women's rights occur – such as Nahid Toubia, the Sudanese surgeon who is now an international advocate for the abolition of FGM – can speak with both direct local knowledge and professional expertise. As Anne Marie Goetz argues regarding the impact of external financial and ideological support for gender and development initiatives nationally:

Where projects and institutions are set up primarily in response to an external initiative, there is little incentive to actively internalise and "own" a policy initiative. Instead, its legitimacy is suspect and even though the funds are welcomed, the imposition of "alien" cultural notions regarding gender is deeply resented ... Cultural imperialism in the projection of Western notions of gender equity to other contexts is an undeniable problem and the resentment this arouses can have the unfortunate effect of stigmatising existing indigenous feminisms as Western derivatives, thereby undermining their local legitimacy. (Goetz 1995: 53)

In this postcolonial era, women in many countries are being asked to choose between their traditional culture or their religion, and their human rights. When they ask for equal human rights with men, they are accused of being "secularist" or betraying their culture or religion and following "Western" ways. As Asma Mohamed Abdel Halim says: "In the Sudan, the notion of the liberation of women is being twisted. Muslim women are being told, by Muslim men, that international law . . . is the real obstacle to women . . ., [that] women should be liberated from western ideas that are subjecting them to the double burden of domestic and public work responsibilities" (1995: 406). Local feminists are forced to choose an allegiance either to the women of their society or to its dominant cultural norms. To be effective at changing local cultural practices, local activists must be in charge (Toubia 1995) and their ideas must have the cultural legitimacy of being their own ideas.

Thus, it is incumbent upon Western feminists to challenge patriarchy in the variety of ways it afflicts the cultures in which women live, in ways that are free of imperialist tone or content. In appropriate cases, this includes giving various kinds of support to women who challenge patriarchy in their own cultures. To challenge patriarchy thus is an especially pressing and heavy burden for those who live under religious fundamentalist regimes, such as those in Iran, Afghanistan, and the Sudan, or who are governed by religious "personal laws" in the context of secular states, such as India and Israel. Here, too, NGOs have been effective in supporting women's rights as human rights, via fostering deliberative inquiry and skeptical scrutiny of religions or cultures that justify and perpetuate the violation of such rights. Some, such as the Arab League for Human Rights, work for human rights in general; others, such as the Sisterhood Is Global Institute, work specifically for women's rights as human rights.

Muslim feminists are taking charge. They are reclaiming for Muslim women the right to interpret Islamic texts, clarifying as point of law and human rights the difference between Islamic law and Muslim practice, and using that distinction to advocate for interpretations of Islamic texts, enactment of laws, and changes in Muslim practices that are respectful to women as equal to men (Zein EdDīn 1982 [1928]; Smith and Haddad 1982; el Saadawi 1982; al-Hibri 1982; Hassan 1991; and Mernissi 1991, 1992, and 1995). Mahnaz Afkhami and Farida Shaheed note the political importance of distinguishing between Islamic practices set forth in the Qur'an and *hadith* (the narrative record of the sayings and actions of Muhammad) from Muslim practices which are more general social, cultural, and economic practices of followers of Islam (Afkhami 1995b; Shaheed 1994). Riffat Hassan distinguishes between the teachings of the Qur'an and the later interpretive texts, arguing that the latter contain faulty scholarship and ideas imported from Judaism and Christianity (Hassan 1991). In theocracies Islamic and Muslim practices are linked by the unified religious and political authority such that Muslim law is both defended as divine law and enforced by the state.[9]

Women Living Under Muslim Laws (WLUML), an international network, uses deliberative inquiry and skeptical scrutiny to point out the many inconsistencies in the ways that Islamic law is used to oppress women (Shaheed 1994 and 1995). Women learn through the network that much of what is claimed to be "Islamic law" or that is required of "Muslim women" varies from country to country. There is great variety among what is required of women to be truly "Muslim," as is the case with dress codes, which vary from the total covering of the head and body, excluding the eyes, to far less stringent requirements to wear a headscarf. Often what is claimed as "Islamic" comes not from Islam, but derives from colonial law, other religious tradition, or local customs of the pre-Islamic period, as is the case (respectively) with the disinheritance of Indian Muslim women, dowry practices in India and Bangladesh, and female genital mutilation in many parts of Africa. Where such alternative laws or customs exist, usually those most oppressive to women are enforced, and justified as required by Islam (Shaheed 1994; also Mayer 1995). Further, in many countries, family or personal law, which has far more drastic life consequences for women than for men, is the *only* aspect of Islamic law that is enforced by the state, which applies secular law in other social contexts (Shaheed 1995; Afkhami 1995a).[10] By fostering contact among women from different Muslim countries or subcultures, WLUML facilitates their learning about the variations among Muslim laws, enabling them to more readily scrutinize and contest the oppressive ones they are subjected to and to suggest alternatives that are applied in other Muslim countries or compatible with other versions of Islam.

[9] See, for example, the text of reservations of Egypt and Morocco upon their ratification of the CEDAW (Mayer 1995).
[10] The inequalities inherent in polygyny are obvious. In some versions, Muslim divorce law makes it far easier for the husband than for the wife to divorce and does not give her economic security even if she has been completely dependent throughout her marriage; the granting of child custody to the husband is also a considerable deterrent to divorce, and therefore source of vulnerability, for Muslim wives in some countries. A few predominantly Muslim countries, such as Indonesia, have modernized their family law and made it more egalitarian. (See Mayer 1995.)

One particularly successful project was the Collectif '95. When the Arab states proposed to enact a uniform family code, WLUML recognized and publicized that the proposed code would codify many of the most oppressive laws affecting women in the various countries. When a sub-group of WLUML, known as the Collectif '95, produced a counter-draft code, which was drawn instead from the least oppressive laws, no uniform code was passed (Shaheed 1994 and 1995). Guided by a belief in the fundamental equal worth of human beings, male and female, the Collectif '95 used deliberative inquiry among women about the Muslim laws in their respective countries to scrutinize the proposed family code.

The feminist methodology of social criticism we have been describing was developed through the observation of a variety of women's activism under conditions of extreme inequality. These activists – the women's rights as human rights activists among them – practice a method of social criticism that challenges values, practices, and norms that perpetuate harm to women based on sharing the knowledge and experiences of women themselves. This method is a formula for informing social change, but does not guarantee it. However, observation of the women's rights as human rights movement allows us to identify a general strategy and particular tactics that have been effective in bringing about social change at the international level of policy-making.

Strategy and tactics

Women's rights as human rights activists have been more than social critics: they have also been agents for social change. As we pointed out earlier, the women's rights as human rights movement achieved substantial change in globally recognized conceptions of human rights. In order to act effectively on the international stage, to transform the existing criteria of androcentric human rights so as to make them fully applicable to women, the movement needed broad international support. The general strategy of the women's rights as human rights movement was to use publicity to heighten local, national, and international awareness of violations of women's human rights and to bring political pressure to bear in order to influence international agreements on human rights policy with an eye toward changing the conditions of women around the world. This strategy proved effective in international policy-making arenas.

Two principal tactics were adopted to achieve the goals of the movement. The first was the publicization of violations of women's rights through the use of testimonials. Feminists had been using deliberative inquiry to canvass a variety of women's experiences and to inform their own arguments. NGOs had been using testimonials to add a human side to their documentation and funding efforts.[11] But testimonials took their most dramatic form at the Global Tribunal on the Violation of Women's Human Rights, which took place on 15 June 1993, as part of the meetings held in conjunction with the Vienna Conference. NGOs concerned with women's well-being, led by the Center for Global Women's Leadership at Rutgers University and the International Women's Tribune Center, had prepared for years for this occasion, which was "the absolute highlight in the NGO section" (Nowak and Schwarz 1994: 6).

In 1990, the idea was born to document violations of women's human rights by collecting individual case histories. The thirty-three cases selected for the Tribunal in Vienna clearly revealed the failure of existing human rights to protect women and demonstrated the many ways in which women experienced violence throughout the world. Women from around the world – or, in instances when they were unable to travel, their representatives – bore witness to the variety of ways in which women's human rights have been violated. The cases included beatings and rape within marriage, incest, dowry murder, murder and neglect of girl children, gender-specific war crimes including rape, and violations of women's physical integrity in the forms of the absence of healthcare and in relation to sexuality and reproduction – including trafficking in women and genital mutilation. Recognizing that each woman who bore witness represented thousands more in a similar situation, the Tribunal displayed "a deeply shocking picture of reality for many women at the end of the twentieth century" (Nowak and Schwarz 1994: 7). The Tribunal's findings and the "verdicts" of its judges were presented to the plenary session of the official Conference in the form of findings and recommendations of the judges to the Conference (Bunch and Reilly 1994: 130–4). Analysts credit the Tribunal as "certainly instrumental in having women's demands included in the final Conference document," which "strengthened measures to protect the human rights of women" (Nowak and Schwarz 1994: 9–10).

The Tribunal was organized for political impact. It was timed with the Fourth UN World Conference on Human Rights. Testimonials were presented to five panels: Human Rights Abuses in the Family, War Crimes Against Women, Violations of Women's Bodily Integrity, Socio-economic Violations of Women's Human Rights, and Gender-based Political Persecution and Discrimination. Due to the traumatic nature of the violations many would describe, each speaker was provided a

---

[11] Keck and Sikkink relate how this method of publicizing violence against women was first used by surviving Korean "comfort women" (1998: 176).

"support" person who facilitated her participation in the Tribunal. Press clippings from around the world during the Tribunal provide evidence that the Tribunal was successful in raising international awareness of the violations of women's human rights. Moreover, the range of examples cited by reporters demonstrate that the Tribunal was successful in conveying not only the variety and extent of the violations of women's human rights but also the failure of conventional understandings of human rights to address many of these violations. The five judges, who were major political actors at the official Conference, reached a verdict which was presented to the full Conference by women's human rights activists and experts, Charlotte Bunch and Florence Butegwa. As noted above, the Tribunal is considered to have had a major impact on the Vienna Conference, such that better recognition of women's rights as human rights became a primary, if not the primary, focus.

In preparation for the Conference and at the Conference itself, media attention was promoted by the organizers. The Global Campaign for Women's Human Rights, the International Women's Tribune Centre, and ISIS International Chile publicized around the world the petition to put women's human rights on the Conference agenda (Bunch and Reilly 1994: 96). Publicity of the Tribunal itself was supported by the Communications Consortium with information packets, press briefings, facilitation of interviews, and a PR effort that, in the United States, landed coverage in *The Washington Post* and *The New York Times*, and a ten-minute piece on CNN (Bunch and Reilly 1994: 97–8). The organizers also displayed and disseminated women's publications, made Conference information available via the Internet, trained women on using the Internet, disseminated information via Feminist International Radio Endeavor (which also allowed women who did not speak at the Tribunal to speak publicly), and organized a video team to document the Tribunal and the broader effort to influence the Conference (Bunch and Reilly 1994: 96–8).

The second tactic of the women's rights as human rights movement was to use the more conventional politics of caucusing and lobbying. Former US Congresswoman and activist Bella Abzug played a leading role in promoting the development of women's political skills over the course of the four UN Conferences before Beijing: Rio, Vienna, Cairo, and Copenhagen (Morgan 1996a and 1996b; Abzug 1996).[12] Governments were lobbied prior to the meetings to include more NGO

[12] Abzug's effect was so apparent to the US right wing that Senator Jesse Helms ensured her absence from the official US delegation at Beijing; she was still, however, a powerful presence at the NGO Forum (Morgan 1996b; Abzug 1996).

representatives on their official delegations, and these delegations were then lobbied throughout the Conferences to include women's perspectives on the matters at hand. At each Conference daily caucuses of NGO representatives were held, to keep on top of and to discuss the issues on the table at the official Conferences – caucuses that "directed, focused, and steered NGOs through sophisticated on-site lobbying efforts so that government delegations were forced to realize that *all* issues are women's issues" (Morgan 1996b: 77). As Abzug describes it, the work was painstaking and unrelenting: "being there side by side with governments, going over the documents, making suggestions line by line" (Abzug 1996: 120).

Even at the Earth Summit in Rio, where these methods were first employed, they were successful in helping to change the two or three mentions of women in the initial document to "about 120 provisions affecting women by the end" (Abzug 1996). In Vienna, where immense and lengthy preparations by women's NGOs preceded the Conference, women had succeeded in getting many of their concerns into the draft agenda, but knew that they needed to continue to apply pressure. At the NGO Forum that preceded the Conference, women from the Global Campaign for Women's Human Rights ensured that they were well represented in all of the five working groups that prepared the NGO document to be addressed to the Conference, but concentrated especially on the group focused on women's human rights, headed by Florence Butegwa of Zimbabwe. Throughout the Conference, two women's caucuses met regularly, to keep close track of its proceedings and their implications for women, to lobby with regard to specific items as they arose, to draft new text for delegates to introduce, and to "explore possible means to collaborate to advance women's human rights at the Conference … as well as afterwards" (Bunch and Reilly 1994: 102–3). One of these caucuses was organized by the NGO Forum and the other by UNIFEM – the UN Development Fund for Women. These two caucuses contributed greatly to the striking focus on women's human rights that marked the Vienna Conference. In Beijing, the draft document that emanated from the preparatory meetings was powerful. However, it went into the conference with many "holy brackets" around 40 percent of it – so-called because these were clauses that were objectionable to a coalition of conservative religious forces, led by the Vatican and the leaders of some Muslim countries. Again, unrelenting political work throughout the Conference was necessary to the success of the feminist agenda. As Abzug relates: "the Linkage Caucus – which is what we called ourselves – linked all of the gains that had been made in the previous conferences and demanded even more, moving beyond the scope of all other platforms" (Abzug 1996: 121). Continuous lobbying from the NGO Forum and by NGO representatives on official delegations ensured that nearly all of the brackets came off in the end.

Thus women, using caucuses and lobbying, worked successfully for the international acceptance of the new, more inclusive account of human rights that resulted from deliberative inquiry and from skeptical scrutiny of the traditional human rights paradigm. Thus, for example, domestic violence, marital rape, and rape during war came to be treated in international law as fundamental human rights violations, as other forms of assault and torture already were (Copelon 1994; Cook 1994), and clitoridectomy came to be seen as a form of mutilation and thus as serious child abuse (Toubia 1995; Winter 1994).[13]

As many theorists of women's rights as human rights have pointed out, these re-envisionings of women's rights violations as serious human rights violations depended on two principal changes: the radical re-thinking of the separation of the public and private spheres that was a (usually tacit) assumption of all early human rights discourse; and the shift from regarding states as the likely violators of most human rights to the recognition that individuals were often human rights violators and that the state needed sometimes to be relied upon to intervene in "private" and "community" practices to stop these violations. Subjecting these assumptions to skeptical scrutiny, based on the experiential reality of women's lives, and translated into global political effectiveness, led to nothing less than a transformation of human rights thinking in the international arena.

While the strategic use of global communication, media, and increased levels of interest in global issues, was effective at bringing international attention to the topic of revising the human rights paradigm so that women's rights are respected as human rights, international attention and pressure have been a less certain strategy for domestic activists. The same strategy that worked to change the international definition of human rights may not work for national or local NGOs trying to influence the agenda of domestic politics (Cook 1994). Respect for women's rights as human rights depends on the cultural legitimacy of the rights paradigm and the specific rights being defended within a given context. Because many practices oppressive to women are directly tied to ethnic or cultural identity, ending those practices requires

---

[13] Following this reasoning, child marriage, coerced marriage, and marriage on extremely unequal terms (for example, easy exit for the husband with guardianship of the children and without continuing financial responsibilities for his former wife, as compared with far more difficult exit for the woman, without economic support or rights to child custody) can be construed as forms of slavery (Okin 1997).

transforming cultural practices without abandoning cultural identity. Radhika Coomaraswamy argues that to do that the women's rights as human rights movement will have to link itself with other social movements (Coomaraswamy 1994). Abdullahi Ahmed An-Na'im concurs that cultural legitimacy is an essential component to achieving the ends of the women's rights as human rights movement within nations (An-Na'im 1994). Although some feminists and feminist organizations have argued that the women's rights as human rights agenda requires divorcing politics from religion, others, such as Women Living Under Muslim Laws and the Sisterhood Is Global Institute recognize that cultural and religious practices have changed and can still change over time. Thus, achieving women's rights as human rights requires evolving existing cultural practices and finding justification for women's equal worth in religious texts and cultural myth (Afkhami and Vaziri 1996; Hassan 1991).

The strategy for influencing the international paradigm of human rights has been effective. However, there were certain failures such as the inability to address the conflict between religious practices and the international covenant at Vienna (Mayer 1995: 118), the failure of many nations to ratify the CEDAW, and the acceptance of the reservations that many countries attached to their ratifications. Yet, as Mayer notes, evidence of the overall success of the women's rights as human rights movement is seen in attempts by conservative US politicians, the Vatican, and Muslim governments to pay lip-service to women's and men's equality while defending unequal rights that disadvantage women on the basis of natural or divine law (Mayer 1995). Success on the domestic level is less obvious. Defenders of practices oppressive to women continue to use arguments for cultural autonomy from Western influence to reject women's rights as human rights (or the human rights paradigm altogether). Conservatives in countries such as the US, China, India, and South Korea have accused "feminists" (in the first instance) or "Westerners" (in the others) of seeking to impose an agenda that undermines deeply held traditional values. As a result they pit many women against their own culture. Activists within nations need to develop their own strategies for promoting the cultural legitimacy of women's rights as human rights. These will probably need to vary according to social context, the politics of opponents, and the availability of allies.

International activists need to develop additional strategies for supporting individual national and local efforts without undermining the necessarily contextual character of those efforts. Though there is no distinctive formula for local success or international support of local efforts, activists for women's human rights will continue to use the feminist method of social criticism comprised of deliberative inquiry, skeptical scrutiny, and guiding criteria (or a single criterion) in their development of such efforts. This method has proven to yield social criticism that is both effective and has cultural legitimacy.

Conclusion

Despite working under conditions of inequality, feminist activists around the world have developed a method of social criticism that is inclusive of diverse perspectives and yet has critical force. Women's rights as human rights activists are examples of such critics. They have used deliberative inquiry to promote understanding among themselves of the ways in which women's rights are violated and to promote awareness in the broader society of an otherwise near-invisible problem. They have used skeptical scrutiny to examine existing cultural and legal norms for their impact on women. Throughout, their work is guided by a criterion of the equal human worth of all people, male and female.

However, more than mere critics, the women's rights as human rights activists have been agents of social change. Through the coordinated actions of national and international NGOs, they have greatly increased women's input into international human rights policy. In the international arena their strategy was to increase public awareness of women's experience of the violations of their human rights. They made particularly effective use of two tactics: highly publicized testimonials and the more conventional political methods of caucusing and lobbying.

The example of the women's rights as human rights activism and political effectiveness suggests that the definition of "civil society" need no longer be used just to refer to domestic society, but can be extended to international politics. Democratic theorists generally have defined civil society as including political parties, the press and other fora of public deliberation, trade unions, associations, educational institutions, religious organizations, and grass-roots and national NGOs where these operate independent of government control (O'Donnell and Schmitter 1986). Some theorists add economic activity to the sphere of civil society and define civil society as all public activity that is not government controlled. Diamond argues, "Civil society is ... distinct from 'society' in general in that it *involves* citizens acting collectively in a public sphere to express their interests, passions, and ideas, exchange information, achieve mutual goals, make demands on the state, and hold state officials accountable" (Diamond 1994: 5). Under either definition, "international civil society," in the form of a network of local, national, and international NGOs sharing a common guiding criterion, has been effective at raising international awareness of the ways in which women's rights are violated. The movement's activism causes theorists to reconsider the definition of civil society. It also cautions national NGO strategies to make adequate use of national information in order to modify their domestic agendas for local particulars, otherwise the fact of international participation might undermine local NGOs' efforts, making them seem too much influenced from outside (or worse, specifically "the West").

Globalization presents problems and challenges for democracy, but it also offers opportunities. Feminist activists have made important use of globalization to promote international and national collective inquiry and scrutiny of human rights policies and practices. Using the feminist method of social criticism, they have expanded public dialogue about human rights such that the views of previously unheard women inform public decision-making. The movement has challenged common understandings of the violations of human rights with examples of the ways in which women's human rights have been violated outside of the purview of the traditional interpretation of human rights law. Their approach has challenged previously heuristically useful distinctions between national and international NGOs and demonstrated that their combined activism can be effective internationally.

REFERENCES

Abzug, Bella. 1996. "A global movement for democracy." In *Beijing and Beyond: Toward the Twenty-first Century of Women. Women's Studies Quarterly* 24: 12, 117–22.
Ackerly, Brooke. 1999. *Political Theory and Feminist Social Criticism.* Cambridge: Cambridge University Press.
Afkhami, Mahnaz (ed.). 1995a. *Faith and Freedom: Women's Human Rights in the Muslim World.* Syracuse, NY: Syracuse University Press.
   1995b. "Introduction." In Mahnaz Afkhami (ed.), *Faith and Freedom: Women's Human Rights in the Muslim World,* pp. 1–15. Syracuse, NY: Syrascuse University Press.
Afkhami, Mahnaz and Haleh Vaziri. 1996. *Claiming Our Rights: A Manual for Women's Human Rights Education in Muslim Societies.* Bethesda, MD: Sisterhood Is Global Institute.
Barriteau, Eudine. 1995. "Postmodernist feminist theorizing and development policy and practice in the anglophone Caribbean: the Barbados case." In Marianne Marchand and Jane Parpart (eds.), *Feminism, Postmodernism, Development,* pp. 142–58. New York: Routledge.
Basu, Amrita. 1995. "Introduction." In Amrita Basu (ed.), *The Challenge of*

Local Feminisms: Women's Movements in Global Perspective, pp. 1–21. Boulder, CO: Westview Press.

Bruce, Judith. 1989. "Homes divided." *World Development* 17(7): 979–91.

Bumiller, Elisabeth. 1990. *May You Be the Mother of a Hundred Sons: A Journey Among the Women of India*. New York: Fawcett Columbine.

Bunch, Charlotte. 1990. "Women's rights as human rights: toward a re-vision of human rights." *Human Rights Quarterly* 12: 486–98.

   1994. "Strengthening human rights of women." In Manfred Nowak (ed.), *World Conference on Human Rights, Vienna, June 1993: The Contribution of NGOs Reports and Documents*, pp. 32–41. Wien: Manzsche Verlags- und Universitatsbuchhandlung.

   1995. "Transforming human rights from a feminist perspective." In Julie Peters and Andrea Wolper (eds.), *Women's Rights, Human Rights: International Feminist Perspectives*, pp. 11–17. New York: Routledge.

Bunch, Charlotte and Niamh Reilly. 1994. *Demanding Accountability: The Global Campaign and Vienna Tribunal for Women's Human Rights*. New Brunswick: The Center for Global Leadership.

Charlesworth, Hilary. 1994. "What are 'women's international human rights?' " In Rebecca J. Cook (ed.), *Human Rights of Women: National and International Perspectives*, pp. 58–84. Philadelphia: University of Pennsylvania Press.

Collins, Patricia Hill. 1997. "Comment on Hekman's 'Truth and method: feminist standpoint theory revisited': where's the power?" *SIGNS: Journal of Women in Society and Culture* 22: 375–81.

Convention on the Elimination of All Forms of Discrimination Against Women. 1979. G.A. Res. 34/180, U.N. Doc. A/Res/34/180. Adopted 18 December 1979.

Cook, Rebecca J. 1994. "Women's international human rights law: the way forward." In Rebecca J. Cook (ed.), *Human Rights of Women: National and International Perspectives*, pp. 3–36. Philadelphia: University of Pennsylvania Press.

Copelon, Rhonda. 1994. "Intimate terror: understanding domestic violence as torture." In Rebecca J. Cook (ed.), *Human Rights of Women: National and International Perspectives*, pp. 116–52. Philadelphia: University of Pennsylvania Press.

Diamond, Larry. 1994. "Rethinking civil society: toward democratic consolidation" *Journal of Democracy* 5(3): 4–17.

Friedman, Elisabeth. 1995. "Womens' human rights: the emergence of a movement." In Julie Peters and Andrea Wolper (eds.), *Women's Rights, Human Rights: International Feminist Perspectives*, pp. 18–35. New York: Routledge.

Goetz, Anne Marie. 1995. "The politics of integrating gender to state development processes: trends, opportunities, and constraints in Bangladesh, Chile, Jamaica, Mali, Morocco, and Uganda." UNRISD Occasional Paper #2, Geneva.

Halim, Asma Mohamed Abdel. 1995. "Challenges to the application of international women's human rights in the Sudan." In Rebecca J. Cook (ed.), *Human Rights of Women: National and International Perspectives*, pp. 397–421. Philadelphia: University of Pennsylvania Press.

Hassan, Riffat. 1991. "The issue of woman–man equality in the Islamic tradition." In Leonard Grob, Riffat Hassan, and Haim Gordon (eds.), *Women's and Men's Liberation: Testimonies of Spirit.* pp. 65–82. New York: Greenwood Press.

al-Hibri, Azizah. 1982. "A study of Islamic herstory: or "How did we ever get into this mess?" *Women's Studies International Forum* 5(2): 207–19.

International Covenant on Civil and Political Rights. 1966. G.A. Res. 2200 (XXI), 21 U.N. GAOR, Supp. (No. 16) at 52, U.N. Doc. A/6316. Adopted 16 December 1966.

Keck, Margaret and Kathryn Sikkink. 1998. *Activists Beyond Borders: Advocacy Networks in International Politics.* Ithaca: Cornell University Press.

Mayer, Ann Elizabeth. 1995. "Rhetorical strategies and official policies on women's rights: the merits and drawbacks of the New World hypocrisy." In Mahnez Afkhami (ed.), *Faith and Freedom: Women's Rights in the Muslim World*, pp. 104–32. Syracuse, NY: Syracuse University Press.

Mernissi, Fatima. 1991. *The Veil and the Male Elite: A Feminist Interpretation of Women's Rights in Islam.* Reading, MA: Addison-Wesley Publishing Company.

   1992. *Islam and Democracy: Fear of the Modern World.* Translated by Mary Jo Lakeland. Reading, MA: Addison-Wesley Publishing Company.

   1995. "Arab women's rights and the Muslim state in the twenty-first century: reflections on Islam as religion and state." In Mahnez Afkhami (ed.), *Faith and Freedom: Women's Rights in the Muslim World*, pp. 33–50. Syracuse, NY: Syracuse University Press.

Morgan, Robin. 1996a. "The NGO Forum: good news and bad." In *Beijing and Beyond: Toward the Twenty-first Century of Women. Women's Studies Quarterly* 24: 1–2, 46–53.

   1996b. "The UN Conference: out of the holy brackets and into the policy mainstream." In *Beijing and Beyond: Toward the Twenty-first Century of Women. Women's Studies Quarterly* 24: 77–83.

An-Na'im, Abdullahi Ahmed. 1994. "State responsibility under international human rights law to change religious and customary laws." In Rebecca J. Cook (ed.), *Human Rights of Women: National and International Perspectives*, pp. 167–88. Philadelphia: University of Pennsylvania Press.

Nowak, Manfred and Ingeborg Schwarz. 1994: "Introduction: the contribution of non-governmental organizations." In Manfred Nowak (ed.), *World Conference on Human Rights, Vienna, June 1993: The Contribution of NGOs Reports and Documents*, pp. 1–11. Wien: Manzsche Verlags- und Universitatsbuchhandlung.

O'Donnell, Guillermo and Philippe C. Schmitter. 1986. *Transitions from Authoritarian Rule: Tentative Conclusions about Uncertain Democracies.* Baltimore, MD: The Johns Hopkins University Press.

Okin, Susan Moller. 1997. "Culture, religion, and female identity formation: responding to a human rights challenge." Unpublished ms.

   1998. "Feminism, women's human rights, and cultural differences." *Hypatia* 13(2): 32–52.

Pala, Achola O. 1977. "Definitions of women and development: an African perspective." *SIGNS: Journal of Women in Culture and Society* 3(1): 9–13.

Parmar, Pratibha (producer and director). 1993. *Warrior Marks*. A Hauer Rawlence Production in association with Our Daughters Have Mothers, Inc. for Channel 4. New York: distributed by Women Make Movies.
Rose, Kalima. 1992. *Where Women are Leaders: The SEWA Movement in India*. London: Zed Books Ltd.
el Saadawi, Nawal. 1982. "Woman and Islam." *Women's Studies International Forum* 5(2): 193–206.
Selliah, S. 1989. *The Self-Employed Women's Association, Ahmedabad, India*. Geneva: International Labour Office.
Sen, Amartya. 1990a. "More than 100 million women are missing." *New York Review of Books* 37: 61–6.
 1990b. "Gender and cooperative conflicts." In Irene Tinker (ed.), *Persistent Inequalities: Women and World Development*, pp. 123–49. New York: Oxford University Press.
Sen, Gita and Caren Grown. 1987. *Development, Crisis, and Alternative Visions: Third World Women's Perspectives*. New York: Monthly Review Press.
Shaheed, Farida. 1994. "Controlled or autonomous: identity and the experience of the network, women living under Muslim laws." *SIGNS: Journal of Women in Society and Culture* 19(4): 997–1019.
Shaheed, Farida. 1995. "Networking for change: the role of women's groups in initiating dialogue on women's issues." In Mahnez Afkhami (ed.), *Faith and Freedom: Women's Rights in the Muslim World*, pp. 78–103. Syracuse, NY: Syracuse University Press.
Smiley, Marion. 1993. "Feminist theory and the question of identity." *Women and Politics* 13(2): 91–122.
Smith, Jane and Yvonne Y. Haddad. 1982. "Eve: Islamic image of woman." *Women's Studies International Forum* 5(2): 135–44.
Soares, Vera, Ana Alice Alcantra Costa, Cristina Maria Buarque, Denise Dourado Dora, and Wania Sant'Anna. 1995. "Brazilian feminism and women's movements: a two-way street." In Amrita Basu (ed.), *The Challenge of Local Feminisms: Women's Movements in Global Perspective*, pp. 302–23. Boulder, CO: Westview Press.
Taylor, Verta. 1989. "Social movement continuity: the women's movement in abeyance." *American Sociological Review* 54: 761–75.
Tinker, Irene. 1990. "A context for the field and for the book." In Irene Tinker (ed.), *Persistent Inequalities: Women and World Development*, pp. 3–13. New York: Oxford University Press.
Toubia, Nahid. 1995. "Female genital mutilation." In Julie Peters and Andrea Wolper (eds.), *Women's Rights, Human Rights: International Feminist Perspectives*, pp. 224–37. New York: Routledge.
United Nations Convention on the Rights of the Child. 1989. Annex G.A. Res. 44/25 Doc. A/Res/4425. Adopted 20 November 1989.
Universal Declaration of Human Rights. 1948. G.A. Res. 217A(III), U.N. Doc. A/810. Adopted 10 December 1948.
Walker, Alice and Pratibha Parmar. 1993. *The Warrior Marks: Female Genital Mutilation and the Sexual Blinding of Women*. New York: Harcourt Brace.
Walzer, Michael. 1983. *Spheres of Justice*. New York: Basic Books.
 1993. "Objectivity and social meaning." In Martha C. Nussbaum and

Amartya Sen (eds.), *The Quality of Life*, pp. 165–77. Oxford: Clarendon Press.

Winter, Bronwyn. 1994. "Women, the law, and cultural relativism in France: the case of excision." *SIGNS: Journal of Women in Culture and Society* 19(4): 939–74.

Zein Ed-Dīn, Nazīrah. 1982 (1928). "Removing the veil and veiling." *Women's Studies International Forum* 5(2): 221–6.

Part II

Inner edges

10   Democratic liberty and the tyrannies of place

Douglas Rae

Until early 1943, a muddy canal near Pike Road, just outside a hamlet called Pantego, had traced the northern rim of Ardie Winsley's[1] life. On the warm evening of Monday, 5 April, she was sent north by train, beyond Beaufort County and even North Carolina itself. The nine-year-old girl's train ride started in the unfamiliar town of Wilson, on the trunk line running up from Florida to Boston and beyond. The Atlantic Coast Line's Train 76 – known to the road's scheduler as the "Havana Special" – all but forbade her the venture:

When we got on the train, it was like "Never enter!" . . . "Restricted!" . . . . It was like you was sitting there and not knowing where you're going and it was really awful. [Uncle] was there and he had never been that way either so he was all excited . . . But then he was a minister and he was looking forward to it. I just wasn't. I was unhappy the whole trip.[2]

Train 76 carried Ardie and her reverend uncle out of Carolina about dusk, and ran on through the darkened silence of Virginia. Richmond, Washington, Baltimore and a score of lesser towns passed in darkness before dawn came near 30th Street Station, Philadelphia. As she tells the story, it is easy to imagine Ardie glued in fascination at the metallic gloom of Trenton, Elizabeth, and Newark, to say nothing of the sub-riparian rush beneath the Hudson and into the catacombs of New York's Penn Station. By late morning, Ardie's train ran out of Connecticut marshlands and delivered her to a gray city of 160,000 strangers.

Place matters

The Winsleys' carefully orchestrated trip carried the family across many boundaries – from south to north, farm to city, from familiar customs to

---

[1] Her maiden name in tricked up spelling.
[2] The story of Ardie's journey was first told to me in November 1988, on several extended occasions in 1989, and during a Fourth of July visit to Beaufort County in 1993. Unless otherwise indicated, direct quotes are from the first interview. The train's name and schedule is inferred from the *Official Guide of the Railways and Steam Navigation Lines of the U.S., Puerto Rico. Canada, Mexico, and Cuba* (1943: 539).

a world of strange ways, from familiar dialect to the stilted sound of urban voices. The family belonged to the vanguard of a great migration, which brought roughly 150,000 southern blacks north annually from World War II's industrial boom until the mid 1970s. It was a trip aimed at liberty of the most concrete and specific sorts. The destination was chosen by Ardie's mother Mary and her aunt Sue, partly because they had heard about the high-paying jobs, driven by the war effort, and partly to escape the paternalism of Beaufort County, a place where being black in 1943 scripted one's place and prospects in some detail, with no serious chance for editorial revision. They might have chosen any of perhaps fifty northern cities – Detroit, Chicago, Cleveland, New York, Indianapolis, Pittsburgh, Philadelphia, Newark – for similar reasons and with roughly equivalent prospects of success; and, having selected New Haven, the Winsleys could have picked any of perhaps fifty city blocks on which to establish a home. But there were a thousand other city blocks not open to them, or to anyone else with no capital, no documented history of steady employment, no ready cash, no access to social security, and a black skin. It was within these constraints that her mother and aunt had signed the family on as subtenants in an upstairs flat in the heart of a low-rent, open-city neighborhood. Ardie recalls the shock of her arrival:

> It was at 30 Gregory Street. At the end of Dixwell Avenue. And I looked at it and I said "No!" I didn't want to see anyone else but my baby brother and sister. And it wasn't pretty to me and I didn't want it. When I came in my mother was working. My brother was there and my sister and my aunt. I knew all of them, but it wasn't my cup of tea.

The flat on Gregory Street stood at the corner of Ashmun Street, which led north toward the Winchester plant, where more than 20,000 hands turned out the weapons of World War II, and south to Majestic Laundry where Mary Winsley worked in the pressing room. Just beyond the industrial laundry, visible across the Grove Street cemetery, was the campus of Yale University. By 1943, that cemetery had come to span the full height of the American class structure. On the burial ground's southern edge, Yale stood ready to admit, educate, and credential three Presidents – Bush, Ford, Clinton – during the Winsleys' fifty-year stay in New Haven. Yale's faculty and administrative staff – all white, nearly all male – lived primarily in a narrow corridor stretching north from Grove Street along Whitney Avenue, an area screened off from the more open neighborhood on the cemetery's other side.

The Dixwell corridor was a quite ordinary working-class neighborhood in 1943, with perhaps 5,000 frame houses – many of them double-deckers – and with a communal life wrapped around the massive

Table 10.1.

	Trip frequency	
Length		
	Long distance	Short distance
Generational time	(1) Migration	(2) Enclave-seeking
Daily or weekly time	(4) Cosmopolitanism	(3) Commuting

demand for labor generated by Winchester and its suppliers. Its people came from southern Italy, from the American south, from Germany and Russia. Like the Winsleys, they were here to be on their way up: and for most, up meant out. This was true in the 1940s, and became more obviously true with the passage of time. Winchester would decline, recover during the Korean conflict, and eventually close. Those with jobs and savings would leave, and Elm Haven public housing – just next to the Winsleys' original flat – would be transformed from a temporary residence for working families into the familiar role of public housing today, a long-term stay for people of color living beneath the lower edge of the mainstream economy. For nearly everyone in Dixwell, the virtually universal American linkage of mobility with liberation was a given.

The trips which brought the Winsleys – like, say, the Forscinni family or most others – to Dixwell were one of three classical moves which define the spatial economy of American liberty. In table 10.1, up–down distinguishes between very infrequent and very frequent trips, while left–right distinguishes longer from shorter trips. Daily or weekly travel over long distances – cosmopolitan jet-setting – has its importance in understanding the upper reaches of American liberty, but for present purposes, attention should be focused on the other three cells.[3]

Migration

The Winsleys' 1943 trip was an act of radical departure, the abandonment of one society for another. Theirs was a story no less dramatic than the immigrant stories of Europeans from Sicily or the Ukraine arriving at Ellis Island. It is the sort of venture a family – most of all a poor family – cannot afford to take lightly or often. It is the sort of trip which can be

---

[3] I, of course, recognize that table 10.1 is far from exhaustive, either in its time–distance schema or in the stories I have elected to emphasize for each of its cells. It is meant as a short-hand or ideal-type condensation of a specific historical process in the twentieth-century United States.

justified only by achieving a major payoff. I will shortly interpret the required payoff as a realization of democratic liberty.

Enclave-seeking

Migration *within* a region, undertaken with the specific purpose of joining a relatively closed community, is what I mean by enclave-seeking. The classic form is, of course, movement from central city to a more or less exclusive suburb, but there are other instances, including central-city gated communities, and high-rise condominia in downtown districts. Detroit's Victoria Park would be a defining instance of the inner-city gated community, and the well-appointed apartments along Chicago's north lakeshore neighborhoods would pretty much typify the latter. Enclave-seeking is dramatic at these top-notch addresses, but is repeated at lower and lower levels everywhere in a way which defines the nation's spatial hierarchy.

Commuting

The revolutionary impact of automobile travel, reaching full force with the Highway Act of 1921, and continuing unabated since, has allowed developers to detach residential living from the workplace in every region of the US (and much of the developed world). This has made it quite unnecessary for people with privileged incomes to confront those without, and has allowed three generations of real-estate developers to construct a hierarchy of neighborhoods in every urban region. Enclave-seeking, made economically viable by commuting, becomes the definitive move in most family histories. With the emergence of the "virtual office," even the car trip to work may become less essential to future developments. The resulting regional hierarchies form a larger system of spatial separation constituting a definitive feature of the US political system. This "viacratic hierarchy," based on differential access to place and movement among places, goes a long way toward explaining the futility of integration efforts that followed *Brown v. Board of Education* (1954), and the continuing isolation of families like the Winsleys and the Browards. This phenomenon is explored briefly below (section on "Liberty's viacratic hierarchy").

Democratic liberty

Where its promise is fully realized, freedom begins at the sidewalk. People are at liberty in walking to the store, talking with neighbors, greeting strangers with trust and good cheer, rearing their children hour by hour, seeking and performing work, enjoying the use of property, finding ways to become what they want to be. These are all things done in real and specific places, places as singular as, say, 135 Webster Street in New Haven, Connecticut.[4] Over the years when Ardie Broward (née Winsley) lived with her children at 135 Webster, her liberty (and theirs) depended as a practical matter on what happened in its narrow hallway, behind its tiny yard, at the elementary school around the corner, and in the rest of the Elm Haven public housing development which surrounded and defined her home. While intangible freedom may travel from one place to another on the power of ideas and laws alone, these very specific liberties are to be fought and won in the places where their beneficiaries live, and can be made real in no other way.

These tangible liberties are never neatly and directly determined by the grand decisions of government. Thus, for example, the US Supreme Court would decide the famous case of *Brown v. Board of Education* (1954) while the Browards went about life on Webster Street. It would be litigated while they continued to live there and at other places in the increasingly segregated Dixwell corridor of New Haven. The question of school segregation which *Brown* addressed would bear heavily on the lives of her children – mainly, as it turned out, in the negative, since the schools they attended remained almost totally segregated as the years went by. More than forty years later another court case, *Shef v. O'Neil* (1996) would quite abstractly require school integration in Connecticut, but would provide no serious means for enforcing that goal.

Over the *Brown* decades, the American hierarchy of neighborhoods was maturing with the help of automobiles, highways, cheap gas, and all the things these permitted – for our purposes, enclave formation and the differential freedom provided by commuting. In 1954, the US was already an automotive civilization with 58.5 million motor vehicles running on 2.2 million miles of paved road. By the 1990s, more than 190 million motor vehicles (some, to be sure, mere motorbikes, others trucks and the like) were at liberty on 3.9 million miles of asphalt and cement (US Department of Commerce, *Statistical Abstracts, and Historical Data* 1994). There is no doubt that the scope of legally permissible segregation – the *de facto* component of it – expanded with the increasing dominance of car travel, allowing as it did a finely detailed hierarchy of neighborhoods in and around any American city.

---

[4] Here Ardie Winsley has grown up, married, divorced, and begun to raise her children. 135 Webster is just 300 yards from her original Gregory Street address, and is part of the Elm Haven public housing development.

In the 1950s – and in every week since then – far more immediate and specific questions of liberty took on greater urgency for the Browards and others like them. Could Ardie, or her mother Mary, get to the store on Dixwell Avenue and home safely? Could her daughter Barbara find opportunity and badly needed encouragement at Winchester Elementary? Could her son Newell get sincere consideration for a dining hall job over at Yale? Would the little TV set still be on its table in the living room when the family got back from its long-planned Fourth of July trip to North Carolina? Would Ardie's dollars open the same opportunity to move into a better building on a quieter street as would the dollars of a white woman? These are all questions about the liberty of one family, living in one neighborhood of a single city. Yet this chapter is about the promotion and preservation of such tangible liberties for that family and for others like it living in thousands of other American neighborhoods.

Liberty has from the beginning functioned as the anthem of American civic life – almost always honored in the libretto, sometimes honored also in the practice. In the earliest decades of European occupation, liberty's claim was staked against religious coercion across the Atlantic (although no small measure of doctrinal coercion was to be found in the puritan colonies of New England). In the formation of the United States (1776 to, say, 1791), liberty was the central prize sought and won (although, to be sure, the institution of slavery was inscribed openly upon the Constitution of 1789). In the era beginning with Abolitionism, running forward through the Civil War and Reconstruction, the great cause of liberty meant the end of slavery and the spread of freedom to former slaves and their descendants. The civil rights movement (1954–68) was a belated and only partially successful attempt to complete that effort. Parallel movements on behalf of women, Hispanic Americans, gay or lesbian persons, and the handicapped have all in one way or another sung the anthem of liberty in recent years.

By clearing out a little space where we are able to make choices on our own, freedom allows us quite literally to become ourselves and invites us to stand up for what we make of our lives. Liberty – meaning that each of us is in some essential ways free from coercion by others[5] – is the basis on which we hold one another accountable in civil society. Where we are free in principle only, these freedoms may be thought to be intangible. Where we are free in actuality, given our concrete position in the world,

---

[5] Recognizing the great complexity of words such as "liberty" and "freedom," I follow the usage proposed by Hayek's classic work. This very conservative view is at pains to distinguish freedom from power and wealth, which suits my analytic purpose nicely. It also should comfort those conservative readers who fear left-handed sophistry in the use of these ideologically precious words. See Hayek 1960.

freedoms become tangible. It is in this tangible form that liberty allows us to become ourselves and makes us properly accountable for our lives as we chose to make them. What I decide freely – without coercion – is what I must be prepared to defend. Where you and I both enjoy tangible liberty, each may justly demand that the other respect her or his right not to be coerced by the other. Given even a modest space of freedom, I can very realistically be expected to gauge my actions against the rights of others, and to figure my responsibilities toward future demands not yet known or visible. Without such a sphere of liberty, it is difficult to expect of me a well-disciplined respect for the rights of others, and even more difficult to suppose that I will act prudently to enlarge my own opportunities in the distant future.

The contrast between tangible and intangible liberty is the contrast between what is actual and what should, in principle, be actual. As an example of liberty in principle, the Fourteenth Amendment to the US Constitution provides for "equal protection of the laws" for all citizens. Leaving aside a library full of juridical complications, the principle here includes the notion that laws which secure individuals against violent coercion in everyday life should be equally available to all. This liberty-in-principle may be made tangible in everyday life by even-handed enforcement and other supporting measures as may be required. For white middle-class families, living in middle-class neighborhoods, liberty-in-principle has generally been made tangible in practice. In contrast, such liberty remained an abstraction for blacks who came into differences of opinion and interest with whites. Thus in Gunnar Myrdal's 1944 *American Dilemma*:

quite apart from laws, or even against the law, there exists a pattern of violence against Negroes in the South upheld by the relative absence of fear of legal reprisal. Any white man can strike or beat a Negro, steal or destroy his property, cheat him in a transaction and even take his life, without much fear of reprisal . . . There is little that Negroes can do to protect themselves, even where they are a majority of the population. They cannot easily secure the protection of police or court against white men. They cannot secure the protection of employers against white men, unless the latter are poor and have had a bad reputation. They can, of course, strike back but they know that means more violent retaliation, often in an organized form and with danger to other Negroes. (Myrdal 1944)

Under these conditions, liberty-in-principle is radically inferior to liberty of a tangible kind. A major accomplishment of the late twentieth century has been to bring principle and practice more closely into line in the protection of blacks and other minorities against violent aggression by race-conscious whites. This is not, as we will see, quite enough to sustain a tangible liberty for those blacks (and whites) who are left at risk to violent aggression by other blacks (and whites) in neighborhoods where the law's protection is radically deficient.

A lawsuit seeking damages for government's failure to protect a homicide victim against a known predator produced a 1982 ruling by Richard Posner whose notion of liberty is the very soul of intangibility. The state of Illinois had released homicidal maniac Tommy Vanda, requiring that he report to a clinic near the Oak Park home of Margie Bowers, whom he eventually killed. Admitting that the Fourteenth Amendment rules out murder by agents of government itself, Posner argues that:

there is no constitutional right to be protected by the state against being murdered by criminals and madmen. It is monstrous if the state fails to protect its residents against such predators but it does not violate the Fourteenth Amendment or, we suppose, any other provision of the Constitution. The Constitution is a charter of negative liberties; it tells the state to let people alone; it does not require the federal government or the state to provide services, even so elementary a service as maintaining law and order. Discrimination in providing protection against private violence could of course violate the equal protection clause of the Fourteenth Amendment. But that is not alleged here. All that is alleged is a failure to protect Miss Bowers from a dangerous madman, and as the state of Illinois has no federal constitutional duty to provide such protection its failure to do so is not actionable. (*Bowers v. DeVito*, 686 F.2d 616 (1982), quoted in Tribe 1985)

This ruling is a credible, or at any rate entirely conventional, rendering of the constitutional question. Judge Posner is careful *not* to deny that the state's release of criminally insane Thomas Vanda created a risk to someone somewhere. He even admits that Vanda posed a risk to Margie Bowers, but not a targeted and specific risk:[6]

We do not want to pretend that the line between [state] action and inaction, between inflicting and failing to prevent the infliction of harm, is clearer than it is. If the state puts a man in a position of danger from private persons and then fails to protect him, it will not be hard to say that its role was merely passive; it is as much an active [culprit][7] as if it had thrown him into a snake pit. But the defendants in this case did not place Miss Bowers in a place or position of danger; they simply failed adequately to protect her, as a member of the public, from a dangerous man.

Posner's opinion greatly understates our aspiration for American life and the real purposes of constitutional government.[8] In suggesting that the Constitution does not "require the federal government or the state

---

[6] The state of Illinois had released Vanda with the stipulation that he visit a mental health clinic near the victim's home regularly.

[7] Posner's word here is "tortfeasor."

[8] See Tribe 1985, which thoughtfully places the *Bowers* case in the broader context of constitutional debate on state action.

to provide services, even so elementary a service as maintaining law and order," Posner is perhaps right technically yet wrong in a more fundamental way. The basis for the authority of governments, more fundamental even than the Constitution itself, must include a benefit of assured liberty to the law-observant citizenry. Whether one reaches back for John Locke, Thomas Hobbes, or Jean-Jacques Rousseau, or consults John Rawls, Robert Nozick, or Bruce Ackerman in our own time, no serious theory of government suggests that the state is entitled to demand obedience and a monopoly on the use of force in exchange for, say, chaos and disorder. This much goes for a quite wide range of societies, including all of the advanced democracies. It applies with special force to the United States, since the prized ideal of liberty stands at the very core of American thought.[9]

Very simple "democratic liberties" are among the most fundamental purposes of governance. The specific details vary between places and moments of history, but the broad requirements persist. The nub of the argument runs as follows. First, society can work only if most of us, most of the time, manage to lead responsible, productive lives within a system of laws which protect the rights of others. We are expected to do this under conditions which include crowded streets, frequent encounters with strangers, the complicated logistics of family life, the need to educate our children, the necessity to accumulate assets in anticipation of hard times and old age, and the need to feel oneself to be a dignified member of some community. Doing these things is what counts as holding up one's end of the bargain in civil society. If we are to do these things, then we must be granted certain key assurances, certain democratic liberties, which provide the basis for responsible conduct by each person and household. Depending on the shape of a national history, the organization of an economy, and the form of a political culture, there will be variations in the specifics of democratic liberty. But, for America in our own era, democratic liberties include five particulars which are absolutely essential:

1. The right to live in a place of our own choosing, subject only to constraints set by our ability to pay and willingness to do so.
2. The right to move about freely without substantial risk of violent coercion and the fear it brings.
3. The right to educate one's children on terms approximating genuine equal opportunity, meaning that individual effort will be encouraged,

---

[9] Liberty is, in American political history, a "prize" in Stanley Fish's sense of the term – an idea to be won for one cause against another, and used to advance one notion of the public's good as against another. See Fish 1994.

and will lead to adult competence in persons of broadly normal ability.

4. The right of a roughly equal opportunity to compete for good jobs, and to accumulate assets through such investments as home ownership.

5. The right to participate on more or less equal terms in the polities which impose laws and other directives on oneself and one's family.

These are not fancy ideas.[10] They are the kinds of things which drew the Winsleys to New Haven. Democratic liberties – the specifics – are also among the considerations which lead so many of us to engage in enclave-seeking. In the act of moving to a place of their own choosing, these people – including suburbanites – exercised the first democratic liberty. In walking about freely, meeting strangers in the street without being attacked, and without fearing attack, they lived out democratic liberty. The actual protection of liberty, in this instance against violent assault of any sort, is its unequivocal concern. Put another way, democratic liberty is concerned with threats and deprivations from all sources, and is not confined to a governmental subset of sources.[11] It is therefore not a valid excuse to say, as does Posner, that government itself had no affirmative part in violating liberty. Democratic liberty must be liberty from coercion whether it comes from a street bully or a barrister.

[10] Virtually all of the content of essential democratic liberty as understood in this book has, at one time or another, been legislated by Congress and read into the Fourteenth Amendment of the Constitution by the Supreme Court. The Civil Rights Act of 1866, which came before the Fourteenth Amendment, contains most of it. The idea of "substantive due process," particularly as articulated in the *Lochner* case, contains virtually *all* of it. Here, for example, is Judge Peckhan for a unanimous court in *Lochner*: "The liberty mentioned in that amendment means not only the right of the citizen to be free from the mere physical restraint of his person, as by incarceration, but the term is deemed to embrace the right of the citizen to be free in the enjoyment of all his faculties; to be free to use them in all lawful ways; to live and work where he will; to earn his livelihood by any lawful calling; to pursue any livelihood or avocation, and for that purpose to enter into all contracts" (quoted in Gunther 1991).

[11] The idea of liberty being a valuable political weapon, it is not shocking to discover a considerable history of conflict over its meaning. One pole in the historical debate defines liberty as "negative" with respect to a single source of potential intervention, typically intervention by government. See, for instance Berlin 1969; Friedman 1980; Hayek 1960; Nozick 1981. This view does not, as it happens, turn out to have a great deal of cohesion, except a general tendency to favor market-based patterns of allocation over government-driven ones (a distinction which is itself quite problematic in light of the entitlements created for market players by government, as in the notorious instances of banking insurance and cost-plus contracting). Looked at closely, most of these views *take democratic liberty for granted* in portraying the behavior of free individuals. A second position, which makes a more explicit statement of democratic liberty, treats liberty as pertaining to all or most sources of potential interference. See, for instance, Bay 1965; Dewey 1935; Hampshire 1975; Macpherson 1962; Mill 1956 (1859); Wolff 1970. For broad analysis of the conceptual battlefield, see Fish 1994; Raz 1986; Shapiro 1986.

This is a stringent requirement. Indeed, as a general rule, it is liberty which formal government cannot secure without active commitment from private citizens. With respect to the fundamental freedom from forcible attack and from the fear of it, Jane Jacobs long ago set things right about what can be expected of government's main arm for law enforcement:

The first thing to understand is that the public peace – the sidewalks and street peace – of cities is not kept primarily by the police, necessary as police are. It is kept primarily by an intricate, almost unconscious, network of voluntary controls and standards among the people themselves, and enforced by the people themselves. (Jacobs 1961: 31–2)

Democratic liberty is meant to be liberty in fact, liberty as a set of choices which can actually be made and carried out.[12] This is not the sort of fact which God creates, or which is cultivated by the invisible hand of market competition. It is the sort of fact that is created by the formation of deeply textured relationships of trust among persons living in neighborhoods. Democratic liberty can be realized as fact only where such trust develops and prospers over time. I will call this textured habit of trust "neighborhood capital."[13] Its essential feature is the way trust allows cooperation without supervision, and this in turn allows support for the specific democratic liberties required by each individual and household. The democratic liberties, in turn, allow behavior which further reinforces trust, so that neighborhood capital is replenished over time. This dramatically localizes the fulfilment of liberty so that place and neighborhood become central determinants. This is the second feature of democratic liberty – its dependence on community support at the neighborhood level. It remains true, of course, that support of regional and even national scope may also be required – as, for instance, with educational opportunity – but in every instance highly localized support is a necessary element.

Democratic liberty is defined and tested from what would once have been called the common man's perspective, not from a judicial or administrative one. Liberty for ordinary people going about the business of regular life is what counts, and only through understanding of their concrete circumstances can the realization of liberty be confirmed. Liberty at this level is quite frequently invisible to governmental decision-makers, even to decision-makers at a local level. This is because it

---

[12] This is not to say that democratic liberty can remove all risk from life, for it cannot and does not pretend to do so. Indeed it guarantees no form of success or gratification. It just assures people of a minimal base from which to seek these things.

[13] This term is used here as a species of "social capital." See, especially, Putnam 1993; Coleman 1990. The intuition traces itself to Jacobs (1961: 189), who is an early user of the term "social capital."

depends on information of many kinds, and on the bundles of facts which form around very specific localities. It is one thing to know the average or general state of a ward or census tract and a very different thing to know about trouble at the corner of Dixwell and Webster, or within the walls of an apartment nearby. It is yet another thing to see that trouble from the eyes of, say, the Broward family. This is one of the reasons why government alone cannot be expected to sustain democratic liberty – though it can do much better at holding its end up than it does now.

Last but not least, democratic liberty should be liberty for all. But it is not, as things stand in American life today, anything like universal in its distribution. The reader no doubt shares the author's outrage at the release of Thomas Vanda, and its deadly consequence for Margie Bowers. Even the chilling effect on her neighbors produces rage if you stop and think long enough. This case is however, utterly unusual, since it constitutes a shattering of freedom in just the sort of place where democratic liberty has the greatest depth of support, and the fewest threats to defeat. The plight of Margie Bowers, like that of Nicole Simpson, is shocking exactly because it occurs in a place where such events are rarest. Our major concern is with the shattering of democratic liberty in places where this implies no shock, and where people are sometimes too worn down to see it as remarkable.

Why should liberty be conceived in such a literal, fact-observant way? Because this is society's part of the deal with each of us. A free society offers each of us this bargain: we will respect your liberty if you will respect the liberties of others. Where the liberty offered is tangible, it is entirely fair to demand acceptance of its terms by everyone as a condition of adult membership in the community. It must, however, be made real and practical in the face of life's facts as they emerge – beginning at the sidewalk and working our way up from there. It is perfectly consistent with the demands of a free society that some households should have much larger incomes than others; it is consistent with the demands of a free society that some should have opportunities based on talent which others do not possess; it is characteristic of a free society that some make wise choices and others foolish ones; but it is inconsistent with the demands of a free society that some should enjoy the tangible rights and opportunities which dignify them as full and accountable members of the community while others do not.

Liberties may, of course, be tangible for some people and intangible for others, depending on their incomes, talents, and connections to people with power and influence. The liberty to eat in an expensive club, for example, has a realizable (tangible) value for people with money, and not for those without. Such a liberty is no less valid for those able to exercise it than any other, but it cannot be mistaken for a generally satisfactory model of liberty for all. It is a case of liberty-in-principle for all, liberty in practice for some. Similarly, the right to compete for admission to an elite university is an invaluably tangible liberty for persons of talent and training sufficient to achieve success. It is also of value as a signal to young people who may be motivated to develop latent talent through years of hard work; and it is of value to perfect strangers who may decades later benefit from the application of intellectual powers so developed for, say, the practice of medicine or neighborhood organizing. But it is not, and can never be, a tangible liberty for persons without the required measure of developed intellectual and academic skills.

It is characteristic of a free society that individuals are free-in-principle to do these things with others, but free-in-practice to do them only with others who make the same choice under specific terms at a given time and place. Thus, in the case of selling you a used 1989 Saab with many dents and bruises, I have a perfect (and tangible) right to ask $10,000 and you have an equally tangible right to send me packing. You have a perfect right to offer $50, and I have the same right to refuse. My right to actually sell you the vehicle is contingent on your acceptance of my terms, and vice versa. Similar reasoning applies to everything we might do together, from shooting craps or playing basketball to making love or playing a duet. In the slightly flippant words of Robert Nozick, "From each as he chooses, to each as he is chosen."

It may well be that Emma Lazarus's poem asks more than we are prepared to deliver, but it has reminded visitors to the Statue of Liberty for more than a century that the power of freedom's promise is for everyone: "Give me your tired, your poor, Your huddled masses yearning to breathe free, The wretched refuse of your teeming shores . . ." Any liberty worthy of the name is a patterning of life for all members of a free society, not for some happy class of winners huddled within enclaves of relative privilege. Looking down from such a perch, it is not good enough to say "Give *them* your huddled masses . . ."

Often, perhaps inevitably, we have allowed our vision to be conveniently limited to the viewpoints of those for whom liberty is most readily achieved. Thus, for example, William Julius Wilson writes of the civil rights movement:

it was the black middle class that provided the leadership and generated the momentum for the civil rights movement during the mid-twentieth century. Thus, the concept of "freedom" quite clearly implied, in the early stages of the movement, the right to swim in certain swimming pools, to eat in certain restaurants, to attend certain movie theaters, and to have the same voting privileges as whites. These basic concerns were reflected in the 1964 Civil Rights Bill which helped to create the illusion that, when the needs of the black middle class were met, so were the needs of the entire black community. (Wilson 1978: 21)

Those wider needs were too often unmet, and some of the people who were trapped in places largely unaffected by the legal victories of the 1960s expressed the omission with burning rage.[14] The 1967 urban riots which foreshadowed the close of the civil rights era were of course complex in their origins, and hence are open to wideranging interpretation. Surely they had something to do with the perception of new possibilities for personal freedom, starkly contrasted with actual conditions at sidewalk level.

What the "civil disturbances" of that summer suggest most obviously in retrospect is what we may call a *"geography of liberty."* Where did they occur? In cities such as Detroit, Newark, Buffalo, Washington, New York, Minneapolis, Milwaukee, Chicago, Houston, Tampa, Cincinnati, Atlanta, New Haven, Birmingham, Flint, Syracuse, Toledo, Philadelphia, and Hartford. And where, within these cities, did the violence erupt? In places such as Detroit's 12th Street, New York's Spanish Harlem, central Newark's vast superblocks of public housing. In New Haven the most dramatic events began on Congress Avenue, but included many other low-income neighborhoods, including Dixwell Avenue just in front of 135 Webster Street.[15] These were places where the liberating effects of the civil rights movement were realized in rhetoric, yet scarcely detectable in local practice. The violence which occurred that hot summer was, it should be remembered, directed symbolically at mainstream America, but in actual fact drew blood largely from low-income persons of color living in very specific and confined sections of urban America. In many instances, the historical record reveals a systematic effort to *preserve by force* the boundaries between these neighborhoods and other places. Thus, for example, a UPI wire service story from 16 July reports that:

Human and barbed wire barricades virtually sealed Newark from its suburbs . . . National Guardsmen were stationed at street corners along a one-mile stretch of the border between Newark and Irvington. Barbed wire was hastily erected on some corners and orders were issued to permit only police and guardsmen into an ever-widening cordoned-off area of trouble.[16] (UPI 1967)

---

[14] Most of the people living in riot-torn neighborhoods did not participate as rioters or looters; many were active as counter-rioters. See Kerner 1988.

[15] The 1968 Kerner report remains a useful source of data on these events. According to that report, the largest disturbances occurred in eight cities: Buffalo, Cincinnati, Detroit, Milwaukee, Minneapolis, Newark, Plainfield, and Tampa (Kerner 1988: 158).

[16] The piece ran as "Newark Area Hit" on page 2 of the *New Haven Register*.

As may be imagined, the point of these barriers was not to keep curiosity-seeking suburbanites from strolling into the burning streets of inner-city neighborhoods. The point was, of course, to keep the trouble and its perpetrators in their places. These barriers sketched out the spatial course of liberty in the 1960s at sidewalk level. Three decades later, as we will see, the geography of tangible liberty follows closely similar contours of urban America.

Inequality rising

Of all the commentaries left over from the 1960s, very few strike closer to the bone than those of Daniel Patrick Moynihan. Writing well before the trouble of 1967, he identified a turning point of immense eventual importance:

The civil rights revolution of our time is entering a new phase, and a new crisis. In the first phase, the demands of the Negro American were directed primarily to those rights associated with the idea of Liberty: the right to vote, the right to free speech, the right to free assembly. In the second phase, the movement must turn to the issue of Equality. This dualism, which has always been present in the civil rights movement, simply reflects the dualism of American democracy. From the outset American society has always been committed to the twin ideals of Liberty and Equality ... But over the years Liberty has enjoyed incomparably the more prestige ... Equality has been suffered rather than espoused: a scullery dream more than a parlor principle; Sam rather than John Adams; a style of the frontier and the slum; for the longest while Irish rather than English; now increasingly Black rather than White. As long as Negro demands concentrated on issues of liberty they enjoyed the unquestioned support of centers of power in American society. Even those who resisted did so in practice, rather than on principle: no one can successfully challenge the principle of Liberty in the United States at this time. However, as demands turn toward those associated with Equality, this support can only dissipate ... Here middle-class support begins to dissipate, principles are not clear, consensus does not exist.[17] (Moynihan 1965: 745–6)

Moynihan was, of course, right in both of his major contentions: (1) the liberty–freedom song of earlier civil rights movement was substantially displaced by egalitarian rhetoric in the late 1960s, and (2) support for equalizing the condition of Americans across race and class started out weak and lost strength with the passage of time. We will conclude, I believe, that he is wrong in a third contention embedded in his choice of

---

[17] One problem with this formulation is that liberty, as opposed, say, to privilege, implies for most of us a broadly equal distribution of its rights to all members of a community. This should not obscure the fact that demands for equality can, have, and do run counter to the implications of liberty. On this point, Moynihan's analysis is profoundly correct.

language, namely, that something like equal liberty is possible in the face of limitless inequality in all the rest of life – of which more anon. As he wrote, Moynihan stood in battlements of Lyndon Johnson's "War on Poverty," declared in 1963, fought on too many fronts with too few dollars for too short a period (from 1964 to 1967) – abandoned in frustration and failure just before the election of Richard Nixon as President in 1968. This program's failure had many causes – perhaps most notable was its creation of Community Action Agencies, which seemed to undermine Democratic Party organizations in city govern-ments across the land – but one of them was certainly what Moynihan suggests. There was very limited public support for equalizing the condition of all Americans, even through the amelioration of poverty – especially if that amelioration extends to the "undeserving poor" (Katz 1989). In his implied prediction for the longer future, Moynihan was right beyond his wildest and most self-indulgent imaginings. What he suggested in 1965, we know as history three decades later.

The civil rights era, and the riots of 1967, occurred toward the end of an unmatched stretch of broadly shared prosperity. This period – opening with the end of World War II (1945) and closing with the first OPEC oil crisis (1973) – is aptly designated the "Golden Age" of the twentieth century (Hobsbawm 1994). America's massive high-wage industrial employment base – epitomized by Detroit's automobile in-dustry – came out of World War II running at full tilt to meet years of pent-up demand, and flourished against limited foreign competition in the 1950s and 1960s. Organized labor continued to demand and get wages which allowed millions of working-class families to own homes and enjoy lifestyles associated in most countries with the professional middle class. From the late 1940s up to about 1970, American incomes were growing rapidly and more or less equally across classes. Over those years, people near the bottom and people near the top of the income curve managed nearly to double their real wages.[18] College education became a standard expectation for more and more families, as did the single-family suburban home, connected only by road and car to the central city.

What we have seen since, in the theory and practice of our decidedly capitalist democracy, has been a steady acceleration of inequality in economic outcomes, combined with an erosion of bargaining power for the lower ranks of the national workforce. High-wage industrial

---

[18] Here is a well-supported summary on this point: "Growth in mean family income was very rapid and widely shared between 1949 and 1969. The inflation-adjusted income of a family in the 20th percentile grew by 92 percent, while the income of a family in the 80th percentile grew by 92 percent" (Danziger and Gottschalk 1993: 6).

employment has declined, as lower-wage imports have risen in importance. The union movement has retreated on most fronts outside
government employment, and even there it took a dramatic hammering
after President Reagan's 1981 firing of the striking flight controllers.[19]
Real wages for workers below the mid-point of the economy have
declined generally.[20] It appears that these falling wages are the consequence of increasingly efficient international competition, with low-skill,
exportable jobs being pressed down toward correspondence with overseas alternatives.[21] Inequality in earnings has risen substantially, as
more households find themselves in very low or very high strata, fewer
remaining in the middle.[22] Inequality in wealth has expanded even
faster and farther than inequality in incomes.[23] Economist Paul Krugman's summary of what happened in the 1980s is at once sober and
sobering:

The growth of inequality is startling. While the incomes of the top 1 percent of
families doubled, that of the bottom fifth of families fell by 10 percent. If one
bears in mind that tax rates for the well-off generally fell in the Reagan years,
while noncash benefits for the poor, like public housing, became increasingly
scarce, one sees a picture of simultaneous growth in wealth and poverty
unprecedented in the twentieth century. Even these numbers fail to capture the
full extent of what happened, because they miss the real extremes. The real
compensation of top executives at major corporations is estimated to have
quadrupled from the mid-1970s to 1990; a few thousand investment bankers
and real estate developers made astonishing fortunes. At the other end, the
amount of sheer misery in America has surely increased much faster than the
official poverty rate, as homelessness and drug addiction have spread.
(Krugman 1995: 24)

Deepening inequality has been felt by every racial and ethnic
grouping.[24] Between 1975 and 1992, the average income of the top 5

---

[19] Since the late 1950s, union labor has fallen steadily as a percentage of total
employment. Beginning at roughly 30 percent, it had fallen to about 16 percent by
1993. See Folbre 1995: 1368, display 2.15.
[20] For a twentieth percentile family, real income fell about 5 percent from 1969 to 1989
(compared to its 92 percent increase in the previous twenty years. See Danziger and
Gottschalk 1993: 6.
[21] See, for instance, Kapstein 1996.
[22] Between 1971 and 1991, the Gini index of inequality in family incomes increased by
about 10 percent, which is among the largest shifts in US economic history. See
Commerce Dept 1992: 1369. See also, among many others: Thurow 1966; Levy 1988;
Holmes 1996.
[23] By the 1990 census, the richest 1 percent of US families accounted for 37 percent of
overall net worth. The poorest 90 percent accounted for 32 percent. See Folbre 1995:
display 1.2.
[24] Thus, for instance, both the number of blacks below $5,000 and the number above
$50,000 grew substantially between 1967 and 1990. See Hobsbawm 1994: 407, or see
his source, *New York Times*, 25 September 1992. See also Hacker 1992.

percent among black families would rise by 35 percent from $76,713 to $103,827 (in 1992 dollars.) Over the same period, the average for bottom-fifth black families would fall by almost a third, from $6,333 to $4,225 (again in 1992 dollars) (Wilson 1996: 195, table 7.1). Think of it in dollar ratios. These top blacks were making $12.11 for every $1.00 for bottom fifth black families in 1975. By 1992 the ratio had become $24.40 to $1.00. These startling changes were in some ways most dramatic among blacks, but occurred also among whites, Hispanics, and other groupings.

The ideological ascendance of economic inequality has been equally stunning. In the Republican 1980s, "supply side" economics justified greatly increased advantages for well-educated persons and well-financed organizations. Tom Wolfe's *Bonfire of the Vanities*, depicting the giddy ascendance of New York investment bankers surrounded by a frightening sea of urban poverty, would become a leading emblem of popular culture when it appeared in 1987. The stunning collapse of the USSR and its principal satellites would signal a worldwide shift to market economics, and would reinforce the belief that planned economies aimed at egalitarian income distributions were doomed to failure. No less progressive a figure than John Kenneth Galbraith would sum up informed opinion thus:

The good society does not seek equality in the distribution of income. Equality is not consistent with either human nature or the character and motivation of modern economic systems ... A strong current of social expression and thought has held that there is, or could be, a higher level of motivation if there were an egalitarian level of reward – "From each according to his ability, to each according to his needs." This hope, one that spread far beyond Marx, has been shown by both history and human experience to be irrelevant. For better or for worse, human beings do not rise to such heights. Generations of socialist and socially oriented leaders have learned this to their disappointment and more often to their sorrow. (Galbraith 1996: 59–60)

It is unlikely in the extreme that a general mood of egalitarian idealism will overtake the nation any time soon, or at any time whatever if market economics remain central to every argument. If this is so, and if our concern with democratic liberty remains, it will be necessary to look at the spatial hierarchy of inequality which is fed by the market engine of polarized incomes and rates of accumulation. As Mickey Kaus correctly observes:

We've always had rich and poor. But money is increasingly something that enables the rich, and even the merely prosperous, to live a life apart from the poor. And the rich and semi-rich increasingly seem to *want* to live a life apart, in part because they are terrified of the poor, in part because they increasingly seem to feel that they deserve such a life, that they are in some sense superior to those with less. An increasingly precious type of equality – equality not of money but in the way we treat each other and live our lives – seems to be disappearing. (Kaus 1992: 5)

For Kaus, the disappearing value is equality of respect; for me, it is democratic liberty. Democratic liberty is democratic in so far as its tangible reality is open to all citizens in roughly equal degree. This does not mean identity, for the rich can always find ways to assure their liberties better than anyone else, and the rich will always be with us. It does, however, mean that the basic democratic liberties will be nearer truth than fiction for people living in the poorest of our neighborhoods.

Liberty's viacratic hierarchy

Many of the practical amenities which bring liberty down to the sidewalk are purchasable as features of residential real estate, and families with equal formal liberties are unequally endowed with the power to buy practical ones. Money differences become mobility differences, and mobility differences become differences of liberty. The term "viacratic" is meant to sum up this set of relationships in which the practical gravamen of governance in all its senses comes down to capacity (or incapacity) for the use of roads. Thus, over the course of generations, there emerges a hierarchy of neighborhoods, scaled from high to low in entry price, and from high to low in the realization of tangible liberty. The relationship between prices and liberty is far from simple, certainly far from linear, but ever so real none the less. Neither is it intelligible apart from the broad sweep of urban history in the United States, of which the following six elements are perhaps most central.

Building core density

Urban cores were once highly valued and highly productive, largely because they provided privileged access to nodes of heavy transportation (rail, river, ocean shipping.) So long as light transportation (from shoe leather through horse-drawn vehicles) remained inferior and limited, high-density housing was developed to meet the needs of workers and managers in industry, who had to live near their place of employment. Work, in turn, had to be near relevant shipping facilities. The resulting core neighborhoods sometimes had densities as high as 20,000 persons per square mile, and a correspondingly tight fabric of supporting institutions – ranging from schools and precinct houses to hardware stores and houses of worship. Where densities were lower, they were nevertheless much higher than in surrounding pre-suburban districts. Over time, the core city's physical environment grows more polluted, less attractive to those with savings enough to seek out alternatives.

Undercutting demand for core density

The competitive advantage of central city location for both production and residence has declined continuously over the course of the century now ending. It depended upon the high quality of heavy transportation (e.g. rail) and the low quality of light, more nimble transportation (horse-drawn carriage, trolley, etc.). The alliance of market and government support for automobile travel and suburban sprawl is substantially responsible for ending the economic advantage of core location. Housing develops at a considerable distance from the core, and productive activity itself can shift to perimeter nodes nourished by the interstate highway system. Where the resulting shift of demand for housing is buffered by new generations of in-migration, or where the initial densities were moderate, gentle decline may result without having any terribly powerful strategic importance. In other cases – those with the paradigm-shifting surplus of housing and no prospect of reversal – something quite different must be confronted. Many eastern and midwestern cities – Baltimore, Philadelphia, St Louis, Detroit, Buffalo, New Haven, and Cleveland, for instance – experienced this much more difficult turn of events.

Racial tipping

The arrival of African-Americans from the rural south in northern cities over the years 1940–75 corresponded more or less to the peak period of out-migration toward suburban living (although, contrary to some, "white flight" began too early to fit its name). As lower-income blacks settled in the now-slack core neighborhoods, they inherited the problems left behind by aged housing stocks and industrial sites with declining, even negative economic value. Jobs often fled core city sites to green-field sites outside city limits, and also drifted south and west toward sunbelt states.

Spatial hierarchy and ideology of place

As all this is occurring, urban regions are developing age-differentiated and quality-differentiated neighborhoods, clustered unevenly into municipalities with quite different central tendencies for age and quality of housing stock. The consequence is a more and more differentiated hierarchy of neighborhoods, and of municipalities. Local decision-making is lodged in increasingly homogeneous communities, often with sharply diminished insight as government, civic, and corporate leadership look top-down through the regional hierarchy. The results include:

- segmental democracy with decisions made by and for relatively homogeneous populations in each municipality;
- sophisticated forms of discrimination in real-estate markets supplanting more vulgar practices made unlawful by the civil rights legislation of the 1960s;
- real-estate markets capitalising the value of the practical conditions necessary for liberty.

Evolution of last-resort neighborhoods

With the passage of time, a bottom tier of neighborhoods forms near the old industrial core of northern cities, and is occupied by an increasingly homogeneous cohort of low-income households. An increasing number are single-parent, female-led families with very limited earning power and a spatial separation from most opportunities for employment. In many cases, densities fall sharply in the late twentieth century, leaving a wasteland of virtually unowned land surrounding the remaining homes. A related pattern turns on the increasing tendency of project-based public housing to strain out all but the poorest of the poor, isolating very low-income people from the rest of civil society.

The politics of localism

Increasingly from about 1980 with the Reagan presidency, accelerating with the odd accommodation between "New Democrats" and a Republican Congress, social policy is shifting downward from nation to states and from states to municipalities. The effect is to increase the ease with which advantaged populations can escape the core problems of last-resort neighborhoods.

Map 10.1 shown below depicts median household incomes in Wayne County, Michigan (Detroit and its suburbs), the top fifth in black, the bottom fifth in white. This configuration is utterly typical of most US urban regions, with the very highest incomes arranged in a driving-distance arc around a central core, to which the lowest income households are confined. Additional low-income neighborhoods lie in distant rural zones, and intermediate incomes are to be found in between.

Map 10.2 showing the same area as the first, is calibrated to indicate the confinement of low-income black households (1990 incomes below $5,000) to core areas. All the tracts shown in black ink (323 out of 632

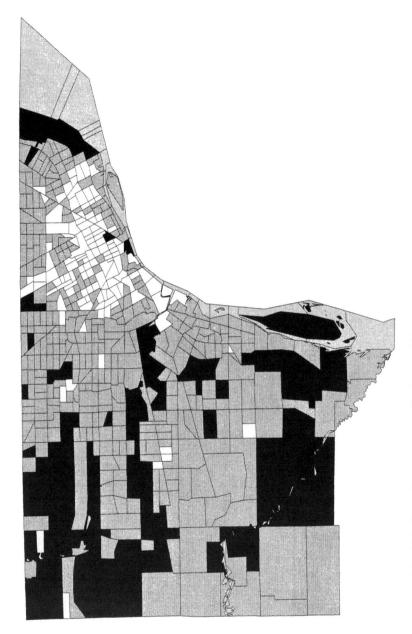

Map 10.1 Wayne County tracts, median household incomes 1990: top 20% black, bottom 20% white, others gray.

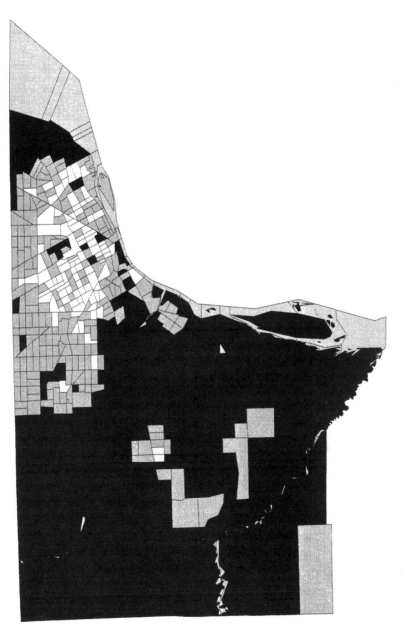

Map 10.2 Wayne County tracts, % of black households below $5,000: below 2% black, above 20% white, others gray

total) have virtually no low-income blacks (fewer than 2 percent of total households). In the tracts shown as white, low-income blacks constitute 20 percent or more of households: these ninety-five tracts contain the great majority of the whole region's low-income blacks, and they occupy neighborhoods of last resort. These are mainly tracts with housing abandonment well above 25 percent of all units, reliance upon public assistance as a plurality occupation, single-parent female-headed households as standard, victimization to crime as a daily prospect. Broadly analogous places can be found in Chicago, New York, Houston, St Louis, Philadelphia, Los Angeles, Washington, Dallas, Pittsburgh, Cleveland, Denver, Baltimore, Milwaukee, Minneapolis, or Kansas City – virtually all older cities outside the deep south, where for historical reasons low-income blacks are spread across the land far more evenly.

In areas like this one, the practical liberties are utterly impracticable. Of the five rights spelled out earlier, only the right to live in a place of one's choosing, subject to ability to pay, is at all real, and it is so only in a hollow and residual way. The right to move about without substantial risk of violent coercion is violated daily. Educational opportunity is minimal, and the majority of children leave adolescence with nothing like adult competence in the skills most essential to earning an income. Participation in the workforce on terms of equal competition is, for all but a few, quite beyond reach; and the meaning of political participation is circumscribed by localism and segmental democracy. People of color may elect some of their number to manage the affairs of core cities, but in the main this occurs just where resources are withdrawn to such an extent that success is all but impossible.

Where's Ardie now?

In fifty years, Ardie twice achieved spatial liberty for herself and the family. Once, in War On Poverty days, she received a federal loan to purchase a modest home on Eagle Street, at the edge of a fine New Haven neighborhood. She and the family kept up payments there for more than a decade. These were good years in better schools for the kids, including the year in which one of her boys – now a college-educated engineer – found himself the chance to attend private school on scholarship. The dream ended when the state of Connecticut discovered a utility lien against the house on Eagle Street, and discovered that welfare dollars were flowing to a homeowner. The relevant agency immediately placed a lien on the property for repayment of AFDC dollars received over the years. These payments were treated as unpaid debt, accumulating compound interest over the years, and the equity she had accumulated in mortgage payments vanished into a lawyer's briefcase.

A second period – running from 1991 into late 1996 – took her to the near-ring suburb of West Haven. There, by pooling incomes with two of her adult children, she managed to rent a modest suburban ranch house in a stable, postwar tract development. There were issues at the neighborhood school about proving that grandson Rasheed really did live there on Cynthia Drive, and the logistics of three jobs with one none-too-reliable old Buick presented a daily struggle. The loss of one job and a backlog of unpaid utilities sent her back to the central city, as a long-term guest of a daughter and her children, where she remains today.

Is her story typical? Of course her life is unique from all others in its details, and in its inner meaning for Ardie and her family. It is not, however, altogether unusual in its relationship to the spatial hierarchy of an urban region. With the exception of her days on Eagle Street and in West Haven, all of her days from the train station in 1943 to the present were spent exactly where the dots on this map happen to fall. All her addresses would be covered by the largest of these dots, indicating the relative homogeneity of her experience. A move north or south a few blocks, west a half mile, but no penetration of enclave spaces except those two.

Democratic liberty and American democracy: adoption of the Twenty-seventh Amendment

Perhaps the most striking feature of American domestic politics over the last four decades of the twentieth century is a nearly complete failure to achieve common purpose among the groups below the midpoint of the economy – the lower-middle class, the working poor, the marginally employed, the so-called underclass. The Democratic Party has discovered that its path to majority status excludes any but the most superficial commitment to the needs of the urban poor (Edsall 1991; see also Greenberg 1996). The GOP has to a very considerable extent based its Congressional strategy on overt hostility to the needs of the urban poor, especially the symbolically visible black urban poor. In so far as political ideology follows relatively narrow self-interest, it is difficult to imagine a systematic strategy which corrects the failures of democratic liberty chronicled above.

Two striking facts need to be addressed in thinking about a way out of

Table 10.2.

Year	Total horsepower x1,000	Automotive as % of vehicular	Vehicular as % of total
1990	34919000	98.97	95.67
1980	28922000	98.91	95.65
1970	20408000	98.68	95.96
1960	11007889	98.98	95.15
1950	4754038	96.57	95.92
1940	2773316	95.83	94.49
1930	1663944	92.10	93.09
1920	453450	76.38	81.10
1900	63952	0.38	41.46
1890	44086	0.00	41.70

this impasse. One is the growing geographic isolation of the liberty-deprived poor. Table 10.2 is one simple summary measure of this phenomenon, namely the percentage of all horsepower in the American economy devoted to automotive travel over the course of the twentieth century.

This two-fold history tells of a society devoting an increasing percentage of total resources to the business of movement, with a simultaneous shift toward the automotive sector of vehicular movement. By 1960, we had all but maximized our commitment to auto travel – 99 percent of 96 percent of the economy's total horsepower being devoted to highway travel in the form of cars, trucks, and buses. This is a commitment so fundamental, so difficult to repeal, that its importance is perhaps understated by imagining it to be the Twenty-seventh Amendment to the Constitution. It is an inarticulate provision, but it sounds like: "In order to reach democratic liberty, purchase a car, purchase a home away from the sight of poor people, and turn the ignition key to your right." Think of a single instance: the room for *de facto* segregation after the *Brown* decision in 1954 as a function of spatial differentiation of regional hierarchies, fueled, as it were, by gasoline. As the economy of movement shifts toward the car, so too does the opportunity for development of enclaves and for the use of commuting to and from these enclaves. If a further shift is to be anticipated – a Twenty-eighth Amendment, if you will – it is toward the movement of information across electronic space as a substitute for actual commuting. This, too, would seem to increase the potential for isolation of a class unable to spend its way into practical democratic liberty.

The other striking fact is the correctness of Moynihan's observation that equality and equalization will not work as ideological configurations of a political movement meant to correct these ills. Liberty is a better bet in rhetoric, and a harder one than it seems in practice.

REFERENCES

Bay, Christian. 1965. *The Structure of Freedom*. New York: Atheneum.
Berlin, Isaiah. 1969. *Four Essays on Liberty*. London: Oxford University Press.
Coleman, James. 1990. *Foundations of Social Theory*. Cambridge, MA: Harvard University Press.
Commerce Dept. 1992. *Money Income of Households, Families, and Persons in the United States: 1991*. Washington, DC: Bureau of the Census.
Danziger, Sheldon and Peter Gottschalk (eds.). 1993. *Uneven Tides: Rising Inequality in America*. New York: Russel Sage Foundation.
Dewey, John. 1935. *Liberalism and Social Action*. New York: G. P. Putnam.
Edsall, Thomas Byrne and Mary D. Edsall. 1991. *Chain Reaction: The Impact of Race, Rights and Taxes on American Politics*. New York: Norton.
Fish, Stanley. 1994. *There's No Such Thing as Free Speech, and It's a Good Thing Too*. New York: Oxford University Press.
Folbre, Nancy. 1995. *The New Field Guide to the U.S. Economic Life in America*. New York: The New Press.
Friedman, Milton and Rose Friedman. 1980. *Free To Choose: A Personal Statement*. New York: Harcourt Brace Jovanovich.
Galbraith, John Kenneth. 1996. *The Good Society: The Humane Agenda*. Boston: Houghton Mifflin Pubs.
Greenberg, Stanley. 1996. *Middle Class Dreams: The Politics and Power of the New American Majority*. New Haven: Yale University Press.
Gunther, Gerald. 1991. *Constitutional Law*. Westbury, NY: Foundation Press.
Hacker, Andrew. 1992. *Two Nations: Black and White, Separate, Hostile, Unequal*. New York, Charles Scribner's Sons.
Hampshire, Stuart. 1975. *Freedom of the Individual*. Princeton: Princeton University Press.
Hayek, Friedrich von. 1960. *The Constitution of Liberty*. Chicago: University of Chicago Press.
Hobsbawm, Eric. 1994. *The Age of Extremes: The Short Twentieth Century, 1914–1991*. New York: Pantheon Books.
Holmes, Stephen A. 1996. "Income disparity between poorest and richest rises." *New York Times*, 4 September, pp. A1, A19.
Jacobs, Jane. 1961. *The Death and Life of Great American Cities*. New York: Vintage.
Kapstein, Ethan B. 1996. "Workers and the world economy." *Foreign Affairs* 75(3): 16–37.
Katz, Michael B. 1989. *The Underserving Poor: From the War on Poverty to the War on Welfare*. New York: Pantheon Books.
Kaus, Mickey. 1992. *The End of Equality*. New York: Basic Books.
Kerner, O. *et al.* 1988. *The 1968 Report of the National Advisory Commission on Civil Disorders*, New York: Pantheon Books.

Krugman, Paul. 1995. *The Age of Diminished Expectations.* Cambridge, MA: MIT Press.

Levy, Frank. 1988. *Dollars and Dreams: The Changing American Income Distribution.* New York: W. W. Norton & Company.

Macpherson, C. B. 1962. *The Political Theory of Possessive Individualism.* Oxford: Clarendon Press.

Mill, John Stuart. 1956 (1859). *On Liberty.* New York: Liberal Arts Press.

Moynihan, Daniel Patrick. 1965. "Employment, income, and the ordeal of the negro family." *Daedalus: Journal of the American Academy of Arts and Sciences* 94: 745–70.

Myrdal, Gunnar. 1944. *An American Dilemma: The Negro Problem and Modern Democracy.* New York: Harper & Row.

New York Times. 25 September 1992.

Nozick, Robert. 1981. *Philosophical Explanations.* Cambridge, MA: Harvard University Press.

Official Guide of the Railways and Steam Navigation Lines of the U.S., Puerto Rico, Canada, Mexico, and Cuba. 1943. New York: National Railway Publications Co.

Putnam, Robert with Robert Leonardi and Raffaella Nanetti. 1993. *Making Democracy Work: Civic Traditions in Modern Italy.* Princeton: Princeton University Press.

Raz, Joseph. 1986. *The Morality of Freedom.* Oxford: Clarendon Press.

Shapiro, Ian. 1986. *The Evolution of Rights in Liberal Theory: An Essay in Critical Anthropology.* Cambridge: Cambridge University Press.

Thurow, Lester C. 1966. *The Future of Capitalism: How Today's Economic Forces Shape Tomorrow's World.* New York: William Morrow & Co.

Tribe, Laurence. 1985. *Constitutional Choices.* Cambridge, MA: Harvard University Press.

United Press International. 16 July 1967.

Wilson, William Julius. 1978. *The Declining Significance of Race: Blacks and Changing American Instututions.* Chicago: University of Chicago Press.

  1996. *When Work Disappears: The World of the New Urban Poor.* New York: Alfred A. Knopf.

Wolfe, Tom. 1987. *Bonfire of the Vanities.* New York: Farrar Strauss Giroux.

Wolff, Robert Paul. 1970. *In Defense of Anarchism.* New York: Harper & Row.

11   Democracy and the politics of recognition

Elizabeth Kiss

One of the liveliest debates engaging democratic theory at century's end concerns the relationship between civic equality and the public recognition of cultural differences among citizens. A number of theorists have begun using the phrase "politics of recognition" (Taylor 1992; Honneth 1992; Fraser 1995a and 1997) to refer to the chorus of claims and aspirations voiced on behalf of groups defined by a sense of shared cultural, national, ethnic, racial, religious, gender, or sexual identity. Proponents of a politics of recognition assert that democratic justice requires affirmative public acceptance of such identities. Mere tolerance of difference is not enough, nor is it sufficient for democratic societies to allow citizens to express different identities in the private realm. Equal moral and political status, and hence democracy, cannot be achieved unless social institutions and sensibilities become more attentive to, and reflective of, cultural differences.

It is important not to exaggerate the historical novelty of the politics of recognition. Democratic struggles have often been fought by, and in the name of, newly assertive identity groups, and democrats have mobilized as much against cultural domination as they have against autocratic rule. For instance, both the European revolutions of 1848 and the anti-colonial struggles of the middle of this century were demands for national or cultural recognition as much as (and often more than) they were efforts to replace autocratic political institutions with democratic ones.

What is new about the contemporary politics of recognition is more a matter of degree than of kind: demands for recognition by identity groups have gained greater immediacy and sharper theoretical focus. A number of historical processes, including increased immigration, colonialism and its aftermath, and the extension of democratic struggles to the domestic and sexual sphere, have brought struggles for recognition closer to home. They feature more and more prominently in the internal political debates of societies which are fully democratic according to standard Schumpeterian criteria. In challenging the status quo in democratic societies, movements for recognition have also explicitly challenged traditional democratic understandings of equal citizenship. According to the ideal-typical conception of a democratic society, it is a social union composed of individuals who enjoy equal civic status and rights in their relations with one another and with the state. The project of democratic equality has often been conceived as involving the progressive elimination of all social distinctions and the creation of an undifferentiated polity of equal individuals. By contrast, the politics of recognition invokes democratic principles of equality to justify what Will Kymlicka has called "group-differentiated" forms of democratic citizenship (Kymlicka 1996).

Does the politics of recognition enhance the project of democratic equality or derail it? Many critics, from progressives such as Todd Gitlin to traditional liberal democrats such as Arthur Schlesinger, have issued warnings about the dangers of a preoccupation with identity and difference (Gitlin 1993; Schlesinger 1992). They argue that a focus on affirming identity produces debilitating political fragmentation, diverts attention from widening material inequality, and leads to a fetishism of identity groups, reinforcing the tendency of such groups to become exclusionary to outsiders and coercive to insiders.

These worries have considerable merit; recent history provides ample proof that political assertions of identity can and do take pathological forms. Nevertheless, it is noteworthy that demands for recognition have arisen within a wide range of democratic movements. The impulse to focus on identity thus comes out of specific practical dilemmas facing people who are struggling for power or resources within different contexts of social inequality. It is a response to experiences of social and political discrimination, inequality, and vulnerability. Awareness of these recognition demands and the circumstances that give rise to them has led a growing number of democratic advocates to argue that traditional democratic frameworks and remedies fail to address some of the processes which prevent citizens from achieving equal status and voice. Of course, all of this may be true without the politics of recognition providing successful or defensible political or legal solutions. But the proliferation of recognition claims within contemporary democratic movements suggests that these claims deserve serious examination for the insights they may bring to the project of democratic equality.

My aim in this chapter is to identify several of these insights, while continuing to emphasize the limitations and potential dangers of a politics of recognition. I examine three ways in which the politics of recognition can enhance democratic theory and practice. First, it can broaden our understanding of sources of inequality by identifying a range of identity-based social and cultural harms which deprive people of equal civic status. Second, it can enhance the institutional repertoire of democratic politics. Efforts to design remedies for identity-based harms have already led to a range of specific proposals for changing democratic practices which, even while we may disagree with some of them, collectively represent an important contribution to democratic theory and practice. The best of these efforts can deepen democratic understandings both of what equal citizenship means and of what is required to institutionalize it within various social contexts. Third, the politics of recognition can teach democrats important lessons in humility, urging us to be vigilant about our prejudices and the ways they can blind us to the needs, vulnerabilities, and legitimate aspirations of those different from ourselves. Humility is also in order, however, for proponents of a politics of recognition. Recognition claims are highly context-specific, and attempts to generalize from them to sweeping accounts of cultural or group "rights to recognition" will almost certainly run afoul of basic democratic values.

Identifying cultural and symbolic sources of inequality

Proponents of the politics of recognition assert that democracy requires affirmative recognition of differences among citizens. But why is such recognition necessary? Some theorists have offered an account of culture as a basic or primary human good, arguing that human well-being depends on people's capacity to express their own, "authentic" cultural identity and to experience an "intact" culture (Taylor 1992 and 1996; Kymlicka 1989). This account is problematic for a number of reasons. It assumes that it is possible to identify a single culture to which a person belongs. But this ignores the cross-cutting complexity of cultural boundaries, the dynamic processes by which identities can gain and lose salience in people's lives, and the ways in which cultural identities are constantly modified (and sometimes created) through political action. The view that culture is a basic good also tends to forget the extent to which cultural values are internally contested, and has difficulty making sense of people's capacity to adopt new cultural identities. Finally, it glosses over the many ways in which culturally sanctioned beliefs and practices can be oppressive, to insiders as well as outsiders.

This is not to deny that cultures shape people's basic beliefs about the sources of well-being, dignity, and value, and hence that actions which demean or destroy cultural practices can cause profound harm. Nor is it to ignore the human suffering which cultural breakdown and forced assimilation have produced, especially in cases of the forced incorporation of traditional societies by more modern ones. But these important examples of harms resulting from disrespect for cultural practices do not entail a positive argument that all cultures deserve respect, nor do they justify the claim that there is a universal need for human beings to express their particular, authentic cultural identity. Such arguments essentialize identity groups, produce a preoccupation with defining and policing cultural boundaries, and legitimate culturally sanctioned patterns of authority and domination regardless of how undemocratic they may be. All of this is deeply troubling from a democratic perspective.

Instead of attempting to defend the view that cultural identity is a basic human good, some recent work on the politics of recognition has begun to focus on identity-based *harms* and their role in creating and sustaining unjust social inequalities. Such harms may occur when membership in a particular group makes people vulnerable to familiar forms of political and economic discrimination, or they may arise through specifically cultural or symbolic processes which deprive people of moral or civic status. Theorists of recognition who focus on identity-based harms argue that democrats have often overlooked the cultural dimensions of oppression. Most contemporary democratic theorists, they contend, conceive injustice in narrowly distributive terms, as a maldistribution of political and legal rights and of economic resources such as property and income. Even democratic theorists who identify core elements of justice which are harder to fit into a distributive framework, such as John Rawls's primary good of "the social bases of self-respect," end up concentrating on goods more easily captured in distributive terms (Rawls 1971: 440; Fraser 1995a: 73.). The problem with these distributive frameworks, according to recognition theorists, is that they miss the ways in which people's status and well-being is influenced by qualitative and interpretive considerations, by culturally authoritative norms and narratives about who and what does, and does not, merit respect.

In a very interesting discussion contrasting the politics of recognition with what she calls the politics of redistribution, Nancy Fraser identifies harms of "misrecognition," which she argues are logically distinct from, though in practice usually intertwined with, unequal distribution of political rights and economic resources. Harms of misrecognition are cultural or symbolic injustices "rooted in social patterns of representation, interpretation and communication" (Fraser 1995a: 71). Examples of misrecognition include cultural domination, which Fraser defines as "being subjected to patterns of interpretation and communication that are associated with another culture and are alien and/or hostile to one's own," non-recognition, which is the process of "being rendered invisible via the authoritative representational, communicative, and interpretive practices of one's culture," and disrespect, "being routinely maligned or disparaged in public cultural representations and/or in everyday life interactions."

Another theorist who emphasizes the role of cultural and symbolic processes in the maintenance of unjust social arrangements is Iris Marion Young. Young identifies what she calls "the five faces of injustice" – exploitation, marginalization, powerlessness, cultural imperialism, and violence – and argues that all five are maintained through symbolic as well as material means. For instance, beliefs about what constitutes respectable versus menial work, or about what forms of work are appropriate to people of a certain race, gender, or ethnicity, support economic hierarchies. Notions of stigma and deviance render some people vulnerable to institutionalized forms of violence. And exclusion from culturally authoritative forms of communication is not only constitutive of what Young calls the injustice of cultural imperialism, but also plays an important role in maintaining conditions in which people are exploited, marginalized, or made powerless (Young 1990: chap. 2).

Fraser and Young disagree over the value of positing a sharp analytical distinction between cultural and material sources of inequality (Fraser 1995b; Young 1997). Fraser acknowledges that, in practice, misrecognition tends to be closely intertwined with political and economic inequalities, and that efforts to remedy misrecognition will usually have a strong redistributive dimension, since they will depend on democratizing access to "the means of interpretation and communication" (Fraser 1989: 164–6). Nevertheless, she argues that it is helpful to draw a dichotomy between recognition and redistribution, for two reasons. First, the harms of misrecognition are at least partially autonomous from material exploitation or deprivation. Cultural domination, non-recognition, and disrespect affect people in ways which are logically distinct from the harms of poverty, political discrimination, or lack of educational opportunity. This becomes clearest in cases of misrecognition in which such traditional distributive injustices play relatively little role. Fraser cites the example of gays and lesbians in the United States, who in her view are not, on the whole, disadvantaged in traditional political or economic terms, but who face systematic cultural and symbolic stigma. Efforts by gays and lesbians to gain public acceptance therefore represent a relatively pure example of the politics of recognition. Second, Fraser argues that drawing the recognition/redistribution dichotomy enables us to better understand some of the tensions which are inherent within the democratic project. According to Fraser, a democratic politics of recognition has its own dynamic, its own logic of means and ends, and under certain conditions these will come into conflict with the internal logic of a redistributive democratic politics. For instance, movements for racial and gender equality have sometimes come to grief over the tension between the difference-affirming logic of the politics of recognition and the difference-denying logic of the politics of redistribution.

Young argues that Fraser's dichotomy between recognition and redistribution is exaggerated and that it distorts social realities more than it clarifies them. She takes issue, for instance, with Fraser's analysis of gay and lesbian activism as a relatively pure case of a democratic politics of recognition, arguing that, while the roots of heterosexism and homophobia may indeed be largely cultural, the goals of gay and lesbian activists include "material, economic and political equality: an end to discrimination in employment, housing, health care; equal protection by police and courts; equal freedom to partner and to raise children" (Young 1997: 158). Young also thinks Fraser's framework exaggerates the tensions between recognition and redistribution. For Young, the politics of recognition should be viewed, not as a separate form of democratic activism with its own logic, but as a means toward the "material goals of equal protection and equal opportunity" (Young 1997: 158). Thus, while it is important to emphasize the cultural dimensions of democratic struggle, the best way to do so, Young argues, is to "reconnect issues of symbols and discourse to their consequences in the material organization of labour, access to resources, and decision-making power, rather than to solidify a dichotomy between them" (Young 1997: 161).

A full assessment of the debate between Young and Fraser is beyond the scope of this chapter, but a few points are worth stressing here. First, Fraser's analysis of misrecognition as a *source* of unjust inequality is illuminating. A society is not truly democratic if it imposes on some of its members, as the price of admission to equal protection and status, the requirement that they deny or hide a deeply felt identity, unless expression of that identity is itself incompatible with democratic equality. The clearest examples of misrecognition occur when people are socially disadvantaged if and only if they engage in, and identify with, socially stigmatized practices such as particular religious observances or sexual practices. The unjust social inequalities which result from misrecognition, as Young rightly stresses, will be political and material, typically including unequal protection and opportunity. However, gay and lesbian activism is an apt example of the politics of recognition, not because the harms gays and lesbians experience have no political or economic dimension, but because their social inequality results from a cultural stigma and would be overcome if cultural changes dissolved that stigma.

Second, Fraser's attempt to isolate the logic of the politics of recognition is also helpful because it highlights how single-minded pursuit of recognition, to the exclusion of considerations of social equality and individual freedom, has deleterious consequences for the democratic project. Conversely, though Fraser does not sufficiently emphasize this point, similar dangers face a politics aimed at achieving distributive equality as an end in itself, as the historical examples of Jacobin and communist excesses demonstrate.

Third, by isolating the harms of cultural domination, non-recognition, and disrespect, Fraser has given greater specificity to the harms of misrecognition. However, more work needs to be done to enable us to distinguish between circumstances in which misrecognition is inimical to democratic equality and those in which processes of cultural domination, non-recognition, and disrespect are morally unproblematic or even appropriate. As different practices, identities, and beliefs come and go, some will become dominant, while others that once enjoyed cultural authority will fade away – so, for instance, the rise of new artistic styles, linguistic conventions, religious movements, and political ideologies entail the displacement of previously dominant ones. Such cultural change usually involves conflict and debate, and participants in debate frequently disparage the practices and beliefs of those different from themselves. Yet these processes of domination, non-recognition, and disrespect, while they may lack kindness or gentility, do not necessarily threaten the moral or civic status of those whose beliefs or practices are being criticized or rendered obsolete. Moreover, when citizens in a democracy are confronted with identities, beliefs, or practices they consider morally abhorrent – for instance, white supremacy or violent pornography – the most appropriate response may be to try to change them through critique or to marginalize them through public disparagement and isolation. In other words, under certain circumstances cultural domination, non-recognition, and disrespect can be appropriate forms of democratic action. A democratic politics of recognition needs, therefore, to be able to distinguish between cases when misrecognition is relatively benign, or even appropriate, and when it is harmful and unjust. Perhaps some identities or cultural differences are so closely linked to social vulnerability that efforts to dominate, ignore, or disparage them will be threats to democratic equality. So, for instance, in a climate of virulent anti-Semitism or homophobia, where Jews or homosexuals are vulnerable to physical attack or intimidation, an article or speech disparaging or ridiculing the habits of Jews or homosexuals can be a powerful resource for social discrimination and marginalization and a catalyst for violence. But similarly negative comments about the habits of golfers may well be viewed as a morally and politically innocuous, even amusing, piece of social satire. This underscores the importance of making democratic equality and respect the regulative ideal of the politics of recognition. Misrecognition is a distinctive social harm, but it becomes a significant social injustice when it is linked to consequences in access to resources, opportunities, power, and voice, and makes people vulnerable to deprivation and abuse. Thus while Fraser's analysis helps to sort out different sources of inequality and injustice, it is Young who best expresses the moral priority which a democratic politics of recognition must give to considerations of equal protection and opportunity. Recognition, Young rightly emphasizes, is a means to equal protection and opportunity, not an end in itself.

Despite their disagreements, Fraser and Young exhibit some important similarities in their approach to the politics of recognition. For both, the appeal to difference arises from a concern with unjust social hierarchies. Both argue that democrats can neither understand nor overcome social inequality without an understanding of the cultural processes which help to constitute and sustain it. Finally, both develop nuanced arguments for how misrecognition can support processes of social subordination.

A politics of recognition centered around cultural sources of harm and inequality, such as the versions developed by Fraser and Young, is a far cry from affirmations of culture as a primary good. It does not assume that cultural identities are fixed, homogeneous, or singular. Nor does it idealize culture, since the harms of misrecognition may be inflicted within as well as across cultures. Finally, and perhaps most importantly, the arguments for recognition developed by Fraser and Young make clear why democrats should be concerned with cultural and symbolic harms in the first place. By focusing on how identity-based harms deprive people of opportunity, status, and voice, these accounts make respect for persons, not for cultures or identities, the centerpiece of their moral concern.

Complex remedies: expanding democracy's institutional repertoire

Just as a detailed analysis of cultural harms contributes to democratic conceptions of injustice, so a fine-grained focus on the political remedies required to address these harms contributes to democratic understanding of the institutional requirements for democratic justice and equal citizenship. While redistributive accounts of democratic justice entail efforts to eliminate, or at least mitigate, social distinctions of class and caste, the politics of recognition calls for social remedies which transcend hierarchies through affirming differences rather than eliminating them. So, for instance, members of stigmatized groups such as gays and Jews demand social respect, and cultural minorities affirm their right to be different, to worship in their own way and teach their children in their own language. Affirmative recognition is at once a means and an end; it enables group members to demand justice and is itself constitutive of justice.

What forms should recognition take? Most arguments for a politics of recognition have been stronger on diagnosis than on prescription. Theorists have argued for a need to take differences into account in democratic practices, but their proposed remedies have been avowedly utopian, such as Nancy Fraser's call for "socialism in the economy plus deconstruction in the culture" (Fraser 1995a: 91), or vague on issues of institutional implementation, such as Iris Young's proposals for group-differentiated democratic participation (Young 1990: chap. 6). It is unclear, for instance, whether Young or Fraser believe that criminal or civil legal remedies should be created to protect vulnerable minorities from egregious forms of misrecognition, making certain forms of hate speech illegal or actionable, or whether such remedies would always be trumped by freedom of speech. Recently, however, efforts to devise remedies for cultural harms have produced a range of specific proposals for democratic institutions, strategies, and practices, which (even when we disagree with them) represent important contributions to democratic theory. What distinguishes the best of these proposals is their specificity: they identify particular harms and devise what Bhikhu Parekh has termed "nuanced and target-specific strategies" to remedy them (Parekh 1994: 101).

Democrats skeptical of the politics of recognition have suggested that all legitimate forms of recognition are already encompassed by individual rights of non-discrimination and free association. Groups subjected to cultural injustice are often discriminated against and denied rights of association, and protection of these rights will go far toward remedying many cultural harms. Nevertheless, struggles for recognition typically involve claims which go beyond demands for non-discrimination and free association, and involve more robust forms of state support or involvement, or substantive changes in policy, legal doctrine, or authoritative cultural narratives.

Take, for instance, the case of the education of deaf children.

Democratic principles dictate that deaf children should be treated as equals. Advocates for the deaf have long argued that equal treatment requires specific attention to the teaching of deaf children, even if this entails additional outlay of resources for them through, for instance, the provision of specially trained teachers. But more recently the debate has centered on how and what deaf children should be taught. One can teach deaf children to speak, though in most cases their speech will remain halting, or, with the same outlay of public resources, one can provide them with the far richer communicative resource of sign language, in which they can attain expressive competence and mastery. Sign language advocates argue that their approach enhances the status and dignity of the deaf by devising a medium of communication that acknowledges and affirms their distinct identity. For them, democratic equality requires a recognition of "deaf culture" and the provision of resources to enable this culture to be cultivated and passed on. Here, the politics of recognition changes the substance of a proposed democratic remedy and challenges culturally authoritative understandings of deafness as nothing more than a misfortune and a disability. The creative remedy of sign language for the expressive disadvantages of deaf people demonstrates how much democratic theory and practice can gain from attentiveness to difference.

However, democratic remedies for cultural harms and vulnerabilities are not easily generalized. The role of contextual judgments in deciding whether democratic equality requires explicit recognition of difference and, if so, in what forms, is particularly evident with gender and ethnic politics. There is, for example, a longstanding debate among feminists over whether gender justice requires gender-neutral or gender-conscious policies. Many theorists have argued that "equal treatment" should not be construed as "uniform treatment," that taking account of gender differences in various contexts is necessary for women to be treated as equals. Guarantees of pregnancy and childbirth leaves and benefits, for instance, may be seen not as departures from a commitment to civic equality but as a way of ensuring that women as well as men have the ability to combine paid employment with raising a family. This reasoning, accepted by the United States Supreme Court, represents a shift in legal understandings of what democratic equality requires in the face of gender difference. This shift has not, however, brought closure to debates over gender-neutral and gender-conscious policies. Instead, it has moved them from the abstract plane of "equality versus difference" to a messier terrain in which complex judgments have to be made about the likely effects of specific policies. So, for instance, in legal debates over whether or not courts should adopt a gender-specific "reasonable woman" standard for adjudicating cases of sexual harassment, feminists who acknowledge that both sides are committed to democratic equality remain divided over whether a gender-specific standard enhances or diminishes women's efforts to attain equal status with men (Abrams 1995).

The democratic rights of members of minority ethnic groups represent a particularly complex set of challenges for the politics of recognition. Ethnicity-based harms and deprivations constitute threats to individual well-being and dignity to a greater or lesser degree in almost all societies. Given that millions of people are rendered socially vulnerable by virtue of their ethnic identity, democrats urgently need to design and support social arrangements that will guarantee equal citizenship for members of minority groups. Moreover, these guarantees must protect not only the right of members of ethnic minority groups to be equal citizens, but also their right to be citizens who are culturally or ethnically distinct. Coerced ethnic or cultural uniformity violates core liberal democratic norms just as enforced religious uniformity does. States which deny people's affirmed ethnic or cultural identities or which make the benefits of equal citizenship contingent on abandoning one's affirmed ethnic or cultural identity violate core democratic norms of equal dignity and respect.

Efforts to devise generalizable institutional protections for ethnic minority communities quickly run into difficulties, however. For instance, in his recent work on multicultural citizenship, largely based on the example of Canada, Will Kymlicka distinguishes sharply between the moral force of recognition claims by national minorities and by immigrant ethnic groups. Kymlicka argues that national minorities such as Native Americans and the Quebecois are entitled to strong self-government rights, but that immigrants have less of a claim to public support for their efforts to maintain their cultural identity. Indeed, he concludes that public subsidies for the ethnic activities of immigrant groups should be seen as a matter of policy, which no one has a right to, or a right against (Kymlicka 1995).

Kymlicka's work is admirable for its close attention to matters of principle and its willingness to offer detailed institutional recommendations. However, his core distinction between national minorities and immigrant groups has come under strong criticism as irrelevant to many other parts of the world. Even in the Canadian context, some have argued that there are immigrant groups, such as Muslims, who have moral claims to stronger forms of recognition because they are subject to cultural stigma and because majority practices disadvantage them or impose burdens on them which are not borne by members of the majority culture (Carens and Williams 1996). But in contexts different from that of Canada, Kymlicka's proposed remedies and distinctions break down even further. For instance, in Eastern and Central Europe, mottled patterns of ethnic settlement, shifting borders, and legacies of mutual distrust have produced situations in which some members of both majority and minority ethnic communities draw on similar forms of justification to make mutually incompatible demands for self-determination.

The case of Central European minority groups, such as the Hungarians of Romania, Serbia, and Slovakia, offers a vivid example of the contextual complexities of the politics of recognition. Ethnic Hungarians in these three countries, who comprise one of Europe's largest national minorities, with 2 million in Romania and about half a million each in Serbia and Slovakia, live in extremely vulnerable circumstances under generally illiberal governments which often play the "ethnic card" against them out of a combination of nationalist conviction and cynical electoral manipulation. Many of the harms they experience are examples of cultural misrecognition. The use of Hungarian is banned on public signs and in schools, cultural monuments are destroyed, and people are forced to change their names. Occasionally, violent rhetoric turns into physical violence, as it did in Tirgu Mures in Romania in 1990, where nearly thirty people died when the local headquarters of the Hungarian party were attacked. Given the far greater ethnic violence occurring elsewhere in Eastern Europe, the grim specter of "ethnic cleansing" hovers in the air.

In Slovakia and Romania, these ethnic tensions are exacerbated by the fact that Slovaks and Romanians were once ethnic minorities within Hungary and were subjected, in the Dual Monarchy period from 1867 to the Treaty of Trianon of 1920, to policies of forced Magyarization, and because Hungary spent the interwar period trying by all available means, including alliances with Hitler, to get Slovakia and Transylvania back. There is, in other words, much grist for the mills of mutual *ressentiment*.

Demands for collective rights to self-determination and autonomy have figured prominently in the rhetoric of the Hungarian ethnic communities of Central Europe since the collapse of communism in 1989. Representatives of the Hungarians of Slovakia, Romania, and Serbia have all claimed various rights to "collective autonomy," including in some cases territorial autonomy, though in all cases short of secession or political independence. These proposed rights to collective self-determination or autonomy have drawn criticism from those inside and outside the minority communities (Craiutu 1995; Biró 1995; Scipiades

1995; Szacsvay 1995; Andreescu, Stan, and Weber, n.d.). But they have many supporters as well. For instance, the absence of explicit references to collective rights to self-determination and autonomy in the bilateral treaty signed by the governments of Hungary and Slovakia in March 1995 led several opposition parties in Hungary, one of which subsequently won the national elections in June 1998, to protest the treaty and pledge to work against its ratification (Nyilatkozat 1995).

On closer examination, the demands encompassed within claims to collective autonomy or self-determination represent a wide range of institutional remedies. In the first instance, they include rights which would clearly be encompassed within standard democratic guarantees of freedom of association and non-discrimination, such as the rights to maintain Hungarian culture and language, to create ethnic institutions and associations, and to form political parties and other organizations on the local, regional, national, and international level. Secondly, they include demands for explicit acknowledgment of the existence of the Hungarian minority in the Romanian constitution. These demands arose in response to a clause in the proposed Romanian constitution which described Romania as a "unitary national state of the Romanian people." It is understandable that members of a large minority will feel threatened when the highest law of the land appears to go out of its way to deny their existence. They will experience this form of symbolic non-recognition as a threat to their civic status. They will also reasonably discern a link between such symbolic actions and policies of destroying Hungarian cultural monuments or of writing official textbooks which ignore or distort the role of Hungarians in Romanian history. At the same time, the positive demand for constitutional recognition, while it seems very reasonable in this context, is harder to generalize. It would be absurd, for instance, to claim that democratic justice requires that every minority group be enumerated in a country's constitution.

A third category of demand made by minority advocates is for access to public resources and institutions to maintain and foster the Hungarian culture and language. These include demands for bilingual street signs, laws mandating that schooling in Hungarian be offered in communities with a certain percentage of Hungarian speakers, access to the state media, and legal protections for the use of the Hungarian language in public life. The force of these demands also depends on contextual factors, from demographics to the ways in which majority cultural institutions are supported. Absence of government funds for minority churches and cultural institutions takes on a very different meaning if majority churches and institutions receive significant public support than if they do not. Finally, a fourth category of demands centers on guaranteeing a political voice to ethnic Hungarians. These demands range from efforts to protect the minority community against ethnic gerrymandering that dilutes its political influence through far more substantial and controversial demands for ethnically based forms of political, legal, or administrative representation or jurisdiction.

Does democratic equality require any or all of these remedies? In each case, proponents of recognition rights argue that the institutional remedies they propose are essential to guarantee their status as equal citizens. This is, indeed, the right question to ask about these remedies. The answer, however, will depend on particularities of context, ranging from the nature and degree of the harms and vulnerabilities experienced by a minority group to probabilistic and strategic judgments concerning the likely intended and unintended consequences of minority demands. Such contextual judgments are difficult to encompass in legal documents. The most sustained and sophisticated efforts to elaborate group rights have specified various degrees of such rights and distinguished between basic requirements that are morally mandatory and more extensive guarantees that would only be politically and institutionally feasible in a narrower range of cases (Draft Convention 1994).

Just as maximalist ethnic demands can exacerbate ethnic tensions and fuel an anti-democratic backlash, so other efforts to enshrine difference can endanger equal citizenship. For instance, gender-specific laws may hurt women who do not, or do not want to, follow the life patterns and aspirations of most women. An assertive politics of recognition can enshrine a particular identity group at the expense of its own members, as happened recently when a small minority of deaf advocates tried to prevent deaf children from receiving implants to partially restore their hearing. It is here that the tensions inherent in a democratic politics of recognition come vividly into view. Equal citizenship can be undermined by ignoring difference, yet it can just as clearly be threatened by efforts to enshrine difference. Arguments over when recognition of difference enhances and when it endangers equal citizenship are likely to occupy democrats for a long time to come.

By "crossing the Rubicon," as Adrian Favell has put it, from more abstract ideal theory to complex contextual judgments, proponents of the politics of recognition find themselves on rough terrain, with a growing need to draw on historical and empirical arguments (Favell 1996). Their standards for evaluating proposed remedies become more complex, requiring them to take into account the way a policy is likely to be perceived or implemented in a particular society, the perverse effects it may produce, its capacity to enhance or destabilize democratic efforts, and the longer-term impact it may have on the dynamic relationship between minority and majority cultures (Brubaker 1995).

This complexity may prompt an uneasy sense that we have moved away from the proper terrain of normative democratic theory. Yet it is through negotiating this rough terrain that the politics of recognition has the most to offer the project of democratic equality. Attention to particular circumstances prompts democratic theorists to refine the meaning and requirements of democratic equality. At its best, the politics of recognition can enrich democratic understandings of social equality. It does this not only by demonstrating that equal treatment does not always require identical treatment, but also by fostering a democratic sensibility in which people will seek to invent creative practices which can enhance the status and dignity of vulnerable or stigmatized groups without threatening the values of shared citizenship.

Lessons in humility

We have seen that the insights which a politics of recognition offers democratic theory carry a considerable price. Attention to cultural injuries renders the project of democratic equality more complex and dilemma-ridden. This is not necessarily a bad thing, however. The politics of recognition can teach democrats important lessons in humility, urging us to be vigilant about our prejudices and the ways they can blind us to the needs, vulnerabilities, and legitimate aspirations of those different from ourselves. Democrats owe no apologies for their core commitments to human dignity and equal citizenship and for their hostility to entrenched social hierarchies. But democratic institutions, practices, and societies have a very mixed record in their willingness to extend respect and protection to alien or unpopular groups. A politics of recognition encourages democrats to re-examine practices to see where they may stigmatize or place unjustified burdens on members of identity groups. It points toward a democratic ideal which Bhikhu Parekh has called "culturally mediated universalism" (Parekh 1994: 106).

Humility is also in order, however, for proponents of a politics of recognition. As we have seen, recognition claims are highly context-specific, and attempts to generalize from them to sweeping accounts of cultural or group "rights to recognition" will almost certainly run afoul of basic democratic values. Proponents must also be vigilant to the ways in which claims to recognition can be self-serving or can mask hostility to democracy in the guise of a democratic politics of recognition.

The position I have sketched here puts democratic commitments first and regards the politics of recognition as a way of extending and deepening these commitments. Democracy's fundamental allegiance is to individuals as equal citizens. That allegiance must be vigorously defended and promoted in the century to come. Its best defense will involve a sympathetic albeit critical engagement with, rather than a dismissal of, the politics of recognition.[1]

REFERENCES

Abrams, Kathryn. 1995. "The reasonable woman: sense and sensibility in harassment law," *Dissent* 421: 50–1.
Andreescu, Gabriel, Valentin Stan, and Renate Weber. n.d. "Draft Law on National Minorities." Bucharest: Centrul Pentru Drepturile Omului.
Biró, Béla. 1995. "Radikális mérsékeltek." *Magyar Hirlap*. (Budapest), 7 June.
Brubaker, Rogers. 1995. "National minorities, nationalizing states and external national homelands in the new Europe." *Daedalus* 124(2): 107–32.
Carens, Joseph and Melissa Williams. 1996. "Muslim minorities in liberal democracies: the politics of misrecognition." In Rainer Baubock, Agnes Heller and Ari Zolberg (eds.), *The Challenge of Diversity: Integration and Pluralism in Societies of Immigration*, pp. 157–86. Aldershot: Avebury Press.
Craiutu, Aurelian. 1995. "A dilemma of dual identity: the democratic alliance of Hungarians in Romania." *East European Constitutional Review* 4(2): 43–9.
Draft Convention on Self-Determination through Self-Administration. 1994. New York: Permanent Mission of the Principality of Liechtenstein to the United Nations.
Favell, Adrian. 1996. "Crossing the Rubicon." Presented at a conference on "Multiculturalism, minorities, and citizenship," European University, Florence, 18–23 April.
Fraser, Nancy, 1989. *Unruly Practices*. Minneapolis: University of Minnesota Press.
  1995a. "From redistribution to recognition? Dilemmas of justice in a 'post-socialist' age." *New Left Review* 212: 68–93.
  1995b. "Recognition or redistribution? A critical reading of Iris Young's *Justice and the Politics of Difference*." *Journal of Political Philosophy* 3(2): 166–80.
  1997. *Justice Interruptus*. New York: Routledge.
Gitlin, Todd. 1993. "The rise of 'identity politics'." *Dissent* 40(2): 172–7.
Honneth, Axel. 1992. "Integrity and disrespect: principles of a conception of morality based on a theory of recognition." *Political Theory* 20: 2.

[1] My thanks to participants at the conference on "Rethinking democracy for a new century," Yale University, 28 February–2 March 1997, and especially to Courtney Jung, John Kane, Ian Shapiro, and Iris Young for thought-provoking comments on the paper which formed the basis of this chapter. It draws on earlier work on group rights supported by the American Council of Learned Societies. I would like to thank Oliver Avens, Aurelian Craiutu, Will Kymlicka, Julie Mostov, Nancy Rosenblum, Yael Tamir, György Tokay, and Bernard Yack for very helpful challenges and comments, and Aurelian Craiutu for his research assistance.

Kymlicka, Will. 1989. *Liberalism, Community and Culture*. Oxford: Oxford University Press.

1995. *Multicultural Citizenship*. Oxford: Oxford University Press.

1996. "Three forms of group-differentiated citizenship in Canada." In Seyla Benhabib (ed.), *Democracy and Difference*, pp. 153–70. Princeton: Princeton University Press.

Nyilatkozat. 1995. Official Statement made by the Alliance of Young Democrats, the Christian Democratic People's Party, and the Hungarian Democratic Party in Budapest on 18 March. The statement appeared in *Szabad Ujság* (Pozsony/Bratislava, Slovakia), 22 March, p. 9.

Parekh, Bhikhu. 1994. "Comment: Minority rights, majority values." In David Milliband (ed.), *Reinventing the Left*, pp. 101–9. Cambridge: Polity Press.

Rawls, John. 1971. *A Theory of Justice*. Cambridge, MA: Harvard University Press.

Schlesinger, Arthur Jr. 1992. *The Disuniting of America*. New York: W. W. Norton.

Scipiades, Iván. 1995. "Ratifikációs csata." *Magyar Hirlap.* (Budapest) 23 May, p. 7.

Szacsvay, Tamás. 1995. "Autonóm nemzeti kisebbség." *Nyugati Magyarság – Hungarians of the West* 13(6): 6.

Taylor, Charles. 1992. *Multiculturalism and the Politics of Recognition*. Princeton: Princeton University Press.

1996. "Modernity and identity." Lecture to the Sawyer Seminar on Religion, Law, and the Construction of Identities, University of Chicago, 17 October.

Young, Iris Marion. 1990. *Justice and the Politics of Difference*. Princeton: Princeton University Press.

1997. "Unruly categories: a critique of Nancy Fraser's dual systems theory." *New Left Review* 222: 147–59.

12   Group aspirations and democratic politics[1]

Ian Shapiro

The question "should there be group rights?" is ill put. Proposed rights cannot be evaluated without reference to the contexts in which they are asserted or to the purposes for which they will be exercised. I believe a further constraint is also necessary, concerning the impact of group aspirations on democratic politics. Because it seems to me to be the most fundamental question, I begin with it, turning second to questions of context and purpose, and concluding with some remarks on institutional design in the light of the intervening discussion.

Democracy's constraint

In most countries of the modern world, democracy exhibits a nonoptional character that other political ideals lack. In the United States, for instance, few would take seriously the proposition that the state may require people to be liberal or conservative, or religious or secular, but equally few would deny the proposition that they can be required to accept the results of appropriately functioning democratic procedures. We are thought free to despise the government, but not its right to be the government. Of course different people understand different things by democracy, and every democratic order will be thought by some not to be functioning as it should, in the corrupt control of an illicit minority, or otherwise in need of repair. But the very terms of such objections to democracy affirm its obligatory character, since it is the malfunction or corruption of democracy which is being objected to. Christian fundamentalists may believe they are acting on God's orders, but the fact that they claim to be a "moral *majority*" indicates that as far as *political* legitimacy is concerned, they understand democracy's nonoptional character. The more or less universal move toward democracy in the ex-Soviet world and much of Africa and Latin America tells a

[1] An earlier version of this chapter was published in *Constellations* 3(3) (January 1997). Thanks are due to Blackwell Publishers Ltd for permission to use it here.

210

similar story: much as they might disagree over the meaning of democracy, and over how best to institutionalize it, the great majority accept its obligatory force.

This force stems from many roots. Part of it is linked to the economic and military successes of twentieth-century democracies when compared to the going alternatives. Part of it derives from agitation by weak and dispossessed groups in undemocratic countries to better their circumstances, and their hope (perhaps, often, naive) that democratization will help bring this about. Part of it flows from the pursuit of democracy in international institutions. The pressure that emanates from the leaders of many poor countries to democratize the UN and other international institutions implicitly affirms democracy's legitimacy. One can scarcely insist on democracy in international institutions without thereby conceding the validity of democratic claims; these then are enhanced willy-nilly in domestic political contexts.

Although democracy means many things to many people, most plausible accounts include two components: that people, collectively, are presumed entitled to an equal say in decisions that affect them, and that opposition to currently prevailing policies is always legitimate. Traditionally, the first of these ideals finds expression in a default – but rebuttable – presumption in favor of majority rule, while the second is institutionalized in the idea of "loyal" opposition. Whatever the procedures by which a decision is arrived at, there must be mechanisms through which those who are dissatisfied with a particular outcome can seek to produce change in the future, so long as they limit their opposition to producing a different decision rather than destroying the democratic order.

If democracy is understood as including these requirements, this still leaves open the question: how should democracy fit with group identities and aspirations? In my view, the best way to think about democracy's place is as a subordinate or conditioning good (see Shapiro 1996: chaps. 5 and 8). Democracy functions best when it shapes the terms of our common interactions without thereby setting their course. Most of the things people value can be pursued in a variety of ways, and it is the challenge of democracy in the modern world to get people to pursue them – even to *want* to pursue them – in more, rather than less, democratic ways. Democracy should be thought of as omnipresent in that it appropriately shapes the pursuit of all goals in which power relations are implicated, but not as omnipotent. Doing things democratically is always important, but it should rarely, if ever, be the point of the exercise. People should be induced to pursue their goals democratically, but not to sacrifice those goals to democracy. The task is to get them to rise to the creative challenge this presents. It is an especially difficult challenge as far as group aspirations are concerned, because these so often do obliterate other considerations. Yet it is all the more urgent for that reason.

Group-based claims

From the perspective of a commitment to democratic politics, we can approach questions about context and purpose. One way to do this is by thinking through examples. In the transition to democracy in South Africa between 1990 and 1994, two groups with intense desires for national self-determination found those desires frustrated as the outgoing National Party (NP) government and the African National Congress (ANC) negotiated a pact, with the enthusiastic blessing of much of the world community. One was the Inkatha Freedom Party (IFP), the ethnic Zulu nationalist party with a significant, though not decisive, power base in Natal. In the old "divide-and-rule" days of apartheid South Africa, particularly in the 1980s, the IFP had received strong support from the NP government in hopes of weakening the ANC which, few seriously doubted, had strong majority support among South Africa's black population. Before the transition began to become a reality, many – including IFP leader Mangosuthu Buthelezi – believed that if the government was to "cut a deal" at all, it would be with the IFP, who would gain control of a substantially autonomous entity, if not an independent country, in Natal. This was, after all, consistent with the Afrikaner ideology of "separate development," and few believed that the NP would ever give up control of the whole of white South Africa to the ANC.

In the event, Buthelezi was as surprised as most observers at the developments that actually unfolded. Following failed "roundtable" negotiations at the Conference for a Democratic South Africa (CODESA) in 1990 and 1991, in mid-1992 the NP and ANC leaderships began negotiating a secret agreement on South Africa's transition to democracy. The IFP was completely excluded from these discussions, whereas it had been a main player at CODESA. The reason was that the IFP had been one of the principal stumbling blocks to an agreement there because they had no real interest in the negotiations succeeding. Throughout, both the ANC and the NP were committed to maintaining the new democratic South Africa as a unitary state. Despite its propoganda about widespread support, the IFP knew what all the other players knew: that it would be a marginal player in such an order. Their own polls told them that they would not even win a majority of the Zulu vote. Consequently, the IFP wanted an independent Zulu nation in Natal, or, failing that result, something as close to it as possible. They denounced the negotiations which resulted in the February 1993 NP/ ANC agreement, began calling for a referendum on self-rule in Natal, and refused – almost to the end – to take part in the April 1994 elections. They hoped, forlornly as it turned out, that somewhere along the line they would be able to scuttle the transition.

In the last days before the election, making the best of it, the IFP added its name to the ballot. The final straw appears in retrospect to have been that President De Klerk transferred some 3 million acres of land to the control of Zulu King Goodwill Zwelitini in Natal. All along the king had insisted on the creation of a Zulu kingdom there with himself on its throne. This bribe was sufficient to buy him off, splitting him from Buthelezi and making any continued thought of opposition obviously fruitless, even to Buthelezi.[2] In the event, the ANC won 62.6 percent of the popular vote, the NP won 20.4 percent and the IFP won 10.5 percent (about a third of the Zulu vote nationally). In Natal, the IFP was declared to have won just over half the vote, despite widespread charges of electoral fraud and violence which the new government – perhaps wisely – decided not to pursue. This vote was sufficient to give the IFP 43 out of the 277 seats in parliament and 3 out of the 27 seats in the Government of National Unity's new cabinet.[3]

A second group, also ethnically based with territorial national ambitions, that had been obstructionist at CODESA and was marginalized in the subsequent negotiations was the white right. Unlike the IFP, they were deluded about the degree of their support. White Afrikaners comprise 7.5 percent of the population (57.5 percent of the white population), yet the Afrikaner separatist Freedom Front (FF) won 2.2 percent of the vote in the April 1994 election, indicating that three out of four white Afrikaners voted for another party – the great majority for the NP.[4] Almost until the end they believed that the majority of South Africans, and particularly the military, would come to see the transition to majority rule as a calamity to be avoided and would turn to them. In the last months before the elections they had tried to take a stand by supporting a black "homeland" leader in Bophuthatswana who opposed the elections, only to be unceremoniously arrested by the army which by this time was manifestly loyal to the transition. Although they continued

[2] *New York Times*, Tuesday 24 May, p. A6.
[3] Election results taken from *Foreign Broadcasting Information Service Daily Report*, 6 May 1994, p. 5. Cabinet portfolios from Associated Press wire, 9 May 1994.
[4] *Foreign Broadcasing Information Service Daily Report*, 6 May 1994, p. 5; Reynolds 1994: 183–220. Population statistics computed from *South Africa 1994*: 14–15.

(and continue) to call for the creation of an Afrikaner "Volksstaad," they have ceased to be a serious force in South African politics.

Both Inkatha and the white right are politicized ethnic groups with national territorial ambitions, yet neither commands much sympathy outside their own constituency in South Africa, on the world stage, or even from intellectuals who champion rights of ethnic self-determination. The reasons why are, I think, instructive. The IFP has shown itself to be manifestly uninterested in democracy, both internally and in its dealings with other groups. Its arguments that a democratic national state is incompatible with "traditional" Zulu society conceal the fact that this society is highly authoritarian and manifestly oppressive of women. For this reason, King Goodwill's periodic claims for reinstatement of his "rightful" kingdom in what is now Natal – first taken from his forefathers by the British in the nineteenth century – win little support. In its dealings with others, the IFP has been warlike and instrumentalist, often bolstered, it should be said, before the transition by South Africa's apartheid government.

No doubt there is plenty of blame to go around as far as anti-democratic politics are concerned, and the NP and ANC historical records are scarcely without blemish in this regard, but Inkatha's opposition to democracy is foundational, even principled. Buthelezi is a member of the Zulu royal family, more interested in consolidating authority of traditional chiefs than any sort of electoral politics. By contrast, both the the ANC and NP leaderships now accept democracy as the governing principle of the country. Despite their histories, and despite the continuing practices of "disloyal" opposition politics within some of their constituencies, they are publicly committed to the essentials of the rule of law within a constitutional democracy. Perhaps democracy is less threatening to them, perhaps they have come to believe that the alternatives to it are all, as Churchill said, worse. Whatever the reason, failures of democracy are, for them, failures to be accounted for, justified, rationalized, or explained away. By contrast, the IFP leadership makes no secret of the fact that its allegiance to democracy is contingent on events. They participated in the 1993 elections only when it became evident that they could not derail them, and they played a similar game of cat-and-mouse with the negotiations on the permanent constitution: refusing to participate unless virtual independence for Kwazulu/Natal was guaranteed, which in Buthelezi's mind includes its own army, which would be under his personal command.[5]

---

[5] See *New York Times*, 7 January 1996, pp. A1, A12.

If democrats have reasonably shed few tears for Inkatha's ethnic ambitions, they have reasonably shed even fewer for those of the white right. Conservative ethnic Afrikaners opposed the democratization of South Africa at every turn, relying substantially on the ideology of separate development of the country's races. Yet the "bantustans" and "homelands" they made available to blacks were not remotely viable economic or political entities, comprising a tiny portion of South Africa's least well-endowed lands. Unsurprisingly, therefore, even in the heyday of apartheid it was envisaged that the white South African economy would be sustained by black migrant labor from these bantustans. One ironic consequence of the disingenuousness of the Afrikaner commitment to separate development is their own geographical dispersion throughout South Africa today. It means that there is no obvious territorial site for the Volksstaad about which they have been talking since the transition became inevitable. The demographic facts make it doubtful that an Afrikaner Volksstaad is viable in the present South African context. The historical facts feed the suspicion that such a Volksstaad would, in any case, be a platform for a relentless war of attrition against the new South African state. The majority of ethnic Afrikaner nationalists do not believe is legitimate, and it is likely that they never will. In such circumstances, why should others defer to their separatist aspirations? Unlike Inkatha, they are not hostile to democracy within their own group. However, they are implacably hostile to the democratic South Africa with which they are at odds; "disloyal" rather than "loyal" opposition. At bottom, this is why their aspirations are fairly resisted by a democratic state.

Separatist demands from hostile groups are not always so easily dismissed, as is indicated by the more intricate problem of the Palestinian aspirations for national self-determination in part or all of what is now Israel. On balance, they may be no less intolerant of Israeli ethnic and nationalist aspirations than the separatist Afrikaners are of the new South Africa, but, unlike the separatist Afrikaners, in the present circumstances of Middle Eastern politics they are a dominated minority who are denied rights of democratic participation in the Israeli state that governs them. I do not mean to deny that Israelis have good reasons to fear Palestinians, given the history of the conflict, and it should be said that commitment to democracy (internal or external) is not high on the agenda of either the PLO or Hamas. In such circumstances separation seems to be the only solution, a reality that was poignantly captured by one cartoon during the Intifada which depicted a prominent Likud politician saying to a foreign reporter: "Our policy concerning the Palestinians is simple. We will keep beating them until they stop hating us!" Israel cannot fairly deny the separatist aspirations of a group that it has no intention ever of recognizing as equal citizens within the Jewish state (how could it?), yet it reasonably fears expansionist Palestinian aspirations that are every bit as potent as right-wing Jewish affirmations of the legitimacy of "greater" Israel. The "two-state solution" seems inescapable in this type of zero-sum circumstance, even if it carries a depressingly Solomonic air.

Some (a small minority) deny this, arguing instead for a secular unitary state in the entire region; but the histories that led both Jews and Palestinians to their circumstances of present mutual hostility renders this unrealistic. Perhaps it would be better in some ultimate sense if the lessons of seventeenth-century England and Europe had led substantial numbers of the present power-brokers in the Middle East to see the virtues of religious disestablishment; personally I wish that this were so. But that is not the present reality, and calling for it is reminiscent of the Western statesman who wondered aloud, during the 1956 Suez Crisis, why Jews and Arabs could not "settle their differences in a Christian fashion?"

Re-engineering identities democratically

It might be said that there is a certain theoretical artificiality to my discussion of the preceding cases. They all involve claims for self-determination that are in various respects extreme and distasteful to democratic sensibilities. As such, perhaps they do not capture much of what defenders of claims to the legitimacy of rights to self-determination have in mind. Such an assertion would be partly justified only: it invites the retort that theoretical literature on this subject is often starry-eyed in ignoring what can be at issue in actual movements that seek self-determination. That said, the intuition that one should not think only about group aspirations that stand in flat contradiction to democratic practice is sound. Indeed, I want to press it further by saying that, for democrats, the creative challenge is to try to structure things so that claims for self-determination will express themselves in ways that are more, rather than less, compatible with democracy. To advance this claim it is necessary to say something about the nature and sources of politicized claims to self-determination. There seem to me to be three principal possibilities.

One is primordialist. If one thinks of identities as unalterable, then the appropriate political stance would be purely instrumental: find ways to prevent people from killing one another by channeling the destructive aspects of their fixed aspirations away from one another. In the "divided society" literature, such thinking gives rise to consociationalism: the injunction is to devise systems of minority vetoes or other mechanisms that force leaders of different national groups to work out a *modus vivendi* and govern as "cartels of elites" (Lijphart 1969: 213–15, 222). If the primordialists are right, instrumental constitutional engineering makes sense. If they are wrong, as I have argued with Courtney Jung in the South African context that they are, then they become vulnerable to the charge that the remedy might actually produce the malady to which it allegedly responds (Jung and Shapiro 1995; Shapiro and Jung 1996). Consociational institutions can manufacture, or exacerbate, ethnic division.

An opposing view stems from the postmodern rejection of primordialism. Postmodernists contend that political identities are "socially constructed"; they are malleable and evolve over time. On this view, there is nothing natural or necessary about ethnic, racial, and other group-based antipathies. They might have developed differently than they have, and can change in the present and future. Although postmodern writers seldom get into the technicalities of how they believe this can be accomplished, it seems reasonable to assume that – on their view – forms of identity might develop that differ radically from those presently prevailing in the world. In particular, people might come to accept, perhaps even celebrate, differences that today are sources of mutual hatred.

Postmodernists can correctly point out that politicized identities evolve with time and circumstance; but to say that types of politicized identity are historically contingent does not entail that they are infinitely malleable. It does not even entail that forms of identity that need not have been mobilized, but have been, can now be demobilized. This is more than the problem of getting the toothpaste back into the tube. The degree to which things are alterable may not vary with the extent to which they are socially constructed at all. Many features of the natural world, ranging from the temperature of our bath water to the genetic structure of our beings, are alterable by conscious human design. Socially constructed phenomena, by contrast, often defy efforts at conscious human control. Markets are human constructions, yet we may have no idea how to design them to operate at full employment with no inflation. Ethnic hatred might concededly be learned behavior, yet we may have no idea how to prevent its being reproduced in the next generation. Postmodernists leap too quickly from the idea of social construction to that of alterability; at best the two are contingently related.

An intermediate, and to me more plausible, view avoids the attendant difficulties of both primordialism and postmodernism. With apologies to philosophical purists, it might be described as a brand of neo-Aristotelian naturalism. On this view, human beings are shaped by context and circumstance, but also constrained by their basic constitutions. These basic constitutions may themselves evolve, but at a given time and place they limit the possibilities of social construction. Human nature is always malleable but never infinitely so, and certain ways of shaping it are likely to be more effective than others. The interesting questions concern what the limits to this malleability are, and which forms of social construction are likely to be more satisfying and effective than others. At bottom these are empirical questions about which there is not a great deal of accumulated knowledge in the social sciences.[6] As a result, it is wise to work at the margins rather than the core, and to think about institutional redesign rather than *tabula rasa* design. Identities are fixed to some – usually unknown – degree, but they also adapt to circumstances, incentives, and institutional rules. The goal should be to reshape such constraints, where possible, so that at the margins identities evolve in ways that are more, rather than less, hospitable to democratic politics.

One mechanism through which this can be pursued is electoral systems. Since ethnic hatred is often mobilized by political leaders in response to what they see as routes to power, it is important, as Donald Horowitz has argued, to shape the incentives for gaining power in ways that will produce a different result. What is needed in ethnically divided societies (assuming partition is not on the agenda), are systems that affect the behavior of elites from one group toward the grass-roots members of other groups (Horowitz 1991: 155). This can be achieved in a variety of ways, all of which require politicians to compete for votes among ethnic groups other than their own. The most obvious is a combination of coalition politics and heterogeneous constituencies. Horowitz describes a successful example of this kind from Malaysia, in which Malay and Chinese politicians were forced to rely in part on votes delivered by politicians belonging to the other ethnic group. The votes would not have been forthcoming "unless leaders could portray the candidates as moderate on issues of concern to the group that was delivering its votes across ethnic lines." In this type of situation, which Horowitz identifies as having operated for considerable periods (and then failed) in countries as different as Lebanon, Sri Lanka, and Nigeria, compromises at the top of a coalition are reinforced by electoral incentives at the bottom (Horowitz 1991).

---

[6] For elaboration, see Shapiro 1990: chaps. 8–9.

Another possible device is geographical distribution requirements, such as the Nigerian formula for presidential elections employed in 1979 and 1983, in which the winning candidate had to get both the largest number of votes and at least 25 percent of the vote in two thirds of the then-nineteen states of the Nigerian Federation. This type of system seems unlikely to work in countries such as South Africa, however, given the territorial racial dispersion. In such circumstances, the two most promising candidates there are proportional representation utilizing the single transferable vote system, and an alternative vote rule that also lists more than one ordered preference, but declares elected only those candidates who receive a majority, rather than a plurality, of votes. Both systems require politicians to cater to voters' choices other than their first preferences, assuming heterogeneous constituencies, so that the internal incentives work in the appropriate moderating directions. Horowitz thinks this will be accentuated further by the alternative vote system, assuming that parties proliferate (Horowitz 1991).

Horowitz makes a convincing case that in many circumstances such vote-pooling systems are more likely to achieve interethnic political cooperation than systems, whether first-past-the-post or proportional, that merely require seat-pooling by politicians in coalition governments. They are also superior, from a democratic point of view, to schemes such as Lani Guinier's cumulative voting as devices for achieving viable diversity in representation.[7] Guinier's proposal is to give each voter in a territory a number of votes equal to the number of representatives. If a state is to have eight congressional representatives, every voter would have eight votes that can be cast however they wish: all for one candidate or spread among several. If there are intense ethnic preferences, members of a minority group can cast all eight votes for the representative of their group; if not, not. This has advantages over racial gerrymandering, which (like consociationalism) can be accused of entrenching ethnic and racial differences. The Guinier approach responds to intense ethnic preferences that might exist in a population, but it does nothing to produce or reinforce them. Yet by the same token it does nothing to undermine or ameliorate potentially polarizing forms of aspirational difference. This is why it is inferior, from a democratic point of view, to systems that give aspiring political leaders active incentives to avoid mobilizing forms of identity that exacerbate cultural competition and to devise, instead, ideologies that can appeal across the divisions of such groups.

Giving leaders electoral incentives to avoid exacerbating inter-group

[7] See Guinier 1991 and 1994a. On the battle over her Senate confirmation to be head of the civil rights division in the Justice Department, see Guinier 1994b.

antipathies will not always work. Parties might proliferate within politicized groups in ways that undermine this dimension of the logic behind transferable vote schemes.[8] Furthermore, some of the worst of what often (misleadingly) gets labeled interethnic violence is actually intra-ethnic violence that results when different parties seek to mobilize support in the same ethnic group. Much of the South African violence that erupted in Natal after 1984 resulted when the United Democratic Front (UDF) was formed and challenged IFP support among Zulus there, and some of the worst violence among white nationalists resulted from comparable competition for the white nationalist vote. There are limits to the degree that intra-ethnic competition of this sort can be ameliorated by transferable vote mechanisms. In theory they may have a positive effect. If parties have incentives to mobilize support in more than one ethnic constituency, they should avoid campaigning as ethnic parties more than they have to. In practice, however, parties such as the IFP – whose *raison d'être* is ethnic – may have little scope to campaign on any other basis. Accordingly, they may resist – perhaps violently – any inroads into their "traditional" sources of support.

Whether this is likely to be the case can be difficult to predict. In the early 1990s, the NP transformed itself in a short time into a viable multi-ethnic party (more than half of whose votes in the 1994 election came from non-whites). It did this because its leaders came to believe that their alternatives were "adapt or die." In Canada, less apocalyptic thinking appears so far to have been sufficient to cause the leaders of ethnic parties to accept that their aspirations must triumph through a democratic process or not at all. By contrast, Bosnia and the Middle East reveal that sometimes even the likelihood – indeed the certainty – of death is not sufficient to head off the pursuit of mutually incompatible group aspirations. Yet most people do not want to die. The challenge, for democrats, is to devise mechanisms that increase the likelihood that people will live in conditions of inclusive participation and non-domination. Group aspirations that by their terms cannot be realized within democratic constraints are to be resisted, but it is better to work for a world in which such aspirations will diminish. Getting rid of institutions that press in the opposite direction seems like a logical place to start.

REFERENCES

Guinier, Lani. 1991. "The triumph of Tokenism: the Voting Rights Act and the theory of black electoral success." *Michigan Law Review* 89(5): 1077–154.

[8] For elaboration of these and related difficulties confronting Horowitz's proposals, see Shapiro 1993: 145–7.

1994a. "(E)rasing democracy: the voting rights cases." *Harvard Law Review* 18(1): 109–37.

1994b. *The Tyranny of the Majority.* New York: Free Press.

Horowitz, Donald L. 1991. *A Democratic South Africa? Constitutional Engineering in a Divided Society.* Berkeley: University of California Press.

Jung, Courtney and Ian Shapiro. 1995. "South Africa's negotiated transition: democracy, opposition, and the new constitutional order." *Politics and Society* 23(3): 269–308.

Lijphardt, Arendt. 1969. "Consociational democracy." *World Politics* 4(2): 213–31.

Reynolds, Andrew. 1994. *Election '94 South Africa.* Cape Town: David Philip.

Shapiro, Ian. 1990. *Political Criticism.* Berkeley: University of California Press.

1993. "Democratic innovation: South Africa in comparative context." *World Politics* 46(1): 21–50.

1996. *Democracy's Place.* Ithaca: Cornell University Press.

Shapiro, Ian and Courtney Jung. 1996. "South African democracy revisited: a reply to Koeble and Reynolds." *Politics and Society* 24(2): 237–47.

South Africa 1994. The South Africa Foundation. Parktown, Johannesburg: The South Africa Foundation.

13 American democracy and the New Christian Right: a critique of apolitical liberalism

Jeffrey C. Isaac, Matthew F. Filner, and Jason C. Bivins

Introduction

The dramatic political rise of religious fundamentalism in American politics, symbolized by the growing political presence and influence of the Christian Coalition, is one sign, among others, of the unravelling of the social contract on which postwar American liberalism rested. This liberalism was distinguished by a preoccupation with solving distributional problems by promoting economic growth and satisfying the demands of a consumerist society, and its breakdown has seen the rise of what has been called a "politics of identity," a politics of proliferating demands for legal and cultural recognition on the part of a range of identity-based groups. Many of these groups – feminists, gays, and Afrocentrists, for example – are outgrowths of the New Left, and of the cultural radicalism of the 1960s, and see themselves, and are widely seen, as "liberatory" or "left-wing" movements.[1]

But equally important have been a number of identity-based groups that have emerged *in reaction to* 1960s cultural radicalism and have sought to counter many of its more liberatory achievements. Among these the New Christian Right stands out, as a loose coalition of groupings, organizations, and movements that have sought to combat what they consider the permissiveness of American society, and to promote "family values," in the name of "decent Americans" and "traditional Christian values." In many ways the New Christian Right has upped the ante of identity politics, by mirroring the New Left in its "grass-roots" organizing strategies, its resolutely ideological style, and in its claim to speak on behalf of purportedly marginalized and victimized Americans.

The conflict of identities is one of the central features of American public life today, as evidenced by recent controversies surrounding Ebonics, the O. J. Simpson verdicts, affirmative action, abortion, the propriety of all-male or all-female academies, gays in the US military,

---

[1] On the legacies of the 1960s, see Gitlin 1995 and Berman 1996.

the legality of gay marriage, popular referenda against the codification of gay rights, the Supreme Court's 1996 *Evans v. Romer* decision challenging such referenda, English-only proposals, immigration law and the treatment of so-called "aliens." It is hard to imagine public discourse today, such as it is, in the absence of these controversies. They raise fundamental questions about race, gender, sexuality, language, citizenship, and what it means to be an "American." They are deeply divisive, implicating competing, and often deeply antagonistic, conceptions of what philosophers call "being" – conceptions of what it means to be a person, of sexual identity, of "blackness" and "whiteness" and a variety of shades in between, of the purposes of law, and of the foundations of political argument, whether appeals be made to the US Constitution, inalienable rights, democracy, and public utility, or to God, biological destiny, historical guilt, or historical innocence.

We are interested in a big question: what are the implications of this kind of politics for thinking about democracy, and in what ways should democratic politics handle, manage, or regulate such controversies? In this chapter we address a small piece of this bigger question, by focusing our attention on the significance of the New Christian Right. The New Christian Right is a *new* Christian Right, rooted in some of the older forms of Christian "fundamentalism" that originated at the turn of the century, but shaped in important ways in reaction to the politics of the New Left. It is this political phenomenon that we wish to discuss here. We are not interested in "religious fundamentalism" in general, but in the particular dilemmas presented by the New Christian Right, in the broader context of the challenges presented by identity politics to American liberalism. What we say here is not intended to illuminate the challenges posed by religious fundamentalism in Afghanistan, Algeria, or Jerusalem, only the challenges posed by the particular kind of politicized Christian fundamentalism that exists in the United States today.[2]

While many self-styled "communitarians" have celebrated the rise of a religiously inspired, value-based politics as an advance on the "thinness" of liberal public life, many liberals have responded to this

---

[2] When this chapter was originally presented as a paper at Yale University, a philosophic eminence responded that it could be read as a whitewashing of all kinds of tyranny. He suggested that if it were Weimar Germany in 1932, and the word "Nazi" were substituted for "New Christian Right," then the paper would clearly be seen as a kind of defense of the Nazis. Our response then, and now, is simple: this paper is not about Weimar Germany but about American democracy in 1999, and that only someone uninformed about the New Christian Right could liken it to the German National Socialists circa 1932. One of our principal intentions in this paper is to repudiate such prejudices about the significance of the religious Right in America, but this hardly makes us "defenders" of the religious Right.

development more defensively and with greater alarm, seeking to retrieve classical liberalism's commitment to "religious liberty" and the separation of Church and state, and to rearticulate liberal political philosophy as a philosophy of civility, compromise, and orderly public life.[3] The most prominent statement of these themes is the "political liberalism" put forth by John Rawls (1993), a view also defended by Stephen Macedo (1995), Stephen Holmes (1988a and 1988b), and others. Political liberalism seeks above all to defend the priority of a certain conception of individual liberty against the political claims of "comprehensive doctrines," such as religious fundamentalism, that seek, in the eyes of political liberals, to intrude into the public sphere. It endorses the use of juridical strategies, especially the deployment of jurisprudential argument and the practice of judicial review by courts, to insulate the political process from religiously inspired conceptions of the good and to limit the politicization of public life on moral grounds. The purpose of this paper is to criticize this political liberalism.

Unlike many "communitarians," we are not unsympathetic to the concerns that motivate political liberalism. We believe that political liberals are properly troubled by the moral absolutism and the sectarianism often characteristic of the religious Right, and correctly consider the religious Right a danger to important historical achievements such as individual freedom of expression and cultural and religious diversity. We believe that political liberals rightly view these achievements as *political* concerns that cannot be sustained by appeal to metaphysical truth-claims and that presuppose certain ways of organizing political power.

Yet we strongly dissent from the *depoliticized* politics that political liberals endorse as a way of dealing with the challenges presented by fundamentalism. In this paper we will argue that the modes of avoidance or "gag rules" by which political liberals seek to insulate public debate and to privatize discourses of the good life are both philosophically and practically deficient. Philosophically, the demand that "public reason" ought to exclude religious modes of justification relies on an implausibly "thin" conception of political identity and of public discourse. Practically, such a demand is unduly reliant on methods, such as judicial review, that are in public disrepute and are in disturbing tension with democratic values of associational freedom, political pluralism, and collective self-government. Furthermore, such strategies of judicial coercion are liable to promote a fundamentalist "backlash" that only exacerbates the problems that motivate political liberalism in the first place.

---

[3] For communitarian views, see, for example, Bellah 1991, Carter 1993, and Cox 1995.

While we dismiss neither the concerns of political liberals nor the importance of judicial review in a democracy, we argue for a more overtly political and democratic way of addressing the problem of religious fundamentalism, and of identity politics more generally, in public life. We argue that the most viable "solutions" to this problem are to be found in civil society, in the form of outlets for healthy but unavoidably fractious discussion and debate about fundamental value questions, and in the form of modes of practical problem-solving and empowerment that help to reduce the alienation and anxiety to which fundamentalisms of various forms often give expression.

Such a robustly democratic politics is more contentious than that preferred by political liberals and, by accepting the kind of value-based public discourse feared by them, it presents the danger of illiberalism in public life. But illiberalism is already in public life – which is, of course, the starting point of political liberalism itself – and we argue that this is partly due to the deficiencies of organized liberalism, especially its aversion to political contestation. Ironically, we argue that the extension of political controversy beyond liberal confines, and the ever-present and often relentless challenging of the boundaries separating what is private and what is public, what is "reasonable" and what is not, might actually work to strengthen liberal values of individual liberty, social pluralism, and public civility.

Our argument has four parts. First, we will delineate what political liberalism is and offer an explanation of the conditions of its emergence. Second, we will consider its theoretical weaknesses. Third, we will criticize the way political liberalism proposes to deal with the problems posed by the New Christian Right, focusing on Stephen Macedo's account of *Mozert v. Hawkins*, a federal court case that has been widely discussed, and that nicely encapsulates many of the problems that concern us.[4] Finally, we will present a more robustly democratic account of the politicization of religion – and morality and identity more generally – in public life.

This is a large and important topic, and our arguments will necessarily be sketchy. Our central point is that political liberalism is too apolitical, and that it wrongly privileges civility and orderliness over democracy in its conception of public life. By defending a more vigorously democratic point of view, we wish to challenge this privileging, not in the name of anti-liberalism, but in the name of a radicalized, robustly democratic

---

[4] *Mozert v. Hawkins* is actually five separate decisions. Although each is significant in its own right, for purposes of simplicity we will condense it into a single decision. For greater detail, see 579 F. Supp. 1051 (1984), 582 F. Supp. 201 (1984), 765 F.2d 75 (1985), 647 F. Supp. 1194 (1986), and 827 F.2d 1058 (1987).

liberalism, one that sees the importance of historically achieved liberties and constitutional limits on public authority, but that also sees these achievements as subjects of chronic democratic contestation.

Political liberalism considered

"Political liberalism" is an interpretation of liberalism, a variant of liberalism principally concerned with the problems of civility and public order. Its most prominent expositor is John Rawls, who coined the term in his essay "Justice as fairness: political, not metaphysical" (1985) and offered a systematic elaboration in his book entitled *Political Liberalism* (1993). While Rawls has most systematically defended this view, he is not alone in supporting it, and similar arguments can be found in the writings of a number of other prominent liberal theorists, among them Judith Shklar (1984 and 1989), Stephen Holmes (1988a, 1993a, 1993b, and 1994), Stephen Macedo (1990), and Richard Rorty (1983).

In what way is "political liberalism" political? There are at least three distinguishable senses in which this kind of liberalism assumes the "political" modifier. The first is the sense announced by Rawls in his above-cited essay, designating his liberalism as "political" rather than "metaphysical." In this sense, political liberalism purportedly rests on no metaphysical claims about the nature of the human self or the human good, and is presented as nothing more than a hermeneutic, an interpretation of the historically evolved political culture of Western liberal democracies.[5]

Second, political liberalism, it is argued, is a juridical rather than a full-fledged moral doctrine. That is, not only is it historically rather than metaphysically grounded; it is also, supposedly, a "thin" conception of basic liberty that deliberately eschews a robust or substantive conception of the good life, and remains open to a wide range of moral conceptions, "reasonable comprehensive doctrines," which are free to flourish in a politically liberal society without fear or favor. Political liberalism, then, represents what Rawls calls an "overlapping consensus" in a broadly pluralistic society based on a multiplicity of religions, cultural forms, and lifestyles (1993: 133–72).

Finally, political liberalism is "political" in its preoccupation with the "basic structure of society," where this is construed as relating to "constitutional essentials and questions of basic justice, especially to

---

[5] See Rawls on the public culture of Western societies (1993: 8, 13–14); on liberalism as a historical tradition (1993: xxlv–xxlx); and on the original position as a device of representation (1993: 25–7). The philosophical perspective underlying this claim has been most elaborately discussed by Rorty (1983 and 1988: 44–72).

questions of civil and political liberty. Rawls's *Political Liberalism* is essentially a book about constitutional liberalism, one that is principally concerned with the juridical organization of the nation state rather than with the structure of power or the distribution of wealth in civil society or with questions of global political or distributive justice (1993: 11–12, 24).

In each of these respects, we believe, political liberalism can only be understood in connection with the kind of liberalism that it seeks to amend, and indeed it must be seen as a substantial modification of this prior liberalism. The liberalism in question is the public philosophy whose most influential statement was none other than Rawls's own *A Theory of Justice*, developed in article form during the 1950s and 1960s, and published in book form in 1971, a different era indeed (see especially 1951, 1958, and 1971: preface; see also Wolff 1977). For our purposes two characteristics of *A Theory of Justice* stand out. One is its widely remarked rationalism, its attempt to derive an axiomatic theory of justice from a certain decision procedure, an "original position" characterized by a "veil of ignorance." The earlier theory offered an updated natural law argument, and was fairly credulous about the possibility that justice could be grounded in the reasoning capabilities of humans as such.[6] The second is the centrality that questions of distributive justice assumed in its argument. While Rawls's "difference principle" was granted secondary lexical status behind the "priority of basic liberty," it is also clear that for the earlier Rawls distributive justice was an essential component of any meaningful political theory of justice. Behind this presumption was an unabashed optimism about the possibility that economic growth could mitigate more radical and contentious conceptions of distributive justice by reconciling the inequalities of a capitalist market system with the economic well-being of the "least well off" members of society, for a rising tide would, it seemed, lift all boats.

It is thus with good reason that Ian Shapiro referred to Rawls's theory as the "Keynesian moment" in modern liberalism (1986: 204–70). As Sheldon Wolin has observed: "Although *Justice* was published in 1971, it was very much a book of the sixties, most especially in its assumptions about continuous economic growth, the existence of a shared consensus centered around New Deal social policy, the defeat of racism, and the good nature of the welfare state" (1996: 113). There is always a danger of reductionism in the attempt to historicize a theoretical argument, but in this case it is quite clear that Rawls's book struck a deep chord among liberals, and offered a philosophically elaborate, and politically

---

[6] Rawls implausibly denies that he ever sought to make such an argument (1993: xv–xvii, 24–8).

appealing, justification for the institutions of postwar liberal democracy. *A Theory of Justice*, in this sense, is emblematic of a particular mode of liberal argument that assumed great prominence among academic political theorists, even when they sought to criticize its details, and that resonated with the "post-ideological" spirit of postwar American liberalism at its height.[7]

In this light the "political liberalism" more recently defended by Rawls and his colleagues must be seen as a substantial revision of the earlier perspective. First, its interpretivist "clarification" of the philosophical status of earlier concepts such as "original position," "veil of ignorance," and "reflexive equilibrium," represents an intellectually more chastened, anti-foundationalist form of theoretical justification, which relativizes liberalism as a response to the religious wars of the sixteenth century (Rawls 1993: xxiv). Even more importantly, the narrative in question focuses on the dangers of civil strife and the need to mitigate these dangers, and in this regard is a markedly less optimistic theory. Indeed, it is, as some of its proponents avow, a "liberalism of fear" (Shklar 1989) rather than a liberalism of social justice, a liberalism very much troubled by the acrimonious forms of conflict that have emerged in the post-1960s period and frightened by the similarities between these forms of conflict and earlier forms of cruelty and violence. Hence it should be unsurprising that this "political liberalism" is much less concerned with the distributive questions that most distinguished its predecessor, and indeed these questions receive only minimal attention and are accorded "constitutional" inferiority.[8]

Political liberalism, then, is a chastened liberalism, a liberalism for hard times, marked by the absence of consensus, by the flourishing of competing conceptions of the good, by the emergence of various

---

[7] In this regard Rawls's book should be seen as echoing sentiments also developed in such post-historical classics as Schlesinger 1949 and Bell 1960. Brinkley (1995) offers a powerful account of the evolution of such a consumerist liberalism and the ways in which it intellectually suppressed more contentious questions of distributive justice and political participation. It bears emphasis that this kind of liberalism is not the only possible kind, and our criticism of it in no way seeks to implicate liberalism as a whole. We do believe that liberalism as a whole has evidenced a longstanding historical suspicion of popular political participation, and an even greater suspicion of efforts to politicize the boundaries separating the public and the private. Yet the liberal tradition is a rich and diverse one, and there are certainly versions of liberalism not liable to the specific critique we develop here. See, for example, Ryan 1993.

[8] This is observed by Stephen Holmes (1993b: 39–47) in his review of Rawls 1993. It is true that Rawls's political liberalism acknowledges the ineliminability of moral and political pluralism and seeks to develop a conception of public discourse capable of institutionalizing conflict. As we argue below, however, this conception of public discourse is a narrow one that seeks to insulate the political process from the most discordant ethical controversies, and to keep much of the discourse and the concern characteristic of identity politics effectively private.

"fundamentalisms," and by an exacerbation of these agonistic tendencies by the decline of economic growth and the political weight of an ever more imposing scarcity (see Dionne 1991; Edsall and Edsall 1992; Phillips 1993; and Gitlin 1995). This difference in tone is obvious, for the central frame of reference of political liberalism is none other than the religious wars of the post-Reformation period, a constantly invoked – and evoked – reminder of the ever-present possibility against which political liberalism stands poised (see Rawls 1993: xxiv and Holmes 1994: 601–2). Indeed, the most important respect in which political liberalism recommends itself, according to Rawls, is that it guards against the coerced imposition of religious belief that remains likely whenever "comprehensive moral doctrines" and contentious conceptions of the good enter the public sphere and make claims upon the organization of political authority (see Rawls 1993: 37 and 1985: 248–51). Political liberalism, then, is an answer to the serious problems thrown up by the cultural politics of the 1960s and by the breakdown of organized liberalism in the ensuing period. It is a jurisprudence for a conflictual polity, fractured along multiple dimensions, where civil confidence is continually disturbed by an inflationary discourse of rights, and competing identity claims threaten to "overload" political authority (see Huntington 1975; Crozier, Huntington, and Watanuki 1975; Glendon 1991; Etzioni 1993; and Elshtain 1995).

If the history of actual liberal politics in the past three decades has been a history of implosion under the pressure of acrimonious conflict, then political liberalism represents what Rawls has candidly described as a "method of avoidance" of such controversies (1985: 231).[9] As one commentator has put it, political liberalism "seeks, purposefully, to avoid the deep metaphysical questions that are a part of a plural society and that are bound to remain so as a permanent feature of modernity characterized by incommensurable and conflicting visions of the good" (Alejandro 1996: 3). The principal category through which political liberalism seeks to effect this "avoidance" of moral controversy and thus to arrest the instability of public life is the category of "public reason."

According to political liberalism, the central imperative of justice is that "we must distinguish between a public basis of justification generally acceptable to citizens on fundamental questions and the many nonpublic bases of justification belonging to the many comprehensive doctrines acceptable only to those who affirm them" (Rawls 1993: xix). Political liberalism thus insists that while individuals in a just society must remain free to believe whatever they choose about the meaning of

---

[9] For an alternative reading of Rawls as supporting a more robustly deliberative and democratic conception of public life, see Cohen 1994.

life and the ultimate sources of that meaning, and even to act upon these beliefs within the limited milieu of their personal lives, it is dangerous whenever these moral beliefs and practices spill over into the political realm and threaten to determine the organization of public authority. For when this occurs, commitments that are by their nature partial and contestable become hegemonic, threatening those others who do not share these commitments, and engendering anxiety, defensiveness, and rancorous hostility. Like Hobbes, political liberals fear the diffidence and divisiveness that deep-seated and particularistic commitments might produce, and, like Hobbes, they believe that it is important to domesticate and to privatize such commitments in order to forestall such dangerous political consequences. Political liberalism thus rests upon a principled and forthright commitment to an institutional and juridical distinction between the domains of public and private life (what Rawls calls, for secondary semantic reasons, "nonpublic" life). And corresponding to this distinction is an equally important distinction between the modes of discourse appropriate to each of these domains.

"Nonpublic reason" is the form of reason appropriate in the realm of the various civil associations – "churches and universities, scientific societies and professional groups" – existing in the broader society. It is distinguished by its plurality, by the fact that it arises in many different contexts and in situationally specific forms. The non-public forms of reason typically draw upon a range of competing and conflicting "comprehensive" conceptions of ultimate value and the way to live a good life. In the domain of the "nonpublic" one can, and typically does, subscribe to deeply held and particularistic creeds and commitments, "strong feelings and zealous aspirations," and acts on these commitments unimpeded (Rawls 1993: 190, 220).

"Public reason," on the other hand, is singular. It applies to the organization of the nation state as a whole. If non-public reasons rest on a plurality of comprehensive value schemes, public reason relies on the articulation of general standards to which all "reasonable" people could and should agree regardless of their non-public aspirations and commitments (Rawls 1993: 217). Public reason is typically abstract and juridical; it is dispassionate and "rational," that is, oriented toward the uncoerced agreement of deliberative interlocutors; it is expressed in a way that is accessible to others in spite of their particular identities. Public reason, in short, is a mode of discourse and deliberation that brackets out the deeply felt and contentious matters of identity and moral concern characteristic of the broader society, that effectively privatizes these concerns and in so doing raises public life to a "higher level" of common agreement.

The domain of "public reason" is public life itself, that is, all forms of public deliberation in which "basic institutions and public policy" are determined (Rawls 1993: 190).[10] As Rawls writes, the limits of public reason

do not apply to our personal deliberations and reflections about political questions, or to the reasoning about them by members of associations, such as churches and universities, all of which is a vital part of the background culture. Plainly, religious, philosophical, and moral considerations of many kinds may here properly play a role. But the ideal of public reason does hold for citizens when they engage in political advocacy in the public forum, and thus for members of political parties and for candidates in their campaigns and for other groups who support them. It holds equally for how citizens are to vote in elections when constitutional essentials and matters of basic justice are at stake. (1993: 215)

The basic point here is that while individuals are free to exercise their civil freedom to think as they wish, in the realm of public debate and policy formation only genuinely public reasons – reasons expunged of their particular religious or moral content and coloration – are fully to count, to be authoritative or valid, and are to carry the force of law.

Rawls is careful not to argue that other kinds of public advocacy should be proscribed, for to do so would be to contravene a basic civil liberty that it is the intent of political liberalism to defend. He thus insists that this ideal of public reason "imposes a moral, not a legal, duty – the duty of civility – to be able to explain to one another" why one's view should be accepted by those with different value commitments, and to be "fairminded" in listening to other perspectives and being willing to compromise with them (Rawls 1993: 217). So political liberalism does not proscribe or prohibit any kind of political speech.

But Rawls also insists that political speech that does not accord with the requirements of "public reason," that does not bracket out fundamental value commitments and calm our passionate attachments to them, lacks constitutional validity. As he writes: "our exercise of political power is proper and hence justifiable only when it is exercised in accordance" with principles acceptable "as reasonable and rational"; and that "strong feelings and zealous aspirations for certain goals do not, as such, give people a claim to social resources, or a claim to design public institutions to achieve these goals. Desires and wants, however intense, are not by themselves reasons in matters of constitutional essentials and basic justice"; and, finally, that "the priority of right gives the principles of justice a strict precedence in citizens' deliberations and

[10] Rawls does equivocate on this question throughout the text, wavering on the subject of whether public reason applies to "constitutional" matters, questions of "constitutional essentials and basic justice," or "basic institutions and public policy."

limits their freedom to advance certain ways of life" (1993: 217, 190, 209). So that while there exists a perfect civil freedom of expression, the role of the ideal of "public reason" is, it would seem, to underprivilege, and indeed politically to *invalidate*, certain modes of discourse.

Public discourse, then, is constrained by political liberalism in the name of civil order. In order that the "basic liberties" of all citizens should be secure, some kinds of exercise of such liberties, paradoxically, must be politically constrained. Political liberalism envisions two principal modes of such constraint. One mode is rhetorical, the other more institutional and sovereign. The first is simply that, for political liberalism, legal argument is the paradigm of public discourse. As Rawls (1993: 254) puts it: "To check whether we are following public reason we might ask: how would our argument strike us presented in the form of a supreme court opinion? Reasonable? Outrageous?" On one level, as Rawls himself clearly knows, this check is an empty formality; and, given the incredible range of US Supreme Court decisions in the past 200 years, it offers precious little guidance. But on another level the medium is the message, and the form is really all that matters; and what Rawls means to tell us is that public reason requires a refinement, formality, and abstractness far removed from the "strong feelings and zealous aspirations" that in fact constitute public discourse in the real world of liberal democracy.

But Rawls's point here is more than rhetorical, and it is far from incidental that he recurs to the example of Supreme Court opinion. For political liberalism it is the courts that ultimately, finally, effectively serve as the arbiters of public reason, in the sense that judicial deliberation exemplifies public reason and, more importantly, in the sense that judicial review adjudicates *when* public reason has been violated and "injustice" has been committed (see Rawls 1993: 231–40).[11] To be more precise, it is the function of judicial review to determine when "comprehensive doctrines" have inappropriately moved beyond their domestic sphere, when they have moved into the public realm and sought to determine "basic questions of justice and public policy." For political liberalism, then, the courts fulfill a crucial role as the "spine" of liberal justice (Macedo 1995: 482).

Political liberalism criticized

What are we to make of such a political liberalism? On the one hand it has the virtue of addressing the changed circumstances of the past thirty

---

[11] The centrality of judicial review to political liberalism is noted by Alejandro (1996: 22) and Wolin (1996: 102).

years, and of theorizing problems of political conflict whose solutions were simply taken for granted by the more optimistic, "end of ideology" liberalism of *A Theory of Justice*. Political liberalism repudiates the idea that there is a natural harmony inscribed in the self or that a metaphysical form of "reason" might unproblematically legislate justice. It acknowledges that justice is a political construction, and that the principal institutions of a liberal democracy – civil freedom and representative government – rely on the exercise of power, that they constitutionally suppress or marginalize alternative ways of being, such as authoritarian forms of government and the kinds of "comprehensive doctrines" that directly promote authoritarian forms of government.

We share the sense that civil liberties are an important achievement worthy of institutional protection, and that it would be an injustice for them to be abridged in the name of a religious or moral creed that sought a monopoly of authority over "basic institutions and public policy," or that sought to exclude certain categories of citizens from the equal protection of the law or from the political process. In particular, we share deep concerns about the way in which political life today is being moralized by the conservative politicization of religion. This moralization threatens important achievements of freedom for racial minorities, women, and gays, and represents a reactionary effort to turn back the political clock on these genuine gains and to reinstate unjust forms of privilege that successfully have been contested.[12] Many – though not all – of the demands of the religious Right, in short, are averse to basic norms of democratic equality as these norms historically have emerged and been institutionalized, and we agree with political liberals that such demands ought to be opposed.

However, we do not believe that political liberalism is a plausible way to promote either the liberty or the "civility" that it prizes (Rawls 1993: 217). Political liberalism has three significant deficiencies. First, it wrongly defines its problem in narrowly jurisprudential terms, in terms of a juridical decision rule for determining the justness of claims once they enter the "public" domain narrowly construed. Like Karl Popper's "falsificationist" philosophy of science, political liberalism wrongly presumes the tenability of a radical separation of the method of discovery and the method of validation; it assumes, in other words, that political theory can concern itself with "public" forms of reason and "public" institutions and policies, and can simply bracket out the institutions and discourses of civil society as "background conditions," relevant to

---

[12] On the reactionary nature of the religious Right, the extent that it is a reaction *to* the political openings of the 1960s, see especially Lienesch 1993.

sociology and perhaps even to political science but not to theorizing the legitimate exercise of public authority in a democratic society.

But this distinction between the "public" and the "nonpublic" – a classically liberal distinction that political liberalism seeks to reinstate in new ways, without the aid of natural law or transcendental reason, but to similar effect – is wholly untenable. Ironically, while it purports to be "political," political liberalism's narrow focus on "public reason" allows it to ignore the social and political sources of contemporary liberalism's difficulties. Yet the causes of the problems that burden liberalism today – the fractiousness, the incivility, the conflict over scarce moral and economic resources – are important for any serious political theory to understand. These problems emerge from a particular civil society at a particular historical moment, they relate to the expression of ethical, cultural, and political demands that exceed liberalism as it currently is organized, and to this extent they can be viewed as symptoms of the limits of liberalism itself. Another way of putting this is that a political theory that proclaims its ethical and explanatory indifference to what is going on in the world of civil society, to the "nonpublic uses of reason," and to the ways in which power is being constituted and contested in society at large, is wholly inadequate to the problems it purports to address. If the optimism of Rawlsian social democratic liberalism circa 1971 is misplaced, then perhaps this suggests the need for a more direct engagement with the limits of that liberalism rather than a retreat, however understandable, behind a pessimistic and more minimalist liberalism whose only answer to its challengers is to exclude them in the name of "public reason." Political liberalism, in short, mistakenly reduces the legitimation problems plaguing liberalism today to the ill manners of agitated constituencies, ignoring the deeper questions of power that they implicate.

Political liberalism's methodological indifference to what is happening in civil society relates to its second defect, its untenable distinction between "public" and "nonpublic" reason. The conceptual strategy of distinguishing considerations or modes of discourse appropriate to public as opposed to non-public processes, and of bracketing fundamental value questions in the name of supposedly public arguments that can command the wider assent of all reasonable people, is one that cannot plausibly be sustained except by arbitrary stipulation. For every political consensus rests on and reinforces background assumptions and fundamental value commitments, and thus the requirement that such commitments be bracketed from public debate only serves to privilege the status quo ante. As Jürgen Habermas has argued:

[if justice were] to require that ethical questions be *bracketed out* of public discourse in general, then such discourse would forfeit its power to rationally change prepolitical attitudes, need interpretations, and value orientations. According to this reading of "conversational restraint," practical questions that are prima facie controversial should simply not be pursued any farther. This amounts to treating questions of the good as "private" affairs ... Such a rigid constraint, which a fortiori excludes ethical questions, would at least implicitly prejudice the agenda in favor of an inherited background of settled traditions. (1996: 309)[13]

The history of modern liberalism is indeed a history of repeated, and often successful, efforts to contest this very strategy of privatization, bursting the bounds of domesticity, violating legally enforced public/private distinctions, refusing to accept as "background conditions" forms of discourse and modes of power that were an affront to a sense of justice, seeking to foreground such matters, to politicize them, and to redress the grievances and injustices that they present. The modern history of feminism is simply one example of this process, whereby activities, concerns, and modes of expression long considered "private" came to be seen as deeply constructed and contestable, and were forced into the public domain (see Evans and Boyte 1986; Fraser 1989; and Young 1990). Indeed, it would be accurate to describe this history of usurpations of this liberal effort to fix a boundary between the public and the non-public as nothing less than a history of the democratization of liberalism.

It is clear that political liberalism seeks to arrest this history, that it sees the problem today as being too much contestation, and that it seeks some juridical mechanism for securing agreement on fundamentals and depoliticizing the disagreements that remain.[14] But this depoliticizing strategy cannot work. For if it is notoriously difficult to give substance to the idea of a distinctively "public" mode of argumentation or deliberation that might bracket out fundamental value commitments and forms of discourse, it is even more difficult to render such a conception consistent with the messy and contentious forms of democratic contestation that have evolved and flourished in the actual course of history. Consider, for example, the discourses associated with abolitionism, or Populism, or Debsian socialism, or the civil rights movement, or second-wave feminism. In each case the public rhetoric and argumentation used to mobilize supporters and to justify controversial demands was deeply moral, deeply contentious, sometimes indeed deeply religious, implicating fundamental values, eliciting passionate response and

---

[13] For an argument that uses Habermas to develop a quite similar critique of Rawls, see Shaw 1997.

[14] A similar criticism has been made by Honig (1993: 126–61). See also Mouffe 1993.

zealous advocacy. These discourses could not at first command wide-spread assent. They were often viewed as fanatical, dogmatic, or "irrational." Martin Luther King's "Letter from Birmingham Jail" (King 1991 [1963]), let us not forget, was written to explain to white so-called moderates "why we can't wait" for civil rights anymore. Endorsing what he called "creative extremism," King invoked the prophetic tradition of the Hebrew and Christian Bibles to support civil disobedience, a form of political resistance that was non-violent to be sure, but that was zealous, contentious, and disturbing to normal "public peace and civility" none the less.[15] In Rawls's terms, such political advocacy would seem appropriate in non-public domains but inappropriate as forms of justification of the exercise of legitimate public authority (1993: 363–91).[16] Yet it is hard to see how liberal democracy could ever have come into existence in the absence of such public discourses, just as it is hard to see, unless one postulates that ethical–political conflict has reached an absolute historical terminus, how it can be said to flourish in any meaningful sense when such discourses are driven outside of the public domain.

Indeed, Rawls himself seems aware of this problem. *Political Liberalism* contains a brief discussion of the abolitionist and civil rights movements, in which Rawls acknowledges the apparent "exclusiveness" of his conception of "public reason," and attempts to reformulate it in a more "inclusive" way. The abolitionists and Martin Luther King, Jr, he allows, did invoke comprehensive moral and religious doctrines that would seem to have exceeded "public reason," and yet he claims that they did not "go against the ideal of public reason." He offers two reasons for this claim. One is that the societies they confronted were not "well ordered," and there thus existed significant and, presumably, legitimate disagreements about the basic structure of society. The second is that if we "view the question conceptually and not historically," we can see that these ethical–political movements exceeded public reason "for the sake of the ideal of public reason itself." As he puts it:

[15] The famous Birmingham campaign was called "Project C," and the "C" was for "Confrontation." See Williams 1988: 182 and Garrow 1986. On the need for a more complex, agonistic conception of public discourse, see Young 1987; Fraser 1992; Villa 1993; and Chaloupka 1993.

[16] Joshua Cohen has reminded us that Rawls (1993: 363–91) does include an interesting discussion of civil disobedience. While we remain unconvinced that this is a topic central to either version of Rawls's theory, our point is not that Rawls's view is inconsistent with civil disobedience, but that the contentiousness and the deeply moral modes of discourse that typically motivate the practice of civil disobedience elude the terms of Rawls's theory.

On this account the abolitionists and the leaders of the civil rights movement did not go against the ideal of public reason; or, rather, they did not provided they thought, or on reflection would have thought (as they certainly could have thought), that the comprehensive reasons they appealed to were required to give sufficient strength to the political conception to be subsequently realized. (1993: 251)

But this account is question-begging in the extreme, and simply will not do. First, it is deeply equivocal. To say that these democratic activists did not go against public reason provided that they thought, or on reflection would have thought, that their moral discourses contributed to public reason is to invoke an utterly hypothetical condition – that they could have or would have endorsed Rawls's "public reason" in spite of the fact that they did not in fact do so – in order to explain an equally hypothetical claim – that they were Rawlsian liberals "provided that they thought" like Rawls does. But in fact they did not talk, and most certainly did not think, as Rawls does, which Rawls himself knows. This is why he constructs his case so equivocally, and why he insists on viewing the question "conceptually and not historically." Rawls wants to incorporate a hypothetical, "conceptual" William Lloyd Garrison or Martin Luther King within his account as a substitute for the real historical protagonists, who elude his account, who pursued their conceptions of freedom by employing a rich vocabulary of moral denunciation and prophetic criticism. Secondly, what can it mean to assert that these figures struggled against societies that were not "well-ordered," if the criteria of a well ordered society are themselves precisely what is in question? On what basis can Rawls confidently assert that the post-Civil War United States, for example, was poorly ordered but that American society today is not? We do not question that slavery was wrong, nor that liberation has been achieved, but we do question the implicit suggestion that liberty has been *realized*, that we have achieved an end of history, in which further contestations have been rendered unnecessary. Indeed, we would go one step further. We question whether such a restrictive, Rawlsian conception of public discourse can even "do justice" to the actual liberatory achievements that Rawls himself seems to prize.

Rawls's effort to use "public reason" as a criterion of legitimate public discourse is thus highly questionable, and there is no reason to support the strategy of discursive containment that his theory endorses. It is possible to take a different tack, and offer a plausible account of a set of ideals and procedures that might constrain public authority, but not on the ground that these procedures are distinctively "reasonable" or beyond comprehensive commitments. These would be the ideals and procedures of procedural democracy itself. Such norms might invalidate certain forms of political conduct, such as those, for example, that involve the use of terrorism or physical intimidation of opponents or the promotion of insurrectionary violence, or those that result in the exercise of governmental authority directly to silence or disenfranchise particular individuals or groups. But it is hard to see how these procedural democratic norms would address the problems of "incivility" that concern political liberalism, for most of the significant and divisive moral conflicts today are debated squarely within the confines of procedural democratic norms.

As Rawls has written, the point of political liberalism is "to appeal to a conception of justice to distinguish between those questions that can be reasonably removed from the political agenda and those that cannot . . . [f]aced with the fact of pluralism . . . a liberal view removes from the political agenda the most divisive issues, pervasive uncertainty and serious contention about which must undermine the bases of social cooperation" (1985: 13, 17). But the difficulty is precisely that there *is* no consensus on which questions "can reasonably removed from the political agenda," or, to the extent that there is such agreement – that slavery is wrong, or that freedom of speech is right, for example (though we wonder about both of these[17]) – this agreement has no bearing on the resolution of those pressing problems on which significant disagreement remains.

The problem with political liberalism is its profound ambiguity in the face of this difficulty. On the one hand it purports to offer a theoretical solution that would resolve the difficulty by specifying a conception of "public reason" that might ease the uncertainty and contention of our time. But it does not, and cannot, offer a plausible conception of public reason that would allow us to say, for example, that the modes of political advocacy typical of Afrocentrism or Christian fundamentalism or radical feminism or queer politics or the critics of affirmative action and abortion rights are "unreasonable." In response, political liberalism wields its other hand; but it turns out to be not a velvet hand of reason but an iron hand of coercion. Political liberals seem to argue that if we want to abate our antagonisms and enjoy the fruits of social cooperation then we *must* have consensus on the value of a minimalist form of liberal

---

[17] The reasons why we wonder about both of these go beyond the scope of this chapter. But the slavery issue raises all kinds of questions about the prevalence of servile and enforced labor in the global economy in which liberal democracies participate and through which they flourish; and the free speech issue raises a thicket of difficulties, related to corporate ownership of the media and to campaign finance legislation. In both cases, the idea that these values have a plain and unproblematic meaning that has already been ascertained strikes us as absurd.

democracy and we *must* agree to depoliticize our other, divisive, differences. The "must" is the imperatival must of philosophy, but it is also the sovereign must of power. In the end it appears that political liberalism requires that such a politics of avoidance must be practiced in spite of the refusal of many constituencies to acknowledge its legitimacy, and that those who cannot be convinced must be coerced. This is why the courts assume such a prominent role in the theory of political liberalism: because they represent a form of power outside of and theoretically above the unruly multitudes of the demos, and a form of "reason" that alone might quiet and harmonize the dissonances of our contentious public life by purging political discourse of its ideological partisanship and thus forcing out the acrimony of politics.

Political liberalism's postulate of "public reason" is thus theoretically untenable. But it is equally deficient from a more practical point of view, for its strategy of containment is anti-democratic in a way that is also self-defeating. To peremptorily insist that political discourse must take a certain form, and that modes of association and activism that fail to do so lack constitutional validity, is to undermine the free flow of debate, and unjustifiably to disempower important constituencies, of a democratic society. It is to privilege the powers of judicial review associated with the court system at the expense of more majoritarian and more conflictive public arenas, in which public debate is likely to overflow the bounds of Rawls's public reason. Yet judicial institutions are in disrepute in American politics today, and the story of this development is also the story of the weakening support for liberalism in America. The juridical remedy that is at the heart of political liberalism is thus deeply suspect, and is likely simply to exacerbate the problems that it seeks to address, and to promote an even more deeply anti-liberal conservative backlash.[18] This is perhaps the most important debility of political liberalism – its inattentiveness to the current weaknesses of organized liberalism and to its own legitimacy deficit, and its ignorance of the political dynamics that have energized the New Christian Right in the first place. We can see this more clearly by looking more closely at how political liberalism treats the phenomenon of the New Christian Right.

The limits of political liberalism: the case of *Mozert v. Hawkins*

In his "Liberal civic education and religious fundamentalism: the case of God v. John Rawls," Stephen Macedo (1995) presents an application of

---

[18] Jeremy Rabkin (1996: 3–26) argues that much of the activity of the New Christian Right was a reaction to liberal court decisions.

political liberalism to the challenges posed by the New Christian Right. The liberalism he defends is "a political liberalism with spine," a liberalism at peace with the idea that "no version of liberalism can make everybody happy," and that in dealing with various forms of fundament-alism liberals are justified in using the coercive powers of the state to invalidate certain fundamentalist demands, in spite of the unhappiness this may cause to those considered fundamentalist.

Macedo's argument centers around an interpretation of five separate federal court rulings in 1983 that came to be known collectively as *Mozert v. Hawkins*. The litigation arose when seven fundamentalist families in Hawkins County, Tennessee, filed a suit against the Hawkins County public schools, alleging that the liberal values being taught in school interfered with their freedom of religious expression and with their constitutional right to raise their children as Christians.[19] According to Vicki Frost and her co-plaintiffs, some of the reading materials used in the schools promoted scientific rationalism, tolerance, "relativism," and other "secular humanist" ideas that contravened their fundamentalist beliefs. According to the *Mozert* parents, the Bible commanded them to avoid "any story or selection which teaches or exposes to children values, beliefs, or concepts which the Bible teaches as being evil" and, because humanistic values were evil, it would infringe on their free exercise of religion for the public schools to require their children to read the materials in question.[20] The *Mozert* parents further argued that the school curriculum violated the First Amendment's establishment clause by promoting a particular religion, the "religion" of "secular humanism." A lengthy litigation ensued, surrounded by an even more complex political spectacle, in which the *Mozert* parents became publicly identified with the New Christian Right's broader agenda of contesting liberalism, represented by Michael Farris of the Concerned Women of America, and in which People for the American Way and other liberal advocacy groups entered the fray on behalf of a strong separation between Church and state.

The US Court of Appeals eventually ruled against the plaintiffs and in favor of the school district, rejecting their claim that the public school curriculum violated their free exercise rights by teaching basic liberal values, and construing their suit as an unacceptable demand for the privileging of their religion by claiming an exemption for it. Macedo argues that the court's ruling epitomizes the argument of political liberalism. The ruling rejected the idea that the teaching of civil tolera-tion promulgates a particular comprehensive doctrine called "secular

---

[19] For an excellent account of this controversy, see Bates 1993.
[20] Complaint filed by attorney Michael Farris, quoted in Bates 1993: 156.

humanism," and defended the right of the liberal state to promote diversity even when such diversity was uncomfortable to some citizens; it asserted that while schools may not teach religious doctrine, such as the idea that all faiths are equal in the eyes of God, it can and should teach that all religions are equal, and none privileged, in the eyes of the state.[21]

According to Macedo, the court recognized that "reasonable people" may disagree about the good life and may profoundly disagree about the value of different religious perspectives, but that these disagreements are not properly public matters, and should legitimately be bracketed out of public discourse and of public education. People may disagree about ultimate values and yet "might nevertheless agree that public aims such as peace, prosperity, and equal liberty are very important." "What political liberalism asks of us," Macedo (1995: 474) goes on, "is not to renounce what we believe to be true but to acknowledge the difficulty of publicly establishing any single account of the whole truth. It invites us to put some of our (true) beliefs aside when it comes to laying the groundwork for common political institutions."

It is thus legitimate for Vicki Frost and her fellow plaintiffs to be expected to abide by public school requirements that their children put their religious beliefs aside in the name of common "public aims," and that they expose themselves to certain literature and learn certain civic skills in spite of their religious convictions. More to the point, it is also legitimate for the plaintiffs to be expected to lay aside their own religious beliefs, however deeply held, when advancing claims in the public arena. If the *Mozert* parents wish to raise their children as fundamentalist Christians that is a private matter, and they should have the right to do so, and to promote and disseminate their point of view as they think fit, in churches, in newsletters, in other forms of voluntary association. But they do not have the right to convert this point of view into public policy. Or, to repeat Rawls's formulation: "strong feeling and zealous aspirations for certain goals do not, as such, give people a claim to social resources, or a claim to design public institutions to achieve these goals. Desires and wants, however intense, are not by themselves reasons in matters of constitutional essentials and basic justice" (1993: 190).

Macedo follows the logic of Rawls's argument, but is more explicit, and thus more revealing of the Hobbesianism of political liberalism's "spine." Political liberals, he maintains, do not seek to exclude religious people or religious speech from the public realm: "The aim, rather, is to suggest that the most basic political rights and institutions should be

---

[21] Macedo's argument focuses on the court opinion written by Judge Lively (Macedo 1995: 470–75).

justified in terms of reasons and arguments that can be shared with reasonable people whose religious and other ultimate commitments differ" (1995: 474). Fundamentalists are as free as anyone else to say what they want, but if they have a desire for their opinions to determine public policy – if they want their opinions politically, rather than metaphysically, to *count* – then they must put aside their passionate religious beliefs and constitutive religious vocabularies and must adopt a more "rational" posture and discourse. "The crux of the matter is not speech at all," Macedo insists, but "the legitimate grounds of coercion." While citizens are free to speak their minds, "at the end of the political day" liberals are justified in recognizing as valid only appropriately articulated, "public justifications" (1995: 475).

According to Macedo, the reasoning of the federal court in the *Mozert* case mirrors the pedagogy of the public school curriculum in Hawkins County. Both "[leave] aside the religious question as such," and deal only with the requirements of liberal public order, with such basic, non-religious, secular aims as the teaching of basic cognitive skills (such as reading, science, and math) and basic civic skills (such as tolerance and civility). This strategy of avoidance is not, Macedo concedes, a "neutral" device; it does, in a way, discriminate against "totalistic faiths" like those of Vicki Frost, which "will be especially resistant to thinking about politics (or anything else) from a perspective that in any way "brackets" the truth of their particular religious views" (1995: 478).[22] But political liberals can do no more than allow such faiths to operate, circumscribed to be sure, in the private sphere, while denying them the political exemptions and entitlements that they seek – exemptions and entitlements that constitute, for the political liberal, nothing but special privileges that are contrary to liberal justice (Macedo 1995: 489). Thus the demand advanced by the plaintiffs in the *Mozert* case, that public life be structured so as to be entirely unburdensome to their particular religious world-view, is illiberal, and ought to be resisted. It ought to be theoretically criticized by political liberals, and it ought to be invalidated by judicial bodies properly committed to politically liberal principles; and less moderate demands – such as demands not simply to limit public burdens on fundamentalism but politically to enact laws that promote fundamentalist values – ought similarly to be invalidated on liberal grounds.

Macedo's argument for the "political promise" of political liberalism has far-reaching implications for thinking about the intersections of

[22] Rawls (1993: 170) admits as much in passing, when he avers that "except for certain kinds of fundamentalism, all the main historical religions" are "reasonable" comprehensive doctrines, that admit their own partiality.

religion and politics in American public life. It suggests that a whole series of demands being currently pressed by the New Christian Right, sometimes in the name of "family values," sometimes in the name of special recognition of "Christian" identity – prayer in the schools, the teaching of "creation science," the banning of books and periodicals deemed offensive to religious sensibilities from public and public school libraries, the involvement of school boards in curricular matters in order to promote so-called "decency" and to eliminate sex education, the provision of "parental rights" of veto over curricular decisions, etc. – might with good reason be considered violations of liberal justice, inappropriate ways of politicizing private, moral matters, introducing "nonpublic reasons" into the public domain and thus producing injustice. It would thus seem to follow that when such efforts meet with political success, and result in the demanded legal enactments by local school boards, state legislatures, or even Congress itself, these successes ought to be invalidated by judicial bodies more sensitive to the demands of "public reason", and done so in the name of peace, prosperity, and equal liberty.

Macedo, to be fair, does not draw these general conclusions from his argument, which is closely centered on *Mozert*. However, the entire point of his "liberalism with spine" *is* that political liberals ought not to shrink from the entailments of their principles, and the principle of "public reasonableness" *does* deprive much of the political discourse of fundamentalist ideologues of its illocutionary force, rendering it invalid as "legitimate grounds of coercion." In the case of *Mozert* the implications of this position are clear – courts should rule against claims such as those made by Vicki Frost and her co-plaintiffs, because such claims involve the inappropriate politicization of "nonpublic" matters and the employment of "irrational" vocabularies.[23]

As we have already indicated, we share the concern of political liberals that the demands of the New Christian Right and other fundamentalist groups, whether religious, ethnic, or racial, are often insensitive to the pluralism of modern life, that they are divisive and indeed often threatening to the liberties of other groups within our society. We share, in other words, the concern about the potentially tyrannical effects of the agendas of many identity-centered movements, especially when

[23] Amy Gutmann and Dennis Thompson (1996: 63–8) present a very similar argument about *Mozert*, contending that the Christian fundamentalist parents invoked reasons that cannot widely be justified, that their anti-humanism is contrary to democracy, and that many of their claims "cannot be sustained by reliable methods of inquiry." While their book is intended to elaborate a robust conception of deliberative democracy, this example suggests that in some important respects their view is not that far removed from that of the political liberals they criticize.

these demands are articulated in a fundamentalist way, as essential or beyond challenge. There is a genuine danger presented by such a fundamentalism. This danger, it is worth emphasizing, is not confined to religious discourses, though there can be no denying that the religious discourses associated with the New Christian Right are particularly dangerous. However, Macedo's argument about the implications of the *Mozert* case is deficient for all of the reasons that Rawls's political liberalism is deficient.

In the first place, while Macedo claims that public policy must be "publicly justified independently of religious and other comprehensive claims," it is less than fully clear that his political liberalism is anything more than an alternative comprehensive doctrine, one undoubtedly more open-minded and tolerant of pluralism and diversity than that of Vicki Frost, but one equally informed by a commitment to certain "ultimate" values, the Rawlsian values of public peace, prosperity, and the enjoyment of "primary goods" by all. This *is* a conception of the good. It is a conception not without its appeal, but it is contestable nonetheless, and in important ways.[24] For is civil amity a good that reasonably should trump all others? Is it plainly unjust for democratic citizens to try to make public education responsive to the demands of morality as they see it? What are the legitimate purposes of education in a democratic society? Is it so clear, as Macedo seems to think, that the teaching of science, math, and reading is unrelated to questions of values, or, to put it perhaps more accurately, that the value of these things is unproblematically fixed and narrowly academic or cognitive? Indeed, what constitutes these seemingly self-evident and staple subjects *as* subjects? Are they not deeply constructed and contested, both at the level of academic discipline and at the level of pedagogy?[25] Couldn't a variant of Macedo's argument, that public schools teach "science" and not "(religious) values," equally be made against the teaching of feminist literature ("we are in the business of teaching reading, not men-bashing") or labor history ("we teach civics here, not Communism")?[26] In other words, are the kinds of issues at stake, and the modes of justification themselves at play, in the *Mozert* case as plainly beyond politics as Macedo suggests? In posing these questions we do not wish to

---

[24] This point is made by Stolzenberg (1993). For an interesting essay that raises similar concerns, see MacIntyre 1990: 344–61.

[25] This argument is made, with great subtlety, about "creation science" in Taylor 1996.

[26] These are crucial issues, nicely explored in Levine 1996, which makes clear just how constructed such pedagogical questions have been in American history, and how impossible it is to bracket out deep value questions and forms of advocacy from "education" and the public domain more broadly.

give credence to the particular answers to them preferred by the Christian Right, but we do wish to insist that Macedo's conception of what constitutes a legitimately public concern is deeply loaded and arguably undemocratic.

This can be highlighted when we consider that the *Mozert* case, which Macedo deploys on behalf of political liberalism, does not deal with the fundamentalism of the Christian Right in its most politically challenging form. First, we will recall, in *Mozert* it was the fundamentalists who were the petitioners of the courts, claiming exemption from the decisions of a democratically elected legislative body. Second, as Macedo indicates but fails sufficiently to theorize, in the *Mozert* case the plaintiffs, far from couching their arguments exclusively in terms of "comprehensive doctrine," embedded their religious claims in a broader narrative fully within the mainstream of liberal constitutionalism, a narrative about the Free Exercise and Establishment Clauses of the US Constitution and what these clauses mean. These facts of the case make it doubly complex. Because the petitioners were clearly an obstreperous minority, the federal court ruling against them has a great deal of intuitive weight for those committed to democratic values, in spite of the fact that their claim, contrary to Macedo's argument, was in many ways "reasonable" and at least comprehensible to liberal ears.[27]

But if we envision a scenario slightly different than the one presented by *Mozert*, then the prescriptions of political liberalism and our democratic intuitions begin to part ways. What if, instead of being presented by an obstreperous petitioner, the argument of Vicki Frost had instead been the argument of the duly constituted authority of Hawkins County? What if the Hawkins County school board, or the Tennessee state legislature, had fallen under the sway of a political party – say, the Republican Party – dominated by the Christian Coalition and groups to its right?[28] What if the Holt reader in question (the reader assigned to students at the school attended by Ms Frost's children) had been eliminated by, or curricular policy more generally had been established by, a democratically elected body of which a majority were committed to acting in the name of "family values" or even "Christian values" (the first being simply a euphemism for the second in any case), and invoked this rhetoric to justify publicly the policy in question? And what if political liberalism were cast in the role of the aggrieved minority and

[27] That the plaintiffs were an obstreperous minority, even within a county that was both deeply Protestant fundamentalist and politically conservative, is a point emphasized by Bates (1993: chaps. 1–3).

[28] On the role of the religious Right in the Republican Party, see Persinos 1994; Barnes 1994; Rozell and Wilcox 1995; Rozell and Wilcox 1996; and Wilcox 1996.

obstreperous petitioner? Would it be right – would it be *just* – to invalidate juridically the decisions of such democratically elected public bodies, and thereby to invalidate the freely expressed and endorsed views of the politically organized majority of the community in question, in the name of "public reason"?[29]

In raising these questions we do not wish to suggest that majority rule in a democracy is always right.[30] We acknowledge the importance of civil and political rights in any democratic society worthy of the name, and thereby acknowledge that institutions such as judicial review play an important role in a democracy by helping to safeguard such rights.[31] Our point is not that anything enacted by an elected body is legitimate. Certainly in a federal system such as the United States there are complex questions regarding competing jurisdictions that severely complicate any judgment and render any legislative enactment legally questionable. And in any constitutional democracy, there are often conflicts between important constitutional principles, such as freedom of expression and equality under the law, that require adjudication. In dealing with questions of public education things are further complicated by the fact that the common "public" school system is a specific institution with a complex set of demands and constituencies, including children who are not yet full citizens and thus do not yet possess effective political rights.[32] But even if we go this route, it is still possible to agree with John Hart Ely's classic argument that the appropriate domain of judicial review is the preservation of basic democratic liberties

[29] In a previous case, *Edwards v. Aguilard* (1987), US Supreme Court Justice Antonin Scalia raised this very question in dissenting from the Court's invalidation of a Louisiana "Creation Act" preventing the teaching of evolution unless "creation science" was taught along side of it. Scalia insisted that "striking down a law approved by the democratically elected representative of the people is no minor matter."

[30] This is itself of course a complex question, that presumes that a clear meaning can be attached to the designation "majority." On the difficulties of this, see Dahl 1956 and Shapiro 1996.

[31] This point is nicely made in Holmes 1988a.

[32] On the complex issues at stake, see Gutmann 1987. On the question of the rights of children, which should not be conflated with the preferences of their parents, see Arneson and Shapiro 1996. On the importance of schools as promoters of democratic values, and on the need to circumvent the opposition of parents who oppose such civic values, see Gutmann 1995: 557–79. We share Gutmann's sense that parents in a democratic society have no exclusive proprietary control over their children, and that the democratic political community has rightful claims through public education. We wonder, however, how truly democratic a political community can be if the preferences of its adult members – parents and other citizens – can easily be overriden in the name of "civic values," for the question is precisely *which* civic values are relevant. While we would not deny that certain forms of indoctrination are inappropriate in a democratic public school, we are wary of the way many liberals would dismiss the results of a procedurally democratic process. But the issues raised by Gutmann are complex matters that go beyond the scope of our argument here.

themselves, that "it can concern itself only with questions of participation, and not with the substantive merits of the political choice under attack" (1980: 181; see also Dahl 1989: 359). To take this position is not to endorse Ely's restrictive conception of the basic civil and political rights essential to democratic self-government. It is simply, but crucially, to commit to a profound skepticism about overriding the decisions of duly constituted and elected legislative bodies, except in extreme cases where basic rights are at stake. In *Mozert* and other similar cases in which questions of fundamentalism are at issue, it is not at all clear that what is at stake is anything other than the "substantive merits of the political choice." If a politically organized majority in a given community, committed to procedural democratic norms, should become politically empowered and proceed to enact political choices consistent with the world-view of Vicki Frost and articulated publicly in the way that she and her colleagues spoke, would it then plainly be legitimate to invalidate juridically such political decisions?

Our answer to this is qualified. We would wisely be inclined, as a matter of historical prudence, to fear the sectarianization of politics, and there are many good reasons why democrats would seek to contest such decisions. It would be foolhardy on pragmatic as well as theoretical grounds to deny that courts are an important arena of contestation in a democratic society, in their capacity as rights-protecting institutions but also in their role as fora for debating matters of principle (see McCann 1994). In some cases there would seem to be clear warrant, following Ely's dictum, for invoking judicial remedies against legislation, if for example a law declared only Christians eligible for office or mandated particular kinds of school prayer or sectarian public display.[33] But there are equally good reasons to be wary of the anti-majoritarianism characteristic of political liberalism and of the way it so peremptorily invokes "public reason" against the most contentious and disruptive political discourses of our time, for judicial remedies may often subvert or inhibit democratic liberty. As Cass Sunstein has argued: "reliance on courts may impair democratic channels for seeking changes, and in two ways. It might divert energy and resources from politics, and the eventual judicial decision may foreclose a political outcome. On both counts, the impairment of democracy can be very serious" (1993: 145; see Burt 1992; Rosenberg 1991; and Shapiro 1995: 13–23). Before we too quickly are moved by fear to foreclose the politicization of religious identity that political liberalism so resists, we should consider, as we have argued above, that the politicization of identity and the redefinition

---

[33] On the history of political debate on these issues, see Kramnick and Moore 1996.

of the public and private realms is the most central defining feature of the history of liberal democratization. It is true, as Bruce Ackerman has pointed out, that once these redefinitions occur they become sedimented in constitutional law and political practice, and a mobilization of bias in their favor ensues; but it is equally true that such redefinitions only occur *because of* the vigorous and passionate "intrusion" of "comprehensive doctrines" into the public realm, thereby unsettling previous mobilizations of bias. Such intrusions have been the principal mechanism of political progress in our society (Ackerman 1991; see Rawls 1993: 233–4). Abolitionism, feminism, Progressivism, trade unionism, New Deal reformism, the civil rights movement, environmentalism – each of these movements represented a redefinition of "the political" that disrupted settled ways and, through the promotion of what Rawls calls "divisive issues, pervasive uncertainty, and serious contention," resulted in the further democratization of American life. It would seem absurd to argue that the political process ought somehow to be insulated from such contention just – as James Madison once noted (1961 [1787]) – as it would be absurd to try to eliminate the dangers of faction by extinguishing the oxygen of liberty.

Democratic politics and the contest of identities

The serious conflicts of values that exist in American society today are different from these earlier ones, in some ways more liberatory, in many ways more fractious and challenging. They are symptoms of a serious institutional and ethical crisis of postwar liberalism and its trinity of peace, prosperity, and equal liberty (Lasch 1991). Political liberalism simply fails to see this. Indeed, for political liberalism this crisis would seem a matter of indifference, a question perhaps of "background conditions" but not of "constitutional essentials." One searches in vain, for example, in Rawls's 390-page book (1993), for any account of the historical and institutional causes of the "incivility" that concerns him. But it is essential to understand these conditions if we want to understand the resurgence of political fundamentalism in American politics. For if "fundamentalism" in American politics signifies anything, it signifies a rejection of the postwar liberal consensus about the limits of politics that political liberalism seeks to reinstate.

This is especially true of the New Christian Right. The objections of people like Vicki Frost to liberal forms of public education did not arise out of thin air. What Macedo calls the threat of "holy war" is not an aberration nor is it an anachronism. It is a reaction to the successes and to the failures of postwar liberalism in America. The New Christian

Right is, among other things, a component of what Christopher Lasch has called "right-wing populism and the revolt against liberalism" (Lasch 1991: 476–532). The liberalism in question is, once again, the liberalism of Rawls circa 1971, a mildly redistributionist and yet individualist liberalism, geared toward the wide distribution of "primary goods" and "basic liberties." The 1960s represented both the apotheosis of this liberalism and the decade in which it fell to pieces, imploded by conflict about the Vietnam War, racial strife, urban violence, and student unrest. The story of American liberalism's decline goes beyond the scope of this chapter,[34] but it is important to note that the New Christian Right emerged as a *response* to this decline.[35] This is true in two important ways. First, the New Christian Right must be seen as a reaction to the New Left, and to the liberatory movements for civil rights and civil liberties, Black Power, student rights, women's rights, and gay rights that defined the New Left and that set it against conventional middle-class "family" values.[36] Second, it emerged as an expression of a growing sentiment, among significant segments of the American population, that liberalism is an inadequate public philosophy, that it is too morally permissive, that in its preoccupation with individual liberties it is too juridical and administrative, too reliant on courts and bureaucracies, and too distant from popular sources of power and conventional moral norms.[37] When Jerry Falwell wrote in *Listen America!* (1980) that "liberal forces such as the abortionists, the homosexuals, the pornographers, secular humanists, and Marxists have made significant inroads" in Christian America, he was (hyperbolically) expressing this sensibility, and articulating a hostility toward liberalism that would help to fuel not simply the growth of a broad network of conservative Christian activists numbering in the millions but also an even broader conservative assault against liberalism, against the Rawlsian idea of equal liberty and against the "big government" that was necessary to guarantee such liberty (Marty and Appelby 1992: 33).[38] To

[34] Excellent overviews are presented in Dionne 1991 and Edsall and Edsall 1992.
[35] The best source on this is Leinisch 1993.
[36] For an interesting discussion of this backlash phenomenon, with particular emphasis on highly charged questions of sexuality, see Bull and Gallagher 1996.
[37] Thus Francis (1982: 68) claimed that a liberal elite had "seized power in the political and economic crisis of the Great Depression ... [and the] chief instrument of its rise to power, then and in the following decades, was the state, especially the federal government, and more especially the executive branch." But this point is recognized by liberals as well. Lind (1995: chap. 4) offers a powerful critique of the reliance of liberals on administrative and juridical remedies for racial inequality.
[38] On the relationships between the New Christian Right and the New Right more generally, see Viguerie 1981 and Crawford 1980. On "big government," see Helms 1976 and Armey 1994: 27–34.

take account of this sensibility, apocalyptic to be sure, is *not* to endorse it, but it is to understand its political power in a way that political liberal moralizing about "irrationality" and "incivility" fails to do.

The New Christian Right is at once a reaction to the growth of a culturally based identity politics in the 1960s and a mirror image of such a politics, in which increasingly self-conscious and self-identified "Christians" are seeking to mobilize political power and to enact legislation in the name of a particular "comprehensive doctrine," in this case a deeply conservative and sectarian doctrine. Like other identity-based movements, the New Christian Right often articulates its demands in a populist idiom, in the name of a collectivity – "decent Americans," or "Christian America" – that is purported to be oppressed by another collectivity – "liberal elites" or "the Washington establishment"[39] But, as the *Mozert* case makes clear, New Christian Right demands often simultaneously adopt the very language of rights that is prized by liberalism itself, asserting that the religious liberties of Christians are being abridged, or that their political speech is denied full constitutional protection by the way in which courts have treated fundamentalist claims.[40]

When we situate the New Christian Right in this way, we see how difficult it is to marginalize it in the way that Macedo proposes. For its fundamentalism is not simply a philosophic conceit, nor is it simply an argument against John Rawls, who most Americans have never heard of and could not care less about; it is a significant reaction to, and rebellion against, organized liberalism itself. In this regard it does not stand alone, but is simply one among many movements contesting postwar, welfare-state liberalism and raising fundamental questions about the legitimacy of the liberal state and its juridical and redistributionist agencies.

As Jürgen Habermas has stated, the welfare state has exhausted its utopian possibilities. It is increasingly viewed as illegitimate not simply by conservatives of various kinds, but by "new social movements" disenchanted with its bureaucratism and political elitism, and seeking to expand the scope and proliferate the sites of political debate (Habermas 1989). The growing literature on civil society addresses many aspects of this legitimacy crisis, treating the associational life of liberal democracy not as the background conditions of politics but as the foreground of

[39] On populist political language, see Kazin 1995. Perhaps the most notorious populist episode in the emergence of the New Christian Right was the uprising against sex education in Kanwaha County, West Virginia, in the early 1970s. See Martin 1996. Binary opposition is, however, a feature of identity language of all sorts. For an excellent critique of this tendency, see Honig 1994.

[40] On the use of "rights talk" by the New Christian Right, see, for example, Moore 1994.

politics.[41] Civil society is increasingly being viewed both as a basis for
the renewal of social cooperation and trust and as a domain in which
new forms of public provision can be delivered. In this light can we so
readily dismiss the claims of religious world-views for public recognition? Many theorists, hardly political liberals to be sure, are raising
important questions in this regard. Can churches, synagogues, and
mosques serve as deliverers of publicly subsidized social services, such
as day care, care of the elderly, or temporary housing? If a flourishing
associational life is an important condition of liberal democratic politics,
is it legitimate to promote religiously based associations or institutions
through public subsidy (indeed, tax exemptions already represent a way
of doing just this), whether these be congregations or local "Y's"? Is it
appropriate for religious student groups to meet in public school
facilities, or for religious groups to use public facilities available to other
forms of association (see Monsma 1996)? Are charter schools creative
alternatives to traditional public schools, and, if so, is there any role to
be played in the charter school movement by religiously affiliated
schools (see Walzer 1994: 185–91)?

These are important questions, to which there are no easy answers.
But public deliberation, debate, and dispute about them exists on the
same moral and legal terrain as debates and disputes about so-called
"family values," sex-education versus the teaching of abstinence, the
importance of "progressive" educational reforms as opposed to traditional rote learning and "restoring discipline," etc. On all of these
questions a serious and meaningful public debate joins, and will continue
to join, many different kinds and levels of discourse, engaging citizens in
passionate contention, and it is hard to see how a Rawlsian conception of
"public reason" helps to make them more tractable. These conflicts will
not go away, nor will they easily be domesticated or discursively con-
tained. As Sheldon Wolin puts it: "Rawlsian democracy might be likened
to a hermetically sealed condition of deliberation that allows rationality
to rule by suppressing certain topics and historical grievances and
excluding diverse languages of protest from public councils. Inadver-
tently, the limitations of Rawlsian reason are exposed: it cannot make
sense of, much less function within, a setting of sharp conflicts, whether
doctrinal, economic, political, or rhetorical" (Wolin 1996: 102).

Contrary to political liberals, we submit that there is no standard for
adjudicating the discordant and unruly controversies of democratic
public life beyond the standards of democracy itself. As Habermas has
maintained: "the theory of rights in no way forbids the citizens of a

---

[41] This literature is immense. See especially Putnam 1995 and 1996, and Cohen and
Arato 1992.

democratic constitutional state to assert a conception of the good in their general legal order, a conception they either already share or have come to agree on through political discussion. It does, however, forbid them to privilege one form of life at the expense of others within the nation" (Habermas 1993). Forms of life – associational, cultural, religious – are entitled to no special privileges, but neither are debates about their value and about their legal recognition in various ways short of privilege to be excluded from politics. Indeed, public debate and contention alone can adjudicate such claims for valuation and recognition. Perhaps this is what Macedo means when he says that "we must listen to dissenters, engage them in political conversation, and indeed encourage them to state their objections publicly. We cannot guarantee that we will do more" (Macedo 1996: 490). But this does describe a politics of avoidance. It describes a robustly democratic politics, where all claimants are empowered to voice their claims and mobilize their supporters, and where public policy is determined by the ebb and flow of argument and influence. It is, after all, one thing to refuse forms of life a guarantee, and quite another to refuse them a political opportunity to voice their concerns and to effect their demands.

It seems to us that political liberalism does not present a convincing or compelling way to address the problems presented by "fundamentalism" in public life. Fundamentalism – whether religious, or Afrocentric, or "queer" – *is* divisive. It is often the expression of serious and historically grounded grievances or a response to deeply felt senses of indignity or suffering. Political fundamentalism of any kind is essentialist, that is to say, it views its own concerns as essential and exclusive, and all others as secondary and inessential, as obstacles to or means of success for its own agenda. In this sense it is averse to the pluralism that is essential to democratic politics. It poses dangers to democratic political culture and to constitutional democracy.

However, we do not believe that fundamentalism can easily be avoided, dismissed, bracketed, or invalidated, for in its various incarnations it is an important force in our political life and gives voice to important and very real concerns. Furthermore, it is part and parcel of an even broader moralization of public life; it raises important questions about the value and meaning of social institutions and practices and the forms of public recognition appropriate for various forms of civic identities that, we have suggested, is endemic to democracy.

To insist that there is no way to manage or to regulate these issues short of democratic politics itself, in all of its uncertainty, divisiveness, and contingency, is not to specify very much, but it is to specify a wariness toward the juridical strategies of avoidance promoted by political liberalism. Legal argumentation and judicial remedies are important and ineliminable features of democratic life, and it is surely appropriate to view the courts as vehicles of justice in cases where fundamental democratic liberties are at stake. But a political philosophy that remains focused on this level of contestation is seriously and needlessly limiting. Rather, the most appropriate and the most effective ways of contesting the dangers of fundamentalism are in the political arena itself, not by seeking to avoid contentious questions of identity and meaning, but by promoting their healthy engagement.

Obviously, when such engagement threatens to turn into civil war then there are reasons to be wary of it. There is, it would be hard to deny, a genuinely "Hobbesian moment" in politics, as current events in Bosnia and Rwanda perhaps indicate. There are moments when forbearance should trump all other values, and when those who refuse to agree might legitimately be forced to obey. But it is a grave mistake to embrace this moment prematurely, and there is no reason to view the conflict characteristic of liberal democracies today as heading in that direction. This is why it is important that engagement in public dispute be healthy. Democracy is not war by other means. It contains its own norms, among which the values of voice, association, and pluralism are central (Elshtain 1995). The most plausible way that political theory can attend to the divisive conflicts that trouble political liberals is for political theory to attend to the problems and prospects for the further democratization of public life, and to promote robust forms of voice, association, and pluralism.

A number of writers currently writing about "deliberative democracy" raise precisely these themes, and we share their conviction that the central problem facing liberal democracy today is not a surfeit but a deficit of meaningful forms of democratic participation (see Barber 1984; Fishkin 1991 and 1995; Gutmann 1993; Gutmann and Thompson 1996; and Habermas 1991 and 1996). Healthy debate about fundamental value questions can, and sometimes does, take place in a range of deliberative fora, from legislatures, courts, public media and public debates, to churches and synagogues, colleges, community arts centers, and newly created citizens' boards and councils. Each of these fora represent a kind of public space where individuals of like mind and of diverging opinions can articulate their points of view, and seek to persuade, and to organize, others. Debates in such contexts are bound to be heated, fractious, and at times openly conflictual. Political antagonists will not always agree, and they will not always even agree to debate with, much less speak with, one another. But the only alternative to the open airing of differences and the freedom to mobilize on behalf of them is an even more acrimonious politics in which the original grievances, so to speak, are only exacerbated by a sense of political powerlessness – grievances not aired and not in some way actualized only multiply. As Martin Luther King said in another context, to justify another kind of disturbance, "like a boil that can never be cured as long as it is covered up but must be opened with all its pus-flowing ugliness to the natural medicines of air and light, injustice must likewise be exposed, with all of the tension its exposing creates, to the light of human conscience and the air of national opinion before it can be cured" (1991 [1963]: 295).

This was a different context. We are not arguing that all political sentiments, however poisonous, ought to be aired. There are certain kinds of advocacy that pose a "clear and present danger" (Holmes 1919) to basic democratic freedoms, and ought to be discouraged and even in extreme cases suppressed. The activities of certain militia groups surely fall into this category (see Coates 1995); but these are not, in general, the kinds of advocacy in question here.

Nor are we asserting that the claims of the New Christian Right have the moral stature of the demands of the civil rights movement. It is true that the New Christian Right often makes this assertion, that its spokespersons perceive themselves to be victimized by the principles of constitutional democracy (see Farris 1992 and Moore 1994). We do not believe this to be the case. There are strong grounds in both historical experience and democratic principle to value such things as the First Amendment's Establishment Clause, a permissive reading of freedom of expression, and a robust interpretation of the Fourteenth Amendment, for example. The liberal democratic state's refusal to privilege Christianity or so-called Christian values, and its enforcement of civil rights legislation on behalf of women, racial and religious minorities, or gays, does not constitute the victimization of Christians. Such measures are institutional commitments essential to a democratic state, commitments backed by the power of politically mobilized majorities, and supported by basic norms of democratic equality. In so far as New Christian Right organizations challenge such commitments, they seek to curtail important democratic achievements. Such challenges ought to be opposed by democrats, in the broader political arena and sometimes through the courts as well.[42]

---

[42] This is why we support the Supreme Court's 1996 decision in *Evans v. Romer* to overturn a Colorado amendment barring localities from treating "homosexual orientation" as a prohibited basis for discrimination, for this amendment denied "equal protection of the laws" to gay citizens, and such a denial is plainly inconsistent with basic norms of democratic equality.

We do, however, believe that the effort to close off public debate on important and controversial value questions can only fuel the sense of indignation that has energized the New Christian Right, and that the best way to counter these energies is to promote a vigorous and open debate whose only constraints are the constraints of democratic freedom itself. While in some respects the New Christian Right does champion patently anti-democratic ideas, it would be a grave error to reduce its politics to such issues as the Christianization of public schools, the curtailment of gay rights, or even an absolute ban on reproductive freedom.[43] For, beyond these very real and very troubling commitments, the New Christian Right has also raised a series of concerns about "public decency," parental authority, and the importance of religious institutions in civil society that cannot and ought not be disparaged and are surely legitimate public concerns.[44] It would equally be mistaken to seek to exclude the modes of advocacy characteristic of the religious Right from the public domain. The public invocation of God or Bible is not necessarily inimical to democracy; and, as the case of Martin Luther King, Jr, indicates, the use of these symbols can often be supremely democratic (see Calloway-Thomas and Lucaites 1993).[45] The political liberal alternative, using juridical mechanisms to under-privilege such discourse and thus to constrain public debate, is both anti-democratic and foolhardy. It is ironic that political liberals would fail to see this, for one of the greatest mistakes of American liberalism in the past thirty years has been its over-reliance on juridical remedies instead of more broadly political ones. From affirmative action to busing to abortion rights, liberals have too readily invoked juridical principles at the expense of substantive political argument, and the result has been

[43] The abortion controversy lies at the heart of New Christian Right advocacy, and a comprehensive treatment of such advocacy would require a full discussion of this issue. While we cannot fully explain below, we do believe that female reproductive freedom is a fundamental democratic liberty, and that court decisions upholding this freedom are democratically justifiable. We are, however, sympathetic to Ruth Bader Ginsburg's argument that in some ways the *Roe* decision went beyond this, and that there is a legitimate democratic public debate to be had about what constitutes an "undue burden" on women, and what state constraints upon abortion, if any, are consistent with female equality (Shapiro 1995: 13–23).

[44] Along these lines is the Bill supported by US Senator Dan Coats (Rep., Indiana), which proposes to use public resources to subsidize private philanthropies, many religiously based, as a way of nurturing civil society. Lively discussions of this idea recently have been published in the Heritage Foundation's bimonthly journal *Policy Review*. On the democratic legitimacy of certain kinds of anti-abortion protest, see Elshtain 1997.

[45] This is, of course, a complex and important topic. See also Diggins 1984, especially the discussion of "the return of the sacred" in the public discourse of Abraham Lincoln.

that liberalism is widely viewed as an elitist philosophy that relies upon the anti-democratic mandates of courts.[46]

How, then, might the discourse of the New Christian Right be more democratically engaged? This is not an easy question to answer, and a full discussion would be beyond the scope of this chapter, but we would argue that there are three ways of pursuing a genuinely democratic engagement.

First, through other, less fundamentalist and more pluralistic modes of politicizing religion, in the domains of both civil society and the state. Magazines such as *Commonweal, New Oxford Review, Tikkun, Sojourners,* and *First Things* represent efforts, from a variety of religious and political perspectives, to promote vigorous debate about the connections between religious practices, ethics, and public life. Liberal forms of religious engagement in public life, such as the Religious Action Center of Reform Judaism, the National Council of Churches, and even in some respects the American Conference of Catholic Bishops – and the many more specialized offshoots of these organizations – similarly promote healthy, democratic debate about a range of issues, from economic justice to the meaning of family. In addition, groups such as the recently formed Interfaith Alliance seek to promote broad-based, ecumenical dialogue, across organized religious boundaries, on the role of religion in a pluralistic, democratic society (see Beckstrom 1996). Efforts such as these represent alternative ways of mobilizing a range of religious discourse to address the issues brought to the fore by the New Religious Right, from educational curricula and policies appropriate to public schools, to the meaning of "family values," "public decency," and "virtue," and the kinds of institutions necessary to support them. Instead of seeking to purge political life of the kind of religio-political discourse advanced by the religious Right, these efforts seek to meet the religious Right on its own terrain, an important terrain in a society such as the United States. It is true that efforts such as these are not juridical; they relate less to the ways the law is organized and deployed than to the ways that democratic citizens understand and organize themselves politically; but they are crucial forms of democratic politics.

Secondly, while it may be neither possible nor desirable to attempt a politics of avoidance of moral controversy, it is both possible and desirable, at least at some times and places, to practice what might be called a "politics of diversion." As we pointed out earlier, one of the

[46] See, for example, Dionne 1991 and Edsall and Edsall 1992, for powerful demonstrations of this. On the jurisprudential arguments to this effect, see Shapiro 1995: 16–23 and Burt 1992. On the weakness of juridical strategies in general, see Rosenberg 1991.

hallmarks of identity politics today is that cultural issues have taken the place of distributional ones at the center of political debate. There are good historical reasons why this has occurred, and it is something to be neither lamented nor repudiated. But it may often be possible to meliorate serious moral and political antagonisms by changing the subject, by shifting the terrain of debate and discussion to issues on which there is a greater likelihood of gaining common agreement. Many writers have argued that a revival of a more robustly social democratic politics, centered around the declining standard of living and the increasing economic insecurity of the broad middle class, might be a way to abate some of the more antagonistic cultural debates of our time. For these writers, what we need is not a more minimalist liberalism of fear but a more activist liberalism of social justice. By addressing questions of social justice, it is argued, it might be possible to create new kinds of common ground; indeed in his best-selling *Why Americans Hate Politics*, E. J. Dionne, Jr, argues that there already exists a good deal of common ground on a range of important socio-economic concerns, and that identity politics represents a kind of "false polarization" that is a symptom of a failure of political leadership and vision (see Dionne 1991; Edsall and Edsall 1992; Lasch 1991; for a critique, see Isaac 1996). Along similar lines, theorists such as Joshua Cohen and Joel Rogers advocate new forms of corporatist intermediation that would empower unions and thus create a more just and more democratic political economy (Cohen and Rogers 1992). Such broadly social democratic strategies seek to sidestep severe cultural conflicts of identity, but not in the name of a politics of avoidance; for they seek to promote new forms of public argumentation about justice and the reordering of socio-economic life that are in their own way deeply ethical and deeply contentious. The point of social democratic politics is not to skirt serious political controversy but to construct a majoritarian consensus through a combination of coalition politics and class conflict. Such an approach faces serious obstacles, and it is never going to eliminate the acrimonious cultural conflicts that characterize public life. It does, however, represent another way of promoting democratic contestation that tackles the moral challenges presented by fundamentalists at a diagonal rather than directly.

Finally, the religious Right can be engaged through the promotion of new forms of public deliberation and participation in which citizens can experience a sense of empowerment, and through this experience lower their level of political anxiety and learn a greater appreciation for the complexities and ambiguities of political life. Political sectarianism and resentment thrive in an environment in which alternative ways of practicing politics are absent or in disrepair, and a political theory truly interested in abating political acrimony must be attentive to such alternatives. Fostering more healthy forms of religious engagement in politics is part of the broader problem of reviving civil society as a dense network of intermediate institutions and associations through which individuals can work toward common goals. Such associations can take many forms: neighborhood associations, community organizations, and community development corporations; national networks, such as ACORN, the Industrial Areas Foundation, and Citizens' Clearinghouse on Hazardous Waste; public educational efforts, such as the Project on Public Work, organized by Harry Boyte and Nancy Kari at the Humphrey School of the University of Minnesota; and experimental efforts, such as the Common Ground Network for Life and Choice and the Public Conversations Project, which seek to bring together activists from across the political divide on controversial issues, such as abortion, and to promote bridge-building dialogue among them. The above-mentioned efforts are simply examples of the kind of creative efforts that are currently under way to promote and enhance concrete forms of public deliberation and empowerment. While these efforts often do not speak directly to the kinds of demands being pressed by the religious Right, they promote openings for dialogue, and new political skills, and forms of practical problem-solving, that might help to take the edge off some of the more fractious cultural conflicts of our time (see, for example, Barber 1996; Boyte 1989; Wallis 1995; Sandel 1996; Amer 1996; Boyte and Kari 1996).[47]

In the end, though, we need frankly to admit that American society is deeply divided along multiple dimensions, that these divisions have a long history, and that there is no solution to them ready at hand. The effort of political liberalism to confine political debate within narrow discursive confines, and to depoliticize the most divisive conflicts of our time, is a hopeless and counterproductive one. A more democratic working out of these conflicts has the virtue at least of acknowledging them for what they are, and for seeking fragile but realistic ways of managing them. Such a politics may contain risks, but all politics contains risk. Thus politics may be imperfect and fragile but, as Hannah Arendt once noted, the only final solution in politics is death.

---

[47] For an invaluable inventory of efforts of this kind, consult The Civic Practices Network, an on-line website produced by Carmen Sirianni in cooperation with the Center for Human Resources at Brandeis University (http//www.cpn.org).

REFERENCES

Ackerman, Bruce. 1991. *We The People: Foundations.* Cambridge, MA: Harvard University Press.

Alejandro, Roberto. 1996. "What is political about Rawls's political liberalism?" *Journal of Politics* 58: 1–24.

Amer, John (ed.). 1996. *Beyond Identity Politics: Emerging Social Justice Movements in Communities of Color.* Boston: South End Press.

Armey, Representative Dick. 1994. "Freedom's Choir." *Policy Review* 67: 27–34.

Arneson, Richard and Ian Shapiro. 1996. "Democratic autonomy and religious freedom: a critique of *Wisconsin v. Yoder.*" In Ian Shapiro (ed.), *Democracy's Place*, pp. 137–74. Ithaca: Cornell University Press.

Barber, Benjamin. 1984. *Strong Democracy.* Berkeley: University of California Press.

　1996. "An American civic forum: civil society between market individuals and the political community." *Social Philosophy and Policy* 13(1): 269–83.

Barnes, James A. 1994. "Rightward march?" *National Journal*: 1847–51.

Bates, Stephen. 1993. *Battleground: One Mother's Crusade, the Religious Right, and the Struggle for Control of Our Classrooms.* New York: Poseidon Press.

Beckstrom, Maja. 1996. "Moral banner subject of tug-of-war among religious groups." *The Bloomington Herald-Times.* 28 December: D4.

Bell, Daniel. 1960. *The End of Ideology.* Glencoe, IL: Free Press.

Bellah, Robert. 1991. "Citizenship, diversity, and the search for the common good." In Robert E. Calvert (ed.), *"The Constitution of the People": Reflections on Citizens and Civil Society*, pp. 47–63. Lawrence: University Press of Kansas.

Berman, Paul. 1996. *A Tale of Two Utopias.* New York: W. W. Norton.

Boyte, Harry C. 1989. *Commonwealth.* New York: Free Press.

Boyte, Harry C. and Nancy N. Kari. 1996. *Building America: The Democratic Promise of Public Work.* Philadelphia: Temple University Press.

Brinkley, Alan. 1995. *The End of Reform.* New York: Norton.

Bull, Chris and Gallagher, John. 1996. *Perfect Enemies: The Religious Right, The Gay Movement, and the Politics of the 1990s.* New York: Crown.

Burt, Robert A. 1992. *The Constitution in Conflict.* Cambridge, MA: Harvard University Press.

Calloway-Thomas, Carolyn and John Louis Lucaites. 1993. *Martin Luther King, Jr., and the Sermonic Power of Public Discourse.* Tuscaloosa: University of Alabama Press.

Carter, Stephen. 1993. *The Culture of Disbelief.* New York: Basic Books.

Chaloupka, William. 1993. "Suppose Kuwait's main product was broccoli?: The street demonstration in U.S. politics." In Frederick M. Dolan and Thomas L. Dumm (eds.), *Rhetorical Republic: Governing Representations in American Politics*, pp. 143–66. Amherst: University of Massachusetts Press.

Coates, James. 1995. *Armed and Dangerous: The Rise of the Survivalist Right.* New York: Hill and Wang.

Cohen, Jean and Andrew Arato. 1992. *Civil Society and Political Theory.* Cambridge, MA: MIT Press.

Cohen, Joshua. 1994. "A more democratic liberalism." *Michigan Law Review* 92: 1502–46.

Cohen, Joshua and Joel Rogers. 1992. "Secondary associations and democratic governance." *Politics and Society* 20: 393–472.

Cox, Harvey. 1995. "The warring visions of the religious Right." *The Atlantic Monthly* 276: 59–68.

Crawford, Alan. 1980. *Thunder on the Right: The "New Right" and the Politics of Resentment*. New York: Pantheon.

Crozier, Michel, Samuel P. Huntington, and Joji Watanuki. 1975. *The Crisis of Democracy: Report on the Governability of Democracies to the Trilateral Commission*. New York: New York University Press.

Dahl, Robert A. 1956. *A Preface to Democratic Theory*. Chicago: University of Chicago Press.

1989. *Democracy and its Critics*. New Haven: Yale University Press.

Diggins, John P. 1984. *The Lost Soul of American Politics*. Chicago: University of Chicago Press.

Dionne, E. J., Jr. 1991. *Why Americans Hate Politics*. New York: Touchstone.

Edwards v. Aguilard. 482 U.S. 578 (1987).

Edsall, Thomas Byrne and Mary Edsall. 1992. *Chain Reaction: The Impact of Race, Rights, and Taxes on American Politics*. New York: W. W. Norton.

Elshtain, Jean Bethke. 1995. *Democracy on Trial*. New York: Basic Books.

1997. "Civil rites." *The New Republic*. 24: 23.

Ely, John Hart. 1980. *Democracy and Distrust*. Cambridge, MA: Harvard University Press.

Etzioni, Amitai. 1993. *The Spirit of Community*. New York: Crown Publishers.

Evans, Sara M. and Harry C. Boyte. 1986. *Free Spaces: The Sources of Democratic Change in America*. New York: Harper & Row.

Falwell, Jerry. 1980. *Listen, America!* Garden City, NY: Doubleday.

Farris, Michael P. 1992. *Where Do I Draw The Line?* Minneapolis: Bethany House.

Fishkin, James. 1991. *Democracy and Deliberation: New Directions for Democratic Reform*. New Haven: Yale University Press.

1995. *The Voice of the People: Public Opinion and Democracy*. New Haven: Yale University Press.

Francis, Samuel T. 1982. "Message from Mars: the social politics of the New Right." In Robert W. Whitaker (ed.), *The New Right Papers*, pp. 64–83. New York: St Martins.

Fraser, Nancy. 1989. *Unruly Practices: Power, Discourse, and Gender in Contemporary Social Theory*. Minneapolis: University of Minnesota Press.

1992. "Rethinking the public sphere: a contribution to the critique of actually existing democracy." In Craig Calhoun (ed.), *Habermas and the Public Sphere*, pp. 109–42. Cambridge, MA: MIT Press.

Garrow, David J. 1986. *Bearing the Cross: Martin Luther King, Jr., and the Southern Christian Leadership Conference*. New York: Random House.

Gitlin, Todd. 1995. *The Twilight of Common Dreams: Why America is Wracked By Culture Wars*. New York: Metropolitan Books.

Glendon, Mary Ann. 1991. *Rights Talk: The Impoverishment of Political Discourse*. New York: Free Press.

Gutmann, Amy. 1987. *Democratic Education*. Princeton: Princeton University Press.

1993. "The disharmony of democracy." In John W. Chapman and Ian Shapiro (eds.), *NOMOS XXXV: Democratic Community*, pp. 126–62. New York: New York University Press.

1995. "Civic education and social diversity." *Ethics* 105: 557–79.

Gutmann, Amy and Dennis Thompson. 1996. *Democracy and Disagreement*. Cambridge, MA: Harvard University Press.

Habermas, Jürgen. 1989. "The new obscurity: the crisis of the welfare state and the exhaustion of utopian energies." In Jürgen Habermas, *The New Conservatism*, pp. 48–70, edited and translated by Shierry Weber Nicholsen. Cambridge, MA: MIT Press.

1991. *Moral Consciousness and Communicative Action*. Cambridge, MA: MIT Press.

1993. "Struggles for recognition in the democratic constitutional state." In Charles Taylor and Amy Gutmann (eds.), *Multiculturalism*, pp. 107–48. Princeton: Princeton University Press.

1996. *Between Facts and Norms: Contributions to a Discourse Theory of Law and Democracy*. Translated by William Rehg. Cambridge, MA: MIT Press.

Helms, Jesse. 1976. *"Where Free Men Shall Stand": A Sobering Look at the Supertaxing, Superspending Superbureaucracy in Washington*. Grand Rapids, MI: Zondervan Publishing.

Holmes, Justice Oliver Wendell. 1919. Minority Opinion in *Schenck v. United States*. 249 U.S. 47.

Holmes, Stephen. 1988a. "Precommitment and the paradox of democracy." In Jon Elster and Rune Slagstad (eds.), *Constitutionalism and Democracy*, pp. 19–58. Cambridge: Cambridge University Press.

1988b. "Gag rules and the politics of omission." In Jon Elster and Rune Slagstad (eds.), *Constitutionalism and Democracy*, pp. 195–240. Cambridge: Cambridge University Press.

1993a. *The Anatomy of Antiliberalism*. Cambridge, MA: Harvard University Press.

1993b. "The gatekeeper: John Rawls and the limits of tolerance." *The New Republic* 209: 39–48.

1994. "Liberalism for a world of ethnic passions and decaying states." *Social Research* 61: 599–611.

Honig, Bonnie. 1993. *Political Theory and the Displacement of Politics*. Ithaca, NY: Cornell University Press.

1994. "Difference, dilemmas, and the politics of home." *Social Research* 61: 563–98.

Huntington, Samuel P. 1975. "The democratic distemper." *The Public Interest* 4: 9–38.

Isaac, Jeffrey C. 1996. "The poverty of progressivism: pessimistic thoughts on the future of democracy in America." *Dissent* 43: 40–9.

Kazin, Michael. 1995. *The Populist Persuasion*. New York: Basic Books.

King, Martin Luther, Jr. 1991 (1963). "Letter from Birmingham Jail." In James M. Washington (ed.), *The Essential Writings and Speeches of Martin Luther King, Jr*, pp. 289–302. New York: HarperCollins.

Kramnick, Isaac and R. Laurence Moore. 1996. *The Godless Constitution: The Case Against Religious Correctness.* New York: W. W. Norton.

Lasch, Christopher. 1991. *The True and Only Heaven: Progress and its Critics.* New York: W. W. Norton.

Levine, Lawrence. 1996. *The Opening of the American Mind.* Boston: Beacon Press.

Lienesch, Michael. 1993. *Redeeming America: Power, Piety and Politics in the New Christian Right.* Chapel Hill: University of North Carolina Press.

Lind, Michael. 1995. *The Next American Nation.* New York: Free Press.

Macedo, Stephen. 1990. *Liberal Virtues: Citizenship, Virtue, and Community in Liberal Constitutionalism.* Oxford: Clarendon Press.

    1995. "Liberal civic education and religious fundamentalism: the case of God v. John Rawls." *Ethics* 105: 468–96.

MacIntyre, Alasdair. 1990. "The privatization of the good: an inaugural lecture." *Review of Politics* 52: 344–61.

Madison, James. 1961 (1787). "Federalist No. 10." In Clinton Rossiter (ed.), *The Federalist Papers,* pp. 77–84. New York: Penguin Books.

Martin, William. 1996. *With God on Our Side: The Rise of the Religious Right in America.* New York: Broadway Books.

Marty, Martin E. and R. Scott Appleby. 1992. *The Glory and the Power: Fundamentalists in the Modern World.* Boston: Beacon Press.

McCann, Michael W. 1994. *Rights at Work: Pay Equity Reform and the Politics of Legal Mobilization.* Chicago: University of Chicago Press.

Monsma, Stephen V. 1996. *When Sacred and Secular Mix: Religious Nonprofit Organizations and Public Money.* Totowa, NJ: Rowman and Littlefield.

Moore, W. John. 1994. "The Lord's litigators." *National Journal* 26(27): 1560–65.

Mouffe, Chantal. 1993. "Rawls: political philosophy without politics." In Chantal Mouffe, *The Return of the Political,* pp. 41–59. London: Verso.

Persinos, John F. 1994. "Has the Christian Right taken over the Republican Party?" *Campaign and Elections* 15(9): 20–4.

Phillips, Kevin. 1993. *Boiling Point: Democrats, Republicans, and the Decline of Middle Class Prosperity.* New York: Harper.

Putnam, Robert D. 1995. "Bowling alone: America's declining social capital." *Journal of Democracy* 6: 65–78.

    1996. "The strange disappearance of civic America." *The American Prospect* 24: 34–48.

Rabkin, Jeremy. 1996. "The Supreme Court in the culture wars." *The Public Interest* 125: 3–26.

Rawls, John. 1951. "Outline of a decision procedure for ethics." *The Philosophical Review* 60(2): 177–97.

    1958. "Justice as fairness." *The Philosophical Review* 67(2): 164–94.

    1971. *A Theory of Justice.* Cambridge, MA: Harvard University Press.

    1985. "Justice as fairness: political, not metaphysical." *Philosophy and Public Affairs* 14: 223–51.

    1993. *Political Liberalism.* New York: Columbia University Press.

Rorty, Richard. 1983. "Postmodernist bourgeois liberalism." *Journal of Philosophy* 80(10): 583–9.

1988. *Contingency, Irony, and Solidarity*. Cambridge: Cambridge University Press.

Rosenberg, Gerald. 1991. *The Hollow Hope*. Chicago: University of Chicago Press.

Rozell, Mark J. and Clyde Wilcox (eds.). 1995. *God at the Grass Roots: The Christian Right in the 1994 Elections*. Lanham, MD: Rowman and Littlefield.

Rozell, Mark J. and Clyde Wilcox. 1996. *Second Coming: The New Christian Right and Virginia Politics*. Baltimore: The Johns Hopkins University Press.

Ryan, Alan. 1993. "The liberal community." In John W. Chapman and Ian Shapiro (eds.), *NOMOS XXXV: Democratic Community*, pp. 91–114. New York: New York University Press.

Sandel, Michael. 1996. *Democracy's Discontent: America in Search of a Public Philosophy*. Cambridge, MA: Harvard University Press.

Schlesinger, Arthur F., Jr. 1949. *The Vital Center* (2nd edn). Boston: Houghton Mifflin.

Shapiro, Ian. 1986. *The Evolution of Rights in Liberal Theory*. Cambridge: Cambridge University Press.

1995. "Editor's introduction." In Ian Shapiro (ed.), *Abortion: The Supreme Court Decisions*, pp. 1–24. Indianapolis: Hackett.

1996. *Democracy's Place*. Ithaca, NY: Cornell University Press.

Shaw, Brian J. 1997. "Liberal neutrality, 'public reason' and religion: Habermas contra Rawls." Lecture delivered at the 1997 Annual Meeting of the Midwest Political Science Association, Chicago, IL, 10–12 April.

Shklar, Judith. 1984. *Ordinary Vices*. Cambridge, MA: Harvard University Press.

1989. "The liberalism of fear." In Nancy Rosenblum (ed.), *Liberalism and the Moral Life*. Cambridge, MA: Harvard University Press.

Stolzenberg, Nomi Maya. 1993. "'He drew a circle that shut me out': assimilation, indoctrination, and the paradox of liberal education." *Harvard Law Review* 106: 581–667.

Sunstein, Cass. 1993. *The Partial Constitution*. Cambridge, MA: Harvard University Press.

Taylor, Charles Alan. 1996. *Defining Science: A Rhetoric of Demarcation*. Madison: University of Wisconsin Press.

Viguerie, Richard. 1981. *The New Right: We're Ready to Lead*. Falls Church, VA: The Viguerie Company.

Villa, Dana. 1993. "Postmodernism and the public sphere." In Frederick M. Dolan and Thomas L. Dumm (eds.), *Rhetorical Republic: Governing Representations in American Politics*, pp. 227–46. Amherst: University of Massachussetts Press.

Wallis, Jim. 1995. *The Soul of Politics: Beyond "Religious Right" and "Secular Left."* New York: Harcourt.

Walzer, Michael. 1994. "Multiculturalism and individualism." *Dissent* 41: 185–91.

Wilcox, Clyde. 1996. *Onward Christian Soldiers?* Boulder, CO: Westview Press.

Williams, Juan. 1988. *Eyes on the Prize: America's Civil Rights Years, 1954–1965*. New York: Penguin Books.

Wolff, Robert Paul. 1977. *Understanding Rawls: A Reconstruction and Critique of A Theory of Justice*. Princeton: Princeton University Press.

Wolin, Sheldon. 1996. "The liberal/democratic divide: on Rawls's 'Political Liberalism'." *Political Theory* 24: 97–120.

Young, Iris Marion. 1987. "Impartiality and the civic public: some implications of feminist critiques of moral and political theory." In Seyla Benhabib and Drucilla Cornell (eds.), *Feminism as Critique*, pp. 56–76. Minneapolis: University of Minnesota Press.

   1990. *Justice and the Politics of Difference*. Princeton: Princeton University Press.

14   Between liberalism and a hard place

Courtney Jung

Much political and democratic theory in the Rawlsian and post-Rawlsian era is located at the site of the tension between liberalism and communitarianism. The perceived tension, simply put, lies in disagreements over the source of morality. Liberals appeal to a universal, supposedly rational, minimal Kantian standard that they believe everyone could agree to (Rawls 1971; Macedo 1990). Communitarians believe that standards of morality derive from community, and are therefore particular. The community must, as a consequence, have a place in public life (Bellah 1991; Walzer 1997; MacIntyre 1984). Partly because this debate does in fact rest on irreconcilable differences regarding fundamental principles, it has largely stalemated. The enterprise now is to find a "third way" between, and yet separate from, the two. This is the project of Isaac, Filner, and Bivins in their contribution to this book. The dominant line of attack in their argument is against political liberalism; yet they hesitate to embrace communitarianism. They invite the community into the public realm and make an appeal to democracy to adjudicate the conflicts their invitation will engender. Democracy, they hope, can include communities, and yet still provide a universal standard.

In order that we begin from the same set of premises, I outline briefly and sympathetically what I take to be the argument of Isaac, Filner, and Bivins, hereafter known as "IFB." IFB's argument is constructed around a critique of Macedo's defense of political liberalism in the case of *Mozert v. Hawkins* (Macedo 1995). Since IFB's positive argument is not actually centrally concerned with this case, however, I present not the structure, but the logic and substance of their argument.

IFB contend that the social contract upon which liberalism was built has unraveled. The politics of distributive justice have given way to the politics of identity. It is the success of liberalism itself, and the fact that its conception of the good excludes other conceptions, that has contributed to the demands of self-identified "excluded" groups for access to the political sphere. Political liberalism deals inadequately with the

265

matter of access to politics by wrongly privileging liberalism over democracy. Liberalism thus depoliticizes much of what should be explicitly political. Identities, for example, should not be bracketed by an appeal to judicial review. The authors argue for the extension of the realm of the public to include identity politics which they believe should be processed in the political sphere. They claim that "there is no standard for adjudicating the fractious and unruly controversies of democratic public life beyond the standards of democracy itself" (p. 251, above).

This argument is well made and persuasive. IFB are engaged in defense of the enterprise of rolling back the sphere of the private. Since the politicization of the private has historically been a route to empowerment for politically (and otherwise) marginalized groups, such as women and gays, the "democratization of liberalism" strikes sympathetic chords. It is in the spirit then, of coinciding commitments, that I comment on IFB's argument. My intention is to expose and question the assumptions on which it rests, and push, rather than discredit, the direction and promise of the paper.

Some of the assumptions that inform IFB's argument are potentially suspect. IFB assume, first of all, that things are different now than they were, in important ways, and that at one time there was a liberal consensus. They claim that it is liberalism itself and its conception of the good that has spawned identity politics. By extension, presumably the end of liberalism would go some way toward attenuating the mobilization of identity. Their argument about the political place of identity presumes that political identity is essential and prior to the political arena itself. They assume that fundamentalisms are of the same order as identity politics and, finally, that an agreement to settle things by democratic means does not also imply some conception of the good. I deal, in the main, with the last three of these underlying premises, all of which I consider more or less problematic for IFB.

The unexamined foundations of IFB's argument may be critically engaged at the level of identity. The conception of identity that informs IFB should be made explicit, at least in part because conflicting notions of the nature of the self are deeply implicated with the larger questions of the communitarian–liberal debate in which IFB are partly embroiled. The authors never make explicit their understanding of the nature of political identity, but they drop some hints which suggest they perceive identities as arising out of the private sphere, as being prior to politics, and natural.[1] People hold identities, based on things such as religion

---

[1] This analysis is based on the following quotes from Isaac, Filner, and Bivins: "The demand that public reason ought to exclude religious modes of justification relies on *an implausibly thin conception of political identity*" (p. 224); "In the domain of the non-public

and culture, which must be accommodated politically. People, and groups, have "fundamental value commitments," "deeply held creeds," and "constitutive religious vocabularies." Political accommodation is necessary because "American society is deeply divided along multiple dimensions" and "these divisions have a long history" (IFB, p. 258, above). To the extent that identities are not allowed expression in the public realm, important constituencies are disempowered.

An alternative set of hypotheses regarding the nature of identities, however, would lead us to a different understanding of what is at stake. Political identity is not something that pre-exists in a natural state and demands recognition. Group membership is not obviously an essential human commitment that structures how and where human beings find meaningful political expression. There is no pure prior self that enters the political arena seeking merely to give voice to constitutive commitments. Where political identity does in fact come from, however, is crucial to claims about what it is owed by democracy.

Rather than being natural and prior, political identity is constructed, at least in part, in the political arena itself. Individuals are the locus of multiple potential identities, most of which will never gain political salience. Political identities may be mobilized around cultural or religious symbols, or they may be lodged in economic or ideological referents, to name but a few possibilities. Political entrepreneurs operating within an incentive structure created by the state (and prior political patterns) mobilize constituencies around particular symbols to maximize their share of the vote. Whether they succeed, and which identities actually emerge as salient, is partly the result of the way the state is organized, how it allocates power and resources, and the way in which opposition to the state identifies and organizes itself. One could make the argument, for example, that as a political identity Christian fundamentalism resonates among a group of previously privileged, downwardly mobile whites who seek to recoup lost social, political, and economic status with regard to other groups. Any one of these markers of group-ness (prior privilege, downward mobility, whiteness) could theoretically be used to constitute a political identity for the same people. Further, Christian fundamentalism makes a different claim, and binds different people as a political identity than it does as a religious identity. Not all people who have religious beliefs that could be

one can and typically does subscribe to *deeply held and particularistic creeds and commitments*" (p. 230); "[Rawls says]...political speech that does not bracket out *fundamental value commitments* lacks constitutional validity" (p. 231); "to insist that political discourse must take a certain form ... is to *disempower important constituencies* ..." (p. 239); "if they want their opinions to count ... they must put aside their *constitutive religious vocabularies*" (p. 242) (emphasis added).

described as Christian fundamentalist ascribe to the political program of Christian fundamentalism. On multiple levels, the space of the political is deeply implicated in the politicization of identity.

This alternative view of political identity leads in two directions. First, it may not be simply a neutral question which identities we allow into the political realm. If it is true that politics itself plays an important role in determining which identities emerge as salient, then access to the state is likely to politicize identities that would otherwise remain politically latent. The formalization of a political place for identities may have the presumably unintended effect of privileging those identities which are sufficiently mobilized and organized to operate politically, while continuing to exclude small or insufficiently constituted identities – such as Christian fundamentalists but not Asian immigrants today, for example. Access to politics and an institutional power base may specifically empower some, by extension disempower others, and further undermine the pluralism on which IFB claim democracy rests.

Second, if political identities are not inherent and natural components of individuals but constructions based on particular symbols, then it is not particular constituencies that liberal democrats want to bracket out of public discourse, but symbols. On this reading of identity, liberals are saying that some discursive moves, such as an appeal to religion or culture perhaps, should not be available to political elites operating in the public realm; and these symbols are not available to anyone. Of course the apparent bias, even on this reading, is that particular symbols are not really unavailable to everyone, they are mostly unavailable to those who want to use them. Excluding some symbols as legitimate mobilizing tools excludes only those who want to use those symbols for mobilizing purposes. Nevertheless, the argument that certain constituencies are excluded falls away. All people have multiple identities and multiple symbols available to them. Groups are not permanently constituted in a given manner, and group boundaries are permeable. As individuals, Christian fundamentalists are not excluded from politics; only the symbols that constitute their group-ness, as fundamentalists, are barred. The argument that liberalism excludes symbols is an apparently lesser charge than the argument that it excludes people.

This leads, however, to a subset of questions that may also need to be negotiated. Is it good or bad that liberal democracy excludes some types of mobilization? Are there good reasons to keep some symbols out of the public domain? Or not? It seems neither normatively nor conceptually obvious that liberal democracy must exclude mobilization around identities from democratic politics. When groups that have been excluded because of objective markers of identity such as race or gender mobilize around such markers to gain access to politics *under the assumption of a liberal value system*, they may be accommodated by both political liberalism and democracy. In fact, they have been. This is where my commitments – toward an expansion of the public realm – coincide with those of IFB. There is no good reason to think that identity politics will subvert democracy, or that groups constituted for political purposes on the basis of language or race are different, in politically determinant ways, from groups constituted for political purposes on the basis of class or ideology. Groups constituted around cultural, racial, sexual, gender, linguistic, or religious symbols are not inherently different, more conflictual, or obviously less compatible with the democratic process, than other groups.

Fundamentalisms, on the other hand, are significantly different from other types of political identities. The authors' unexamined conflation of fundamentalist and identity politics, as if they were all the same thing, is a mistake. Fundamentalisms are articulated as essentialist, all-encompassing, totalitarian, and exclusive. Be they religious, economic, ideological, or cultural identities, their construction as fundamentalisms demands strict and literal adherence to a basic set of principles in every realm, including the political. Any group other than "democratic fundamentalists" is constitutively at odds with democracy because it holds some other basic set of principles as the appropriate currency of politics. Christian fundamentalists would presumably appeal to their reading of the Bible rather than majority rule to settle political conflicts or allocate resources, for example. Fundamentalists of any stripe do not hold democracy as their highest good, or even as a "subordinate foundational good."[2] When identities are articulated in a fundamentalist way, they represent an alternative to democracy, and therefore cannot be processed within democracy.

IFB present a hypothetical example of what I take to be the incompatibility of fundamentalisms and democracy. They speculate that if the plaintiff in *Mozert v. Hawkins*, Vicki Frost, were the democratically elected representative of Hawkins County, rather than the leader of an "obstreperous minority," it would be illegitimate, on democratic terms, to overturn her decision to allow some children to opt out of the reading program. They make this argument to demonstrate that liberalism interferes with the democratic process. We may carry their hypothetical example further, however, to make a different point. If Vicki Frost swept

---

[2] Shapiro argues, for example, that the place of democracy is not that of highest good (Shapiro 1996). Democracy should condition our actions, but should not be our only, or even always highest, commitment. Fundamentalists would presumably reject either option.

into office on a Christian fundamentalist platform, she would probably hasten to install a Christian fundamentalist school curriculum. Such a curriculum would certainly be exclusive, and it would probably also undermine the exercise of reason, and values of free association and equality, which some of us, including, I think, Isaac, Filner, and Bivins, think of as underpinning democracy. And what reason do we have to believe that Vicki Frost, a committed fundamentalist, would yield to election results if she were voted out of office? Ultimately, if the Christian Right swept into power, and there was no private space or domain that was not available to them to change, could we still have a democratic system? The answer is probably no.[3] It is in this sense that opening the public realm to those who would undermine it is a dangerous proposition.

How then do we adjudicate among recognition claims? If Christian fundamentalist values are intolerant and in contradiction with the necessary tolerance of democracy, if they are "divisive and threatening to the liberties of other groups" (IFB, p. 243, above), they may not deserve the same access to politics we might want to afford other less exclusive and intolerant groups. IFB seem to feel some tension about this very question. They compare Christian fundamentalist claims for recognition to identity politics in the 1960s. They say that the space of politics should be expanded now just as it has been in the past to include women and African Americans. They *also* say that the claims of the new Christian Right lack the moral stature of the civil rights movement (IFB, p. 254, above). But if we have no standard to adjudicate among claims, how are we to privilege some as legitimate over those that are illegitimate? Once equal access to the public realm, and voice, have been provided, we are implicitly, and even explicitly, legitimating claims equally, stamping them all with equivalent merit in politics.

IFB contend that the democratic process itself must function as the standard of legitimation. They contend that part of the problem with liberalism is not simply that it *claims* to be neutral, or that liberals are wrong about what their politics includes, but it is the *fact* that liberalism is not neutral itself which is a problem. It is the fact that liberalism is not neutral, that it includes a conception of the good and thereby excludes other conceptions of the good, that has given rise to what they call the

---

[3] It is this point, taken further, that the so-called "philosophic eminence" (IFB, p. 223, above), Brian Barry, made at the Yale conference. Isaac's retort – that we are not talking about Germany in the 1930s, but rather the United States in the 1990s – is weak in the sense that it says nothing about the philosophical grounds on which the Nazi Germany outcome is precluded. He makes an empirical claim that "it could not happen here," failing to take into account that we did not exactly predict it would happen there. But it did.

cacophony of identity claims that characterize our fractious public life. They say, "for if fundamentalism signifies anything ... it signifies a rejection of the liberal consensus about public reason that political liberalism seeks to reinstate" (IFB, p. 248, above).

If this is true, then certainly at least part of what must recommend democracy as a better standard of adjudicating controversy is that it is neutral. This claim cannot be sustained, however, even if the democracy to which we appeal is purely procedural. Even minimalist democracy would not necessarily be agreed to by "reasonable people" as an appropriate decision rule. Democracy includes an agreement to process decisions by appealing to voting mechanisms in which a majority, plurality, or cartel of victors win, and implement their policies. Those who lose must submit to the will of the winners, at least until the next election. These are clearly conceptions of the good that, however thin, not all people would agree to. Crucially, fundamentalists would be unlikely to agree to such decision rules.

IFB claim, further, that "there is no standard for adjudicating the fractious and unruly controversies of democratic public life beyond the standards of democracy itself" (IFB, p. 251, above). But what are the standards of democracy itself? If we rely on procedural democracy alone for adjudication, democracy being what it is, it will be more available to those groups that are (a) well organized, (b) rich; and/or (c) big. Democracy also excludes, and it excludes on the basis of size and wealth alone, which seems an even less valid standard than that of liberalism. Moreover, if we settle on procedural democracy as our highest standard for adjudicating among competing claims, we would probably soon be forced to embrace some uncomfortable, or difficult to defend, outcomes. Majorities have, after all, been known to contain hatred, prejudice, and malice. Democracy does not by definition lead to legitimate outcomes. If democracy and justice of recognition do not necessarily go together, if the former does not lead naturally to the latter, it is not obviously true that democracy should always trump.

Nevertheless, the authors clearly have in mind a richer, thicker conception of democracy that rests on norms they call the values of voice, association, and pluralism. Substantive democracy holds a conception of the good that includes freedom of expression, association, and worship, critical thought, and opposition. It includes a thin commitment to something more open-minded and tolerant of pluralism and diversity, without which democracy could not be sustained. Once IFB embrace a more substantive democracy, it becomes clear that democracy does not carry any more weight as a neutral standard than did liberalism. Democracy must also exclude groups that do not endorse its foundations or that undermine those things required to uphold it. A substantive democracy that embraced values of voice, association, and pluralism would also exclude Christian fundamentalists, for example, to the extent that the latter fail to uphold such values.

There is a tension between democracy and liberalism that IFB have done an excellent job of fully exposing. Their critique of liberalism is well taken. A call to question where we have drawn the lines separating public and private, and to expand the sphere of democracy, is something many of us can probably agree to. Nevertheless, it is possible that the way forward is to live with that tension, and that the debate over what is political is a fine place for democracy to continue to operate and play itself out. It is not clear that democracy can afford to include fundamentalisms in its broad reach. To the extent that fundamentalisms are articulated in such a way that they stand in totalitarian opposition to democracy, they cannot be processed within a democratic system. Finally, democracy itself cannot stand as the "solution" to liberalism. It suffers from the same flaw as liberalism, namely that it is not neutral among conceptions of the good, and it does not include universally defensible standards for adjudication. Where liberalism and democracy struggle, democracy is not obviously the moral victor.

REFERENCES

Bellah, Robert. 1991. "Citizenship, diversity, and the search for the common good." In Robert E. Calvert (ed.), *The Constitution of the People: Reflections on Citizens and Civil Society*. Lawrence: University Press of Kansas.
Macedo, Stephen. 1990. *Liberal Virtues: Citizenship, Virtue, and Community in Liberal Constitutionalism*. Oxford: Clarendon Press.
    1995. "Liberal civic education and religious fundamentalism: the case of God v. John Rawls?" *Ethics* 105: 468–96.
MacIntyre, Alasdair. 1984. *After Virtue: A Study in Moral Theory*. Notre Dame, IN: University of Notre Dame Press.
Rawls, John. 1971. *A Theory of Justice*. Cambridge, MA: Harvard University Press.
Shapiro, Ian. 1996. "Elements of democratic justice." In Ian Shapiro (ed.), *Democracy's Place*, pp. 222–62. Ithaca: Cornell University Press.
Walzer, Michael. 1997. "Response to Kukathas." In Ian Shapiro and Will Kymlicka (eds.), *NOMOS XXXIX: Ethnicity and Group Rights*, pp. 105–11. New York: New York University Press.

15 Rationality, democracy, and leaky boundaries: vertical vs horizontal modularity*

Susan L. Hurley

Are boundary issues raised by processes of globalization exogenous or endogenous to the theory of democracy?

Can democracy be adequately understood in terms of majoritarian procedures? Majoritarian procedures depend on certain parameters to be well defined, in particular, on specifications of boundaries and of units. For a given issue, we can ask: should majoritarian procedures be applied within local or national boundaries, or internationally? And should the units represented equally by such procedures be individuals, or other units such as families, regions in a federal system, or states? These critical parameters are obviously not fixed by nature. No one boundary or set of units is simply given, nor is there necessarily any one correct specification of them for all political purposes. Especially if we take a global view, various familiar boundaries and units display complexity of structure and relativity to purpose: they overlap and layer and nest and cut across one another.

How should boundaries and units be specified, an agenda of issues be divided up, and particular types of issue be assigned to particular decision-making domains, identified in part by the choice of boundary and unit? As Robert Dahl (1982) and others have pointed out, we cannot appeal simply to majoritarianism to resolve such jurisdictional questions: a majority of *what* units, and within *which* boundaries? So the question arises: are the values that guide these jurisdiction-setting tasks properly seen as exogenous or endogenous to democracy?

The exogenous view would be as follows. Various forces and powers

* I am grateful to Michael Bacharach, Jose Bermudez, John Broome, Gordon Brown, Gerald Cohen, Ronald Dworkin, Diego Gambetta, Russell Hardin, David Held, Richard Higgott, Ramin Nakisi, Derek Parfit, Kim Plunkett, Joelle Proust, Adam Przeworski, Joseph Raz, John Roemer, Paul Seabright, Ian Shapiro, Tim Smithers, Bernard Williams, and members of various audiences to which this material has been presented, for comments and discussion of these ideas.

operate to set boundaries and units and to assign issues to domains. We are not necessarily in control of this process, and the values that guide it, to the extent it is guided at all, are independent of the values of democracy. We should not confuse democracy with other values. Democracy presupposes these parameters, but it does not determine them. Dahl writes: "The fact is that one cannot decide from within democratic theory what constitutes the proper unit for the democratic process" (1983: 103ff).

Here is a contrasting, endogenous view. (In developing this contrast, I will put the endogenous view more forcefully, since the exogenous view has been made familiar and has been forcefully expressed by others.) Democracy does bear on jurisdictional questions; democracy is more than majoritarianism with presupposed parameters. Gerrymandering can have anti-democratic or pro-democratic effects. Distinctively democratic values, such as values of self-determination, autonomy, respect for rights, equality, and contestability, are already at stake in the choice of boundaries and units and the assignments of issues to domains so defined: for example, in the relationships of political boundaries to ethnic groupings, in the treatment of refugees, in the assignment of certain issues to referenda, to individuals for private decision, to judicial review, to a body of representatives of regions, and so on. Some choices of boundaries and units and assignments of jurisdiction might tend to repress and others to foster the autonomy of individuals, respect for their rights, and their deliberative and rational capacities. Some choices of boundaries and units and assignments of jurisdiction might involve built-in tendencies toward bias or cooperative failure that hinder self-determination, while others might avoid them. The values that illuminate these issues and guide heterarchical institutional design cannot plausibly be segregated from the values of democracy (Hurley 1989: chap. 15, and 1999). Rather, they should be integral to our best understanding of democracy itself. Otherwise, democracy will be handicapped in its ability to provide a coherent ideal in the face of global complexity. It will be only a fragment of a political ideal.

On the endogenous view, heterarchical complexity *per se* is not undemocratic. It is not undemocratic *per se* to fix a boundary for majoritarian procedures to operate within. Some boundaries may be more democratic, others less. It is no more undemocratic *per se* to assign jurisdiction over issues in a complex, overlapping, layered, nested way, with different units and boundaries for different types of issue. Of course, there is scope for disagreement about jurisdictional issues, whether their structure is simple or complex. And whether simple or complex, such issues can be resolved in more or less democratic ways.

We cannot, however, understand how one assignment of jurisdiction or choice of boundary is more democratic than another in terms simply of majoritarianism. If we try to do so, we face a regress: this move embeds the very questions about jurisdiction, boundaries, and units that we are trying to answer.

The issue between the exogenous and endogenous views arises, *inter alia*, in the course of considering how the theory of democracy should deal with the undermining of traditional state boundaries by processes of globalization.[1] Globalization makes it increasingly the case not only that people beyond state boundaries can be profoundly affected by internal decisions, but also that external factors can wrench power and control away from internal decision procedures. Functional power networks specific to various particular domains of activity – economic, political, environmental, informational, technological, legal, etc. – increasingly cut across traditional state boundaries (see and cf. Held, above,[2] and Held 1996: chap. 10; Altvater, above;[3] Dahl, above[4]). If the theory of democracy traditionally presupposes the type of state

[1] As Ian Shapiro has pointed out (personal communication), localism also undermines traditional national boundaries. It need not do so just by creating new less inclusive boundaries (as in secession), but may also do so in a piecemeal domain-relative way, and so increase the net permeability of boundaries.

[2] Held is sceptical about the uncritically appropriated concept of the territorial political community at the center of dominant theoretical approaches to democracy. Given increasing globalization, the traditional conception of democracy in terms of a circumscribed self-determining community of citizens begins to appear strained. Held's view, like the view taken here, is that globalization does not so much defeat democracy as force us to rethink it in less boundary-presupposing terms than are traditional. He also indicates what is here called the "horizontally modular" character of the global scenario, though he also agrees in effect that vertical modularity does not disappear: that the "rhetoric of hyperglobalization" is sometimes overdone and that nation states continue to be immensely powerful. Held's own conception of cosmopolitan democracy strips the idea of sovereignty away from the idea of fixed borders and territories, and recognizes the multiple citizenships of people.

[3] Altvater writes: "More important for the question of the procedural rationality of democracy is the difference between national political *borders* and the principal *boundlessness* of economic processes. ... democracy requires coordinates in space and time to secure 'governability.' ... Borders are necessary to secure the formal democratic working of the procedures. ... the perforation of national borders is shaping the democracy's space and time, and thus the *meaning of sovereignty* is changing" (pp. 42–3, above). He emphasizes the effects of economic and ecological factors on political boundaries and processes.

[4] In his skeptical view, Dahl writes: "In sum: if it is difficult enough for ordinary citizens to exercise much influence over decisions about foreign affairs in their own countries, should we not conclude that the obstacles will be far greater in international organization? Just as many important policy decisions in democratic countries are in effect delegated by citizens to the political elites, will not the citizens of countries engaged in an international association delegate effective control to the international policy elites? And won't the extent of delegation in international organizations go well beyond any acceptable threshold of democracy?" (p. 32, above).

boundaries that globalization undermines, what could or should take their place?

On the exogenous view, we cannot appeal to the values of democracy to answer this question. But what can we appeal to? Perhaps a maximally expanded boundary, in effect that of a world state, could reinstate majoritarian democratic theory at the global level. But why presuppose this state boundary? On reflection, it is no more given by nature than any other. The domain-specific power networks that tend to undermine state boundaries may well not support a world state either. So globalization plus the exogenous view tend to support a kind of skepticism about democracy. If the essential procedural presuppositions of democracy are not met, its demands are indeterminate. Perhaps some ways of responding to the boundary-undermining effects of globalization are better than others, but they are not more democratic. We should not confuse democracy with other values.

By contrast, the endogenous view can in principle respond to the consequences of globalization in terms of democratic values. A world state, even a majoritarian one, may be unattractive on many grounds, some internal to the values of democracy itself. Some ways of arranging higher-order power relationships among domain-specific power networks may be more democratic than others.

The way the exogenous/endogenous issue arises in the context of globalization suggests that the contrast may be too sharp. The concept of democracy may not be static, but may itself demand dynamic adaptability. As we rethink democracy in the global context, perhaps what we need is something more like an idea of continuity in the evolution of democratic values, where the normative relationships of procedural and substantive component values have an essentially dynamic aspect.[5]

Recall at this point the still-fruitful classical idea that there may be analogies between social and political structure, on the one hand, and the structure of the mind, on the other.[6] Boundary issues have become a recent focus of attention in cognitive science as well as in political theory. Some interdisciplinary lateral thinking may aid the search for the legitimate descendants of democratic values and procedures in the global context. To this end, consider an analogy between rationality and democracy: between the way rationality is conceived in cognitive science

---

[5] This suggestion is broadly in harmony with Held's views on cosmopolitan democracy and the boundary problem (above, pp. 84–11).

[6] This idea was revived in the contemporary context by Hurley (1989), so the suggestions made here can be seen as an extension of that project. For a precursor of the horizontal/vertical distinction developed here, see especially chap. 15.

and the way democracy is conceived in political theory. Questions familiar from recent philosophy of mind are these: is it essential to rationality, cognition, and thought that the internal causal processes underwriting them have a certain structure? In the absence of that causal structure, are true rationality and thought eliminated? (See Stich 1996.) Consider the parallels with our questions about democracy: is it essential to democracy that internal political procedures have a certain structure? In the absence of that procedural structure, is true democracy eliminated?

Vertical vs horizontal modularity in cognitive science: rethinking rationality[7]

In traditional cognitive science, the mind is seen as dependent on underlying processes, the overall structure of which is *vertically modular*. Each vertical module performs a broad function, then passes the resulting representations on to the next. Within the perceptual module, information about location, color, motion, and so on, is extracted from inputs by various streams of domain-specific perceptual processing. The representations produced by the various streams of input processing converge and are combined by perception. The unified result is sent on to cognition, the central module that interfaces between perception and action. This is where the processes occur on which rational thought and deliberation depend. Rationality is conceived as depending on internal procedures, such as the manipulation of internal symbols or representations, including those passed on by perception. Based on current and stored input and cognitive processing, a motor plan is formulated, and it is passed on to motor programming processes for execution. There is a linear sequence of separate processing stages, from perception to cognition to action. There may be parallel processing within each stage, for example, before information about color and about motion are combined within perception. Nevertheless, the overall functional structure is vertically modular.

We should not confuse talk about the mental states of a person with talk about the underlying subpersonal processes on which those personal-level mental states causally depend. The vertical modularity view is a view about the functional structure of subpersonal causal processes. We can, however, understand why the vertically modular view has seemed natural. At the personal level, we distinguish between a person's

---

[7] Some material in this section is taken from *Consciousness in Action* by Susan Hurley, copyright © 1998 by the President and Fellows of Harvard College, reprinted by permission of Harvard University Press.

perceptions, her reasoning, her intentions. Vertical modularity finds similar distinctions at the level of subpersonal functions and causal processes. It may be natural to assume such an isomorphism between one level of description and another.

Nevertheless, this vertically modular conception of subpersonal causal processes is coming under pressure in recent cognitive science and philosophy of mind, from neural network and dynamical systems approaches (Thelen and Smith 1994: 174, 220; Elman *et al.* 1996; Plunkett and Elman 1997; Kelso 1995; Port and van Gelder 1995; Brooks 1991; Clark 1997: 13ff, 58; Hutchins 1995: 292, 316, 364ff; Milner and Goodale 1995: 10–13, 26, 41–6, 65, 163, 170, 179, 200; Hurley 1998b, etc.). These suggest a contrasting conception of the mind as depending on distributed subpersonal processes that are functionally *horizontally modular* in structure.[8] One way of thinking of these is in terms of layer upon layer of content-specific networks. Each layer or horizontal module is dynamic: it extends from input through output and back to input in various feedback loops. Layers are dedicated to particular kinds of task – for example, one network may govern spatial perception and the orientation of action (the so-called "where" system), another may govern food recognition and acquisition-type behavior (part of the so-called "what" system), another may govern predator recognition and fleeing-type behavior (another part of the "what" system), another may govern imitative responses to the observed behavior of others, and so on. We can think of evolution and/or development as selecting for each layer. Since each subpersonal layer is a complete input–output–input loop, essentially continuous and dynamic, involving external as well as internal feedback, not only are sensory and

---

[8] A technical clarification: the vertical/horizontal contrast drawn in this section should not be confused with the vertical/horizontal contrast drawn by Fodor (1983: part 1). It is closer to, but not identical with, the vertical/horizontal contrast drawn by Clark (1997: 12–14) and elsewhere, and to that implied by Goodale and Milner (1992) when they suggest that functional modularity extends from input right through to output (this would count as horizontal modularity, in present terms); see also Milner and Goodale 1995. It is closer still to some of the contrasts developed by Brooks (1991) between the horizontal domain-specific layering of his subsumption architectures and the traditional artificial intelligence approach. Note that in present terms, Fodor's view counts as vertically modular: he functionally distinguishes transducers, input systems, central processors, motor systems, and supposes the flow of information becomes available to these systems in about that order; input systems mediate between transducer output and central cognition by producing mental representations on which central cognition then operates; input systems are "informationally encapsulated," while the central system is not (Fodor 1983: 41–2). However, in present terms, horizontal modules are domain specific. We do not give up domain specificity by moving from vertical to horizontal modularity. See and cf. Thelen and Smith 1994: 174, 220; Elman *et al.* 1996: 37, 40–1, 100, 108, 158; Hurley 1989: chap. 15. A horizontally modular view of the mind is controversial and unorthodox; it is not argued for here, merely reflected on.

motor processes coupled, but the neural network is directly coupled to the creature's environment. Horizontal modules are essentially "situated." Each dynamic layer is a system that is distributed across perceiving and acting organism and relevant parts of its environment (perhaps including other organisms: see Hutchins 1995 on socially distributed natural cognition). However, just as a given environmental object or feature can be presented in personal-level content in different ways, it can also feature in more than one subpersonal horizontal layer or module or system of relations.

On a horizontally modular view, what happens to vertical boundaries? Vertical boundaries, such as those around sensory or motor processes, or around central cognitive processes, or indeed around the organism as a whole, are relatively transparent and permeable. The mind is "leaky," as Andy Clark puts it (1997). It does not follow that vertical boundaries disappear entirely. But they share functional significance with horizontal boundaries, and the tendency of the recent work mentioned is to emphasize the latter at the expense of the former, on both empirical and theoretical grounds.

Can a horizontally modular view accommodate cognition and rationality? *If* our minds were dependent on horizontal layers dedicated to particular tasks, would our rationality be an illusion? If shown to be correct, would it eliminate rationality?[9]

Though this may be our first reaction, recent work has argued that properties of cognition and rationality can emerge from what are, in effect, horizontally modular systems. But these properties need to be rethought, in a way that does not depend on a linear sequence of separate stages or on procedures internal to a central interface between input and output. Rationality might instead emerge from a complex system of decentralized, higher-order relations of inhibition, facilitation,

---

[9] What is the relationship of these questions to questions about whether the truth of connectionism and lack of internal classical structure would eliminate thought or merely alter our views of what thought is? (For a recent discussion and references see Stich 1996; see also Hurley 1998a and 1998b). The threat to rationality from horizontal modularity is a local threat to the holism of practical reason, in the way explained in the text. Holism is seen as necessary for rationality on a wide variety of views, so the threat to holism needs to be disarmed. By contrast, the threat to thought from connectionism supposedly derives from lack of classical causal systematicity, of syntactical subpersonal structure isomorphic with the conceptual structure of thought. The view that such isomorphism between the personal and subpersonal levels is necessary for thought is more controversial than the view that holism is necessary for rationality. In this sense the need to disarm a threat to holism is more urgent. This threat is more fundamental than the threat posed by connectionism to an internal language of thought. Notice that these points are put in terms of a need to defeat a threat to a necessary condition for rationality. It is not suggested that holism is sufficient for rationality.

and coordination among different horizontal layers, each of which is dynamic and environmentally situated. Just as evolution and development can select a network at each layer that can do the job wanted, they can also operate on relations between the layers to favor rationally flexible responses to problems that the environment sets the organism.

However, rationality conceived in this way is substantively related to the world. It does not depend only on internal procedures that mediate between input and output, either for the organism as a whole or for a vertically bounded central cognitive module. Rather, it depends on complex relationships between dedicated, world-involving layers that monitor and respond to specific aspects of the natural and social environment and of the neural network, and register feedback from responses (see Hurley 1998b on the idea of an organism-centered dynamic singularity). Among the aspects of the environment included in these feedback loops may be events that amount to the actions of others and, for language-using creatures, to uses of natural language by others. Very crudely, some layers get turned on and others turned off, in a totality of ways that count as rational overall in the circumstances. Rationality on this view is a higher-order property of complex patterns of response, which emerges from the layers of direct dynamic couplings between organisms and their structured environments.

Imitation, rationality, and evolutionary search

It may be helpful to consider a more specific illustration of how horizontal modularity might seem to threaten rationality and how the threat can be responded to. Take as an example of a horizontal layer the imitation system (or systems). First, some facts.

Newborn infants imitate gestures made to them: for example, they will stick out their tongues reliably when they see someone sticking out his or her tongue. Various empirical reasons have been given for regarding this as intentional behavior, not as merely reflexive (Meltzoff 1995; Meltzoff and Moore 1977, 1983a, 1983b, 1985, and 1995).

Patients with certain kinds of frontal brain damage can be affected by an imitation behavior syndrome, in which they persistently imitate gestures the experimenter makes, even when these are socially unacceptable. When asked why they imitate, since they had not been asked to imitate, patients display a degree of cognitive entrapment: they say they feel they have to, that it is their duty, that the gestures they see somehow include an order to imitate them, that their response is a natural reaction. They do not disown their behavior and may attempt to justify it. Though their behavior reflects a loss of autonomy and rationality, it has been viewed as voluntary and not reflexive. For example, a patient with the frontal imitation syndrome might refuse to imitate hair combing because he wore a wig that would come off: so his imitative behavior is not simply reflexive, and is subject to some voluntary control. But there is still a loss of rationality: in this example, there was no reason to imitate to begin with, so no need to have a reason for refusing. (By contrast, echo-reaction apraxia patients, with a different kind of brain damage, have immediate, automatic, reflexive imitative reactions, which the patient himself may criticize but cannot control.) It has been suggested that these frontal patients have damage to an area that normally functions to inhibit the activity of a system that makes particular connections between perceptions and actions. On this view, damage to the inhibitory area can release imitative patterns of behavior, among others (Lhermitte, Pillon, and Serdaru 1986; Lhermitte 1986; Stengel, Vienna, and Edin 1947).

However, the tendency to imitate is not confined to the young and the brain-damaged. Normal experimental subjects instructed to point to their noses when they hear "nose!" or to a lamp when they hear "lamp" perform correctly while watching the experimenter perform correctly. But they are unable to avoid mistakes when they observe the experimenter doing the wrong thing: they tend to imitate what they see rather than follow the instruction heard, even though they have been clearly instructed to follow the verbal command (Eidelberg 1929; Prinz 1990). The underlying tendency to imitate is inhibited in normal adults under many conditions, but it is still there, and its influence can be revealed experimentally. It may operate under a range of natural conditions as well; dysfunction may reveal aspects of normal function.[10]

[10] Imitation appears to involve an immensely complex mapping from visual inputs to motor outputs. It is tempting to speculate about how the observed tendency to imitate might be achieved by the nervous system. There are various possibilities involving stronger or weaker forms of shared neural coding for perception and for action (Prinz 1990; Hurley 1998b). Mirror neurons have been discovered in monkeys (di Pellegrino et al. 1992; Jeannerod 1997). These, like many other neurons, have both perceptual and motor fields: that is, their firing correlates with certain perceptions as well as with certain motor intentions. But mirror neurons also have the feature that their perceptual and motor fields match: they fire when the agent perceives someone acting in a certain way or when she does the same thing herself (or both). For example, certain cells might fire when the monkey sees the experimenter bring food to the mouth with his hand *or* when the monkey does the same.

It is also tempting to speculate about why the nervous system should be wired in such a way as to facilitate imitation. To address this question we can invoke a distinction between the architecture, or general structural features, of neural networks, and the variable degree and direction of fine-grained synaptic connectivities within a network of a given fixed architecture (argued for in Elman et al. 1996). In nature, evolution can operate on types of architectural starting points, despite a degree of plasticity of architecture with development and experience. So perhaps it can select for structures

A tendency to imitation involves a certain threat to rationality. Imitation need not be merely reflexive, but can entrap cognitive processes. The potential threat to rationality is typical of a horizontal module, considered in isolation from others (for other examples and discussion, see Hurley 1998b: essays 9, 10). The connections it makes between perception and action are too rigid and may not be rationally mediated by someone's desires or intentions, as in the imitation syndrome patients. Imitation is often counterproductive or an irrelevant distraction from the task at hand. More generally, a tight imitative mapping between external stimuli and responses threatens, with respect to imitative responses, the holism of practical rationality: the way intentional action depends on the rational interaction of beliefs and desires, or of perceptions and intentions.

A closely related point is often made in criticizing behaviorism. No given perception by itself can determine what someone should do, because different purposes will rationally lead to different intentional actions, and purposes are not fixed by perception. Behaviorism tries to take a short cut through the rational interaction of perception and intention, belief and desire. It makes too tight a connection between the content of a perceptual experience and its manifestations in action, which fails to respect a rational agent's degrees of freedom. The type of behavior that is apt in a given environment is relative to a purpose. The "wrong" purpose can always interpose itself between given perceptions and behavior, creating an obstacle to any smooth behaviorist transition from content of perception to type of behavior.

Yet despite these points, a tendency to imitate may have important and beneficial functions. Why might evolution favor neural or subpersonal structures with imitative tendencies? This is not hard to see. Variations in the inherited behavioral traits of adults may slightly favor some members of a given generation over others, so that some reproduce and others do not. Offspring may benefit if they can acquire the

that have general or default phenotypic tendencies, such as the presence of potential mirror neurons. However, empirical evidence suggests that fine-grained synaptic connectivities are not innate (Elman *et al.* 1996: 315). Rather, they are a function of development and experience, within the interactive constraints set by neural, bodily, and environmental structures. For example, the co-firing of connected neurons, which may have an environmental source, may increase their positive degree of connectivity, so that the firing of one facilitates the firing of the other. Physical growth may change co-firing patterns, resulting in developmental changes in connectivity (Thelen and Smith 1994). Suppose, for reasons considered in the text, evolution favors architectures that have default imitative tendencies, even if these are slight. For example, suppose "weak" mirror neurons are selected by evolution: these create a slight tendency to favor imitation in certain contexts. With experience, this tendency could be reinforced as connectivities alter to facilitate the co-firing of connected neurons.

I emphasize that these possibilities are purely speculative, but they may make the complex mappings that imitation involves seem slightly less inexplicable.

behavioral traits of their successful parents through imitation as well as through inheritance. A young creature that has an innate tendency to act the way it observes others act will, through observing its parents, tend to pick up the behavior of creatures that have survived long enough to reproduce. A tendency to imitate would permit adaptation within, as well as between, lifetimes (see also and cf. Boyd and Richerson 1985). In the human case, in particular, imitation may play an important role in the acquisition of language.[11]

So, we should consider how minds are made up as well as how we make up our minds. The tendency to imitate may be among the developmental means by which sensorimotor systems are calibrated and by which people acquire a basic vocabulary of intentional actions, both linguistic and non-linguistic, so as to become the kinds of mature agents to whom the principles of rationality and autonomy generally apply.

How can we have it both ways? How can the beneficial functions of imitation be secured without creating a general threat to rationality? Imitation needs to be inhibited and facilitated appropriately in relation to other systems, if the subject/agent is to achieve rationality, at least under a range of normal conditions. There could be motivational or other mechanisms to override or inhibit the imitative tendency, while releasing it in certain circumstances or developmental periods. In addition to a variety of dedicated horizontal layers, we need higher-order structures that connect these layers, facilitating or inhibiting their functions when they are related to one another in certain ways, or under various environmental conditions.

Now the higher-order structures that connect the horizontal imitation system with other horizontal layers can also have beneficial functions, and so can also be the objects of evolutionary search. Evolution can search the space of higher-order structural possibilities for sets of relationships between horizontal modules that inhibit and facilitate their operation in appropriate environmental contexts and at appropriate developmental stages, in ways that increase overall fitness. One (over-simple) supposition might be that the beneficial functions of imitation are concentrated in early development. Thereafter, the imitative tendency may be inhibited and overlaid in a wide range of normal

---

[11] Development and evolution may work together. A weak innate imitative tendency might be strengthened as a result of imitative experience, if connections between sensory and motor neurons that fire together are strengthened. As a result, neural connections would be calibrated on meaningful and functional gestures and behaviors, which would facilitate the emergence of more complex intentions and compound behaviors. It is interesting to note that the area of the monkey brain in which mirror neurons have been found corresponds to Broca's area in the human brain, one of the areas on which linguistic abilities depend (di Pellegrino *et al.* 1992).

circumstances (though not necessarily all). Even so, its underlying influence could still be revealed under non-normal conditions and by brain damage. Another hypothesis is that it may be evolutionarily advantageous to mimic certain behaviors in certain circumstances in order to obtain the benefits of cooperation without incurring its costs. For example, the imitation system might be switched on to mimic the behavioral appearances or signals used by cooperators to identify one another, in order to receive cooperation, then switched off by the cheater just before it comes to the point of reciprocation.[12]

Rationality can be conceived in general terms as an emergent property of such a complex system, distributed across organisms and their structured environments. Despite the potential conflicts between imitation and rationality, rationality may build on and develop out of the imitative tendency, among others. Rationality may emerge from complex relationships between horizontally modular subpersonal systems which, considered in isolation, generate behavior that is less than rational.[13] More would, of course, need to be done to provide a positive account of rationality in these general terms. The aim here is not to do that, but rather to suggest how a threat to a widely endorsed necessary condition for rationality, namely, holism, might in principle be disarmed.[14]

The moral of our consideration of imitation is: we can rethink

[12] Thanks to Diego Gambetta for discussion of these points; on "greenbeard" genes and their vulnerability to imitative cheater mutants, see, e.g., Dawkins 1982: 144–5.

[13] As Hutchins (1995: chap. 5) has emphasized in his work on network simulations of socially distributed cognition, the rationality of the whole cognitive system does not require the rationality of the components of the system. Overall rationality may be an emergent property of the whole system. For example, confirmation bias is a propensity for a cognitive system to affirm prior views and to discount, ignore, or reinterpret evidence that runs counter to an already formed view. However, even given confirmation bias in individuals, certain structural conditions on communication within the group may enhance the cognitive performance of the overall system so that it does not display confirmation bias as a whole. Confirmation bias in individuals with different starting points and limited intercommunication produces a diversity of views. The trick then is to find a way of airing these diverse views in a way that facilitates finding and settling on the correct resolution.

Reflection on Hutchins's fascinating study of navigation as socially distributed cognition suggests various other possibilities. For example, could the legal system be understood as socially distributed cognition; could something like what Hutchins does for navigation be done for law?

[14] Perhaps the suggested line of thought would be more compatible with some views of rationality, such as reliabilist views, than others. Moreover, in developing this line of thought further it would probably be helpful to disaggregate rationality. The horizontally modular view may accommodate practical rationality in the way suggested more readily than theoretical rationality – but consider rational action of a special kind: action and interaction in the public space of natural language. Through action in this public space we acquire theoretical rationality. Having done so, we tend to project this public space of theoretical rationality inwardly, perhaps thereby creating an illusion of a central vertical module.

rationality. Rationality need not be conceived to depend on procedures internal to vertical boundaries. It is not eliminated by and can even depend on, horizontal modularity.

Vertical vs horizontal modularity in political theory: rethinking democracy

I hope this is all sounding a bit familiar, and that the analogy between these boundary issues about rationality and the issues about democracy we began with is beginning to make itself apparent. To be explicit: on the one hand, there is a vertically modular view of the subpersonal causal structures on which minds depend. Rationality is seen as depending on procedures internal to such structures. On the other hand, there is a vertically modular conception of the power structures on which governance depends. Democracy is seen as depending on procedures internal to such structures. On the latter view, the political world is presumed to be divided into individuals and states; majoritarian procedures are defined by reference to these units and boundaries. The analogy is not perfect, and should not be pressed too far. But it is suggestive, and may help us to see how democracy, too, can be rethought in the face of boundary problems. It is arguable that the demise of the classical, vertically modular conception of the causal processes that underwrite the mind does not eliminate rationality so much as challenge certain views of what rationality is, of its nature. Similarly, a horizontal conception of the processes that underwrite political decision and action need not been seen as eliminating democracy so much as challenging prevalent views of what it is, of its nature. Arguments about elimination in cognitive science are complex and I do not pretend to do justice to them, or resolve them, here. The point is rather to suggest the analogy (see figure 15.1).

As we have seen, vertical modularity is under pressure in political theory, as a result of increasing globalization. This in turn puts pressure on the applicability of a conception of democracy in terms of internal procedures that presuppose exogenously fixed units and boundaries. Globalization creates structures and complex dynamic processes that distribute power across state boundaries. When we view the world in this way, national boundaries go transparent and permeable – leaky – even though they do not disappear entirely.

While the functional power networks thrown up by processes of globalization do not necessarily respect traditional vertical distinctions between nations, they often do reflect horizontal distinctions between specific domains. Like the horizontal layers in a dynamic systems

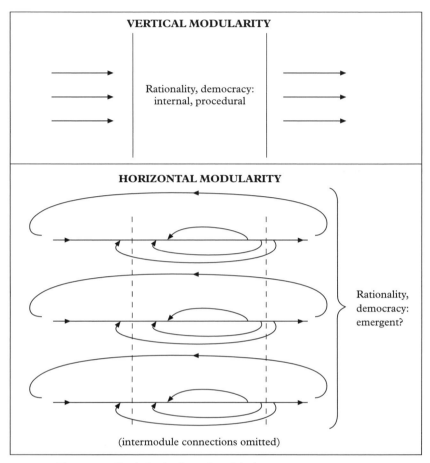

Figure 15.1 Vertical vs horizontal modularity

conception of the subpersonal processes on which mind depends, global processes are often dedicated or domain-specific. Consider the global organizations and processes that deal with banking, trade, information technology, human rights, environmental issues, and so on.

Now what is the place of democracy in this view of a horizontally layered world, where vertical boundaries are shifting and increasingly permeable? Is the concept of democracy still applicable? If we presuppose an internal, procedural conception of democracy our first response may be "no." But consider the possibility that the correct answer might be "yes," as for the parallel question about rationality. Democracy also needs to be rethought. It can no longer be conceived strictly in terms of internal procedures, can no longer be conceived to presuppose fixed units and vertical boundaries. But democracy no more requires vertically modular power structures than rationality requires vertically modular subpersonal structures. We need to understand how the various horizontal layers of activity, which can themselves be more or less democratic, can also be related to one another more or less democratically. Democracy might be an emergent property of the higher-order system of relations between various functional power networks, global institutions, and processes, which may or may not be democratic considered in isolation. The operation of "external" forces can be democratized, appropriately inhibited and facilitated, not just by "internal" control, but also, or instead, by being embedded in a larger system with a complex structure and dynamics.[15]

For example: what kinds of relationships between the international networks concerned with human rights law, information technology, ecological issues, trade and finance and industry, etc., would generate more or less democracy? To answer such a question, we need a way of evaluating resulting states of affairs as more or less democratic. But we also need to know what states of affairs are possible: what the consequences over time of various arrangements would be. Evolution cannot search the space of possibilities for us here. We only have one world, and cannot afford to expend it in evolution. Moreover, deliberate design of a global system of institutions to serve certain goals may well be frustrated by the characteristic and fundamental unpredictability of complex dynamic systems: the only way to find out how they will behave is to let them run and see. How can the space of possible relations among various international processes be searched effectively, with the aim of finding complex relationships from which more rather than less democracy emerges?

Ways the world might be: simulation and imagination in normative political theory

Different sets of relations among global institutions played out over time may give rise to different tendencies (again, cf. Hutchins 1995). Some

[15] As well as being in harmony with Held's position on cosmopolitan democracy and boundaries, there is a sense in which this view can also be regarded as a radical extension of Dahl's (1982) notion of democratic polyarchy, in which there is "a complex system with several or more layers of democratic government, each operating with a somewhat different agenda"; but compare his skeptical view set out in this volume. It also constitutes a variation on Hutchin's (1995) point that the cognitive properties of a group depend not just on the cognitive properties of individuals, but also on the way they are related.

oversimplified examples may convey the gist. Suppose that the ratio of certain international economic variables is correlated with some measure of the rate of environmental damage. Suppose then that if that ratio is used in a certain role as a parameter in the lending policy of the IMF, and we let the system run, over time it develops so that the economic autonomy of certain impoverished and dependent areas of the world is increased while the rate of environmental damage is reduced. On the other hand, if this ratio is used in a different parametric role, the opposite tendencies are produced. How can these different tendencies be predicted in advance? Or consider a choice between information technology policies: should nations that censor information about human rights and refuse to cooperate with international human rights organizations have full access to the Internet? What would be the effect, for example, of granting tax subsidies or other favors to commercial Internet users that voluntarily refrain from doing business via the Internet with organizations in censoring nations? The effects on respect for human rights and on individual autonomy are hard to predict. These illustrations are, in fact, vastly too simple; the complexity of the real world does not lend itself to easy examples.

It is well known that complex dynamic systems, as modelled using neural network techniques among others, can display striking forms of emergent self-organization despite the lack of a central controlling module (Kelso 1995; Thelen and Smith 1994). Given the non-linear complexity involved, these patterns of self-organization may be opaque to an unaided design perspective, and may best be discovered by computationally simulating evolution. Emergent order may be unpredictable by any means other than simulation, even in a fully deterministic system. We can harness the power of evolution as a mechanism of search without running the risks of extinction by simulating evolution. Computational evolution can search the space of possible complex systems using genetic algorithms, under selective pressure that we provide. Evolutionary techniques are being applied to design robots (for a summary, see Clark 1997: chap. 5). Could they not also be applied to global institutional design?

Some of the ways a horizontally modular world might be arranged are substantively different in normative respects from other ways it might be arranged. For example, to invoke a republican conception of democratic citizenship, suppose that some institutional arrangements are better than others at fostering autonomy, deliberative capacities, public-spiritedness, and other civic virtues in citizens, at encouraging thoughtful and widespread participation in public life and decision-making within a variety of fora, at facilitating fair contestability, and at avoiding concentrations of power in biased hands. Suppose that some such differences count as ways in which the world might be more substantively democratic. Of course, other values may also be relevant. The supposition is that among the various applicable values are distinctively democratic values. If this premise is granted, then we may be able to use simulation techniques to work backward from such substantive judgments to an understanding of what structures and procedures count as democratic in a horizontally modular world. On such a view, norms of substance and of procedure would be dynamically and adaptively related within the concept of democracy, in application to a changing world. The short essentialist argument from lack of certain traditionally presupposed vertical structures and procedures to the elimination of democracy is too short. We can do better.

We might model various institutions, organizations, and processes that constitute the horizontal layers of the global system, in ways that benefit from experience at network modelling in cognitive science. We could first build various subnets, and then build a supernet out of them.[16]

Suppose first that various horizontal layers were modelled separately, each one by a neural network trained to simulate dynamic empirical data about the given area: a subnet. One such subnet might model international banking processes, another might model processes in the international legal system, and so on. We would try out various subnet structures or "architectures" for each horizontal domain, and attempt to train up a subnet (algorithmically adjust the connections between its units) until its performance simulates the specific horizontal layer we are modelling. Subnet training could be guided by detailed specifications of the empirical data to be simulated.[17] An adequate subnet itself could be very complex. "Context units" of subnets might reflect important remaining aspects of vertical modularity, such as the distribution of population and GNP across nations, so that vertical modularity does not disappear entirely. But vertical modules could be treated as the context within which horizontal modules operate, rather than vice versa.

Second, consider how these different horizontal subnet layers interact when we connect them up in various ways into a big supernetwork and let the supernet run. Even holding the subnets' internal structure and connections fixed and varying only the connections between subnets, we may find that some of the resulting tendencies may be more desirable in

---

[16] "If one thinks of the brain as a network of networks, global architectural constraints concern the manner in which these networks are interconnected" (Elman *et al.* 1996: 29).

[17] Using, for example, standard backpropogation techniques. See also and cf. Casti 1997.

terms of democratic values than others. At this stage our modelling goes heavily normative. We are not simply trying to model the world as it is, but to use simulation to help us to imagine, understand, and evaluate ways the world might be. So we cannot rely on empirical data to supply detailed specifications of our aims, and simply adjust the supernet algorithmically until it simulates the detailed empirical data.

We can, of course, also evaluate the subnets separately with respect to how democratic they are, and perhaps find ways to improve them. We could then enter the stage of supernet modelling with normatively improved subnets. Arguably it matters how democratic certain horizontal layers are internally, and not just how democratic the overall system is in its tendencies. That is compatible with recognizing that the overall system might also have democratic tendencies resulting from interaction of subnets that may not themselves all be especially democratic.

Again, we can benefit from experience within cognitive science: of applying genetic algorithms and fitness functions to evolve complex nets with desired properties. A genetic algorithm would throw up a variety of supernets by random variations on relations between subnets. We could let the supernet simulations run, see what they do, and choose the ones we like to apply the next round of mutation to. By this means we might succeed in evolving an ultra-complex supernet with attractive emergent properties but which we would have been hard put to design deliberately.[18]

In order to simulate evolution, however, we need to provide a fitness function. Rationality may emerge under evolutionary pressure, but democracy needs guidance from us to emerge at the global level. A fitness function expresses our selection among the supernet possibilities the genetic algorithm throws up. It can reflect substantive values continuous with those of democracy as traditionally conceived, even if these cannot be understood in the internal, procedural terms that presupposed a vertically modular world. That is, the same substantive values of self-determination, autonomy, respect for rights, equality, contestability, etc., that motivate internal democratic procedures can also bear on processes that are not internal but that relate people across different nations. The fitness function would be devised so as to search for emergent patterns and processes that tend to satisfy such values.

In order to decide what relations between international networks would count as more or less democratic, we need both a way of

---

[18] No suggestion is intended that precisely the same network structures and weights that do some piece of cognitive work would also do normative political work. I am indebted to Bernard Williams for revealing this possible misunderstanding to me.

evaluating resulting states of affairs for their democratic character and a way of knowing what the resulting states of affairs would be. It is natural to suppose that we need first to develop our conception of democratic values and then to figure out how best to serve them in a global context: to specify the end or goal, and then determine the means. The first problem may seem to be the normative problem, the second merely technical. It may seem that simulation techniques borrowed from cognitive science can contribute only to solving the technical problem, not to solving the normative problem. That would be worthwhile in itself. But I suspect that simulation might have a contribution to make in solving both problems, and that they are not so sharply separable.[19] The complexity of subject-matter, and the need to adapt norms of democracy to the global context, may make it better to think about norms and techniques more interactively. The concept of imagination seems particularly appropriate here: simulation may aid our normative imagination, our abilities to envisage and evaluate alternatives in a complex world. Learning what is possible, what properties emerge from various ways of connecting up international networks, may help us to develop our conception of democracy, to specify more sensitively the emergent properties that count as democratic in a global context. Evolving a complex system to satisfy one specification of a democratic norm and comparing the way it works with alternative systems thrown up en route may alter our conception of the norm.

The difficulties of coding and interpretation in such a simulation project would be significant, but perhaps not insuperable. It is worth investigating further the feasibility of such a new approach to the design of cosmopolitan democracy. There may also be other areas of potential cross-fertilization of modelling and simulation techniques between the cognitive and social sciences.

I have exploited the analogy between boundary issues in cognitive science and in political theory in order to suggest how democracy could be rethought as an emergent property of a complex globally distributed dynamic system or supernetwork. Like rationality, it need not be conceived in internal and procedural terms. It is not wedded to vertical modularity. Democracy is not eliminated by, and can even depend on, horizontal modularity.

REFERENCES

Boyd, Robert and Peter Richerson. 1985. *Culture and the Evolutionary Process.* Chicago: University of Chicago Press.

[19] I am grateful to Ronald Dworkin for comments that prompted this clarification.

292   *Susan L. Hurley*

Brooks, Rodney. 1991. "Intelligence without reason." In the *Proceedings of the Twelfth International Joint Conference on Artificial Intelligence*, pp. 569–95. San Mateo, CA: Morgan Kaufman.

Casti, John L. 1977. *Would-be Worlds*. New York: Wiley.

Clark, Andy. 1997. *Being There*. Cambridge, MA: MIT Press.

Dahl, Robert A. 1982. *Dilemmas of Pluralist Democracy*. New Haven: Yale University Press.

1983. "Federalism and the democratic process." In Roland Pennock and John Chapman (eds.), *Liberal Democracy*. New York: New York University Press.

Dawkins, Richard. 1982. *The Extended Phenotype*. Oxford: Oxford University Press.

di Pellegrino, G., L. Fadiga, L. Fogassi, V. Gallese, and G. Rizzolatti. 1992. "Understanding motor events: a neurophysiological study." *Experimental Brain Research* 91: 176–80.

Eidelberg, L. 1929. "Experimenteller Beitrag zum Mechanismus der Imitations-bewegung." *Jahresbucher fur Psychiatrie und Neurologie* 45: 170–3.

Elman, Jeffrey L., Elizabeth A. Bates, Mark H. Johnson, Annette Karmiloff-Smith, Domenico Parisi, and Kim Plunkett. 1996. *Rethinking Innateness: A Connectionist Perspective on Development*. Cambridge, MA: MIT Press.

Fodor, Jerry A. 1983. *The Modularity of Mind*. Cambridge, MA: MIT Press.

Goodale, Melvyn A. and A. David Milner. 1992. "Separate visual pathways for perception and action." *Trends in Neuroscience* 15: 20–5.

Held, David. 1996. *Models of Democracy* (2nd edn). Cambridge: Polity Press.

Hurley, Susan L. 1989. *Natural Reasons: Personality and Polity*. New York: Oxford University Press.

1998a. "Vehicles, contents, conceptual structure, and externalism." *Analysis* 58(1): 1–6.

1998b. *Consciousness in Action*. Cambridge, MA: Harvard University Press.

1999. "Cognitivism in political philosophy." In Brad Hooker and Roger Crisp (eds.), *Well-being and Morality: Essays in Honour of James Griffin*. Oxford: Oxford University Press.

Hutchins, Edwin. 1995. *Cognition in the Wild*. Cambridge, MA: MIT Press.

Jeannerod, Marc. 1997. *The Cognitive Neuroscience of Action*. Oxford: Blackwell.

Kelso, J. A. Scott. 1995. *Dynamic Patterns: The Self-Organization of Brain and Behavior*. Cambridge, MA: MIT Press.

Lhermitte, F. 1986. "Human autonomy and the frontal lobes, Part II." *Annals of Neurology* 19: 325–43.

Lhermitte, F., B. Pillon, and M. Sedaru. 1986. "Human autonomy and the frontal lobes, Part 1: Imitation and utilization behavior: a neuropsychological study of 75 patients." *Annals of Neurology* 19(4): 326–34.

Meltzoff, Andrew N. 1995. "Understanding the intentions of others: re-enactment of intended acts by 18-month-old children." *Developmental Psychology* 31: 838–50.

Meltzoff, Andrew N. and M. Keith Moore. 1977. "Imitation of facial and manual gestures by human neonates." *Science* 198: 75–8.

1983a. "Newborn infants imitate adult facial gestures." *Child Development* 54: 702–9.

1983b. "The origins of imitation in infancy: paradigm, phenomena, and theories." *Advances in Infancy Research* 2: 266–88.

1985. "Cognitive foundations and social functions of imitation and inter-modal representation in infancy." In J. Mehler and R. Fox (eds.), *Neonate Cognition: Beyond the Blooming Buzzing Confusion*. Hillsdale, NJ: Erlbaum.

1995. "Infants' understanding of people and things: From body imitation to folk psychology." In J. L. Bermudez, A. Marcel, and N. Eilan (eds.), *The Body and the Self*. Cambridge, MA: MIT Press.

Milner, A. David and Melvyn A. Goodale. 1995. *The Visual Brain in Action*. Oxford: Oxford University Press.

Plunkett, Kim and Jeffrey L. Elman. 1997. *Exercises in Rethinking Innateness: A Handbook for Connectionist Simulations*. Cambridge, MA: MIT Press.

Port, Robert F. and Timothy van Gelder (eds.), 1995. *Mind as Motion: Explanations in the Dynamics of Cognition*. Cambridge, MA: MIT Press.

Prinz, Wolfgang. 1990. "A common coding approach to perception and action." In O. Neumann and Wolfgang Prinz (eds.), *Relations Between Perception and Action: Current Approaches*, pp. 167–201. Berlin: Springer.

Stengel, E., M. D. Vienna, and L. R. C. P. Edin. 1947. "A clinical and psychological study of echo-reactions." *Journal of Mental Science* 93: 598–612.

Stich, Stephen P. 1996. *Deconstructing the Mind*. New York: Oxford University Press.

Thelen, Esther and Smith, Linda B. 1994. *A Dynamic Systems Approach to the Development of Cognition and Action*. Cambridge, MA: MIT Press.

Index

Abrams, Kathryn 203
absolutism 86–9
Abu-Lughod, Janet 85
Abzug, Bella 153, 154
Ackerly, Brooke A. 9–10, 135, 139
Ackerman, Bruce 173
Afkhami, Mhnaz 149
Alejandro, Roberto 229
Almond, Gabriel 23–4
Altvater, Elmar 5, 6, 8, 58, 275
Anderson, Benedict 130
Anderson, Perry 86
Archibugi, Daniele 22–3
Arendt, Hannah 258
Arneson, Richard 246

Banting, Keith 114
Barber, Benjamin 253
Barry, Brian 270
Beck, Ulrich 59
Beetham, David 42, 43, 51, 101
Beitz, Charles 88
Beuilly, John 91
Bivins, Jason 12–13, 265–72
Bobbio, Norberto 46, 47, 89, 90
Brubaker, Rogers 207
Bull, Hedley 86, 104
Bunch, Charlotte 153
Butegwa, Florence 153

capitalism 41–2, 49–51, 57–60
Carens, Joseph 131, 204
Cassese, Antonio 87
Charlesworth, Hilary 140
citizenship 8, 45–51, 107, 112–25, 200–8
civil society 57, 105–8, 108, 121, 134–5,
    143–58, 170–1, 250–2
Clark, Andy 279
Cohen, Joshua 236, 257
collective bads 6, 63–5, 67–83
collective goods 65–7, 69, 73–4
Comte, Auguste 45
Connolly, William 90

constitutionalism 38, 46, 105–8, 121–2
cosmopolitan democracy 8–9, 84, 104–8,
    119, 127, 131
cultural harm 195–207, 232–58
    remedies for 200–7, 216–20, 248–58

Dahl, Robert 3–4, 5, 8, 37–9, 89, 90, 130,
    246, 247, 273, 274, 275, 287
Dahrendorf, Ralf 50
de facto internationalization 9, 34, 128–9
definition of democracy 19–21
delegation 21–2, 31–2
deliberative democracy 106, 133–7, 138,
    143–6, 253–4
democratic accountability 84, 89–91,
    105–8, 131
    lack of 2–3, 5, 8, 13, 23–8, 45–51
democratic deficit 30, 34
democratic liberties 10–11, 105–8,
    168–77, 183–8, 189–91
    tangibility and intangibility of 10–11, 42,
    51, 171–2, 176–89,
democratic public law 7–8, 105–8
Diamond, Larry 157
Dionne, E. J. 257

ecological democracy 56–7
economic democracy 33, 38, 57–60
Economist, The 25
Ely, John Hart 246–7
environmental deterioration 5, 6, 41, 44,
    52–7, 63, 99–100
environmental regulation 5, 6, 44–9, 52–7,
    64–5, 69, 70, 71–3, 74–5, 77–8,
    80–3
exit, costs of 4–5, 37

Falk, Richard 87, 88
Falwell, Jerry 249
Favell, Adrian 206
feminist criticism 135–50
Fernàndez-Armesto, Felipe 85, 93
Filner, Matthew 12–13, 265–72

295

Fishkin, James 253
Fordism and post-Fordism 58–60
foreign affairs and policy 23–30, 64, 102
Fraser, Nancy 193, 196, 197–200, 201
freedom: *see* democratic liberties
fundamental rights 20, 41, 43–4, 45–51

Galbraith, John Kenneth 180
Giddens, Anthony 86, 92
Gitlin, Todd 194
global communications networks 98–9
global inequality 5, 6, 44, 48, 55, 60, 132
global political economy 4, 5, 7, 41–60,
    91–104, 113–14
globalization 5, 6–7, 8–10, 34, 41–2,
    45–51, 52–7, 91–104, 112–25,
    129–30, 134, 275–7, 285–7
Goodin, Robert 132
Gramsci, Antonio 57
Grimm, Dieter 121, 125
group rights 9, 11–12, 132, 148, 193–5,
    200–7, 210, 211–20
Guttmann, Amy 243, 253

Habermas, Jürgen 234–5, 250, 251–2,
    253
Halim, Asma Mohamed Abdel 149
Hall, John 88
Hardin, Garrett 44
Hardin, Russell 6
Harrod, Roy 44, 55
Harvey, David 52, 53
Hassan, Riffat 150
Hawthorn, Geoffrey 88–9
Hayek, Friedrich 97
Hegel, G. W. F. 57
Held, David 6–8, 9, 11, 22–3, 34, 46, 49,
    88, 89, 90, 103, 105, 106, 107,
    112–13, 115, 119, 120, 123, 127,
    131, 275, 276, 287
Hirsch, Fred 44
Hirschman, Albert 4
Hirst, Paul 93, 97
Hobbes, Thomas 7, 11, 67, 173, 230, 241,
    253
Hobsbawm, Eric 58, 180
Holmes, Justice Oliver Wendell 254
Holmes, Stephen 12, 224, 227, 246
Honig, Bonnie 235
Honneth, Axel 132, 193
human rights 45–51
    and women's rights 101, 105–8, 119
Hurley, Susan 14–15, 274
Hutchins, Edwin 287

identity politics 1–2, 11–13, 38–9, 120,
    148–51, 193–208, 211–20, 222–64,
    265–72
immigration 1, 5, 10–11, 31, 165–6,
    167–8
industrial democracy, prospects for 57
inequality 39–60, 179–91, 195–200
    see also global inequality
international democracy 8–9, 80, 127,
    131–2
international institutions 2–4, 6–8, 10, 19,
    22–3, 30–4, 37, 45, 50, 101–2,
    124–5, 134–58, 211
international law 7, 9, 86, 100–2
international security 102
Isaac, Jeffrey 12–13, 265–72

Jacobs, Jane 173
Jung, Courtney 13

Kant, Immanuel 42
Kaus, Mickey 182–3
Kennedy, Paul 85
King, Martin Luther 236, 237
Kiss, Elizabeth 11, 13
Krugman, Paul 181
Kymlicka, Will 8, 132, 193, 195, 203–4

Lasch, Christopher 248, 249
Lazarus, Emma 177
legitimacy 4, 9, 12, 13, 32–4, 37–9, 46,
    104–8
Lenin, Vladimir 48
liberal democracy 12, 12–13, 42, 89–91,
    104–5, 222–64
Lipset, Seymour Martin 54, 58
Locke, John 79–80, 173
Luttwak, Edward 48
Luxemburg, Rosa 48

Macedo, Stephen 224, 225, 232, 239–46,
    248, 250, 252, 265
MacIntyre, Alasdair 244
majority rule 38
Mann, Michael 48, 85, 86, 92
market economy 32–3, 41–2, 46, 57
Marx, Karl 42, 58
McGrew, Anthony 90, 100
Mill, James 89
Mill, John Stuart 121
mind, nature of 14–15, 277–91
minority rights: *see* group rights
monetary politics 4–5, 39
Mouffe, Chantal 235
Moynihan, Daniel Patrick 179, 180,
    190–1
Mozert v. Hawkins 239–48

multinational corporations 96–8
Myrdal, Gunnar 157

An-Na'im, Abdullahi Ahmed 156
nation state 3–4, 5, 6–7, 23–8, 30, 34,
    38–9, 41, 44–51, 75–8, 79–80,
    86–91, 91–104, 106–8, 119–25,
    155–88, 127–32
  and policy autonomy 5, 6–7, 45–51, 86,
    103, 114
  and sovereignty 5, 7, 41, 47–9, 79,
    86–8, 102–3
nationhood 90–1, 115–18, 119–25
Neumann, Franz 52
Nozick, Robert 173, 177

O'Donnell, Guillermo 21, 49
Offe, Claus 92, 103
Okin, Susan Moller 9–10
oligarchic goods 55–6
Olson, Mancur 65

Paine, Thomas 89
Parekh, Bhikhu 201, 208
participatory democracy 107
Plato 27
Poggi, Gianfranco 85
Polanyi, Karl 43, 45
political boundaries 1–2, 14, 15, 38–9, 41,
    43–4, 45–51, 52–3, 75–6, 86–102,
    273–7, 285–7
  see also identity politics
political liberalism 226–39, 265–72
  and religious fundamentalism 239–48
Popper, Karl 233
popular control 20, 28–30
  lack of 2–3, 5, 8, 13, 23–8, 49–51
Posner, Richard 171
Przeworski, Adam 54
public good 25–8, 65–7
  in foreign affairs 27–8
  procedural and substantive conceptions
    of 25–6
public reason 230–2, 233–9

Rae, Douglas 10–11
rationality 14–15, 42–4, 54, 277–85
Rawls, John 12, 173, 196, 224, 226–39,
    241, 248, 250, 265
religious fundamentalism 12, 13, 149–51,
    222–64, 265–72
representative democracy 89–91
representative government 7, 89–91
Rogers, Joel 257

Rorty, Richard 226
Rousseau, Jean-Jacques 173
Ryan, Alan 228

Samuelson, Paul 65
Schattschneider, E. E. 67
Schlesinger, Arthur 194
Schmitt, Carl 41, 45
Schmitter, Philippe 23, 49
secession 11–12, 200–7, 212–16
Shaheed, Farida 149
Shapiro, Ian 11–12, 13, 42, 130, 227, 246
Shklar, Judith 239–48
Shore, Chris 130
Simpson, O. J. 222
Smith, Adam 41, 45, 46, 53
Smith, Anthony 91
sovereignty 107, 128–9
Spencer, Herbert 45
status harm 195–207
Stich, Stephen 277
suburbanization 10–11, 183–8
Sunstein, Cass 247
symbolic harm 195–207

Tamir, Yael 132
Taylor, Charles 193, 195
Thompson, Dennis 243, 253
Thompson, Grahame 93, 97
Tilly, Charles 85, 86
Tobin, James 4–5, 11
toleration 12, 13
transition to democracy, and global
    economy 49–50
transnational democracy 5, 6–10, 31–2,
    55–7, 80, 81–3, 84, 119, 134–58
transnational forces 2–3, 5, 6–7, 8, 45–51,
    56–7, 91–108, 128–30

urban decay 10–11, 183–8

Walker, R. B. J. 90
Weber, Max 43
Wendt, Alexander 8–9, 129, 132
Wessels, Bernhard 27–8
Whitehead, Laurence 49
Williams, Melissa 204
Wilson, William Julius 177–8
Wolfe, Tom 182
Wolin, Sheldon 227, 251
women's rights 9–10, 135–8, 140–3, 146,
    151–8

Young, Iris Marion 197–200, 201